NATURALISM:
A CRITICAL APPRAISAL

Naturalism
A Critical Appraisal

Steven J. Wagner and Richard Warner
Editors

University of Notre Dame, Notre Dame, Indiana

Library of Congress Cataloging-in-Publication Data

Naturalism : a critical appraisal / edited by Steven J. Wagner,
Richard Warner.
    p.   cm.
    Includes bibliographical references and index.
    Contents: Naturalism and teleology / Mark Bedau —
Honorable intensions [sic] / Mark Wilson — Ethical naturalism and the explanatory power of moral concepts /
Robert Audi — Skepticism and naturalized epistemology /
David Shatz — What am I to believe? / Richard Foley —
The incoherence of empiricism / George Bealer — Aspects
of acceptability / George Myro — Why realism can't be
naturalized / Steven J. Wagner — Is the body a physical
object? / Richard Warner — Analysis and the attitudes /
Ian Pratt — Nonreductive materialism and the explanatory
autonomy of psychology / Terence Horgan — What beliefs
are not / Lynne Rudder Baker.
    ISBN 0-268-01472-8
    1. Naturalism.   I. Wagner, Steven J., 1952– .
II. Wagner, Richard, 1946– .
B828.2.N37   1993
146 — dc20   91-51119
                                   CIP

Manufactured in the United States of America

THE EDITORS DEDICATE THIS VOLUME TO THE MEMORY OF
PAUL GRICE AND GEORGE MYRO

Contents

Introduction

Steven J. Wagner and Richard Warner

1

Most readers of this volume will associate the notion of naturalism (and the closely related notion of physicalism) with Quine and the school of American philosophy that has flourished after *Word and Object*.[1] The issues arising in that context are our principal concern. As a preliminary characterization, we take naturalism to be the view that only natural science deserves full and unqualified credence. 'Physicalism' would seem to connote a narrower view that privileges specifically physics, as opposed to natural science in general. However, since self-described physicalists also endorse chemistry, ecology, neuroanatomy, and the like, the line between the two classifications blurs. We will simply speak of naturalism. (The precise boundaries of the "natural" will not matter in this introduction.[2]) Our volume, then, addresses issues arising in American discussions of naturalism since 1960.

But Quinian naturalism is just one of many strands in an argument that has preoccupied philosophers since Kant. At issue have been the relations among a range of human endeavors: among philosophy, science, and the arts, and among various branches of or ways of doing philosophy, science, and art. The roots of this problematic are familiar in outline. They lie, most prominently, in the establishment of physical science as a substantially autonomous institution between (roughly) 1600 and 1850; Kant's reassessment of philosophy; the transformation in our thinking about art due to Kant and the antipositivism of the romantic movement; and the rise of such social sciences as history, economics, and psychology in the eighteenth and nineteenth centuries. French positivism and German naturalism are the main nineteenth-century precursors to naturalism in the sense of this volume.[3]

The relation of science to philosophy, and of each of these to a somewhat amorphous third player one might call 'common sense', is arguably the principal concern of philosophy in the past century. An astonishing variety of positions on this issue have been occupied by Nietzsche, Frege, Wittgenstein, Russell, Husserl, Heidegger, Carnap, Dewey, Strawson, Quine, Goodman, Derrida, and others. Clearly, we are in the midst of a grand and often chaotic transformation of our understanding of our various creative pursuits, hence of our selves.

A survey of the issues directly pertinent to naturalism would therefore hardly differ from a survey of all the main recent schools of philosophy. An attempt to resolve these issues would hardly be distinct from a resolution of all problems these schools address. The survey must obviously be beyond the scope of this introduction and the resolution beyond the scope of this book. Hence our narrower ambitions. But an awareness of the broader philosophical context will guide us in several ways.

(i) Participants in current discussions of naturalism seem to assume that the meaning of 'naturalism' ('naturalist program', etc.), its motivation and — often — its correctness, one way or the other, are almost obvious. The historical situation makes such assumptions exceedingly unlikely. Philosophers have taken just about every possible stance with some measure of justification, and all of the main programs within this area ("naturalism," "phenomenology," "analytic philosophy," and so forth) have been open to sharp differences of interpretation by their adherents.

(ii) In view of the historical situation, systematic reflection on naturalism must lead us to confront the broadest possible issues — such issues as our proper self-image as human beings. It would be naive to expect any simple resolution.

(iii) Just for these reasons, a conservative procedure recommends itself. Given the welter of conflicting claims and interpretations, the best hope of progress lies in thoroughly examining a specific variety of naturalism. Not that there is only one variety to be studied, but the present stage of our understanding prohibits any attempt to evaluate "naturalism" in general. Hence our focus on a particular realization of the naturalist idea.

Our target is, as announced, taken from Quine's *Word and Object* and the body of work done in its shadow. This conception is itself programmatic and flexible, yet is still a specific moment in the history of philosophy. The emphasis of this volume is in one way pure accident, a result of the philosophical education and development of the contributors. But the accident is felicitous. A signal feature of the debates over naturalism in current American philosophy is that the centrality of classical problems — mind and body, causation, apriority, fact and value, skepticism, and the like — is upheld. This is in sharp contrast to the stances of rival schools, which have held the classical issues to be in some way irrelevant or outmoded — to rest on linguistic error, to admit of some kind of dissolution, or to presuppose fundamental misunderstandings of our position in the world. Insofar as the classical problems define our tradition, any philosopher should consider the possibility of salvaging them within a contemporary framework. That salvage is what Quine—after Russell, perhaps the most traditional of the major figures of this century—promised. We want to study naturalistic approaches, in substantially his sense, to philosophical problems.

Our collection takes a critical view of naturalism. This would need no apology in any case, since criticism benefits even the most plausible and fruitful philosophical view. However, the contributors' general stance (this does not apply equally or in the same way to all) is that naturalism should be criticized not just as a salutary exercise but because it does face grave difficulties. These criticisms tend to fall into two main categories.

On the one hand, naturalism usually involves a doubtful aim. A naturalist would characteristically claim that such key philosophical notions as mind, cause, self, or knowledge are indeed important objects of study but that their serious use requires, at least in the long run, "naturalization." That is, such notions are to be defined strictly from terms of established science (perhaps some science of the future). Alternatively, one might hold that naturalistic counterparts or analogs of these notions should ultimately replace them. Either way, the commitment is to making our talk of mind, self, and allied notions scientific. Now this idea provokes various questions. One may well ask just *when* the naturalization is expected or required, just what follows if it is not forthcoming, and, in any case, just what counts as "naturalization." It is, however, clear that the demand for naturalizations is central to most philosophy in a naturalistic vein.

Consider, then, naturalistic work on the circle of concepts surrounding mind and meaning: belief, reference, perception, and so on. Intensive efforts have produced nothing like a clear indication, even in principle, of how to naturalize these terms. Instead, each of a range of proposals is bogged down in its own characteristic difficulties. Although the controversies may just signal healthy ferment, the track record of attempted naturalization certainly invites skeptical challenges. And this holds not just with regard to psychological and semantic notions but for the various other terms (e.g., from ethics or metaphysics) that have occupied naturalists.

Here a comparison of naturalism with conceptual analysis is instructive. These schools are often cast as opponents, since the former privileges science at the expense of common sense while the latter inverts this relation. Also, naturalists deny the interests or the existence of the conceptually necessary and sufficient conditions that analysis aims to produce. But both schools are, in their usual forms, committed to a search for definitions. Just as continued failure to produce counterexample-free analyses

raised doubts about the analytic program, so an unrelieved dearth of naturalizations provokes second thoughts about naturalism. In neither case does
a lack of results at any point spell refutation. There is no way of knowing
in advance whether a satisfactory conceptual analysis or naturalization of,
say, belief should take five years, or fifty, or five thousand. Still, nothing
is as encouraging as success, and its absence breeds doubt.

A second kind of difficulty for naturalism arises not from the attempt to carry out its project but from the fundamental, openly adver-
tised character of the naturalist ideal. The naturalist's paradigm is science:
what cannot be brought under that heading merits less than full credence.
Yet a natural reaction is that this viewpoint must be too narrow, that too
much of what we value and find deeply illuminating is being rejected. One
might be particularly concerned about the status of common sense, of art,
of philosophy, or of various empirical inquiries, such as anthropology, that
lie outside of hard science. Indeed, several of our contributors argue that
the naturalist's strictures are outright self-refuting, since naturalism itself
is no scientific view. Thus one might hope to move from naturalism to some
viewpoint more tolerant of our diverse cognitive pursuits. The question
then becomes just how far naturalism is to be condemned, or what kind
of compromise with its demands might be appropriate.

2

Of course naturalism already has its critics — not just philosophers
well outside the movement but many who have been immersed in it and
have some sympathy for its claims. Yet the extant criticisms do not readily
add up to a satisfactory perspective. We wish to point out some main features of our collection, while at the same time conveying a sense of the
open problems via a comparison with two of the leading antinaturalist
positions now in the field.

Richard Rorty has established himself as a critic of naturalist ambitions.[4] Not that he entirely rejects the naturalist premises. On the contrary.
Rorty holds, with many other philosophers, that philosophy as traditionally understood will disappear, and he believes that science will pursue some
of its concerns in some form — by empirically studying phenomena of mind
and language, for example. But Rorty denies that empirical results could
answer characteristically philosophical questions — the mind-body problem,
the nature of truth, questions about skepticism or objectivity. He rather
takes it to be an insight of the pragmatists that these are not good questions; that there are no interesting answers to be given. This is a key difference with naturalism, since the typical naturalist accepts the questions and
seeks scientific solutions.

Further, instead of taking science as the paradigmatic discourse, Rorty gives at least equal worth to other forms of thought and speech, notably to literature. Indeed, these forms may be assigned cognitive (as opposed to, say, purely sensual or emotive) value, albeit of a kind different from science.[5] One consequence is that science cannot be our intellectual center: it cannot assess the truth or rationality of discourse in other areas. A scientific critique of political discourse is as nonsensical as a poet's critique of the periodic table.

A crucial premise for Rorty is the failure of positivist epistemology. Two fundamental positivist ideas were, first, the existence of a well-defined, epistemically privileged set of observation beliefs, and, second, the possibility of generating science from these beliefs through inductive logic. Thus beliefs founded on observation were seen as more worthy of credence than other (synthetic) beliefs. And among the observation-based beliefs, we could in turn distinguish those with high degrees of confirmation. The scientific doctrines that positivism favored were simply taken to be the result of making good inductive inferences from observation. In this way, positivist epistemology aimed to demarcate science and justify its elevated status. But Rorty rejects this picture. There is, for him, no "scientific method." Scientists attack their problems using procedures tied to a specific context and theory. For example, a basic method in recursion theory is to try to reduce a question to the halting problem. A method of elementary mechanics is to ignore various "small" forces, such as friction or the gravitational pull of distant stars. Such methods have no general application: it is nonsense to look for methods common to recursion theory, mechanics, and population biology. On the other hand, poets, historians, and bridge players have their context-specific methods, too. So there is no useful distinction between scientific and nonscientific methods. A fortiori, one cannot propose that the use of scientific methods yields a higher grade of belief.

This is not to deny science its proper place. Rorty would of course agree that designers of radio telescopes should not rely on poetry or commonsense physics. But on this view, science is just a set of beliefs and techniques used to solve certain problems. It is not an epistemically significant category. Philosophical naturalism therefore makes no sense.

A study of Rorty's views would take us far afield. But we see reasons for pursuing alternative critiques of naturalism while leaving the ultimate validity of Rorty's position open.

We have already mentioned Rorty's dismissal of the classical problems of philosophy — mind and body, truth, causation, and so forth. These belong to a philosophical problematic that Dewey, Heidegger, Wittgenstein, Quine, and other philosophers have, in his view, laid to rest: one originating with Plato, continuing through Descartes and Kant, and still showing decadent manifestations now. Among the signatures of this tradition are, for Rorty, epistemological foundationalism; a belief in first-person authority about mental states; a view that thought can mirror reality; categories of analyticity and apriority; a search for philosophical theories (say, of justification or truth); and belief in philosophical hegemony, that is, in the right of philosophy to sit in judgment on other disciplines. But Rorty's historical interpretations are highly controversial. One question is whether he caricatures the tradition. Another is whether he does not considerably underestimate the traditional elements in the modern figures to whom he appeals. Whatever the resolution of these issues, antinaturalists may hope to avoid such heavy interpretive and substantive commitments.

Moreover, the various traditional views that Rorty lumps together are at best loosely related. For example, foundationalism, an image of mind as mirror, and an interest in philosophical theories seem almost completely independent of each other. The traditional philosopher might therefore survive by avoiding some of the commitments that Rorty attacks. This is directly relevant to the issue of naturalism: if one need not buy into an entire, dubious package in order to pose, say, the mind-body problem, then the naturalist's efforts to solve that problem are not automatically misguided.

Similarly for Rorty's attack on positivism. Although few philosophers today accept positivist views of observation and inductive logic, a favored epistemic status for natural science is not so easily dismissed. A principled, albeit rough, demarcation of natural science from other forms of inquiry still seems possible — the category is not arbitrary. It is also hard to deny that science enjoys particularly close ties to observation, or that telling good from bad reasoning is easier in science than elsewhere. These features give rise to certain salient features of science: relative clarity, objectivity, and the (generally) cumulative growth of knowledge. For contemporary naturalists, these are doxastic virtues sufficient to establish the epistemic superiority of science.

Such a relatively modest viewpoint promises to escape standard critiques of positivism. We will return to this matter below. Worth noting in this connection is that naturalists are not committed philistines. They do not hold that literature or anthropology are worthless or even that these offer no *cognitive* gains. Rather, they find nonscientific doctrine inferior by reasonable epistemic standards. We may still need and even take a deep interest in such doctrines, but they do not merit full and unqualified credence.

In short, Rorty draws strong conclusions from the failures of certain highly committal views — of positivism and of a version of traditional philosophy. Hence the force of his attack on more circumspect forms of naturalism is unclear, as are the attractions of his radical alternative. We therefore recommend a more detailed and exploratory investigation of naturalism. And our volume suggests that the ideas Rorty lumps together and discards include useful antinaturalist weapons. Richard Warner, for example, argues that a qualified form of first-person authority is genuine and resists naturalistic explanation. George Bealer defends a range of seemingly *a priori* beliefs as falling outside of natural knowledge. Richard Foley argues that a quite general, Cartesian question about what to believe still makes good sense — yet naturalism is powerless to deal with it. Perhaps, then, a radical break with the past is not the best way to advance philosophy. Assessing naturalism may require a delicate separation of the correct from incorrect elements in the tradition out of which this movement arose.

We turn to the critique of naturalism developed in Hilary Putnam's writings since 1978.[6] Putnam, too, holds a complex position of which we can only sketch certain relevant aspects.

Putnam rejects the attempt to make science the prime arbiter of truth. He advocates a centerless pluralism that recognizes the human value of diverse inquiries. Scientific rationality is not the preferred route to a comprehensive theory of the world. It is simply one way to solve various problems and to enhance our life. As such, it coexists with poetry, history, psychotherapy, and our other efforts. In these respects, Putnam's position is very close to Rorty's.[7] A critical difference, however, lies in Putnam's views on scientific rationality.[8]

Putnam represents the naturalist as assigning full cognitive value, or objectivity, to science and none to anything else. To him this illustrates the philosopher's penchant for pernicious dichotomizing. His own model is a continuum of objectivity, with mathematics and physics at the top and history or ethics much farther down. Thus he does not entirely dismiss the positivist idea of objectivity. It remains desirable for him. He also keeps the view that the social sciences and humanities lack objectivity. The point is that they are not fatally deficient. By allowing degrees of objectivity, he can place hard science at the top while leaving other disciplines enough objectivity to make them worth taking seriously.[9]

Putnam's antinaturalist campaign appears to be driven by a sense of dangers — a fear that the epistemic demotion of politics, literature, and anthropology will encourage their devaluation. If we accept the naturalist critique, we may attach less importance to nonscientific forms of discourse. This would pave the way for the technocrats who will trample culture and treat people like things. Putnam's opposition to naturalism is therefore at once a vote for human culture. By crediting nonscientific inquiry with some measure of objectivity, he aims to get us to take it seriously.

But Putnam's strategy is quite curious. Suppose, on the one hand, that the connection between objectivity and importance is real: that a denial of objectivity can or should lead to diminished regard for human values. Then Putnam has conceded too much. Although he has gained some objectivity for nonscientific inquiries, he allows them to be placed far below science. Hence it would seem reasonable to place human values far below scientific ones, even though we do not entirely disregard them. Such a defense borders on surrender. On the other hand, if the connection is spurious, then we lose Putnam's original worry. If a lack of objectivity for, say, politics should not diminish our political concerns or undermine our political beliefs, then there is no call to defend the objectivity of politics. Serious political commitments would be acceptable in any case.

A notable feature of Putnam's position is, therefore, his retention of a positivist premise deeper than the one he attacks. Putnam sees the positivist as denying the objectivity, hence the importance, of politics. In response, Putnam upholds importance by defending objectivity. But the error may lie in the shared premise — objectivity may be one thing, importance another. Quite generally, the antinaturalist strategy of arguing that nonscience makes contributions fundamentally similar to those of science may buy too much of the positivist model. A pertinent illustration of this problem is the position of Nelson Goodman, to whom Putnam is heavily indebted.[10] Goodman defends the arts on the grounds that they make cognitive contributions fundamentally similar to those of science; he goes on to advocate the clarification of a general notion of rightness that applies both to scientific theories and artistic creations. Yet the arts may not at all enhance cognition in the ways that science does (indeed, various arts may differ radically from each other). An account of their value might need to emphasize precisely the differences. Trying to show that cinema and politics are more like physics than we had thought may be the wrong idea.

We believe Rorty would sympathize. Thus a fundamental division among antinaturalists emerges: does naturalism underestimate the resemblances between science and nonscience (Putnam), or are the scientific standards generally irrelevant (Rorty)? Here our collection overall takes an intermediate position. Our contributors are generally closer to Putnam in their sense that science still represents an ideal of knowledge. Although this is not true for Baker and Warner, it applies somewhat to most of the authors and strongly to several, such as Horgan, Pratt, Wagner, and Wilson. But the defenses of nonscientific belief in this volume do not appeal to anything like Putnam's continuum of objectivity. Baker, Foley, and Warner, for example, all find that scientific criteria are at best weakly relevant in certain areas of inquiry. Also, our contributors are not explicitly concerned with naturalism as a cultural pathology. They pursue, instead, the rigorous scrutiny of the naturalist's epistemological and metaphysical claims.

Underlying this last difference is a reluctance to offer such bold assessments as characterize Putnam's (as well as Rorty's) discussions of naturalism. Putnam has categorically dismissed naturalism and proposed an alternative view: "pragmatic realism."[11] Yet his new position has proved elusive. Its various statements have been obscure both in themselves and in their relations to each other. Moreover, Putnam's recent writings stress an idea hard to reconcile with logical theory: the existence of incompatible yet equivalent systems of belief. In our view, his difficulties reflect the need to examine naturalism with more care and discrimination before drawing large conclusions. The tenor of our collection is that a precise view of the insights and failures of naturalism still lies some distance away.

3

Objectivity has been a recurring theme of our remarks. We now wish to examine the idea more closely and to stress its role in motivating naturalism.

Consider these lines from Israel Scheffler:

> A fundamental feature of science is its ideal of objectivity, an ideal that subjects all scientific statements to the test of independent and impartial criteria, recognizing no authority of persons in the realm of cognition. The claimant to scientific knowledge is . . . trying to meet independent standards, to satisfy factual requirements whose fulfillment cannot be guaranteed in advance.[12]

This is hardly a definition, since such terms as 'independent' and 'impartial' require as much elucidation as 'objectivity' itself. Still, Scheffler's formulation is compelling. The science we hold is substantially unaffected by such things as cultural or personal prejudices, and the continuous testing of its theories is a model of critical examination. The occasions when scientific practice falls short of this ideal are hardly worth mentioning here. The point is the contrast with nonscientific inquiry. Whereas the distortion of theory by prejudice is news in physics, in anthropology or art criticism it is simply the order of the day.[13]

A critic might deny that science is objective in any significant, nonarbitrary sense. As long as a philosophical theory of objectivity is lacking, the features Scheffler mentions can be dismissed, in one way or another, as illusions. Yet while Rorty and others defend such a line, it is unpromising. The impression that science resolves its disagreements efficiently, and that its doctrines are conspicuously open to criticism and refutation, endures. Here, as often in philosophy, the fact seems obvious even in the absence of a clear analysis.

Having argued that scientific objectivity is real, the naturalist will go on to propose that it is plainly a virtue of inquiry. Scientific discourse appears as an improvement on the confusion and cross purposes of other disciplines. Now add to this the demonstrated ability of science to correct opinions originating elsewhere — say, from philosophy or common sense. Then it becomes clear why one might elevate scientific rationality above other forms; why one might *hope* for an eventual scientific adjudication of all significant questions. This is the fundamental appeal of naturalism: an endorsement of epistemic order and progress.

Yet a taste for objectivity does not, by itself, yield naturalism. First, essential to any naturalism is an exclusionary clause: *only* objectively grounded statements merit full and unqualified credence. For one might otherwise accept scientific objectivity as a good but deny that fully justified belief requires it. One might, for example, hold that beliefs are fully justified when they are not open to reasonable objections — even if they lack a scientific foundation. Such statements as that Illinois summers are unpleasant or that Hegel influenced Georg Büchner would then be fully justified, in spite of not being naturalistic at all. The naturalist must therefore explain why relaxing scientific standards for (full and unqualified) belief is always wrong. Simply appreciating the merits of objectivity is not enough for that.

Second, we are still lacking a distinctive element in the naturalist idea of objectivity. So far, objectivity involves impartiality, the possibility of criticism and refutation, and the interpersonal acceptability of results. Areas outside of science can exhibit these, perhaps even to an equal degree. Theological disputation, for example, could be disciplined enough to count as objective in this sense. So could debates about the law in a sophisticated legal culture such as our own. Yet for naturalists, legal knowledge would still not rank with science.

The missing element is, presumably, observation. On the naturalist view, science aims to explain observations. Indeed the business of science in principle is to explain whatever can be observed. Thus science must answer to a comprehensive set of perceptual data. This grounding in observation is what distinguishes science even from ideally objective legal inquiry. Although observation in various senses plays a role in the law, the fundamental determinants of legality are decisions — the acts of legislators, the opinions of judges, the exercise of prosecutorial discretion, and so on. In no relevant sense are judgments of legality grounded in their ability to systemize observed data. Likewise for judgments in theology or any other field of rule-governed disputation. Essential to naturalism, then, is the idea of science as a confrontation with the observable world.

Naturalists must therefore also explicate the notion of observation and defend its privileged status. As regards explication, the very existence of observation in the naturalist's sense is disputed. Once we abandon naive forms of an observation-theory distinction, it is no longer obvious that a significant line between these categories can be drawn. Still, the idea that science is founded on perceptual observations seems neither trivial nor arbitrary. It is unlikely to prove fatal to naturalism. Similarly for the epistemic merits of observation. Observational testing is the key to the stunning growth of scientific knowledge over the past few centuries. Although we are far from a clear philosophical account of this development, the role of observation in promoting progress and insight is not really in doubt.

We have now partially recovered both of the main principles of positivist epistemology. The idea of an inductive logic survives in our admittedly inchoate view of science as an objective mode of inquiry. Similarly, observation remains an epistemologically significant category. From the naturalist's viewpoint, positivism erred not in its basic vision of science but in its premature, simplistic analysis. Thus standard dismissals of positivism are simplistic in turn, as are the consequent dismissals of naturalism. [14]

But this does not solve the naturalist's problems. Even if we grant the reality and benefits of observation in some neo-positivist sense, the naturalist's exclusionary clause is still unexplained. Why should full and unqualified credence *require* an observational basis?

At the heart of naturalism is the idea that observation is our access to an independent world. The senses present us with a reality that is not of our making and not shaped by our beliefs or wills. (Thus it is unlike, say, legal reality.) Subjecting our theories to sensory testing is a way of giving this reality substantial control over our thoughts. This is the connection between observation and objectivity — or so naturalists will claim. They will then add an exclusionary clause as before: inquiry should be directed at an objective reality. The reason now would be that no other inquiries can have a claim to truth, properly speaking. And that inquiry should aim at truth may, perhaps, serve as an ultimate premise.

Of course these ideas are problematic, if not outright mysterious. The problem of truth is one more tangle into which our exploration of naturalism has led. Yet a link between objectivity and truth was to be expected; and the naturalist's concern with objectivity has been clear all along. So the foregoing may at least serve to indicate the possible sources of naturalism. Although we have no intention of clearing up the attendant mysteries here, we caution against underestimating the naturalist perspective. The power of naturalism lies ultimately in its vision of objectivity. Essential to any critique is a thorough and sympathetic understanding of that vision.

4

Contemporary naturalists may take either an epistemological or an ontological starting point. Basic to the epistemological approach are the epistemic merits of science: one thinks that physics (particularly) is good theory in a certain sense and holds that only theories good in that way fully merit belief. Underlying the ontological approach is the idea that reality is physical reality. The thrust of naturalism, on this view, is that we should believe only in physical things. Although many philosophers combine these ideas (indeed, an entailment seems to run at least from epistemological to ontological naturalism), they represent somewhat distinct fundamental intuitions. A likely source for this bifurcation is the possibility of emphasizing either of two elements in the conception of objectivity sketched above. A focus on the idea of an objective world may lead to an ontological formulation of naturalism. Focusing on the process of scientific inquiry would tend to yield an epistemological version.

In any case, the duality is prominent in the literature on naturalism. Our collection illustrates the point. Several essays confront one version of naturalism only; others separate the two and judge them somewhat unequally (e.g., Horgan or Audi). Evidently critics of naturalism as well as proponents vary in their sense of where the interest and appeal or danger of naturalism lies.

Constant throughout these variations, however, is the preoccupation with a particular nonscientific domain: commonsense discourse about psychology and epistemic justification. This is indeed one domain, since the psychological notion of belief and the normative notion of rationality are inseparable. The study of reason, or justification, concerns beliefs and desires (as well as conjectures, hopes, intentions, and so forth), hence presupposes folk psychology. Conversely, to regard a system as holding beliefs and desires is to see it as a reasoning thing. But identifying reasons means judging them to be good or poor, that is, justified or unjustified. Thus a single viewpoint makes us thinkers and subjects of epistemic evaluation. Since this view is, further, reflexively applied — we take it of ourselves — the familiar description of us as being conscious rational agents nicely summarizes the folk picture. This inherited self-image is the primary target of naturalism. It is the common element in the diverse areas of thought that do not count as natural science — sociology, art criticism, economics, history, ethics, and so on.

But why the skepticism about intentional (and epistemological) notions? One common answer is that the trouble lies with the intentional notion of mental representation: that it is mysterious how an internal state can represent something "out there." This, however, is clearly uninformative, since naturalists recognize all kinds of relations among objects or states. What makes representation (as opposed to, say, distance) nonnatural? One would need to show how some feature of this relation distinguishes it from those discussed in science. Simply pointing out that it involves representation is useless. A better answer is that naturalists compare our intentional descriptions with descriptions in the language of physics and find the former deficient in point of precision, clarity, empirical power, and the like. Folk psychology is judged as science and falls short.

Such considerations often lead naturalists to eliminative materialism. The alternatives are to defend folk psychology as being good science or to argue that scientific standards are not properly applied to it. The former amounts of nonskeptical naturalism, the latter to rejecting naturalism in order to affirm folk concepts.

All of these positions are well represented in the literature. Noted eliminative materialists include Patricia Churchland and Stephen Stich, both of whom follow the lead of *Word and Object*.[15] The defense of folk psychology on naturalist terms is principally due to Jerry Fodor, whose main idea is that fully scientific cognitive theories presuppose folk concepts.[16] Rorty and Putnam, both strongly influenced by the later Wittgenstein, represent the third option. Donald Davidson is another prominent member of that camp.[17] The classification of folk psychology as bad science also comes under fire (from a variety of directions) in most of the essays to follow.

This issue, too, has provoked hasty judgments. Eliminativists and proponents of folk theory tend to communicate through short dismissals of each other's positions. In fact, our folk scheme is not yet well understood. Its very familiarity hides its complexity and the problematic character of its concepts. As we proceed with its defense, gaps, confusions, and errors will come to light. The scheme that best survives naturalist criticism will be some distance from what we started out with, and it must in turn be open to further elaborations and corrections. Hence a reasonable antinaturalism may, in the end, amount to this: the view of human beings as rational agents is right enough to warrant its persistence, in *some* recognizable form, across all conceptual and scientific evolution. This is less than many critics of naturalism would ask for, but categorical judgments in this area have a poor track record. Besides, it is really quite a strong claim.

Let us recall the comparison of naturalism with conceptual analysis. Both are revolutionary agendas that promised to sweep out cobwebs, settle old questions, and give philosophy a fresh purpose. It turns out that both suffer from foundational ills as well as a simple shortage of results. Another common element is that these programs are deeply rooted in the philosophical tradition which they have attacked in rather ahistoric terms.

And we find them quite alike in their positive contributions. The analytic philosophers' exhaustive studies of such notions as meaning, freedom, knowledge, and justice have revealed fascinating connections (and disconnections) among ideas. Whatever the fate of the analytic program, the light shed on our ways of thinking justified the enterprise. Similarly, the benefit of naturalism has been its logical and empirical scrutiny of folk concepts. By asking how well our human self-image would serve as science, naturalism compels attention to its role(s), its defining features, its defects and merits. Each program is therefore one more contribution to the Socratic project. Since that project is enmeshed in the folk perspective, it lacks ultimate validity for naturalists, but that does not lessen our own appreciation of their work.

We now turn to a summary of the essays.

5

Mark Bedau, "Naturalism and Teleology": Bedau is a self-confessed antinaturalist. Nonetheless, his contribution turns on a careful examination of actual scientific practice. (It is ironic that those skeptical of naturalism often seem to pay more attention to actual science than do naturalism's proponents.) Bedau takes the guiding principle of naturalism to be that "everything in the world is within the scope of scientific investigation." He points out that it is widely agreed among naturalists that values are not part of the natural order while teleology is. The difficulty is that teleology presupposes the notion of value. Hence, teleology falls outside the natural order. Either that, or value is part of the natural order.

Mark Wilson, "Honorable Intensions": Wilson shows that an examination of the actual history and practice of science casts serious doubt on prevalent philosophical assumptions about the nature of physical properties. These assumptions provide the background for much of the contemporary discussion of the mind-body problem, and Wilson argues persuasively that this background is confused. For example, he contends that the notion of a functional property and the notion of supervenience should be "dropped as both unnecessary . . . and ill-conceived." More generally, Wilson's work is a much needed antidote to uncritical and uninformed versions of naturalism that purport to find in science ready-made tools to turn to naturalizing projects. The purported tools are not there. Wilson considers himself to be a physicalist and believes his view of properties makes naturalism almost unavoidable, yet he also thinks that that same view of properties shows that naturalism lacks the methodological cutting edge normally ascribed to it.

Robert Audi, "Ethical Naturalism and the Explanatory Power of Moral Concepts": Audi rejects the position that moral properties are "substantively naturalistic"—that is, the view that moral facts are empirically confirmable. He suggests instead that moral properties may be "conceptually naturalistic"—that is, explicable in a way that employs no irreducibly normative concepts. On this view, moral judgments attribute real properties that are naturalistically based (since they supervene on natural properties). However, the connection between the moral property and the base on which it supervenes is *a priori*. This is a departure from a Quinian naturalism that eschews the *a priori*. The departure is a major one. Many naturalists hold that logic and mathematics are *a priori,* but far fewer would subscribe to the claim that there are *a priori* explications of moral terms. Audi's goal is to naturalize moral explanations while holding that moral properties are non-natural.

David Shatz, "Skepticism and Naturalized Epistemology": Shatz focuses on science—like Bedau and Wilson; unlike them, his concern is more general and abstract. Shatz is concerned with "methodological naturalism." This is the three-part thesis that, in epistemological inquiries into the justifications for our beliefs: (1) philosophers *must* use empirical data; (2) they may *only* use such data; and, (3) the use of such data is unproblematic. This is naturalism in the form Quine endorses in "Epistemology Naturalized" and subsequent writings. Shatz questions the third claim (he does not in this piece take a position on the first two). He argues that, when methodological naturalists address Cartesian skepticism about the external world, their use of empirical data turns out to be question-begging, if not simply circular. If the use of such data is to be legitimate more needs to be said. The "more" is the thesis of "dialectical naturalism." Dialectical naturalism allows the use of empirical data in epistemology only when that use is demonstrably unproblematic. While Shatz is hopeful about the prospects of such a naturalism, he does not try to show that the use of empirical data is demonstrably unproblematic. His point is that, where skepticism is concerned, the only real alternatives for naturalism are dialectical naturalism or despair, the abandonment of the claim that empirical data can support non–question-begging arguments against the skeptic.

Richard Foley, "What Am I to Believe?": Like Shatz, Foley is concerned with relations between epistemology and science. He asks the "intensely personal" question, "What am I to believe?" Naturalists have a ready answer, "Whatever science asserts." Of course, so baldly stated this is much too crude. Or perhaps not *much* too crude; consider Quine: "Physics is the arbiter of what is, that it is; and of what is not, that it is not." Foley argues that the claim cannot be an answer to the question asked. When

Descartes asks, "What am I to believe?" he is asking for *self-legitimating methods of inquiry* which will determine what he is to believe. Foley, in line with naturalists, grants—indeed emphasizes—that there are no self-legitimating methods of inquiry, but his point is that the question still calls for a method of inquiry. Saying "What science asserts" cannot answer *this* question unless we mean the answer to recommend science as a method of inquiry. But what if we do mean just that? Then we can still ask, "Why accept science as a method of inquiry?" This question still makes sense, even if there are no self-legitimating methods. And it is a question to which there cannot be an answer from within science, an answer that presupposes the very method of inquiry it is to validate. Nonetheless, it is a question we *must* answer if we are coherently to back our beliefs and decisions with reasons. Each person's answer is an exercise of intellectual autonomy.

George Bealer, "The Incoherence of Empiricism": Bealer takes naturalism to be the thesis that the natural sciences constitute the simplest comprehensive theory that explains all, or most, of a person's experiences. He combines naturalism with empiricism (a person's experiences comprise that person's *prima facie* evidence) and holism (a theory is justified for a person if and only if it is, or belongs to, the simplest comprehensive theory that explains all, or most, of a person's *prima facie* evidence) to derive: a theory is justified for a person if and only if it is, or belongs to, the natural sciences. Bealer rejects this conclusion on two grounds. First, there are, he argues, justified claims that are not part of natural science, and the empiricism-holism-naturalism trinity cannot coherently deny this. Second, the trinity itself makes claims that are not part of natural science: namely, the theses of empiricism, holism, and naturalism. The trinity is self-defeating. Thus, Bealer and Foley arrive at similar positions: There are legitimate claims about the nature of justification that lie outside the bounds of natural science.

George Myro, "Aspects of Acceptability": Myro acknowledges the power and attractiveness of naturalism; indeed, he says it represents a half of his philosophical perspective. The other half is a commitment to the irreducibility of psychological theory to naturalistically acceptable terms. Against the first half of this split perspective, Myro argues that naturalism is self-defeating: a naturalist cannot coherently assert the thesis of naturalism; indeed, from a naturalist point of view, there is no reason to think that the thesis is true. The similarity with Bealer is not accidental; as Bealer notes Myro's argument predates and inspires Bealer's own argument that naturalism is self-defeating. Myro concludes by suggesting a way to resolve, to some extent at least, the tension between two halves of his thought. He argues that psychological facts cannot merely amount to physical facts.

He points out that we have reason to accept the natural sciences only because we have reasons to interpret certain sounds natural scientists make as assertions that we have reason to accept. We have grounds for such an interpretation only because we view such sounds from the perspective of a psychological theory. Myro suggests that if the acceptability of one theory depends on the antecedent acceptability of another, the latter theory cannot reduce to the former. This idea (also favored by Paul Grice) deserves further investigation.

Steven Wagner, "Why Realism Can't Be Naturalized": While Myro claims that naturalism cannot coherently regard itself as second-rate ("grade B," not "serious") theory, Wagner follows Quine in permitting this move. Naturalists can propose naturalism as the best view that our imperfect language of mind and justification will allow, hence as meriting qualified credence. Although a straightforward self-defeat objection is thus blocked, subtler variations still work. Wagner distinguishes between soft naturalism, which allows intentional concepts to gain serious acceptability through reduction, and hard naturalism, which assigns them a permanent grade B status. Hard naturalism fails because it does not offer the pragmatic or empirical benefits that grade B beliefs need for their justification. Soft naturalism might avoid this problem in an ideal state of knowledge, where it could (naturalists assume) be stated in naturalistic, seriously acceptable terms. But even there, it would simultaneously presuppose and question intentional concepts in an incoherent way. Woven into this critique is an analysis of Putnam's "model-theoretic argument" against naturalist realism. Although Wagner agrees that Putnam is responding to a genuine difficulty in that position, the problems seem to lie strictly with its naturalist component.

Richard Warner, "Is the Body a Physical Object?": Like several of the other contributors, Warner takes up the theme that there are justified claims that cannot be part of natural science. But he argues for this on rather different grounds. Warner begins by noting that the physical, and more generally the natural, sciences aspire to objectivity, and he argues that this aspiration is inconsistent with recognizing incorrigible claims. The reason is that the aspiration to objectivity means that the subject matter of the natural sciences is the mind-independent world; however, items that are the subjects of incorrigible beliefs cannot be mind-independent. Warner then argues that certain beliefs about the positions of one's limbs can enjoy a kind of qualified incorrigibility. Since, for naturalists, the natural world is the mind-independent world, it follows that the body is not a physical or natural object. This absurd result, Warner contends, shows that contemporary naturalism does not have a coherent account of either the body, the physical, or the mind-independent.

Ian Pratt, "Analysis and the Attitudes": With Pratt's contribution we turn from the general consideration of science to criticisms of particular naturalist projects. One such project is to give an account of the propositional attitudes in non-intentional terms. Pratt argues that there is no reason whatsoever to think that this is possible. Many naturalists think there is. They contend that only an account in non-intentional terms could explain our systematic grasp of the meaning of sentences that attribute propositional attitudes. Pratt counters by providing an alternate way of explaining our grasp of the attitudes. He suggests that we each use ourselves and our own self-understanding to model the thought and behavior of others. This idea has been in the air for some time. What is new and convincing about Pratt is the detail and persuasiveness with which he develops the idea. It is noteworthy that Pratt draws heavily on ideas from computer science, a field many naturalists look to for ideas about how to naturalize the attitudes.

Terence Horgan, "Nonreductive Materialism and the Explanatory Autonomy of Psychology": Horgan describes himself as a "metaphysical naturalist": "Metaphysical naturalism . . . includes the view that the facts of physics diachronically fix, or determine, all the facts about our world — and about any other physically possible world too." In addition, Horgan thinks that all human behavior is explainable in neurobiological terms, and that, although the mental is not reducible to the neurobiological, mental properties supervene on neurobiological ones. So far, so naturalistic. However, Horgan also emphasizes, first, that for naturalism, supervenience facts should be naturalistically explainable and, second, that it is not at all clear how to give such explanations. "So supervenience does not solve the mind-body problem, but only points us toward another version of it." Horgan does not, in this essay, address how to give naturalistic explanations of supervenience. The main burden of the essay is to argue for a "non-reductive form of naturalism . . . that is robustly realist about mentality itself, about mental causation, and about mentalistic causal explanation."

Lynne Rudder Baker, "What Beliefs Are Not": Like Horgan, Baker holds that the mental is not reducible to the physical. Unlike Horgan, Baker rejects mind-brain supervenience. Focusing on belief and desire, she argues that "the belief/desire pattern of explanation does not require justification in terms of underlying mechanisms." The idea that it does is a confusion fostered by the Cartesian split between mind and matter. This split has led many to think of beliefs as "internal entities"; from the perspective of naturalism, the way to understand the nature of an entity is by investigating the underlying stuff that composes it. Science suggests to naturalists that the relevant underlying stuff in the case of belief is neurobiological. Baker raises serious difficulties for current naturalistic attempts to develop such a reductive understanding of belief.

6

The contributions divide into general and specific criticisms of naturalism. The general criticisms are: crucial assumptions that naturalists make about science are not borne about by actual scientific practice (Wilson, Bedau); naturalism is self-defeating in that it asserts more than its own strictures allow it to assert (Bealer, Foley, Myro, Wagner); naturalism is inconsistent with other things we are clearly justified in thinking (Baker, Bealer, Bedau, Foley, Warner). The specific criticisms assess specific attempts to "naturalize" crucial philosophical concepts: epistemological concepts (Bedau, Shatz); ethical concepts (Audi); propositional attitudes (Baker, Pratt); the mental generally and supervenience in particular (Horgan).

Clearly, the contributors critique naturalism across a wide front. There are also other ways in which the front is broad. In particular, the contributors differ in their attitude toward the "authority of science." By such an attitude, we mean the way in which one is inclined to resolve a conflict between a scientifically validated claim and one not so validated, say a claim of common sense. Those who unqualifiedly accept the authority of science think that the scientifically unvalidated claim must always yield. Several contributors do not accept the authority of science in this sense (Bealer, Foley, Myro, Warner); others do (Horgan, Wagner, and Wilson, although the latter two with *caveats*); others are noncommittal (Audi, Bedau, Pratt, Shatz); one (Baker) thinks each case should be separately evaluated and that many conflicts may be illusory.[18] This difference certainly underlies another, a difference in attitude towards naturalism itself; for, to accept naturalism fully is (in part) to accept the authority of science. Some hold out hope for some sort of naturalism, or at least hold positions not inconsistent with such a hope (Audi, Foley, Horgan, Shatz); others reject naturalism outright (Baker, Bealer, Bedau, Myro [ultimately], Wagner, Warner); one contributor (Wilson) considers himself a physicalist but views the matter as relatively unimportant.

While some philosophers see traditional philosophy dissolving into a variety of different camps or "conversations," and lament or applaud the dissolution, we see vitality in the vigorous critique of naturalism from a variety of perspectives. The reexamination of the recent roots of contemporary philosophy promises new directions for fruitful inquiry. It is noteworthy that the reexamination sounds many familiar, traditional themes —

skepticism, incorrigibility, the nature and role of science, the justification of belief, the place of value and the mind in the natural world.

Notes

1. W. V. Quine, *Word and Object* (Cambridge, Mass.: MIT Press, 1960).

2. We will also use 'science' as shorthand for 'natural science'. This is strictly for brevity and reflects no endorsement of naturalist classifications.

3. The problematic of German philosophy in the decades after Hegel turns out to be remarkably similar to that of English-speaking philosophers now. See Hans Schnädelbach, *Philosophy in Germany: 1831–1933* (Cambridge: Cambridge University Press, 1984).

4. Esp. in *Philosophy and the Mirror of Nature* (Princeton, N.J.: Princeton University Press, 1979), *Consequences of Pragmatism* (Minneapolis: University of Minnesota Press, 1982), and *Contingency, Irony, Solidarity* (Cambridge: Cambridge University Press, 1989).

5. For Rorty, the idea of distinctively cognitive value already implies the error of restricting "factuality" to some preferred area of discourse (such as science). Our point here is that there is no general sense in which literature is supposed to be less informative or valuable than science.

6. See esp. Hilary Putnam, *Realism and Reason* (Cambridge: Cambridge University Press, 1983); *The Many Faces of Realism* (La Salle, Ill.: Open Court, 1987); *Representation and Reality* (Cambridge, Mass.: MIT Press, 1988); and *Realism with a Human Face* (Cambridge, Mass.: Harvard University Press, 1990).

7. Putnam's critique of positivism was one of the influences on Rorty. There seems to have been some influence in the other direction concerning pragmatism and the cultural significance of naturalism.

8. *The Many Faces of Realism* is the main source for the next two paragraphs. See also *Realism with a Human Face,* e.g., essay 11.

9. This suggests that at some point — some distance below music criticism, perhaps — an area of discourse will suffer from a fatal lack of objectivity. That is apparently Putnam's view, although he does not elaborate.

10. E.g., Nelson Goodman, *Ways of Worldmaking* (Indianapolis: Hackett, 1978).

11. *Representation and Reality* (p. 114) offers this name as an improvement on Putnam's older 'internal realism' (while still keeping the latter term). Given the historical opposition between pragmatism and metaphysics, we suggest that the very concept of "pragmatic realism" signals a fundamental ambivalence in Putnam.

12. Israel Scheffler, *Science and Subjectivity* (Indianapolis: Bobbs-Merrill, 1967), 1.

13. Note that we are speaking of the effects of prejudice on the content of established physical theory. Of course racial, political, and gender biases (among other factors) affect the training and hiring of physicists, the composition of editorial boards for journals, and so forth.

14. There are sharp differences between naturalism and positivism. Naturalism, unlike positivism, aims to solve traditional problems of philosophy. Also, it neither holds a positivist view of meaning nor rests on any theory of meaning at all. So the evolution from positivism to naturalism is a complex one that deserves a separate investigation.

15. E.g., Patricia Churchland, *Neurophilosophy* (Cambridge, Mass.: MIT Press, 1986); Stephen Stich, *From Folk Psychology to Cognitive Science* (Cambridge, Mass.: MIT Press, 1983).

16. E.g., Jerry Fodor, *Psychosemantics* (Cambridge, Mass.: MIT Press, 1987).

17. E.g., Donald Davidson, *Inquiries into Truth and Interpretation* (Oxford: Oxford University Press, 1984).

18. This is the position Professor Baker adopted in a recent conversation about the position taken in her essay.

Naturalism and Teleology

Mark Bedau

1. Naturalism, Mind, and Biological Teleology

Naturalism is less a specific doctrine than an intellectual movement guided by the principle that everything real is at least in principle within the scope of a purely scientific description of the world.[1] Consider Armstrong, who defends a naturalism defined as "the doctrine that reality consists of nothing but a single all-embracing spacio-temporal system,"[2] and Fodor, who worries about how "the semantic/intentional properties of things . . . supervene upon their physical properties."[3] Although there is ample room for divergent positions under the naturalistic umbrella, it is widely agreed to exclude moral and, more generally, evaluative matters. A naturalistic theory must, as Millikan insists, be "nonnormative."[4] Some form of a relatively rigid fact-value distinction is erected, with "transcendent standards of value," to use Armstrong's words, banished from the natural order.[5] Let *narrow naturalism* be this naturalism-*cum*-descriptivism. (References to unqualified naturalism in what follows are always to apply to narrow naturalism.)

Most criticisms of naturalism have focused on whether there can be a place in a narrowly natural world for self-conscious, morally responsible agents.[6] It is striking, then, that almost *no* criticism has focused on biological teleology. Both mental agency and biological teleology are typified by purposes, goals, and the like, but only biological teleology seems to fit neatly within the naturalistic fold. It is true that some biologists avoid all teleological explanations, believing them to be unscientific, Aristotelian throwbacks, even though this causes the intellectual tension expressed by J. B. S. Haldane's quip that "Teleology is like a mistress to a biologist: he cannot live without her but he's unwilling to be seen with her in public." However, most naturalistically inclined philosophers publicly embrace biological teleology without embarrassment, for they believe that it is now clear at least in rough outline how teleological explanations fit within the

23

legitimate explanatory patterns employed by the physical sciences generally.[7] Contemporary naturalistic treatments of biological teleology tend
to fall into two broad groups, one inspired by the dramatic success of cybernetics and general systems theory, the other largely modeled after natural selection. Although specialists still debate the details and the relative
merits of these two approaches to teleology, the majority conviction is
that ultimately some version of one of these approaches will emerge vic-
torious. Either way, a naturalistic treatment of biological teleology would
be secured.

This essay aims to undermine this consensus of confidence in naturalized teleology and suggest that problems for naturalism arise at a level
prior to morals and the mind. Upon examination, the two naturalistic approaches to teleology are seen to be inadequate. Their failures can be traced
specifically to their inability to give an appropriate role for evaluative notions. Although the rough outline of a value-centered approach to teleology
can be pieced together from the following discussion, the details of the
theory must be developed elsewhere.[8] Instead, the aim here will be to reveal the evaluative barrier to naturalistic approaches to biological teleology.

This barrier to naturalism in teleology is significant in part because
it robs the naturalistic movement of what was banked on as a naturalistic
done deal. The success of naturalism in teleology has not only been held
up as a model and a source of inspiration in more difficult battles still under-
way; it also has itself been wielded by naturalists as a weapon in those
very battles. Most notable, perhaps, is how biological teleology has been
invoked recently in the attempt to save naturalism in contemporary philosophy of mind.

Functionalism in one form or another is the position favored by
most naturalistically inclined philosophers of mind. Recently, functionalists have been attracted by the idea of explicitly appealing to biological
(also called "natural") teleology.[9] For example, it has been hoped that the
excessive liberality that leaves functionalism open to counterexamples,
such as Block's well-known example involving the Chinese nation, can be
avoided by

> imposing a teleological requirement on realization: a physical state of an
> organism will count as realizing such-and-such a functional description only
> if the organism has genuine organic integrity and the state plays its func-
> tional role properly *for* the organism, in the teleological sense of "for" and
> in the teleological sense of "function." The state must do what it does as
> a matter of, so to speak, its biological purpose.[10]

In addition, it has been hoped that teleology will help provide a naturalistic account of the intentionality or representative content of mental states.[11]

Let us baptize this naturalistic wedding of functionalism and natural teleology as *teleo-functionalism*.

Teleo-functionalists typically appeal to an intuitive notion of biological teleology. They confidently assume that one of the standard naturalistic theories of teleology will prove adequate and leave it to the specialists to settle the details. But if it should prove true that natural teleology is essentially value-centered, then teleo-functionalism must immediately confront two problems. First, teleo-functionalists sharply distinguish intentional or mental teleology from natural or biological teleology, emphasizing that they appeal to natural teleology.[12] The reason for this is plain; if a functionalist account of the mind is to employ a teleological condition, then on pain of vicious circularity the teleology had better not be mental. But if natural teleology involves value, then the threat of vicious circularity arises anew, for the analysis of value might itself appeal to mental considerations. At the very least, teleo-functionalists must show that the value considerations embedded in natural teleology are not mentalistic. The teleo-functionalist's second problem would be to give value a naturalistic interpretation. Without providing this, the value-centered theory of teleology, and the fusion of functionalism and biological teleology, would be off limits for naturalists. This is an apparently insurmountable hurdle for narrow naturalism. Even if teleo-functionalists were willing to embrace broader forms of naturalism, naturalism in the philosophy of mind would not be home free unless and until a suitable naturalistic interpretation of value had been provided. At the very least, teleo-functionalism depends on an unacknowledged and undefended thesis to the effect that the fact-value distinction can be breached and value can be naturalistically construed.

For these reasons, if the naturalistic approaches to teleology fail, an attractive avenue leading to naturalism in the philosophy of mind appears to be blocked. But do they fail? We will consider each in turn.

2. Cybernetic Systems

Goal-directedness is a central kind of telic phenomena. We can readily identify goal-directed systems and distinguish them from systems that are not goal directed. A woodpecker hunting for grubs gives an intuitively clear example of the first, a pendulum returning to rest gives an intuitively clear example of the second. But what is it to be a goal-directed system? One popular construal of the intuitive notion of a goal-directed system is inspired by systems theories like cybernetics.[13] Other telic phenomena are then construed by reference to goal-directed systems.[14] If sound, this systems approach would show that telic phenomena fall within the naturalistic fold and can be explained by (a special subset of) the kind of efficient causal explanations used in the physical sciences generally. It would then be appropriate to view telic phenomena in a purely descriptive, nonevaluative light. Furthermore, these purely descriptive characterizations of telic phenomena would tend to be expressible in quantitative terms, thus promoting the kind of scientific progress enabled by the shift from qualitative to quantitative methods. It is ironic that the flaw with the systems approach derives precisely from its value-free, quantitative form.[15]

The basic idea of the systems approach is that goal-directed systems are, roughly, those systems that have a tendency to maintain a state (called the "goal state") in the face of external and internal perturbations.[16] Not all goal-maintaining systems successfully maintain their goal states, so it is sufficient for a goal-directed system to attain, oscillate around, or approach its goal state. There are two traditional behavioral signs of goal-directed systems: plasticity and persistence.[17] According to the traditional view, goal-directed systems are systems with the capacity for exhibiting a plastic and persistent range of behaviors that result in the production of the "goal state."[18] It is convenient to distinguish two kinds of forces (or variables) in goal-directed systems. *Deflecting* forces deflect a system from its goal state, and *restoring* forces restore the system to its goal state. The behavior of a goal-directed system is *plastic,* then, if restoring forces can come in a variety of strengths and from a variety of directions; and its behavior is *persistent* if (within certain limits) a deflecting force is eventually balanced by equally strong and oppositely directed restoring forces.

Much of the discussion of the systems approach is couched in terms of artifacts — steam engines with governors, homing torpedoes — reflecting its outgrowth from cybernetic engineering. But one of the strong points of the approach is that it would apply univocally to biological systems as well. A nice biological illustration of the approach is the biological system that keeps the concentration of water in the blood of mammals at about 90 percent.[19] The system has two main components: the kidneys, which remove water from the blood, and the muscles, which release water into the blood. If the organism drinks some water, perspires, or does something else that makes the concentration of water in the blood rise much above or sink much below 90 percent, then there is a corresponding change in the rate at which the kidneys take water out of the blood and the rate at which muscles release water into the blood. The direction and magnitude of these changes is such that, due to their combined effect, the system has a plastic and persistent disposition to maintain a narrowly circumscribed goal state, so that, unless the system breaks down, the concentration of water in the blood constantly hovers near 90 percent.

The systems approach has been the target of many criticisms, but with suitable modifications it can handle a wide variety of problems.[20] However, there is a fundamental flaw that continually recurs: systems that nobody would think are genuinely goal directed pass the systems tests for being goal directed. The counterexamples are certain systems that tend toward some steady state or state of equilibrium; such systems can be called *equilibrium systems.* Some equilibrium states are states of rest, states in which all motion stops. A pendulum that is damped by friction, for example, is an equilibrium system and its equilibrium state is the state in which the bob is motionless at the bottom of its arc. Other equilibrium states consist of regular cyclic motion, such as the constant swinging back and forth of the bob of a frictionless pendulum.

Many equilibrium systems are not goal directed, intuitively, even though they exhibit persistent and plastic behavior with respect to a state that one can label the "goal state." Two familiar examples are a marble inside a bowl and a simple pendulum. Intuitively, the system consisting of a marble in a bowl is not really directed to any goal, even though the system plastically and persistently pursues the "goal state" of keeping the marble in the bottom of the bowl. The behavior of the system is plastic, since the goal can be reached from many different directions and initial conditions; it is persistent, since the marble's behavior automatically adjusts if it is deflected from its goal state. Similarly, a damped pendulum persistently and plastically pursues a "goal state" if given impulses by gusts of wind. Intuitively, however, the pendulum system is no more goal directed than the marble in the bowl. Equilibrium system counterexamples are easy to find. In fact, defenders of the systems approach have admitted that persistence and plasticity apply in "well nigh all processes in which some equilibrium state is restored."[21] So, if persistence and plasticity alone were signs of goal-directedness, then virtually everything would be goal directed and, as Nagel puts it, "the concept of being goal-directed would not be differentiating, and would therefore be superfluous."[22] The task of excluding non-goal-directed equilibrium systems can be called the *equilibrium problem.*

A natural hypothesis is that equilibrium systems are too simple to be goal directed; the persistent and plastic behavior of genuinely goal-directed systems must have a more complicated explanation. Following this line of thought, Nagel proposed supplementing the requirements of persistence and plasticity with the condition that the behavior of goal-directed systems is governed by "orthogonal" or independent variables; that is, "within certain limits the value of a variable at a given moment is compatible with *any* value of the other [system controlling] variables at the *same* moment."[23] It is natural to interpret this condition as the requirement that the deflecting and restoring forces must be independent. Although this requirement rules out many equilibrium systems, it does not save the systems approach, for it is also rules out most genuinely goal-directed systems.[24] Recall that the behavior of goal-directed systems is persistent because deflecting forces are balanced by equally strong but oppositely directed restoring forces. That is, goal-directed systems are structured in a way that guarantees that, as long as the system does not break down, the deflecting force and the restoring force are balanced. Thus, the deflecting and restoring forces in (well-functioning) genuinely goal-directed systems are not independent.

Defenders of the systems approach have tried to identify exactly which *kind* of factors bring about the balance between deflecting and restoring forces in goal-directed systems. Thus, in order to handle the problem above, Nagel has recently proposed the following condition:[25]

[S1] Apart from the balance between the variables brought about by the system itself (because of their role in goal-directed processes), the deflecting variables must be independent of the restoring variables.

This condition requires the restoring force and the deflecting force in goal-directed systems to be balanced not merely because of background laws of nature; rather, the balance must be something that the system itself brings about. A goal-directed system has the disposition to reorient itself toward its goal specifically because of the particular way in which the system is configured (designed or structured). When a goal-directed system is dismantled, the system loses its capacity to balance the deflecting and restoring forces and maintain its goal. For example, consider how Nagel explains what would happen if a Watt governor were dismantled:

[W]hen the so-called "Watt governor" of a steam engine is not hitched up to the engine, any speed of the engine is compatible with any spread of the arms of the governor; for there are no known laws of nature according to which, in the assumed circumstances, the spread of the arms depends on the engine speed. . . . [This system, if intact,] is goal-directed with respect to a certain rotation speed of the engine's driving wheel. But if the relations holding between the behavior of the governor and the engine speed were included among the laws of nature, that system could no longer be so characterized.[26]

The deflecting and restoring forces are balanced because of the general laws of nature *and various facts about the structure of the system*. If the structure of the system changes (because the governor is dismantled, for example), restoring forces will no longer balance deflecting forces. Nagel has defended condition [S1] against the criticism that it depends on a dis-

tinction between laws of nature and laws that hold only for various spe-
cialized structures.[27] But there is a more fundamental problem: it fails to
rule out certain equilibrium systems. Nagel considered the effect of changing the internal structure of a steam engine. In like fashion, consider the
effect of changing the internal structure of a marble-plus-bowl system by,
for example, shattering the bowl or slicing off the sides of the bowl. Changing the system in this way destroys the system's capacity to balance deflecting forces by restoring forces. Thus, in the "dismantled" marble-plus-bowl
system the deflecting and restoring forces are independent, and the system
satisfies condition [S1]. Similarly, dismantle or destroy any other equilibrium system and restoring forces will no longer balance deflecting forces.
Equilibrium systems balance deflecting forces with restoring forces in part
because of the system's internal structure. So [S1] fails to rule out non-
goal-directed equilibrium systems.

   Defenders of the systems approach might try another tack and hypothesize that equilibrium systems are not goal directed because the cause
of their behavior is too simple or too direct, which suggests the following
condition as a solution to the equilibrium problem.[28]

   [S2] The causal connection between the deflecting variables and the
         restoring variables must not be simple and direct.

Although it is not completely clear what "simple and direct" causal connections are, it is plausible that there is a simple and direct causal connection between the deflecting and restoring variables in the marble-plus-bowl
system and other simple equilibrium systems, so it is plausible that condition [S2] (correctly) rules them out. The condition also seems to correctly
rule in goal-directed systems, such as the kidney-plus-muscle system, a
guided missile, or a woodpecker searching for grubs; whatever the causal
connection between deflecting forces and restoring forces is like, it certainly
is not simple and direct. However, condition [S2] will not save the systems
approach. Highly complex and indirect causal connections are not sufficient
to make a system genuinely goal directed. It is easy to construct more and
more elaborate modifications of a simple pendulum, in which there are
more and more complex and remote causal connections between deflecting and restoring forces. For example, consider a pendulum suspended from
a balloon with a steel bob hanging from a rubber band and swinging above
an electromagnet powered by a battery. Then, couple this pendulum with
another one by suspending the first from the bob of the second. Next, isolate the whole apparatus inside a gravity-free chamber, and power the electromagnet with a generator turned by a waterfall far outside the chamber.
Finally, concoct a mechanism that makes the temperature in the chamber
(and, thus, the length of the rubber band) a function of, say, the number

of vehicles on the Golden Gate Bridge. By now, there would be a quite complex and indirect causal connection between the pendulum's deflecting and restoring variables. Furthermore, it would be easy to make the connections infinitely more complex and indirect. But making the causal dynamics of a non-goal-directed pendulum more complex and indirect does not turn it into a goal-directed system. Thus, the degree of complexity and degree of remoteness of causal connection do not provide a sign of goal-directed systems.

No doubt there are other possible system-theoretic conditions besides those just examined and rejected, so rejecting those conditions does not by itself prove that the systems approach cannot solve the equilibrium problem. However, if one could provide a recipe for constructing new counterexamples for each possible new system condition, then one could argue against the sufficiency of all possible systems-theoretic conditions.

A preliminary glimpse of such a recipe comes from considering whether what we might call *pseudo-bridges* have functions. Out in an uninhabited desert there could be a physical object that is causally structured just like a bridge, but which is the result of an accidental collision of the purely impersonal forces of nature—no goal-directed behavior plays any role in the object's origin. So-called "natural bridges" are very crude illustrations of what pseudo-bridges can be like. A pseudo-bridge presumably "bridges" some chasm, river, etc., and it might be structured in such a way that it is ideally suited to be used as a bridge. The question is whether a pseudo-bridge has the function of a bridge. If it came to be used as a bridge, then it would acquire the function of a bridge. Even if never used as a bridge, if someone noticed it and intended to use it as a bridge, then it might acquire the function of a bridge. But being ideally suited to be used as a bridge does not all by itself bestow it with that function. Many stones are ideally suited to be used as paperweights, but most are not paperweights and lack any such function. Similarly, if a pseudo-bridge is never used as a bridge and never intended to be used as a bridge, then it lacks the function of a bridge.[29]

An analogous conclusion can be drawn about goal-directed systems. Call a *pseudo-goal system* any system with two features: (i) it has the same systems-theoretic structure and the same apparently goal-directed behavior as some (actual or merely possible) genuinely goal-directed system, but (ii) goal-directed behavior plays no role in the origin or the (actual or intended) use of the system. Notice that, because of condition (ii), none of the standard examples of genuinely goal-directed systems qualify as pseudo-goal systems. Goal-directed organisms (e.g., a woodpecker hunting for grubs), goal-directed organs and biological systems inside organisms (e.g., a mammal's temperature regulating system), and goal-directed artifacts (e.g., a guided missile) arise from processes involving goal-directed behavior. However, because of condition (i), pseudo-goal systems are indistinguishable from genuinely goal-directed systems, from the systems-theoretic point of view.

A realistic example of a pseudo-goal system is Lost Cave, which was prominent in the media recently.[30] This cave, located in southeastern New Mexico, remains at a constant climate of 69 degrees Fahrenheit and 99 percent humidity, regardless of the fluctuations in the temperature outside. Because of its natural climate control (and its proximity to NASA's Johnson Space Center and the medical school in Houston), it is used in experiments for determining the effects of isolation on humans. If Lost Cave had not existed, scientists might have created something just like it in order to have a climatically constant isolation chamber. Is Lost Cave a goal-directed system with the goal of climate control? The cave has acquired certain telic properties, since people use it as an isolation chamber. But, intuitively, before it was used it was not directed to any goal, even though it maintained a constant climate in just the way that a genuinely goal-directed system might. Likewise for other caves that similarly remain at a constant climate. Miners in the Australian outback construct dwellings underground in order to escape the heat, and the climate control that ensues is the result of an intentionally created goal-directed system. But exactly the same kind of climate control might result accidentally. Caverns that would be ideally suited for underground dwellings are not goal-directed systems if nobody is aware of them.

In general, pseudo-goal systems merely appear to be goal directed. But the systems approach cannot distinguish pseudo-goal systems from the genuinely goal-directed systems that they match. Any systems condition could be met by an appropriate physical structure created and formed by an accidental collision of forces. In an extreme case, a cosmic accident could produce an object structured just like a house with thermostatically controlled central heating. Nevertheless, this accidental structure would no more be goal directed than an accidentally bridge-shaped structure would have the function of a bridge.

The previous section's glance at systems diagnoses of the equilibrium problem revealed some inadequate systems signs of goal-directedness. The pseudo-goal system argument shows that this pattern of failures is no fluke. Every possible systems condition will fail to be a sign of goal-directedness because no systems-theoretic condition can exclude pseudo-goal systems. The intuitive notion of goal-directedness is not (solely) a systems condition. The goal-directedness of a system does not supervene on the system's systems-theoretic (physical, naturalistic) features. Any systems-theoretic condition met by any goal-directed system could be met by some non-goal-directed pseudo-goal system. It is true that, by accident, some systems-theoretic condition might happen to be true of all and only the actual goal-directed systems because no appropriate pseudo-goal system exists. But an appropriate pseudo-goal system might have existed and might come to exist. Therefore, any systems-theoretic condition that happened to be true for the moment would be just an accident.

It is one thing to know that the systems approach cannot solve the equilibrium problem; it is another thing to know why. What do equilibrium systems lack? What must be added to a pseudo-goal equilibrium system in order to make it genuinely goal directed? The system diagnosis would be to situate the equilibrium system inside another system that was suitably more complex. I will briefly defend an alternative diagnosis: Equilibrium systems fail to be genuinely goal directed when as a matter of fact their equilibrium-maintaining behavior is of no value for anything.[31]

Preliminary support for this value diagnosis comes from a twofold pattern involving the role of value in examples of genuine and spurious goal-directed systems. On the one hand, systems that are not goal directed can be value free. Water flowing downhill, a marble rolling around in a bowl, a pendulum returning to rest — nothing in things like these need be of any value to anyone or anything. One can easily conceive of cases in which the behavior of these things *does* benefit someone or something, but value *need* play no such role. In general, the behavior of equilibrium systems that are not goal directed either does not, or need not, benefit anything. On the other hand, value standardly plays a central role in genuinely goal-directed systems. It is no accident that the grub-seeking behavior of a woodpecker benefits the woodpecker, the self-regulation of a steam engine with a governor benefits the people using the engine, or a mammal's temperature regulation system benefits the organism. This pattern of goal-directedness standing or falling with a suitable role for value suggests that the right role for value is at least part of what is missing from equilibrium systems.

Further support for the value diagnosis comes from considering how to turn an equilibrium system that is not goal directed, such as a simple marble-plus-bowl, into one that is. According to the value diagnosis, the shortcoming of the marble-plus-bowl system is that the behavior of the system provides no benefit to anyone or anything. To test this diagnosis, consider the effect of changing the system so that its behavior does provide value by benefiting either an organism containing the system or a person using the system. As an illustration of the first possibility, consider a creature with a marble-plus-bowl system as a proprioceptive organ — call it the *marble-plus-bowl organ*. The creature maintains its balance if the marble-like-object is kept at the bottom of the bowllike object. It is good for our hypothetical creature to have a good sense of balance, and the marble-plus-bowl organ is structured in such a way that (under normal conditions) it provides a good sense of balance. So, the behavior of the marble-plus-bowl organ is good for the creature. As an illustration of the second way in which the behavior of a marble-plus-bowl system can provide a benefit, consider people who measure the stability of surfaces with a marble-plus-bowl system — call it the *marble-plus-bowl instrument*. It is used by placing it on a flat surface and checking the marble's behavior, thereby measuring the stability of the surface. Since knowing how stable a surface is benefits these people, the behavior of the marble-plus-bowl instrument is of value for them.

Intuitively, a simple marble-plus-bowl system is not only not goal directed; it also lacks all other teleological properties. It has no function, no purpose, is not for the sake of anything, etc. But, when value is added, as in the marble-plus-bowl organ and instrument, teleology emerges. The marble-plus-bowl organ and instrument clearly have functions, and, while intuitions may vary about whether they are themselves goal-directed systems, they clearly are at least parts of goal-directed systems. The marble-plus-bowl organ is part of a creature's proprioceptive system, which is a classic example of a goal-directed system, on a par with the system that regulates the concentration of water in the blood. The marble-plus-bowl instrument is part of a goal-directed system consisting of the people who are using it to accomplish their goals. Furthermore, even if the marble-plus-bowl organ and instrument are not themselves goal-directed systems, their behavior has a goal-directed quality because it contributes to the goals of these larger systems. The behavior of the marble in the organ contributes to the creature's goal of balance, and the behavior of the marble in the instrument helps achieve the person's goal of measuring stability. The causal dynamics of a marble-plus-bowl system is not altered when it becomes an organ or an instrument. Instead, that dynamics is exploited to provide some benefit. Thus, making the behavior of an equilibrium system provide a benefit can be enough to make the equilibrium system part of a goal-directed system. In other words, what seems to be missing from equilibrium systems is an appropriate role for value.

Adherents to the systems approach tend to try to couch the distinction between goal-directed and non-goal-directed systems in *quantitative* terms. The number of (kinds of) variables governing a system, the degree of complexity and directness of (kinds of) causal connections that the system brings about — conditions like these are interesting in part just because they are quantitative. However, intuitively, there is a fundamentally *qualitative* difference between a genuine goal-directed system and a system that merely behaves as if it were goal directed. A non-goal-directed system cannot be turned into a goal-directed system merely by adding more independent variables or making the connection between deflecting and restoring variables more complex and indirect. The equilibrium problem shows that the intrinsic causal dynamics of a system do not determine whether the system's behavior is goal directed. No systems condition is sufficient for all actual and possible goal-directed systems. Thus, the systems approach does not fulfill the hope for a naturalistic, purely descriptive theory of teleology.

3. Consequence Etiology and Natural Selection

Reflecting on the pseudo-goal argument suggests that details of etiology matter to teleological systems. In fact, the second contemporary naturalistic approach to teleology is keyed to certain kinds of etiologies — "consequence" etiologies. The idea behind this etiological approach to teleology is, roughly, that something happens in order to achieve a goal when (i) it tends to bring about that goal and (ii) it happens because of its tendency to bring about the goal.[32] To get a feel for this approach, consider the heart pumping blood in order to circulate it. According to the etiological approach, this means that (i) the heart's pumping of the blood tends to circulate the blood and (ii) the heart pumps blood because doing so contributes to circulating it. Certainly, the heart's pumping does circulate the blood, but why does the heart pump blood? Well, the heart would not be pumping unless the creature possessing it were alive, and the creature would not be alive unless its blood were being circulated. If the heart were to stop circulating the blood, the creature would die and its heart would stop pumping. So, the heart pumps in part because doing so contributes to circulating the blood.

There is much to be said for the etiological approach to teleology,[33] but as it stands it is not sufficient — something that is not teleological might nevertheless have an etiology like the heart's. Consider a stick floating down a stream that brushes against a rock and comes to be pinned there by the backwash it creates.[34] The stick is creating the backwash because of a number of factors, including the flow of the water, the shape and mass of the stick, etc., but part of the explanation of why it creates the backwash is that the stick is pinned in a certain way on the rock by the water. Why is it pinned in that way? The stick originally became pinned there accidentally, and it remained pinned there because that way of being pinned is self-perpetuating. Therefore, once pinned, part of the explanation for why the stick is creating the backwash is that the backwash keeps it pinned there and being pinned there causes the backwash. In this case, the stick meets the etiological conditions: creating the backwash tends to pin the stick on the rock and the stick creates the backwash because doing so contributes to pinning it. However, clearly the stick does not create the backwash *in order to* keep itself pinned on the rock. The stick's behavior has no teleological explanation.

Given that the heart example and the stick example involve a similar sort of etiology, why is only the heart example teleological? There are two ways to answer this question, both involving a revision of the etiological approach: to appeal to value, or to appeal to natural selection. One clear difference between the two cases is that the heart's pumping is *good* for the creature, but the stick's backwash is not good for the stick (and it need not be good for anything whatsoever). Thus, one diagnosis of the stick in the stream counterexample is that teleology must involve an appropriate role for value. Teleology involves not merely effects that tend to bring about their own production, but *good* effects that tend to bring about their own production.[35]

Those sympathetic with the etiological approach might offer an alternative diagnosis in terms of natural selection. Roughly, the idea would be that a feature is for the sake of any effect by virtue of which it is naturally selected, i.e., by virtue of which it is favored by natural selection.[36] Appealing to natural selection would handle the stick example because natural selection does not explain why the stick is stuck on the rock. Sticks floating in streams do not reproduce their kind. Being (able to be) stuck on a rock is not a trait inherited from parent sticks, nor is it a trait that affects a stick's "fitness." So, the stick in the stream is not a counterexample to a version of the etiological approach that explicitly invokes natural selection. Perhaps the value diagnosis is wrong and teleology can be naturalized by appeal to natural selection.

Both the value diagnosis and the natural selection diagnosis rule out the stick in the stream. To decide between these diagnoses, we need a case that drives a wedge between them. But it is difficult to find a value-free case of natural selection. The familiar biological examples of natural selection will not do, since they typically involve traits that are *beneficial* to biological organisms. Typically, the traits by virtue of which natural selection favors an organism benefit the organism. For example, once the forests around industrial centers in England became besooted by industrial pollution, the whitish forms of the peppered moth *Biston betularia* became much easier for predatory birds to find. In those environments, industrial melanism (black coloration) benefited the peppered moth by camouflaging them.[37] What we need is a case of natural selection in which value clearly plays no role whatsoever.

To find such a case, it is helpful first to focus on the idea of a value-

free situation. It seems that, everything else being equal, surviving is good
for an organism. An organism seems worse off if it is barely eking out
an existence; it seems better off to the extent that it is flourishing. One
way to guarantee a value-free situation would be to have one free from
all forms of life. So, my strategy in the following pages will be first to describe a lifeless planet, devoid of teleology, and also devoid of natural selection. Then I will add to the planet what is required for natural selection
to occur among certain inorganic minerals. But at no stage will the planet
contain any form of life.

Consider a planet containing land and sea masses surrounded by an
atmosphere. In addition to certain atmospheric gases (oxygen, hydrogen),
the planet contains various relatively simple mineral compounds, such as
those found in rocks and sand (silicate, aluminium, etc.). The stuff on this
planet is subject to the familiar orchestra of physico-chemical processes,
from Born repulsion to covalent bonding. Sand and dust are blown about,
rains fall, rocks weather, particles become suspended in water and then
are sedimented, minerals dissolve and crystallize out of solution, chemical
bonds form and break. Various physico-chemical equilibria are disturbed
and restored; various cyclical physical processes occur (a water cycle, a tidal
cycle, daily and seasonal temperature cycles; etc.). But the planet is lifeless.
It contains absolutely no forms of life, not even any organic molecules.

Not only is this dead planet value free, I take it to be uncontroversial
that there is nothing teleological on it. Nothing has any purpose, nothing
is for the sake of anything. Everything that happens on the dead planet
is a paradigm of an ordinary efficient causal process. The dead planet would
be thought to involve teleology only by someone, perhaps like Teilhard
de Chardin,[38] who finds teleology in virtually every merely physical process—in water flowing downhill or in the cycle of the tides.

In addition to lacking value and teleology, the dead planet also lacks
natural selection. Specifically, it lacks each of the following four necessary
and jointly sufficient conditions for natural selection:[39]

(1) There must be a population of *reproducing entities*. Each member of the population has a kind of individual identity, a "life"
of its own. New members of the population are created from existing members when "parents" give "birth" to "children."

(2) Members of the population will possess various kinds of traits.
Some traits will be shared across the board; all moths have a pair
of wings. Other traits will be unique to a few; individual moths
have idiosyncratically specific numbers of bristles on their bodies.
There must be *random variation* among some of the traits possessed by the members of the population, as there is among col-

oration in peppered moths. These variations must be random, not in being uncaused, but in that which of the variable traits will change is unpredictable and in that there is no connection between the specific changes that occur and their potential significance for the organism.[40]

(3) "Children" must *inherit* some traits from their "parents," including at least some that are subject to random variation. Some traits cannot be inherited at all, such as characteristics acquired in response to environmental contingencies. Others are inherited by all members of a population, such as a moth's trait of having a pair of wings. But some of the traits which randomly vary from individual to individual, such as a moth's coloration, must also be inherited.

(4) Some of the randomly varying inherited traits must be *adaptive* in the sense that they can causally influence the extent to which the entities with the traits proliferate. That is, the traits must affect a lineage's fitness. A trait's adaptivity can be relative to the local environmental context. For example, whereas whitish coloration benefits peppered moths in an environment of lichen-covered trees, this coloration is harmful in an environment besooted by industrial pollution.

It turns out that each of these prerequisites for natural selection can be added (step-by-step, or all at once) to the dead planet. What is rather surprising is that in the process the planet remains entirely devoid of life. Thus, natural selection can take place in an entirely inorganic setting.[41] This is possible because of the nature of crystals, specifically, the microscopic crystallites of inorganic materials out of which clays and muds are composed.[42] When we think of crystals, we tend to think of something on the order of fingernail or fist-sized chunks of quartz, amethyst, mica, or possibly diamond. The last thing that comes to mind is clay. But if you were to magnify particles of clay thousands of times with a scanning electron microscope, you would see an amazing diversity of tiny crystallites.[43]

Populations of clay crystals have each of the four features necessary for natural selection. In fact, natural selection is occurring in populations of clay crystals all over the earth right now. Consider each prerequisite for natural selection in turn.

Step 1: Reproduction. Crystals are simply layers of orderly arrays of molecules, which grow as new layers are added on top of existing layers. Clay crystals are formed basically from silicic acid (SiO_4) and hydrated cations (positively charged ions). These crystals can form in the presence of a supersaturated silica solution if crystal "seeds" (small pieces of crystal) are present. A new layer grows as silica atoms from the solution become affixed to the surface of the seed. When a crystal becomes big enough it cleaves and pieces break off, becoming seeds for new crystals. In this fashion, crystals reproduce. Clay crystals tend to break up easily during their formation as a result of cyclical and sporadic variations in ambient conditions, similar to the way in which the layers of a mica crystal (not a clay, but a relatively easily studied prototype for clays) can separate because of changes in external conditions, such as the presence of certain ions.[44] Cairns-Smith describes how to perform a simple experiment that illustrates this process of reproduction on a macroscopic scale.

> Take about 250 grams of photographer's 'hypo' (sodium thiosulphate penta-hydrate) and put it in a clean 250 millilitre beaker together with 75 millilitres of distilled water. Heat to near boiling, stirring the solution. . . . Remove the beaker from the heat and cover it immediately with a loose-fitting lid to keep out the dust . . . and leave strictly alone for several hours, for the solution to cool. . . . Carefully take the lid off the beaker, drop one tiny piece of 'hypo' crystal onto the surface of the solution, and watch amazed at what happens. Your crystal grows visibly: it breaks up from time to time and the pieces also grow. . . . Soon your beaker is crowded with crystals, some several centimetres long. Then after a few minutes it all stops.[45]

The reproduction process in this experiment stops when the solution ceases to be supersaturated. If crystals were continually removed from the beaker and the supersaturated solution were continually refreshed, a population of crystals could reseed and reproduce indefinitely. (In fact, this is roughly what happens in the continuous crystallizers used to produce crystals commercially.) Just as a population of reproducing biological organisms is the setting for biological evolution, a population of reproducing crystals can be the setting for crystal evolution.

Step 2: Variation. In an ideal world all crystals of a given substance would be exactly alike in structure. Each part of an ideal crystal would have a molecular lattice structure that is just like that found in every other part. In our actual world, all crystals have flaws.[46] Some flaws are physical imperfections, such as edge dislocations (a slip at right angles to a line defect), screw dislocations (a slipping of lattice units parallel to a line defect), and grain boundaries (a mismatch between two separate lattices). Flaws can also be chemical imperfections, such as interstitial flaws in which "foreign" atoms are found in spaces between normal lattice constituents, and substitutional flaws in which foreign atoms replace some of the normal lattice constituents. These crystal defects are produced haphazardly, "randomly," just as genetic mutations are, and the potential variety of crystalline defects is enormous. These flaws can be a source of novel information in the evolution of crystal populations, just as genetic mutations are in organic evolution. Flaw-produced novelties can be expressed in a wide variety of "phenotypic" traits. For example, physical defects in crystals can affect a crystal's shape, its growth rate, and the conditions under which it cleaves. In addition, the chemical defects in microscopic crystallites can play a dominant part in determining their physico-chemical properties, such as whether they remain dispersed, coalesce into loose clusters, or form a gel; even the density of the gel can be affected.[47] Thus, crystalline defects cause the sort of random variation in phenotypic traits required by natural selection.

Step 3: Heredity. When a new layer of a crystal grows, it copies the geometrical arrangement of atoms occurring in the layer below. For example, new layers in a graphite crystal copy the flat hexagonal pattern of the carbon atoms in the lower layers of graphite, while new layers in a diamond crystal copy the tetrahedral pattern of the carbon atoms in the lower layers of diamond. Crystalline defects can be copied in the same way. For example, as atoms in new layers align with the atoms below, any grain boundaries or dislocations tend to be copied and, thus, the defect propagates in subsequently added layers. When a crystal with such a defect cleaves and reproduces, the crystalline offspring will contain the same defect, and the defect will then propagate through the layers as these new crystals grow. When these new crystals themselves cleave, the defect will be passed on to their offspring. In this way, the defects and the phenotypic traits they cause can propagate from generation to generation. If further defects occur, these too can propagate through the crystal population. Many "mutations" later, a population of crystals can contain many different crystal "species," each with its own characteristic pattern of crystalline flaws and resulting phenotypic traits. These different species can provide the subpopulations among which natural selection can make its selections.

Step 4: Adaptivity. For natural selection to get a grip on the subpopulations, the inherited variations must have the ability to affect the crystal's survival and reproductive success — its fitness. There are many ways in which crystalline phenotypic traits might accomplish this. A crystal's shape, the rate at which it grows, and the conditions under which it cleaves (reseeds) can all affect the rate at which that crystal "species" proliferates. A crystallite species' physico-chemical properties, such as whether the particles remain dispersed, coalesce into loose clusters, or form a gel, can affect their dispersal tendencies. The density of such gels can affect the diffusion rate of the clay-forming solution and thus the rate at which they reproduce. These are just some of the ways in which crystal traits can bear on the relative fitness of different crystal "species."

The idea that a clay crystal's defect-driven traits can be adaptive can take some getting used to. Cairns-Smith gives a nice example clearly illustrating how the shapes of crystallites can affect their fitness. It is worth quoting this example at some length.

> Clay crystals growing under such conditions [in the pores within a piece of sandstone] have, often, distinctive and elaborate forms . . . and it is not too difficult to imagine circumstances in which simply the shapes and sizes of crystals could have a bearing on their ability to grow quickly, or break up in the right way, or survive difficult conditions — or otherwise be a success. . . .
>
> The shapes and sizes of clay crystals can greatly affect the porosity of a sandstone that contains them. This allows one to imagine a process of natural selection operating at a very simple level. Imagine a piece of sandstone that has initially two different crystal genes in it. Each of these soon makes a little zone containing thousands of tiny crystals, all the crystals in one zone having similar features of shape and size and hence giving a characteristic porosity to that zone. The crystals in one of these zones are so shaped that they clog the pores completely. The flow of nutrient (supersaturated) solution stops in that zone, the flow now being channelled elsewhere. These crystals stop growing. The crystals in the other zone have a different characteristic shape which is being replicated — a rather spindly shape, perhaps, that allows the crystals to grow without completely filling the space in which they are growing, so that solutions can still flow through to continue the supply of nutrients. It is this second form which thus tends to spread to fill the sandstone with its characteristic mass of loosely woven crystals. Bits of this fabric break off, perhaps, to carry the secret of how to grow effectively to other pieces of sandstone, which then become infected. Inevitable mistakes in the replication process would ensure that there was always some spread of types. I dare say that the detailed shapes would not have much effect on performance: but real cloggers would always drop out of the race, as would, for example, crystals that were too small and hence too easily washed out of the growth region altogether. . . . In the end you would expect, not always one exact shape within the sandstone of a given region, but a general style or perhaps a few styles if there was a spread of types of sandstone, or a spread of flow rates, or more generally a spread of niches calling for somewhat different optimal shape characteristics.[48]

Since the adaptivity of crystal traits is such a central pillar in my argument, it is worth quoting another vivid example given by Dawkins of how natural selection could operate in a population of clay crystals. Dawkins's example will also serve to illustrate the argument that follows.

> Clays are made from chemical building blocks such a silicic acid and metal ions, which are in solution in rivers and streams having been dissolved —

'weathered'—out of rocks further upstream. If conditions are right they crystalize out of solution again downstream, forming clays. . . . Whether or not a particular type of clay crystal is allowed to build up depends, among other things, upon the rate and pattern of flow of the stream. But deposits of clay can also *influence* the flow of the stream. They do this inadvertently by changing the level, shape and texture of the ground through which the water is flowing. Consider a variant of clay that just happens to have the property of reshaping the structure of the soil so that the flow speeds up. The consequence is that the clay concerned gets washed away again. This kind of clay, by definition, is not very 'successful'. Another unsuccessful clay would be one that changed the flow in such a way that a rival variant of clay was favoured. . . .

To speculate a little further, suppose that a variant of a clay improves its own chances of being deposited by damming up streams. This is an inadvertent consequence of the particular defect structure of the clay. In any stream in which this kind of clay exists, large, stagnant shallow pools form above dams, and the main flow of water is diverted into a new course. In these still pools, more of the same kind of clay is laid down. A succession of such shallow pools proliferates along the length of any stream that happens to be 'infected' by seeding crystals of this kind of clay. Now, because the main flow is diverted, during the dry season the shallow pools tend to dry up. The clay dries and cracks in the sun, and the top layers are blown off as dust. Each dust particle inherits the characteristic defect structure of the parent clay that did the damming, the structure that gave it its damming properties. . . . The dust spreads far and wide in the wind, and there is a good chance that some particles of it will happen to land in another stream, hitherto not 'infected' with the seeds of this kind of dam-making clay. Once infected by the right sort of dust, a new stream starts to grow crystals of dam-making clay, and the whole depositing, damming, drying, eroding cycle begins again.[49]

Now that we appreciate the possibility (indeed, actuality) of natural selection among crystals, we have the ingredients of a value-free case of natural selection. Thus, we can finally assess the version of the etiological approach to teleology that appeals to natural selection, for we can now drive a wedge between the value diagnosis and the natural selection diagnosis of the stick in the stream counterexample. We have seen that populations of clay crystals can have all the elements necessary for evolution by natural selection. Consider the crystalline defect (call it D) that is responsible for the damming action of Dawkins's clay. Notice that natural selection causes D to persist in the clay population because of its "advantageous" dam-making effects. In short, just as natural selection favors the black subpopulation of the peppered moth in those environments blackened by industrial pollution, in the environment described by Dawkins natural selection favors the clay species containing *D*. But, while we are inclined to say that the moth's dark coloring is to camouflage them from predatory birds, we would *not* want to say that, as a matter of natural teleology, the *purpose* of *D* is to make dams, that *D* is there *for the sake of* making dams or *in order to* make dams. Thus, when a process of natural selection causes a trait to persist in a population because of its effects, there is no guarantee that the trait will be for the sake of that effect. The trait might not be for the sake of anything. So, even though the dead planet has the physico-chemical resources to support a full-blown process of natural selection, it is still not the kind of place where there is any teleology. Merely having a population of replicating entities will not produce teleology, not even if the entities have random variations that are heritable, not even if those variations can affect the degree to which those entities proliferate. What happens on the dead planet has no purpose and is for the sake of nothing; it is merely a physico-chemical process. Therefore, contrary to those versions of the etiological approach to teleology that are couched in terms of natural selection, natural selection is not sufficient for teleology. A feature might not be for the sake of the effect by virtue of which is has been favored by natural selection; a feature that has been naturally selected might not be for the sake of anything.

To summarize: The presence of natural selection in populations of crystals allows us to check whether the etiological approach to teleology that appeals to natural selection captures a sufficient condition, for each condition in the approach can be satisfied by features of crystals. But intuitively, features of crystals are not the sort of things that fall within the realm of teleology. Thus, we have a clear-cut counterexample to the natural selection version of the etiological approach to teleology.

4. The Value Diagnosis Again

With this counterexample to the natural selection version of the etiological approach in hand, we should next try to diagnose its failure. We do think that the peppered moth's dark coloring is for the sake of protecting it from predators, that the heart pumps blood in order to circulate it — in general, that those traits in biological organisms favored by natural selection are clear-cut instances of natural teleology. This raises the question of what differentiates natural selection in crystal populations and natural selection in biological populations. If natural selection among crystals is insufficient for teleology, then why is there genuine teleology in the biological products of natural selection? Here the value diagnosis reasserts itself: Value notions apply in the biological world but not on the dead planet. Dark coloring is good for peppered moths in industrial environments; but it is clearly a metaphor at best to say that mineral property D is "good" for Dawkins's dam-making crystals. Value notions apply to living things, even those that are not human. For horses, birds, bees, even plants, even amoebas, the notion of being made better or worse off by a trait makes sense. On the other hand, crystals, rocks, and other bits of inorganic matter are not the kinds of things for which the notion of being better or worse off makes sense, except metaphorically. So, as with the original stick in the stream counterexample, the value diagnosis explains away the crystal counterexample by pointing to the absence of an appropriate role for value.

The intuition behind the value diagnosis might strike some as implausible. Someone might question whether value notions are inextricably linked to the organic world on the grounds that it seems that value notions could apply meaningfully to entities that are not composed out of hydrocarbons, and possibly even to entities that are not alive at all. For example, it seems possible for there to be a community of self-reproducing robots that would have sophisticated enough mental lives and social relations for the notions of being better or worse off to apply to them. But the robots would be constructed out of metal and silicon circuitry rather than hydrocarbons; furthermore, although this might be controversial, someone might hold that our hypothetical mental and social robots would not even be alive. Or consider Cartesian angels that, although lacking all sensations, still enjoy purely intellectual pleasures and suffer purely intellectual pains. Again, Cartesian angels are not composed of hydrocarbons (or any other material substance); and, although again this might be controversial, someone might hold that Cartesian angels are not alive. But these possibilities do not undermine the intuition on which the value diagnosis rests, for that intuition is *not* the thesis that value notions apply only to those entities that are either composed of hydrocarbons or alive. The scope of the intuition concerns life in whatever forms it might take and out of whatever it might be composed. Second, the direction of the intuitive link is not from value to life but from life to value; the intuition claims being alive is not necessary but *sufficient* for an entity to be the kind of thing to which value notions can be correctly attributed. So, possible non-vital subjects of value are beside the point.

It must be admitted that the value diagnosis remains quite schematic. The details of a positive value-centered account of teleology are yet to be provided;[50] further discussion about value must await another occasion. The intuition, however, does at least yield this thesis: There is a certain essential conceptual link between teleology and value, and the specific contour exhibited by the theory of teleology will depend on the specific shape possessed by the view of value to which it is connected.

In response to natural selection among crystals, some naturalists might simply bite the bullet and insist that there is teleology in the crystals on the dead planet. From the perspective of the value diagnosis, such a response is under-described and can be filled out in two incompatible ways. First, someone might think that crystals can have teleology because it is appropriate to view crystals in an evaluative light. On this view, a trait that increased a crystal species' reproductive fitness would literally *benefit* crystals of that kind, would literally be *good* for them, would literally make them *better off*. For myself, I do not know how to take such value attributions literally; they strike me as only metaphors. But this is merely a report on my intuitions about value; I have presented no argument to show that it would be incoherent to attribute value to crystals literally. So, it is just possible that this (to me) strange view is coherent. However, if so, this would not undermine but actually *support* the value diagnosis. The value diagnosis insists that there is no teleology without value, and this first response supports teleology in the crystals on the dead planet by insisting on the propriety of value attributions in that setting.

But there is a second possible response to the crystal example that directly challenges the value diagnosis. Naturalists dubious about the prospects of a naturalistic theory of value for crystals might still believe that natural selection among crystals on the dead planet can give rise to genuine teleology. The difficulty with this second response is to explain the emergence of teleology. Presumably, those making this second response are not intending to embrace radical pan-teleologism, so they agree that the original dead planet, free of natural selection, is also free of teleology. Then, if adding natural selection to the dead planet does give rise to teleology, and if natural selection can be introduced to the dead planet by adding the four conditions of reproduction, variation, inheritance, and adaptivity, which of these conditions is responsible for the rise of teleology? Merely adding a reproducing population of mineral entities seems insufficient to create teleology, even if the entities have randomly varying heritable traits, even if a trait increases the representation of that kind of mineral in the general population. So, those who think the crystals involve a value-free form of teleology place themselves on a slippery slope with radical pan-teleologism awaiting them at the bottom.

Other naturalists might have a quite different reaction to natural selection among crystals. Agreeing that the crystals on the dead planet lack teleology, and agreeing that the reason for this is that the crystals are not alive, they might conclude that the natural selection approach to biological teleology simply needs an additional condition restricting it to living populations. The need for this restriction has gone unrecognized until now, they might add, because it is only after contemplating clay crystallites that we realize that natural selection could occur in non-living populations. A naturalist should have no scruples against incorporating this condition, for surely life is a respectable naturalistic concept. After all, biology is a thoroughly naturalistic science of life. So, the naturalist might conclude, the restriction to living populations rules out the crystal counterexample, and the natural selection approach to biological teleology is back on its feet.

But what is life? If naturalists want to refer to life in an account of biological teleology, they must provide some account of it, and doing so in the present context is not easy. Interestingly enough, there is no consensus among biologists about how to define life. One prominent characteristic of living beings that biologists typically mention is none other than purposeful or teleological behavior.[51] But a definition of life in terms of biological teleology will generate vicious circularity for the naturalist who contemplates appealing to life in an account of biological teleology. Although acknowledging the intuitive connection between life and teleology, biologists themselves are usually unhappy to account for life in these terms, thinking teleology to be vague at best and unscientific at worst, so they often retreat to the position that living beings are simply those that evolve by natural selection.[52] But this is even less helpful to our naturalist, for the life condition would then fail in its appointed task of excluding clay crystals. So, on closer examination, naturalists who contemplate using a life condition to save the natural selection account of biological teleology are simply spinning their wheels.

A naturalist who would attempt to appeal to life in an account of biological teleology must also address the value diagnosis. That diagnosis rests on an intuition to the effect that life in some way is essentially connected with value; living beings are by their nature the kind of things to which it makes sense to apply the notions of being better or worse off. Naturalists who appeal to life in a definition of teleology must show that they are not covertly helping themselves to a value notion with dubious naturalistic credentials.

Reminding us that biology is the naturalistic science of life, the naturalist might respond that life *must* be a naturalistic notion. But that response would be fallacious. Even though biology is a natural science that studies life, life could still be a complex notion with some non-naturalistic components. Consider two analogous cases, the first quite artificial, the second less so. First, as with other abstract notions of pure mathematics, it is arguable that the notion of being a prime number is not a notion derived from the spacio-temporal natural world; at least, we can safely assume this for the sake of argument. But the notion of being prime can be a component of a more complex notion instances of which can be studied naturalistically. Consider the notion of a *physical prime,* defined as the notion of a prime number of physically proximate similar objects. (To make the notion more precise, take physical proximity to be a distance no greater than the sum of the diameters of the similar objects, where similar means that the objects all fall under the same relatively specific natural kind.) Since the mathematical notion of being prime is not naturalistic, the stipulated notion of being a physical prime is not completely naturalistic. Still, one could perfectly well embark on a naturalistic investigation of physical primes, studying instances in the field and the laboratory, looking for regularities involving them, and so on. There might be no interesting body of theory about physical primes to be discovered, but nothing would stand in the way of a naturalistic investigation of them.

Next, consider a less artificial but more controversial case. According to some people the notion of the self-conscious, rational mind is not naturalistic; we may assume for the sake of argument that these people are right. Even if so, it would be perfectly possible to conduct a naturalistic study of entities that have such minds; behaviorists have been doing this for the better part of a century. No matter what view one takes about the fruits of behavioral science, there is no doubt that it is the naturalistic study of mental entities. Thus, by analogy, even though biologists study living entities naturalistically, it does not follow that the notion of life is itself purely naturalistic. The naturalistic practice of the science of life is consistent with the hypothesis that the notion of life contains a non-naturalistic, evaluative component.[53]

Thus, the etiological approach to teleology is inadequate. Even if appeal is made to natural selection, etiological considerations alone are insufficient to capture biological teleology. Just as with the systems approach, the flaw with the etiological approach can be traced to its failure to provide an appropriate role for value; neither approach fulfills the hope for a naturalistic, purely descriptive theory of teleology. With the two naturalistic approaches to teleology proven to be unsound, the movement to naturalize biological teleology is left without a leg to stand on.

5. Can Naturalism Be Reclaimed?

Naturalism has been thought to be on safe ground at the level of biological teleology. If it encounters any problems, they are thought to arise only after ascending to the level of self-conscious, morally responsible agents. But on closer examination, the prospect for a naturalistic treatment of biological teleology is clouded by the ineliminable presence of

evaluative notions. Whether one pursues the cybernetic systems approach
or the approach grounded in natural selection, the need to appeal to evaluative notions emerges. Not only does this overturn what has been adver-
tised as a naturalistic victory; it undermines the possibility of using that
victory to help win ongoing naturalistic battles in the philosophy of mind.

These difficulties arise not for all forms of naturalism, but specifically for narrow naturalism — the "non-normative" naturalism that ban-
ishes "transcendent standards of value" from nature. But naturalists need
not be narrow. A broader view of nature, perhaps roughly Aristotelian in
outlook, could reckon objective standards of value as part of the natural
order. According to this broader form of naturalism, which would contrast with supernaturalism and would reject the miraculous in nature, values
would be real ineliminable natural properties, subject to broadly scientific
investigation. If sense could be made of this broad form of naturalism,
biological teleology and life could be fully naturalized. In addition, naturalism in the philosophy of mind would have new hope; teleo-functionalism
would flourish, and its rich value condition would promise to help handle
the familiar Chinese nation and Chinese room counterexamples of Block
and Searle.[54] The attractions of a naturalistic treatment of biological teleology would be many, but they are available only to naturalism broadly
construed.

Notes

Many thanks to George Bealer, Hugo Bedau, Mark Hinchliff, Jim Moor,
Jim Page, Geoffrey Sayre-McCord, and Carol Voeller.

1. E.g., see A. Danto, "Naturalism," in P. Edwards, ed., *The Encyclopedia
of Philosophy,* vol. 5 (New York: Macmillan, 1967); L. Baker, *Saving Belief: A
Critique of Physicalism* (Princeton, N.J.: Princeton University Press, 1987), 173;
and J. Bigelow and R. Pargetter, "Functions," *Journal of Philosophy* 84 (1987):
181–196, esp. 182.

2. D. Armstrong, "Naturalism, Materialism, and First Philosophy," *Philosophia* 8 (1978): 261–276, p. 261.

3. J. Fodor, "Semantics, Wisconsin Style," *Synthese* 59 (1984): 231–250, p.
232.

4. R. Millikan, *Language, Thought and Other Biological Categories* (Cambridge, Mass.: MIT Press, 1984), 17.

5. Armstrong, "Naturalism, Materialism, and First Philosophy," 263.

6. To pick just two examples, see C. Taylor, *Philosophical Papers,* 2 vols
(New York: Cambridge University Press, 1985); and Baker, *Saving Belief.*

7. For statements to this effect by proponents of the two leading naturalistic approaches to teleology, see E. Nagel, "Teleology Revisited," *Journal of Phi-*

losophy 74 (1977): 261–301, pp. 276, 298; and L. Wright, *Teleological Explanations* (Berkeley: University of California Press, 1976), 26, 56.

8. I have attempted to do this in my "Where's the Good in Teleology?" *Philosophy and Phenomenological Research,* forthcoming. For more or less similar attempts, see F. Ayala, "Teleological Explanations in Evolutionary Biology," *Philosophy of Science* 37 (1970): 1–15; and A. Woodfield, *Teleology* (Cambridge: Cambridge University Press, 1976).

9. W. Lycan explains a number of ways in which contemporary functionalists have invoked teleology in an introductory section of his recent anthology *Mind and Cognition, A Reader* (Cambridge, Mass.: Basil Blackwell, 1990), 59f.

10. Lycan, *Mind and Cognition,* 60. For example, Lycan ("Form, Function, and Feel," *Journal of Philosophy* 78 [1981]: 24–50; *Consciousness* [Cambridge, Mass.: MIT Press, 1987]) and E. Sober, ("Panglossian Functionalism and the Philosophy of Mind," *Synthese* 64 [1985]: 165–193) make this sort of response to the criticisms of functionalism in N. Block, "Troubles with Functionalism," in C. W. Savage, ed., *Perception and Cognition,* Minnesota Studies in the Philosophy of Science, vol. 9 (Minneapolis: University of Minnesota Press, 1978).

11. Proponents of this project include D. Stampe, "Toward a Causal Theory of Linguistic Representation," *Midwest Studies in Philosophy* 2 (1977): 42–63; R. Van Gulick, "Functionalism, Information and Content," *Nature and System* 2 (1980): 139–162, and "A Functionalist Plea for Self-Consciousness," *Philosophical Review* 97 (1988): 149–181; R. Millikan, *Language, Thought and Other Biological Categories,* and "Biosemantics," *Journal of Philosophy* 86 (1989): 281–297; D. Papineau, "Representation and Explanation," *Philosophy of Science* 51 (1984): 550–572, and *Reality and Representation* (Oxford: Basil Blackwell, 1987); J. Fodor, "Semantics, Wisconsin Style," and "Psychosemantics, or: Where Do Truth Conditions Come From?" in Lycan, *Mind and Cognition;* F. Dretske, "Misrepresentation," in R. Bogdan, ed., *Belief: Form, Content, and Function* (Oxford: Oxford University Press, 1986), and *Explaining Behavior: Reasons in a World of Causes* (Cambridge, Mass.: MIT Press, 1988); and C. McGinn, *Mental Content* (New York: Basil Blackwell, 1989).

12. Lycan, "Form, Function, and Feel," 32, and Dretske, "Misrepresentation," 25.

13. The ability of systems theories like cybernetics to give efficient causal explanations of apparently goal-directed phenomena has been used to explicate the notion of being goal directed. The founder of cybernetics, Norbert Wiener, first attempted this: see A. Rosenblueth, N. Wiener, and J. Bigelow, "Behavior, Purpose, and Teleology," *Philosophy of Science* 10 (1943): 18–24; and N. Wiener, *Cybernetics, or Control and Communication in the Animal and the Machine* (New York: Wiley, 1948). Similar attempts have since been made by many others: G. Sommerhoff, *Analytical Biology* (New York: Oxford University Press, 1950); and R. B. Braithwaite, *Scientific Explanation* (Cambridge: Cambridge University Press, 1953); E. Nagel, *The Structure of Science* (New York: Harcourt, Brace and World, 1961), and "Teleology Revisited"; C. Hempel, "The Logic of Functional Analysis," in his *Aspects of Scientific Explanation* (New York: Free Press, 1965); M. Beckner, *The Biological Way of Thought* (Berkeley: University of California Press, 1968);

L. Von Bertalanffy, *General System Theory* (New York: George Brazillier, 1968); C. Boorse, "Wright on Functions," *Philosophical Review* 85 (1976): 70–86; R. Van Gulick, "Functionalism, Information and Content," and "A Functionalist Plea for Self-Consciousness"; A. Falk, "Purpose, Feedback, and Evolution," *Philosophy of Science* 48 (1981): 198–217; A. Collins, "Action, Causality, and Teleological Explanation," *Midwest Studies in Philosophy* 9 (1984): 345–369; and Bigelow and Pargetter, "Functions." The general methodology followed by the systems approach is to identify the simplest systems-theoretic condition shared by all (and only) goal-directed systems.

Given that systems theories provide teleology-free explanations of apparently teleological phenomena, some are tempted to use systems theories to *eliminate* teleological explanations. See, e.g., R. Dawkins, *The Selfish Gene* (New York: Oxford University Press, 1976), and *The Blind Watchmaker: Why the Evidence of Evolution Reveals a Universe without Design* (New York: Norton, 1986).

14. E.g., Nagel, *The Structure of Science,* and "Teleology Revisited"; Hempel, "The Logic of Functional Analysis"; and Boorse, "Wright on Functions."

15. The issues covered in this section are treated more fully in my "Goal-Directed Systems and the Good," *Monist,* forthcoming.

16. What follows focuses on systems that maintain goals; analogous remarks would apply to systems that merely seek or aim at goals.

17. Nagel, "Teleology Revisited," 272. Some advocates of the systems approach propose an internal sign of goal-directedness, rather than a behavioral sign. They characterize goal-directed systems in terms of certain general features of their internal causal structure, such as negative feedback loops, that are responsible for producing the characteristic goal-directed behavior. See, e.g., Rosenblueth et al., "Behavior, Purpose, and Teleology," and Falk, "Purpose, Feedback, and Evolution." I will focus on the more prevalent behavioral forms of the approach; the internal formulations are subject to analogous conclusions.

18. Nagel, *The Structure of Science,* 411; Hempel, "The Logic of Functional Analysis," 323.

19. Nagel, "Teleology Revisited," 272.

20. For a number of traditional problems and responses, including goal-failure, non-existent goals, and multiple goals, see R. Taylor, "Purposeful and Non-Purposeful Behavior," *Philosophy of Science* 17 (1950): 327–332; I. Scheffler, "Thoughts on Teleology," *British Journal for the Philosophy of Science* 9 (1959): 265–284; J. Canfield, "Introduction," in *Purpose in Nature* (Englewood Cliffs, N.J.: Prentice-Hall, 1966), 1–7; Beckner, *The Biological Ways of Thought;* Boorse, "Wright on Functions"; and Nagel, "Teleology Revisited."

21. Nagel, "Teleology Revisited," 274.

22. Ibid.

23. Nagel, "Teleology Revisited," 273, following Sommerhoff, *Analytical Biology.*

24. Woodfield, *Teleology,* 67–72.

25. Nagel, "Teleology Revisited," 275.

26. Ibid.

27. Ibid.

28. Van Gulick, "Functionalism, Information, and Content," especially 143–145.

29. Similar considerations are explored at greater length in my "Against Mentalism in Teleology," *American Philosophical Quarterly* 27 (1990): 61–70.

30. E.g., *San Francisco Chronicle,* May 24, 1989; *Time,* June 5, 1989; *Newsweek,* June 5, 1989.

31. This value condition is intended to be necessary but not sufficient. (In fact, as stated, it is not even quite a necessary condition.) To get a sufficient condition, one must require (for reasons to be suggested in section three below) that the value produced by the system's behavior is a (suitable) part of the explanation of why the system exhibits that behavior. Presenting and defending these details is beyond the scope of the present discussion, which is intended to suggest only that *some* appropriate role for value is the missing ingredient in equilibrium systems. For development and defense of strict necessary and sufficient value conditions, see my "Where's the Good in Teleology?"

32. Larry Wright ("Functions," *Philosophical Review* 82 [1973]: 139–168, and *Teleological Explanations*) has offered what is probably the best known version of the approach. For various other more or less similar versions of the etiological approach, see C. Taylor, *The Explanation of Behavior* (New York: Routledge & Kegan Paul, 1964); W. Wimsatt, "Teleology and the Logical Structure of Function Statements," *Studies in the History and Philosophy of Science* 3 (1972): 1–80; J. Bennett, *Linguistic Behavior* (Cambridge: Cambridge University Press, 1976); G. Cohen, *Karl Marx's Theory of History* (Princeton: Princeton University Press, 1978); Millikan, *Language, Thought, and Other Biological Categories;* R. de Sousa, "Teleology and the Great Shift," *Journal of Philosophy* 81 (1984): 647–653; and M. Matthen, "Biological Functions and Perceptual Content," *Journal of Philosophy* 85 (1988): 5–27.

33. In fact, what I take to be the correct view of teleology, defended in my "Where's the Good in Teleology?" can be viewed as a modification of Wright's analysis to which a value condition has been added.

34. This example (though not its diagnosis) is due to Robert Van Gulick.

35. For a detailed development of this etiology-plus-value approach to teleology, see my "Where's the Good in Teleology?"

36. Wright points out that his analysis can be understood in terms of natural selection ("Functions," 159; *Teleological Explanations,* 69f). Others, inspired by Wright, explicitly refer to natural selection in accounts of natural teleology; e.g., see Dretske, "Misrepresentation," 25; Papineau, *Reality and Representation,* 65; and Matthen, "Biological Functions and Perceptual Content," 14, 17. See also S. Wagner, "The Liberal and the Lycanthrope," *Pacific Philosophical Quarterly* 69 (1988): 165–174. For a more or less similar definition, see Millikan, *Language, Thought, and Other Biological Categories,* and "In Defense of Proper Functions," *Philosophy of Science* 56 (1989): 288–302. Bigelow and Pargetter, "Functions," also explicitly appeal to natural selection, but their view differs more substantially from Wright's.

Although I will not pursue this criticism here, anyone who proposes a natural selection account of biological teleology would be well advised to accommodate the critique of the adaptionalist program launched by S. J. Gould and R. Lewontin, "The Spandrals of San Marco and the Panglossian Paradigm: A Critique of the Adaptationist Programme," *Proceedings of the Royal Society of London* B205 (1979): 581–598, especially the possibilities that selection and adaptation can be decoupled, that differences among adaptations can lack a selective basis, and that adaptations can result as secondary utilization of parts present for reasons of architecture, development, or history.

37. A nice review of empirical evidence for this famous example of natural selection in wild populations can be found in J. Maynard Smith, *The Theory of Evolution,* 3d. ed. (Hammondsworth, England: Penguin, 1975), 150–154.

38. P. Teilhard de Chardin, *The Phenomenon of Man,* trans. B. Wall (New York: Harper, 1959).

39. For example, see R. Lewontin, "The Units of Selection," *Annual Review of Ecology and Systematics* 1 (1970): 1–18, p. 1; A. G. Cairns- Smith, *Seven Clues to the Origin of Life* (Cambridge: Cambridge University Press, 1985), 2; Dawkins, *The Blind Watchmaker,* 150f.

40. E. Mayr, *Populations, Species, and Evolution* (Cambridge, Mass.: Harvard University Press, 1963), 102, and *The Growth of Biological Thought* (Cambridge, Mass.: Harvard University Press, 1982), 58; also, Falk, "Purpose, Feedback, and Evolution," 212f.

41. This is news not only to philosophers (e.g., Falk, "Purpose, Feedback, and Evolution," 205) but, apparently, even to a student of evolution as astute as Mayr (*The Growth of Biological Thought,* 52).

42. My information about crystals in general, and clay crystallites in particular, is due to A. G. Cairns-Smith, "The Origin of Life and the Nature of the Primitive Gene," *Journal of Theoretical Biology* 10 (1965): 53–88; *Genetic Takeover and the Mineral Origins of Life* (Cambridge: Cambridge University Press, 1982); *Seven Clues to the Origin of Life;* and "The First Organisms," *Scientific American* 252, no. 6 (1985): 90–100. I had long thought that the natural selection version of the etiological approach was vulnerable to hypothetical counterexamples involving value-free cases of natural selection, and I had speculated that crystals might be an appropriate setting for such hypothetical cases. Upon discovering Cairns-Smith's discussion of natural selection among clay crystallites (written with completely different aims in mind), I was pleased to learn that my counterexample was not merely hypothetical but actual.

Honorable Intensions

MARK WILSON

> Among the innumerable mortifications which waylay human arrogance on every side may well be reckoned our ignorance of the most common objects and effects, a defect of which we become more sensible by every attempt to supply it. Vulgar and inactive minds confound familiarity with knowledge and conceive themselves informed of the whole nature of things when they are shown their form or told their use; but the specialist, who is not content with superficial views, harasses himself with fruitless curiosity, and still, as he inquires more, perceives that he knows less.
>
> Samuel Johnson, *The Idler*

1

A growing contingent of philosophers has urged that *properties* (or, synonymously in this essay's usage, *attributes, traits,* or *universals*) be liberated from the philosophy of language shackles in which these entities have long languished. Some of the leaders in this emancipation are Hilary Putnam, David Armstrong, Sydney Shoemaker, and David Lewis,[1] with John Locke often cited as a historical inspiration. Armstrong, for example, writes in his *Theory of Universals:* "The study of the semantics of predicates must be distinguished from the theory of universals"[2] and repeatedly warns against "the old, bad equation of universals with meaning." The central contention is that our judgments about the character of universals should no longer be based upon their fortuitous linguistic associations. Assume that universals φ and ψ correspond to predicates "P" and "Q". Armstrong holds that the mere fact that *language* permits formation of the complex predicate "P or Q" provides no reason for supposing that the realm of *universals* contains a disjunctive φ *or* ψ. Similarly, the fact that the predicates "being water" and "being H_2O" are non-synonymous in no way shows that distinct physical properties must correspond to these two terms.

53

Emancipationist approaches to universals likewise dismiss as inconsequential an allied host of considerations deriving from philosophy of mind, considerations involving "content" et al. too familiar to require recitation here. The basic strain running throughout the emancipationist criticism is that the *mode of presentation* which envelops a universal as we learn or think about it is irrelevant to the attribute's true *character,* where the term "character" covers the internal characteristics and/or identity conditions essential to a property as such. For an emancipationist, the "character" of a universal should embody only those factors which directly influence (or, more minimally, correlate with) the behavior of objects that exemplify it; we might label these factors "the universal's power to influence its object's behavior." Many emancipationists use phrases like "causal characteristics" or "causal integrity" to pick out the desired character cluster needed in a true universal. Shoemaker evokes these themes when he writes, "genuine properties . . . are individuated by the ways they contribute to the causal powers of the things that have them, and also by the ways their own instantiation can be caused."[3]

Throughout this essay, I shall dub as an "intensionality" any consideration that can be viewed as distinguishing true properties from mere sets. Armstrong grants that certain disjunctive predicates "*P* or *Q*" manage to denote genuine traits. What distinguishes the acceptable "*P* or *Q*" from the unacceptable "grue"? Some writers claim that the former possesses a "unitary causal character" not found in the latter. If so, "unitary causal character" counts an *intensionality* required in a genuine property. In this jargon, our project is to determine what kind of total "intensional character" is proper for emancipated universals.

Although this essay's viewpoint is assuredly emancipationist, it has little faith in the vagaries of "cause" and "causal powers." Indeed, its main claim to novelty will lie in showing that there is a better route to emancipated universals than "causal power."

Emancipationism, in its various forms, is of manifest importance to questions of the relationship between mind and body and to doctrines like the Kripke-Putnam theories of "natural kind" reference which do not make much sense unless some view akin to emancipationism is accepted. In *theory,* a large gulf ought to separate emancipationists from views of "property" deriving from the more classical perspectives (a paragon of a "classical view" is Bertrand Russell's *The Problems of Philosophy*[4]). In *practice,* however, self-proclaimed emancipationists often stoop to considerations resting upon linguistic or psychological matters, frequently without comment upon the apparent inconsistency. This is really not surprising, for views like Russell's offer crisp treatments of many important questions — what happens when two people share a thought; how one goes about achieving rigor within a science—that a truly unbending emancipationist can approach only in a vastly more convoluted fashion. Russellian answers tempt believers from the narrow way so frequently that it is often difficult to determine whether a given writer qualifies as a proper emancipationist or not. Most of this essay will be devoted to the articulation of a clean form of emancipationism; I will reserve my limited comments upon questions of mind-body identity until the end.

2

As far as opening fanfare goes, our proclamation of emancipationism sounds well and good, but the view has been formulated in largely negative terms: the traditional considerations of synonymy, logical form, etc. show little about the true characteristics of universals. How might we provide a more positive account of properties? Most emancipationists expect *Science* (with a capital "S") to rescue the situation. Yet, judging from the literature, Science must speak as an uncharacteristically delphic oracle, for the emancipationist authors I have cited disagree wildly on the lessons it proscribes (compare Putnam's conclusions with Armstrong's, for instance).

In truth, few of the considerations that shape the accounts of universals sketched in the emancipationist tracts count as straightforwardly "scientific." Often the only task assigned to "Science" is one of passing a list of "primitive terms" or "fundamental magnitudes" to philosophy. The list provided is so hopelessly brief that it does not account for the full inventory of attributes utilized within any real life science. This incompleteness leaves philosophy much discretion in framing a realm of properties to suit its own desires. In practice, the motivations which influence a particular emancipationist's treatment tend to be drawn from philosophy of science or general metaphysics. Armstrong, for example, hopes that Nelson Goodman's "grue" will not count as an emancipated trait, on the grounds that an adequate account of induction cannot be constructed otherwise. Putnam's interests seem to lie in articulating an adequate treatment of "theoretical reduction."

However persuasive these last considerations may seem, they represent motivations drawn from philosophy, rather than from working science *per se*. I believe that science cannot let philosophy tamper with its allotment of properties in this way. Most developed physical theories directly quantify over extensive domains of properties whose contents can be ascertained straightforwardly. The range of properties posited invariably turns out to be much richer than philosophers generally presume. The unexpected feature of these enlarged domains is that their sheer size practically forces the attributes therein to abandon the sorts of intensionality needed in the philosophical projects dear to most emancipationists.

But what do I mean by "the attributes lack the intensionality needed to support standard philosophical projects"? Consider the tensions that affect Bertrand Russell's approach to universals. For Russell, linguistic and psychological considerations explicitly frame the primary determinants of the intensional characteristics of universals. He assumes that a basic range of properties can be known in a very direct fashion — in his evocative terminology, we are *acquainted* with them. When we become acquainted with the concept **red,** we apprehend its internal nature in an intrinsically robust way, a type of understanding forever denied to the permanently unsighted. If a universal is derived from a disjunctive predicate such as "is red or green," it will possess an internal "disjunctive nature," for our natural path to understanding **red or green** seems to travel through the legs of the disjunction. "Intrinsic disjunctive nature" is an example of an intensionality assigned to traits based upon considerations of a quasi-linguistic nature. Utilizing such intensionalities, Russell sketches tempting answers to a wide range of philosophical questions, answers that the honest emancipationist cannot easily duplicate.

But when we turn to Russell's philosophy of mathematics, signs of strain begin to appear. As is well known, Russell's original "no class" view hoped to base mathematics upon concept-universals, rather than sets (sets were introduced as essentially equivalent classes of coextensive concepts). But mathematical analysis requires that the universe of mathematics embrace a rather extensive complement of sets, including quite randomly disjointed members of the power set of the integers. It seems hard to imagine what sort of "concept" might collect such disjointed sets together, at least if we construe "collect" according to the naive model in which the universal **red** collects the set $\{x \mid x$ is red$\}$. Pretending that God "grasps" concepts that collect the uncollectible is not very helpful; how many concepts of this theological type will God entertain relative to a given set? It seems more plausible to maintain that we have a fairly direct purchase upon the idea of "set," without a prior journey through a Shangri-la of unreachable concepts.

Accordingly, over the great universe of sets, there are comparatively few ($\aleph_0$, say) which can plausibly derive from universals with a Russellian intensional character. A randomly selected set is simply too "thin" to carry an "acquaintance"-based character. Russell paints all of his sets with the intensionality of **red** but, like the roses in the Queen of Hearts' garden, the objects underneath do not take the coloration.

3

Russell was forced to accept properties with a thin, set-like character because otherwise he would not have supplied mathematical analysis with enough properties. In fact, most modern texts simply *identify* "properties" (or relations) with sets of n-tuples extracted from a given domain. W. V. Quine's well-known brief against "intensional entities" bases its case exactly upon the fact that mathematics construes its "properties" in this set-like way.[5] Since mathematics converts properties to sets, Quine urges, so should physics. This obligation arises as a product of science's ongoing fondness for extensionality; in its relentless pursuit of clarity and ontological economy, it eschews fuzzy intensional entities wherever possible. Mathematics and the sciences endeavor to "flee from intension," although, because of pesky propositional attitudes and the like, perhaps only mathematics and physics have totally effected their escapes. The example most frequently cited by Quine as evidence of "the flight from intension" is the decision by mathematicians, *circa* 1920, that Russell's theory of types had been unnecessarily encumbered with its "concept" accretions.

In my opinion, Quine's argument is wrongly put — it is mysticism pure and simple to proscribe an eventual destiny for all science, extensional or not. From what font do we extract this neo-Hegelian ability to divine the future meandering of the Scientific Spirit? Gruff authoritarianism merely invites rebellion; it is no wonder that devotees of more robust traits retort, "Well, I don't feel like converting my properties to sets, thank you."

In truth, an effective investigation of attributes must look beyond the brute fact of mathematics' growing extensionality to the deeper reasons that originally forced the field to develop in an extensional direction. We will find that much of the true story of "extensionality" derives from a symbiosis between mathematics and physics. As this entanglement is retraced, we will find that the underlying considerations leave scientific properties, as distinct from those of mathematics, with a residue of inherent "intensionality," an intensionality born of the notions of physical possibility and law. But this triumph over the Quinean extensionalist should not be reckoned as a complete victory for standard intensionalism, for the modal soil in which physical attributes must live is too impoverished to support the luxuriant foliage that philosophers have hoped to plant in the realms of the possible. Quine's overarching purpose has been to warn philosophy against uncritically relying upon vague and ill-defined conceptions of "intensionality." The story told here does not carry such an unyielding moral as Quine's, but nonetheless suggests that many of the intensionalities deplored by Quine are genuinely ill conceived.

As far as I am aware, philosophers rarely object to mathematics' extensional approach to attributes, although this absence of cavil may stem more from oversight than endorsement. Elliott Sober, however, has explicitly rejected extensionality on the grounds that the properties of **being an equilateral triangle** and **being an equiangular triangle** are "obviously different."[6] He tells a tale of two machines: (a) which, in a first stage of operation, inspects geometrical figures for **equality of sides** and (b) which begins instead by checking for **equality of angles.** In a second stage, (a) and (b) both check for **triangle.** Sober claims that device (a) clearly detects the property **being an equilateral triangle** but not **being an equiangular triangle,** whereas machine (b) does exactly the opposite. He concludes that the two properties should not be identified.

As stated, these considerations are unlikely to sway many emancipationists because they baldly turn upon "modes-of-presentation" of the properties (albeit presentations to machines, rather than to human beings). The distinction Sober draws rests upon the dissimilar manners of response to a common property on the part of detection devices; the difference lies in the instruments, not the property. Mercury thermometers and thermocouples detect the presence of **70°F** in radically different ways; coherent talk of objective measurement would prove impossible if traits had to embody the structures of the devices which detect them.

But at a deeper level, Sober's deliberations do not appear totally dissimilar to arguments frequently cited by emancipationists. For example: pendulums obey the "law"[7] that x is a pendulum of length L if and only if x is a pendulum with a period $2\pi \sqrt{L/g}$ (g is a gravitational constant). The two properties **pendulum of length L** and **pendulum of period $2\pi\sqrt{L/g}$** are accordingly coextensive — nay, *nomologically coextensive* — yet they seem obviously different properties. Why? The length property is "causally responsible" for the presence of the period property, but not *vice versa.* Yet if this kind of argument is acceptable in physics, why isn't Sober correct in distinguishing the mathematical properties **equilateral triangle** and **equiangular triangle** on the basis of their "causal powers"?

It is not sufficient to retort that mathematical objects cannot "cause" anything: a better diagnosis of the triangle case points to the role that the syntactic structure of property names plays in eliciting Sober's "intuitions." Note that machines (a) and (b) both work in two clearly demarcated stages. Sober uses the syntactic structure of the phrase "S and T" to code the fact that machine (a) checks, in its two stages, first for S and then for T. If Sober had wished, he might have correlated the commuted "T and S" with the devices that, unlike (a), first check for T and then check for S. When rendered explicit, this method of syntactically coding information about measurement instruments seems a bit strange, but, in the appropriate circumstances, it is perfectly well defined. Sober's mistake is to transfer these features, which really pertain to measurement instruments, over to the objects to which the measuring devices respond. That a misallocation of intensionality has occurred can be readily seen when we consider devices which avoid sorting out the shapes through two-stage processes — say, a sieve in which the figures pass through appropriately shaped holes. Which of Sober's two triangle properties is "responsible" for the behavior of the sieve? In truth, Sober's "intuition" that "the property **equilateral triangle** is causally responsible for the behavior of machine (a)" simply represents a telescoped version of the longer claim, "In stage 1 of (a), **equal sides** is detected; in stage 2, **triangle** is detected; the net effect of both operations is to check for **equilateral triangle**." Our "intuitions" vanish in the sieve case because there is no obvious way to correlate the operation of a sieve with the syntactic structure of a property name.

In general, we must expect that misleading "intuitions" about property identity can easily transfer from extraneous sources. In fact a related variety of syntactic coding is utilized in the pendulum example. If the pendulum law is to hold (approximately), the term "pendulum" must be understood in a strict sense, viz. "mass that maintains constant distance from a pivot under the combined influence of a potential field mgy and a tension V_T in the string." Gadgets we ordinarily consider "pendulums" — a bob in someone's hand or in some irregular gravitational field — will not qualify, for they do not obey the strict description. In most cases, when we set up our pendulums, we begin with bobs and strings of fixed length. In such circumstances, it is natural, I suppose, to claim, "The string having length L in the past is causally responsible for the system, which now meets the conditions for 'pendulum', having a period of $2\pi\sqrt{L/g}$." Presumably, the bob displayed no periodicity until it was installed in the conditions that now qualify it as a pendulum. I believe that the temporally distinct times at which the simple properties **length** and **period** enter into the standard prehistory of a pendulum are the source of the "intuition" that **pendulum of length L** and **pendulum of period $2\pi\sqrt{L/g}$** behave in "causally" dissimilar manners. The syntax of the phrase "pendulum of length L" has been used to encode a fact about that property's prehistory. Such intuitions about causal efficacy fade if the pendulum is set up in unusual ways, e.g., it forms as a swinging blob of plastic filament hardens.

Moral: the intensionality of an emancipated trait does not lie in the eye of the beholder.

4

Further motivation for distrusting initial "intuitions" about properties can be extracted from a consideration of normal definitional practices in physics. All of the sciences, as does mathematics itself, tolerate a wide variety of alternative definitions for a given property. For example, the trait **kinetic reaction** (or **total force**) in the x direction can be defined in Newtonian fashion as simply "$m\ddot{x}$" or in Lagrangian fashion as "$-\partial V/\partial x$", where V is the total potential for the system. Presumably, a trait F should not be defined as G unless the terms "Fx" and "Gx" denote the same property. Since a property often can be expected to bear more than one name in a formalism, a science should be permitted some latitude in framing its definitions (and, for that matter, in its selection of primitive vocabulary as well).

These simple considerations are virtually sufficient to force the correctness of our disputed pendulum identity, despite its alleged non-intuitiveness. By combining the two definitions cited of **kinetic reaction** in x and y directions, we learn that:

(1) $m\ddot{x} = -\partial V/\partial x$ and $m\ddot{y} = -\partial V/\partial y$.

Following the strict meaning of "pendulum" delineated in section 3, we find that, definitionally, a pendulum must obey (in polar coordinates):

(2) $\partial(V_T + mgy)/\partial r = 0$ and $\partial V_T/\partial\Theta = 0$

(i.e., the tension potential V_T is balanced by gravity in the direction of the bob and it contributes no force transversal to the rod). Multiply the formulas in (1) by $\dot{x}$ and $\dot{y}$ respectively and add:

(3) $m(\dot{x}\ddot{x} + \dot{y}\ddot{y}) = -m(\dot{x}\ \partial(V_T + gy)/\partial x + \dot{y}\ \partial(V_T + gy)/\partial y)$.

It is a tedious exercise in polar coordinates to convert (3), utilizing (2), to:

(4) $m\dot{\Theta}L^2\ddot{\Theta} = -mL\dot{\Theta}\sin\Theta$.

Notice that V_T has dropped out. Making the small angle approximation $\sin\Theta \simeq \Theta$ and simplifying, we obtain the standard pendulum equation:

(5) $\ddot{\Theta} = -L/g\ \Theta$.

(3) and (5) have the same content, but the switch from x and y to the polar quantity Θ simplifies matters considerably.

To summarize: relying upon definitional property identities and mathematics alone, we have shown that any pendulum must obey equation (5). But all solutions to (5) have period $2\pi\sqrt{L/g}$. Conclusion: we can move betwixt the phrases "pendulum of length L" and "pendulum of period $2\pi\sqrt{L/g}$" by transitions that rely only upon accepted definitions or purely mathematical manipulations. It would seem, then, that our two predicates must denote the same property.

There is nothing special to the pendulum case here; a bit of further reflection will show that virtually any "nomological equivalence" can be converted to a property identity by these techniques. It should not surprise us that definitional practice can force the "nomological" property identities. Although the addition of a *single* definition can be expected to add no essential content to a theory, we recognize that the simultaneous employment of *two* acceptable definitions for a term may carry a good deal of inherent substance. In the case at hand, the combination of our two definitions for "kinetic reaction" is sufficient to convey the basic content of Newton's Second Law, which in turn provides the framework upon which differential equations can be set up through an appeal to the definition of "pendulum." This basic pattern can be harnessed to convert virtually any "nomological equivalence" to an identity.

Emancipationists need to confront the consequences of customary definitional practice more squarely. Hilary Putnam, in "On Properties," explicitly asserts that (i) standard definitions report correct property identities and (ii) logical and mathematical manipulations preserve property identity, yet he hopes, at the same time, that mere "nomological equivalences" such as the pendulum case will not stand as identities. This does not appear to be a viable position.

In conversation, I have encountered those who would reject Putnam's (i) on the grounds that science often says wrong things "for the sake of its own convenience." To paraphrase Mae West, convenience has nothin' to do with it; the wellsprings of "nomological equivalence" run deeper. In this essay, we will attempt to trace these waters to their sources.

5

If someone steadfastly maintains that "some definitions in science are right, some wrong," she should recognize that a distinction has been superadded to science, not extracted from it. Some philosophers do not play altogether fairly in this regard. It is not uncommon to find an author who berates her opponents on the grounds that "Our Best Scientific Theories teach us that ***," yet, when scientific shoes are on the other feet and the deliverances of Best Theories prove awkward, she retreats to "Oh, Science says *that* merely for convenience."

This is not to say that "Science" should be viewed as a Solomon to settle every metaphysical dispute. Indeed, I find rarified talk of "Science" or "Best Theories" distasteful; so often the "Science" cited is simply Philosophy in dark glasses with a phoney passport. If science, with a little "s," has anything to teach us about properties, it must arise at the lowly level of overlooked fact, rather than appear as a lesson blown in with a methodological wind. I shall maintain that our philosphical conception of emancipated properties must be reshaped to accommodate the rich assortment of attributes found in the world around us. The only role for "science" in this argument is simply to remind us how many unsuspected properties lurk in the behavior of the most familiar objects — a dropped garbage can lid or the waves on a canal.

In dealing with a branch of science, the considerations of section 4 suggest an important constraint on an adequate theory of universals, namely, if, from a theory we can extract a particular list of attributes, we should obtain this same listing if we had operated instead with a variant formulation of the same scientific content. A Hamiltonian recasting of classical physics should be expected to supply the same universals as a Lagrangian formulation. In short, a theory of universals should be *invariant* under theory reformulation. *Prima facie,* most philosophical approaches fail this test. Consider Hilary Putnam's approach in "On Properties." He begins with a list of the "fundamental magnitudes" of physics, which he takes to be the primitive vocabulary utilized within some formalization of the theory. The range of properties is extended beyond this initial basis by declaring that further properties correspond to every syntactic form that can be constructed within the language of the theory. Since he wishes to identify $2 \cdot \textbf{temp}(x) = 37$ and $\textbf{temp}(x) \cdot 2 = 37$ (i.e., properties differing only in their order of multiplication), but not our two pendulum quantities, Putnam proposes that predicate expressions be grouped into equivalent classes if they are "logically or mathematically equivalent."

This approach arranges properties in a hierarchy based upon a set of canonical *names.* Two questions naturally arise: First, how far do the syntactic constructions extend before physics' realm is left behind? Can quantifications appear in the canonical forms? Putnam allows quantifiers ranging over physical objects, but none over properties or quantities. Admitting property quantification would accept purely functional properties (such as **instantiates Turing machine m**) as legitimate physical traits, a conclusion that Putnam, quite famously, rejects. A large literature has sprung up trying to ascertain how "higher" properties such as the "functional" ones relate to the lower physical traits in Putnam's hierarchy; many authors have found the term "supervenience" useful in this connection.

Secondly, do all of the linguistic forms built in Putnam's hierarchy correspond to genuine properties? Putnam's approach, for example, readily constructs disjunctive predicates of the "grue" type, properties that Armstrong, *inter alia,* wishes to dismiss as non-genuine. Perhaps some kind of filter is needed to throw out the phoney properties arising in the hierarchy or, more minimally, to grade them according to their acceptability — their "naturalness" in David Lewis's terminology.

On the face of it, these kinds of procedures run the risk of failing our "invariance principle." Can we be sure that the same hierarchy, and the same degrees of "naturalness," will be constructed if we begin with an alternative formulation of our theory? Will the same predicates prove "mathematically or logically equivalent" within a Hamiltonian formulation as in a Lagrangian formulation? *Prima facie,* the answer is "no" because classical mechanics' symplectic structure (which arises as the product of a scientific law) is needed to pair off the proper Hamiltonian replacements. Are we entitled to expect that **grue** can be invariantly classified as "inherently disjunctive," given that Putnam's approach aligns properties with equivalence classes of names? How do we determine which name in the bunch is "canonical"? Will we get the same results if our theory is reexpressed in terms of an alternative set of primitives?

For that matter, can we really make sense of the notion of the "fundamental magnitudes" of a theory? The usual gloss on this expression is that they represent the "properties mentioned in the fundamental laws of a theory." Of course, what laws are "fundamental" typically alters under theory reformulation. More importantly, in both Lagrangian and Hamiltonian presentations, the "fundamental laws" contain explicit quantifiers ranging over *all* of the properties admitted by the theory. Note that, in dealing with the pendulum case above, it proved advantageous to switch quantities from our original x and y position variables to the polar quantities Θ and r. In doing so, the troublesome term "V_T" dropped out. The basic genius of the methods pioneered by Lagrange is to formulate "basic laws" in such a way that terms like "V_T" never appear in one's equations (it is much easier to set up the pendulum equation within a Lagrangian format than in the more Newtonian framework that we followed). But if we parse "fundamental magnitude" as "quantity mentioned in the basic laws," a Lagrangian starting point immediately gives us all properties at ground level, with no need to proceed to further stages of Putnam's hierarchy.

Lagrange's basic insight, that physics must render itself flexible enough to locate the right quantities for expressing a problem, will prove central in what follows.

6

On the face of it, no true-hearted emancipationist should wish to treat properties in the manifestly language-dependent manner of section 5.

Why have hierarchy-like views of property proved so appealing to philosophers? The answer seems to trace primarily to the worry that, unless intensional structure of a quasi-linguistic kind is assigned to properties, they will be insufficiently *rich* or *controllable* to serve any useful scientific or philosophical purpose. Here are two examples of this kind of worry.

David Lewis hopes that the notion of determinism can be defined roughly as follows:[8]

> Theory T is deterministic if and only if for every emancipated quantity Θ and all pairs of possible systems S and S' permitted by T, if the value of Θ on $S =$ the value of Θ on S' and t_0, then S and S' will continue to agree in Θ values at every time subsequent to t_0.

But if the range of quantifications tolerates too many phoney properties, this definition will fail. Suppose that T is a theory that should come out indeterministic (e.g., quantum mechanics). If **evolves from t_0 to t_1 in the manner of system S** is accepted as a genuine property, theory T is wrongly classified as "deterministic" according to Lewis's definition. Why? Let S' be a possible system that, properly speaking, should represent a legitimate alternative development of S from its condition at t_0. But S and S' clearly disagree on the "property" mentioned at t_0, thus preventing S' from demonstrating that S is indeterministic. Lewis claims that physics should not tolerate dubious "properties" such as this.

But what are the precise grounds for dismissing the problematic **evolves from t_0 to t_1 in the manner of system S**? Lewis, unfortunately, does not tell us; he simply presumes that some intensionality desired in a genuine property is missing. Presumably, the unstated exclusionist principle runs something like "No legitimate property should refer to a system's *de facto* evolution from present state to its future or past temporal position." Note how naturally an appeal to "reference" emerges in the prohibition, despite the fact that reference seems an activity native to language and thought, rather than to emancipated universals. The syntactic structure of "evolves from time $t_0 . . . ,$" with its explicit mention of future times, seems to pinpoint what is wrong with the intensionality of the unwanted property.

As a second example, consider the problem of segregating "good" disjunctive properties from "bad." Look at the "complex" predicate "has energy E_1 or energy E_2 or . . . or energy E_n," where $E_1, . . . , E_n$ represent a band of energies available to the system. When we measure the "energy" of the system, we invariably detect a property with some disjunctive spread in it; we never detect a sharp **has energy E_i** property. But how might we distinguish between the "causal efficacy" found in our "good" disjunctive energy property from the lack of efficacy seen in the "bad" disjunction "grue"? Doesn't the correct answer have to be that, in the energy property, the "causal efficacies" of its sundry E_i legs amalgamate neatly as one works towards the full disjunction, whereas in "grue," the blending process becomes blocked because the individual "causal efficacies" of **green** and **blue** are too disparate to supply the disjunction with any causal power to call its own? Doesn't this observation show that properties must carry an intrinsic intensionality that determines how well they can be amalgamated into one another?

The general concern expressed in both examples is that properties can be useful only insofar as they embody a much higher degree of "intensional content" than mere sets do. David Lewis puts the point this way:

> Because [sets] are so abundant, they are undiscriminating. Any two things [belong to] infinitely many [sets], and fail to [belong] to infinitely many others. This is so whether the two things are perfect duplicates or utterly dissimilar. Thus [sets] do nothing to capture facts of resemblance. That is work more suited to the sparse universals. Likewise, [sets] do nothing to capture the causal power of things. Almost all properties are causally irrelevant, and there is nothing to make the relevant ones stand out from the crowd.[9]

By "sparseness," Lewis intends the thesis that there are far fewer universals in the world than sets — he claims that this is the key reason why science needs to accept "universals" at all. His chief worry is the notion that bare sets are "too thin" — in his phrase, "nondiscriminating" — to prove useful for most scientific purposes. Sets lack the essential character — or "soul" — that properties need to be useful.

But how can we expect to gain access to "intensional content" unless we look beyond the raw extension of a predicate into the structures revealed in its meaning? By such reasoning, the valiant emancipationist is pulled, against her will, back into the lair of linguistically centered universals.

Fortunately mathematical physics long ago found a better approach to such issues. Historically, physics' initial attempts to develop a systematic account of properties followed a quasi-syntactic strategy akin to Putnam's. A richer appreciation of the sound reasons why such accounts proved inadequate should remove the appearance of oddity from many aspects of scientific practice — its tolerance of definitional variation; mathematics' identification of "property" with "set," etc. On a modern treatment, virtually every philosophical presumption articulated in this section winds up being rejected: (1) syntactic structure is not an optimal guide to the ties that bind attributes together; (2) properties cannot be "sparse"; multiple properties will correspond to any selected set of real world objects; (3) the basic intensionality of properties may seem nearly as "thin" as that of "set" (although appearances in this regard can be rather deceiving); (4) the alleged intensionalities cited in the discussions of **evolves from . . .** and **grue** should be dismissed as fuzzy and improper; emancipated universals have been judged by wholly inappropriate standards. We will appreciate better the nature of this error after section 11, where the status of the **evolves from . . .** property is examined in greater detail.

The reader has probably found our discussion of "property intensionality" in this section to be rather vague. Such haziness is not entirely the fault of the inarticulate author of "Honorable Intensions"; the emancipationist writings from which the alleged intensionalities have been extracted are rarely explicit about the systematic features they have in mind. Discussion instead tends to run at a "candy store" level, viz., "I like this one; I don't like that." To me, this reticence is no accident, for I see the alleged intensionalities of the last section as fuzzy misallocations of linguistic or mentalistic distinctions pretending to be neither linguistic nor mentalistic. Obviously, most emancipationists will regard my diagnosis of their claims as slanderous; they view the intensionalities they cite as directly reflecting the "causal characteristics" of universals, free of any excursion through unwanted "modes of presentation," linguistic or otherwise. We will table further discussion of "causal character" until section 13.

7

I have just claimed that physics embraces a very rich ontology of properties, in contrast to the "sparse" views of most emancipationists. It is here that the critical differences between the approach followed here and those of other philosophical writers begin to emerge. The evolution of physics' treatment of property has been largely shaped by a need to ratify various *existence claims* about properties—that is, statements dominated by *existential quantifications* over properties ("there are properties such that . . ."). Most philosophical discussions instead stress applications involving *universal quantifications* ("all properties are such that . . ."). Lewis's suggested definition of determinism is a case in point. The pressure of existential statements tends to enlarge the domain of properties and render them "thinner"; the universal statements, smaller and "thicker."

Where do the existence claims come from? They originate in unprepossessing data such as the following: in the late 1700s, the craftsman E. F. F. Chlandi found that struck metal plates vibrate in a combination of special patterns called "modes," rather as plucked strings vibrate in a superimposed pattern of pure note frequencies. Chlandi uncovered these unsuspected vibrational properties by sprinkling sand upon plates held in specially clamped positions; the resulting sand patterns revealed the spe-

Figure 1 Plate Modes

cial modes in which the plates vibrate. (See figure 1.) For our purposes, the salient fact is that Chlandi clearly *discovered* some unexpected properties hidden in the plates. But, once these traits are revealed, it becomes clear that they represent some of the plate's most *important* attributes, in the sense that they best determine how the plate will absorb energy, when it will rupture, and so forth.

It turns out that a wide variety of physical systems own their own private stock of mode-like properties; many of the key successes in nineteenth-century physics represented the elucidation and exploitation of these hidden traits. The investigations of Joseph Fourier and his school (particularly those by C. Sturm and J. Liouville in the 1830s) revealed the mathematical basis for these behaviors. If a physical system is suitably modeled by a set of equations of "Sturm-Liouville type," then its "mode" properties can be calculated. If this is done, an experiment can be run—sprinkling sand, shaking the material with a frequency generator—that looks for the predicted traits. These experiments typically meet with success. Once recognized, the hidden qualities prove most helpful in understanding the system's composite behavior.

Here we have an existence claim of the sort I wish to emphasize: "For any system of Sturm-Liouville type, a set of mode properties exists such that. . . ." An adequate physics, clearly, should predict the existence of these hidden properties. Since the specific set of relevant properties tends to vary from system to system, Chlandi's discovery and its aftermath forces physics to become generous in its allotment of properties. Other existential discoveries—the "constants of motion" discussed below—stretch physics' attribute domain along other dimensions of enlargement. It turns out that, by our usual standards for nameability, many of the predicted traits cannot possess preexisting names within a Putnamesque syntactic hierarchy. Physics has found that it needs to rely upon more sophisticated mathematical tools if it hopes to frame a conception of property that can ratify the existence claims it needs. At the time of Chlandi's and Fourier's discoveries, mathematics itself was unprepared to meet rigorously the demands that physics had begun to place upon it. The spectacular recasting that analysis saw in the period following Fourier was motivated, in no small part, by a desire to bring a wide variety of existence claims, within both mathematics and physics, into proper adjustment. A deep and pervasive collaboration between mathematics and physics was created that simultaneously induces mathematics to treat "property" in a set-like manner and physics to utilize attributes that, in spite of their stronger "intensional" character, do not wear the popular intensionalities of philosophy well. The object of this essay is to rehearse some of the key considerations involved in this history and to elucidate the basic reasonableness of the solution obtained.

The extent to which other emancipationist authors have been aware of physics' existential demands is unclear. Putnam, who is largely concerned with "reduction," displays more generosity than Armstrong, who often writes as if attributes adhere in the world like coins in a miserly pudding. Yet even Putnam seems unaware of how artificially limited are the existence principles that his approach supports. On the other hand, in spite of his official "sparseness," Armstrong is sometimes willing to tolerate a pool of "second rank universals" beyond the genuine ones. How far this extension reaches, how it is to be controlled (i.e., does **grue** get in?), and what are its purposes are left rather nebulous. Nor is it obvious, in any real life science, what the "real universals" are supposed to be. Sometimes I think that Armstrong intends the "fundamental coupling parameters" — e.g., **mass, charge, spin** — that occur in some (but not all) approaches to physics. But such a reading would exclude **energy** and **momentum,** which I doubt is Armstrong's intention. Since Armstrong rather proudly abjures real life examples, it is impossible to determine what he might have in mind. It seems fair to say that few emancipationists display much awareness of the range of existential claims commonly utilized in physics.

8

To proceed to the history, we must introduce a slight adjustment in the parameters of our discussion. The original drive towards extensionality in mathematics directly concerned the notion of *function,* rather than *property.* Here the term "function" represents a many-one association between mathematical objects, such as provided by the addition mapping "+". Like properties, functions are treated totally extensionally in modern mathematics: two functions are identified if they agree in their courses of values (i.e., they map objects to the same images). But the puzzling fact about functions is that their existence is treated in the same "thin" manner as sets — a modern mathematician will accept *any* many-one pairing of input values with outputs as a "function," no matter how disconnected the mapping may appear. This "set-like" view of function is commonly credited to an 1837 paper by L.-J. Dirichlet, although, in truth, it is unclear whether Dirichlet would have actually accepted all of the modern ramifications of the approach (widespread acceptance of completely general mappings as functions did not occur until the 1890s).

On physics' side, we need to discuss so-called *physical quantities,* rather than properties *per se.* Quantities are physics' analogs of functions —quantities like **mass, position,** and **frequency** involve maps from physical systems and times to numerical values (or to more complicated mathematical objects such as vectors). Here the term "function" will always be restricted to "mathematical function"; "quantity" confined to "physical quantity."

In general, the notions of "property" and "function"/"quantity" are interchangeable. A property can be coded by its so-called "characteristic" function or quantity and *vice versa.* Despite this equivalence, it is better to study functions and quantities, for they represent the more natural entities in mathematics and physics. Generally, a discipline's approach to "property" tags along with its treatment of "function" or "quantity." Our discussion of emancipationism will largely center upon functions and quantities, leaving the transcription to properties to the reader.

On the face of it, the identification of "mathematical function" with an arbitrary extensional course of values seems as aberrant as the collapse of "properties" into sets. Shouldn't functions be characterized as *rules* for calculating values? (After all, introductory calculus texts still explain "function" in this way.) *Prima facie,* a "rule" should possess a richer intensional character than a mere course of values.

Indeed, mathematicians originally found Dirichlet's account to be excessively inclusive. Thus, James Harkness and Frank Morley complained in a popular analysis text of 1893:

> According to Dirichlet's definition, the value of y, when x = a, may be entirely unrelated to the value of y for any other value of x, x = b. This definition, in contrast to those used before Dirichlet's time, errs on the side of excessive generality; for it does not of itself confer properties on the function. The functions so defined must be subjected to restrictive conditions before they can be used in analysis.[10]

Their claim is that, in our eagerness to ensure that the net of "function" misses no important examples, the term has been defined in such a way that all of the specific properties—e.g., differentiability, continuity—which enable a function to act *as a function* in practice have been eliminated from its definition. One of the major ways in which functions "act as functions" is shown by their role in physics. But to play this role, they must be "regular." Some quick explanations: for a function f to be *differentiable* with respect to a variable t, f must change sufficiently smoothly as t varies so that one can meaningfully consider *the rate at which f is changing with respect to t* (written df/dt or $\dot{f}$). The **velocity** of a particle, for example, represents the derivative of its **position** with respect to time. If f changes its values at $t=t_0$ suddenly, then df/dt may not be defined. It may or may not happen that df/dt itself varies smoothly enough to enjoy its own rate of change (written $d^2f(t)/dt^2$ or $\ddot{f}$). The depth to which this process of taking further derivatives can be carried is called f's "degree of smoothness." If f happens to be a function of several variables (e.g., x as well as t), it may possess derivatives with respect to variations in x as well (the so-called "partial derivative" $\delta f/\delta x$). Requirements on the differentiability of f (and allied constraints such as Lifschitz conditions) are labeled *regularity conditions*.

In these terms, Harkness and Morley presume that if a function does not include sufficient regularity in its "character," it will be useless in mathematics — *a fortiori*, in physics. Consider the following "wild" function (suggested by Dirichlet) that is licensed by the modern treatment:

$$d(x) = \begin{cases} 1 \text{ if } x \text{ is rational} \\ 0 \text{ if } x \text{ is irrational} \end{cases}$$

(Indeed, it is easy to construct mappings vastly more unruly than this example.) How might science have any use for "monster" functions like this? Classical physics predicts the future, after all, using differential equations — equations which state the rate at which a function f of interest will change in response to changes in the surrounding conditions. If df/dt is undefined, no differential equation for f will make sense. But the Dirichlet function $d(x)$ has no derivative anywhere. Why do mathematicians dignify such useless rubble with the title of "function"?

Viewed this way the modern approach to functions appears too *thin*; it eschews the very regularity properties which allow a function to perform useful work. Harkness and Morley's worries can be seen as related to the trepidations that David Lewis expresses in regard to the identification of physical properties with sets. The shared concern is that existence standards for functions and quantities have been so relaxed that they now ignore the central core (or "intensional character") that supplies these entities with utility. To put the matter metaphorically, functions and quantities need a "soul" such as the robust content of a concept or rule seems to supply.

In fact, concern with the nature of functional utility led early mathematicians to define "function" in a quasi-linguistic manner quite similar to that discussed in section 5: they tried to construct the complete class of functions by utilizing reiterated linguistic operations over a set of fundamental elements. Thus Euler wrote in 1744:

> A function of a variable quantity (e.g., x, y, t, etc.) is an analytic expression composed in any way from this variable quantity and numbers. [11]

That is, one starts with x and y, say, and uses operations like $+$, $\bullet$, cos, exponentiation to build up expressions such as "$x^5 y + \cos(3x/6y)$." As it stands, the definition is careless about use/mention considerations and, if taken literally, would distinguish between $2 + x$ and $x + 2$. (Euler would have presumably been happy to follow Putnam in grouping these expressions into a common equivalence class.)

For reasons we shall discuss in the next section, Euler eventually recognized that his syntax-based treatment would not encompass all entities commonly treated as "functions" in application. Nonetheless many early mathematicians felt that Euler's basic approach was unavoidable. There seemed to be no other way that the "usefulness" of functions could be preserved. Recall that functions must be differentiable if they are to serve in differential equations. But how is the notion of "derivative" to be explained? In this period, it was customary to explicate "derivative" simply in terms of the "cookbook" calculus rules for obtaining the derivative, i.e., $x^2 \rightarrow 2x$, etc. This account makes sense only if functions internally embody an inherent "syntactic form" or "rule-like intensionality," that provides a texture to which the cookbook rules can attach.

9

What forced mathematicians to abandon this treatment of "function"? I have already claimed that a large part of the answer sprang from mathematics' symbiosis with physics. As early as Descartes, it was noted that the curvilinear trajectory of a stone—that is, its changing quantity of **position**—was quite unlikely to be modeled by the stock of functions nameable in the usual mathematical vocabulary. Descartes himself drew the conclusion that mathematics could model a physical system only when the system's behavior was especially simple. But it was gradually recognized that this conclusion was too pessimistic. A famous (and often bitter) dispute on these issues arose between Euler and d'Alembert. It concerned the class of functions that can be regarded as solving the standard equation for a vibrating string. Euler argued, on physical grounds, that a function representing a *plucked* string needs to be defined by a piecemeal formula such as "$1/16x$ if $0<x<1/2$; $(1-x)/16$ if $1/2<x<1$." As Euler was well aware, this formula does not fully conform to his official definition of "function" — it is defined in pieces, equivalent to a use of the logical operation of "or." D'Alembert agreed that a physical string might assume a bent shape, but noted that the derivatives appearing in his string equation could not be completely defined for such curves, on the grounds that the "rule" for the function "switched" at the midpoint $1/2$ (the cookbook rules for derivatives break down there). Plucked strings, for d'Alembert, represented just another example of the physical processes exceeding the grasp of mathematics. Euler, however, claimed that the *true* realm of "functions" ought to include his plucked specimen. Most mathematicians accepted Euler's conclusion, although it was not until the late nineteenth century that d'Alembert's worries about the absence of derivatives were answered rigorously.

It is Euler's altered vision of mathematics' potential power that informs our modern conception of an all-encompassing "mathematical physics." The realm of mathematics must be rich enough to provide enough objects — functions or whatever — to model *all* quantities that might arise in physical applications; mathematical physics should not be restricted to the narrow class of physical occurrences that happen to fit its preexisting tools. It is unlikely, were the doctrine to have occurred to him, that Euler would have immediately embraced Dirichlet's set-based approach; he would have worried that "function" is drawn too "thin" and characterless to sustain its customary chores in mathematics. The hundred years after Euler represented a period in which functions not satisfying his "official" constraints were frequently smuggled into mathematics through fudgy considerations involving infinite series expansions and the like.

The sloppy tolerance of contraband functions slowly began causing problems in analysis, eventually forcing a more judicious weighing of basic questions of functional existence at the hands of A.-L. Cauchy and others. Consider the simple equation $E - \sin E = n(t - T)$ where n, T are constants; $n \neq 0$, which arises in celestial mechanics. By trivial rearrangement, this equation can be solved to produce a function $\varphi(E)$ mapping the E values to the t values. Indeed, $\varphi(E)$ has a simple name fulfilling Euler's demands on function "$E/n - \sin E/n + T$." Will there also be an *inverse* function $\psi(t)$ that maps the t values to the E values? One should beware of the ready reply, "Certainly, it is called φ^{-1}," for many functions lack inverses. Consider $t = x^2$, for example. No function $f(t)$ exists to map t values inversely to x values because most t's are associated with two x values, disqualifying the would-be inverse from counting as a function. (See figure 2.) Indeed, this suggests an important distinction: the phrase "$E/n - \sin E/n + T$" is *an expression of self-guaranteeing reference* in the sense that the constructions indicated by "sin", "+", etc. are all guaranteed to carry functions to further well-defined functions. On the other hand, "φ^{-1}" is

Figure 2

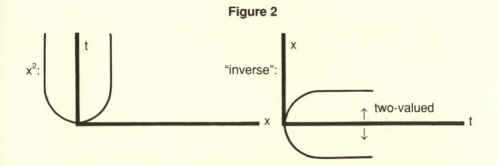

not a phrase of "self-guaranteeing reference," for no such function is guaranteed to exist even if φ does. If Euler's approach is to delineate genuine existence conditions for functions, it must operate only with self-guaranteeing expressions.

As noted, early mathematicians were less than scrupulous in heeding this warning. By performing various manipulations on the equation for E, an expression for ψ can be obtained by "solving" it with an infinite series expansion, viz. $E = n(t-T) + \Sigma 2/k J_k (ke)\sin kn(t-T)$ (the J_k are Bessel functions). But once again, expressions containing the sign for infinite summation "Σ" cannot be regarded as self-guaranteeing. Series expansion, no matter how impeccable the manner in which they are derived, often fail to converge and accordingly delineate no function whatsoever. Put another way, phoney infinite series "inverses" can be plausibly obtained for functions that do not possess inverses at all. Indeed, terrible errors in eighteenth-century mathematics arose through the uncritical habit of treating series expansions as automatically representing well-determined functions. Much of Cauchy's original motivations for tackling the problems of function existence stemmed from unhappy experiences of this sort.

Euler in fact suspected that no formula expressible in the self-guaranteeing language tolerated by his official definition would name our needed inverse ψ. In 1833, J. Liouville confirmed this hunch. Indeed $\psi(t)$'s unpleasant behavior turns out to be the norm for functions arising in the context of differential equations. If we wish to tolerate $\psi(t)$ and its kin as functions, a new account of functional existence must be found. Cauchy pioneered an approach that dealt with the problem in a manner that completely eschews any consideration of whether a formula exists to denote the desired ψ or not.

In simple terms, here is how Cauchy would try to build an inverse for a function f. He tries to construct f^{-1} as a limit of broken line approximations to it. Divide the domain desired for f^{-1} (here the y axis, see figure 3) into n intervals. At each node i, find the derivative s_i (= slope) of

Figure 3

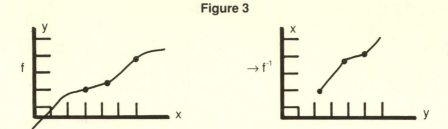

f. Then draw a broken line consisting of segments with the inverse slope $1/s_i$. With luck, this broken line function will go to f^{-1} as $n \to \infty$. The limit being reached will depend upon regularity conditions on f: e.g., df/dx must not vanish in the interval; it must also be continuous. Cauchy also proved that if f is sufficiently smooth, f^{-1} will also be. The idea, roughly, is that as the angles between the broken line approximations to f grow smaller with increasing n, so will the angles in the approximations to f^{-1}.

Note that linguistic expressions are not used to build f^{-1} — instead, an infinite host of approximating functions "squeeze in" upon it. The "existence conditions" for functions now rely upon the usual Cauchy standards for determining when a sequence has a limit, not whether a linguistic form exists. Indeed, functions produced as limits will usually not possess names; at least, in the precise sense of a self-guaranteeing "name."

Although the Cauchy approach to existence claims does not force one to embrace the full "thinness" of the Dirichlet treatment, the introduction of the "limit" concept carries the notion of "function" considerably closer to that of "set." In particular, taking the limit of a sequence of functions displays a remarkable tendency to strip away features present in the sequence's members. One of the great surprises in the history of mathematics came when Joseph Fourier showed that a well-defined sequence of sine waves (= rolling curves like that of a string sounding a pure tone) can add up in a limit to a function that takes a completely discontinuous jump. That is, a series of continuous (= connected) functions will pop out as a discontinuous function in the limit. Riemann later showed how the Dirichlet function can be obtained as a limit at "nicer" functions.

Naively, one expects that, if the qualities of the "components" of a sequence are understood, the character of the function emerging from their limit can be readily foreseen. The examples just mentioned show that this assumption is deeply wrong (much of the nineteenth-century work on the foundations of analysis was devoted to straightening these matters out). Taking a limit tends to destroy the characters (or "intensionalities") of the functions thrown into the hopper of the limit-taking machine. The inverse function f^{-1} constructed in Cauchy's proof usually assumes regularity properties similar to the starting f, but this regularity is not automatically inherited from f by a simple process where the regularity is passed undiminished along the sequence of functions intermediate between f and f^{-1}. Indeed, the mediating functions, being broken lines, are not fully regular themselves, so it is rather surprising that smoothness can reassert itself in the limit. Among partial differential equations, the question of the extent to which one function transfers regularity to another is apt to prove an enormously difficult problem. For our purposes, the crucial observation is that, after Cauchy, syntactic expression no longer serves as an infallible guide to functional character—one must *prove* that a function possesses a characteristic such as regularity on the basis of how it *behaves*. Note that the worries that wedded Euler, against his better instincts, to a hierarchial approach to "function" have now been resolved.

Allowing that a genuine function can be constructed solely as a limit of broken lines ties "function" closely to "set" (even if it does not force a complete Dirichlet-style identification). In my opinion, it is this linkage that stands chiefly at the root of the "thin" and extensional character of the modern approach to "function." We have seen that much of the motivation for accepting limit constructions was the desire to model quantities that physics seems to need. Why, after all, did Cauchy regard the inverse function $\varphi(t)$ as a creature that deserves a place in mathematics? Why had not Liouville's proof simply shown that $\varphi(E)$ has no inverse? Answer: $\psi(t)$ constitutes the natural model of an important physical quantity, the **eccentric anomaly** of celestial mechanics (the "eccentric anomaly" of a planet, roughly speaking, supplies its angular position in the solar sky as a function of time). The quantity obviously exists; we want a function to match it.

But we still have not responded adequately to the worry that our new standards of functional existence are too tolerant and fail to provide genuinely useful functions. Before we answer this, we need to look at how modern treatments of classical physics handle its indigenous range of quantities.

10

Standard texts in classical physics have long offered an explicit treatment of "physical quantity" that eschews linguistic considerations altogether. Essentially, the method piggybacks upon mathematics' well-articulated treatment of "function," a linkage that is unsurprising given the historical symbiosis between "function" and "quantity."

To understand the approach, we must first explain the notion of "phase space." Consider the possible states (or "phases") that a mechanical system S of a particular construction might assume. "Particular construction" means that factors such as the following must be settled: the number of particles in S; values of "parameter" quantities like **charge, mass, spring constant;** the types of force, external and internal, acting on S and so forth. This leaves wide latitude in selection of a "phase" for a system instantiating the S recipe (think of how widely the nine planets might have been scattered around the universe without altering the stipulations that classify them as the same kind of system). A *phase space* Γ is essentially the collection of all states possible for S. I say "essentially" because it is important to understand that the S recipe inscribes Γ with additional structure — in particular, the points of Γ are painted with little "arrows" which tell a system currently in state S_0 how to move to its "next" (= infinitesimally neighboring) state S_1. The *trajectory* of a particular system is just the locus of states it passes through in time, pushed from one arrow to the next (this talk of "arrows" is simply a geometrical way of picturing what differential equations tell us about S). In sum, phase space is a collection of states physically open to a system, interwoven with a bunch of arrows and trajectories. Except in cases of constraints, one can inscribe coordinate axes q_i and p_i corresponding to the position (q) and momentum (p) of each particle in S (i.e., 6 coordinate axes for each member of S), for a system's state is determined by its current q_i and p_i values (see figure 4). (Sometimes it is fruitful to collect larger groups of possibilities into a common space — e.g., a *control space* where parameter values like **mass** and **charge** vary.)

The following gloss on "physical quantity" can be found in many texts, for example, Thirring or Sudarshan and Mukinda:

> In order to interpret the formalism it must first be agreed what the observable quantities are. . . . We should therefore allow arbitrary functions of coordinates and momenta as observables, subject only to boundedness and, for mathematical convenience, differentiability.[12]

Or

> The observables or dynamic variables of the system are all real functions on phase space (or they may be a subset chosen according to some criterion).[13]

Reformulated as an existence postulate for quantities, the quotations above suggest an Existence Postulate (EP):

> If (q_i, p_i) are physical quantities sufficient to fix the state of a system S, then $f(q_i, p_i)$ will be a well-defined quantity for S, where f is an arbitrary mathematical function.[14]

Figure 4

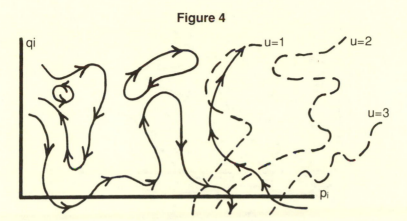

EP might be restricted by limiting the range of permissible *f*; in fact, the Thirring quotation mentions a regularity requirement that we will discuss later. I might add that EP, generous as it is, does not supply all of the quantities of physics — in particular, parameter quantities like **mass** do not have an adequate representation within a single phase space (they instead appear in the "control spaces"). But we will not worry about these ramifications here, because they do not affect the basic content of what is claimed.

We can picture the quantities accepted by EP as follows: in the previous diagram (fig. 4) mark lines (called "level surfaces") where a quantity **u** assumes the same values, in the manner of the isobars on a weather map. EP states that a distinct quantity should correspond to every conceivable inscription of level surfaces within the phase space (if **u** is not required to be regular, the "level surfaces" may fragment into a disconnected mass of points).

Here is a sketch of how these ideas work. Suppose the possible trajectories of some collection of *S* systems move in irregular concentric loops like a squashed onion (figure 5). If we are given a continuous printout of such a system's changing *p* and *q* values, the results would appear haphazard and disorderly. But now introduce a quantity *u* supplying the *path the system is on* and a quantity *v* marking *the system's current place around that path,* measured as an angle. That is, the trajectory travels on a level surface for *u*. Viewed from *u* and *v*'s perspective, the motion looks very regular. Figure six is a picture of the same phase space as before but based upon a different choice of coordinates (think of the various appearances of Greenland in maps based upon different projection rules). By changing to *u* and *v* (officially called "action/angle coordinates"), an important hid-

Figure 5

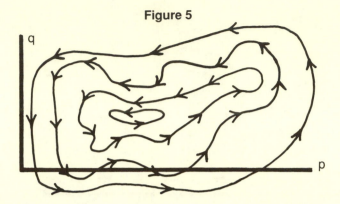

den order is revealed in our systems, an order that makes such systems especially tractable.

Here we have worked within a phase space of two dimensions. Suppose our system instead requires a four-dimensional phase space. In analogy to the previous case, we can ask whether any *u* exists that slices the space into neat leaves, so that each trajectory of our system remains upon a fixed leaf of *u*. *v*, as before, supplies the system's current location along its leaf (mathematicians call such slicings "foliations"). It may happen that a further quantity *w* exists that slices the phase space transversally to *u*, so that each trajectory now runs along the intersection of a *u* leaf and a *w* leaf. The phase space is now "fully foliated." Obviously these ideas can be repeated in higher dimensional spaces.

It turns out that the basic character of a physical system's behavior will depend strongly upon whether such "foliating" quantities exist or not. If they do, the physical system will be "practically predictable" in the sense that a computer can be used to track its motion without being quickly overwhelmed by roundoff error. In such cases, the *u*'s correspond to what older mathematicians called "constants of the motion" (a system will retain the same *u* value because it is confined to a level surface for *u*). The sun and moon system is "predictable" because its phase space is foliated by enough "constants of the motion." But such neat slicings are rather rare; a system may behave chaotically with respect to predictability if no underlying foliations exist.

Even when suitable foliating quantities exist, they can be the devil to uncover. In the earth-sun case, some of the "constants" are easy to find (e.g., **energy, linear momentum**), but others (**orbital plane**) require some mathematical cleverness. Chlandi's "modes," too, foliate their relevant phase spaces and we have seen that, historically, their existence was a complete surprise. In general, finding a complete set of foliating quantities evinces

Figure 6

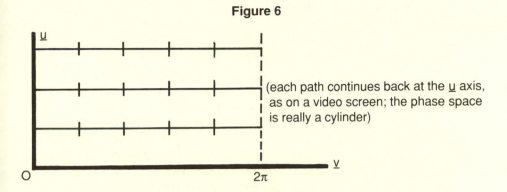

(each path continues back at the u axis, as on a video screen; the phase space is really a cylinder)

a skill in mathematical gerrymandering comparable to that of our best party bosses. Such quantities could potentially range anywhere within the bounds set by EP, which is an important motivation for its generosity.

A set of foliating quantities automatically provides a collection of "good coordinates" for a system, in the same sense that the polar trait Θ is better suited to a pendulum than the *x* and *y* with which the discussion of section 4 began. The fact that "good coordinates" may potentially lurk anywhere within the bounds of EP can be understood as follows: as one forms a system out of a collection of component molecules, their interactions may lead various sorts of "ordering" to lock in among them. Analogy: if one assembles complex shapes by hinging triangles along their edges, certain configurations (e.g., Buckminster Fuller's famous "geodesic domes") will "lock in" a rigidity absent in most of the otherwise floppy complexes that one builds. Similarly, the intermolecular ties within Chlandi's plates manage to "freeze in" patterns of cooperation extending across all the molecules of the plate. This cooperation allows us to meaningfully ask how much energy is stored in each mode, giving rise to a set of good coordinates for the system. The "locking in" of a good coordinate can be so startling that physicists are sometimes tempted to speak of "the emergence of traits." Tap the side of a glass of supercooled water. Almost instantly it will turn entirely to ice. The jarring allows a new type of order to extend over the water molecules. In EP's terms, the underlying system has been modified in such a way that, very roughly speaking, the ice system has become confined to the leaves of an "ordering parameter" quantity for the system. It is not that such leaves did not exist while the water was liquid; rather the system was then not disposed to travel in their directions.

Notice that in all of these examples we ask: how do the system's trajectories align with the "level surfaces" of *u*? This innocent observation turns out to be central to the superiority of EP over a quasi-syntactic approach to quantity.

Before we take up these matters, I will make a passing remark on the connections between EP and smoothness. In the above examples, the "level surfaces" of a quantity indicate the presence of "predictability" only if they are smooth—i.e., one cannot jump immediately from a "$u = 1$" leaf to a "$u = 3$" layer. Nonsmooth u do not trap the system sufficiently to count as a foliation. Nevertheless, I regard u as a perfectly acceptable quantity nonetheless, but some authors (e.g., Thirring above) withhold the honorific term "quantity" when u is not smooth. There are many fascinating issues buried here, but it would take us too far afield to discuss them. If one follows Thirring's version of EP, "quantities" acquire a somewhat thicker "basic intensionality" than I have assumed here (viz., regularity), but the basic tenor of our discussion, *mutatis mutandis,* remains the same. Actually I suspect that Thirring would readily concede that nonsmooth u can represent genuine, and sometimes important, "aspects" of a physical system, so our disagreement about "quantity" is largely a quibble about the best use of a name.[15]

11

We can now begin to understand what is wrong with the "hierarchial" approach to properties discussed in section 5. That approach tried to evaluate a quantity's varying dimensions of intensional virtue *in advance* of looking at the *behavior* of the mechanical systems to which the quantity will apply. That is, an attempt is made to order quantities into a lattice so that the intensional character of a quantity is revealed through its ties to other quantities within the hierarchy. The disjunctive property **has energy in a range from E_0 to E_{37}** qualifies as an "acceptably unified" trait because it builds upon its base (the specific **has energy E_j** properties) in a coherent way, whereas unacceptable **grue** fails to do this. Likewise, the insertion of reference to particular times in **evolves from t_0 to t_1 in the manner of system S** commits an intensional sin which was avoided in its acceptable progenitor, **evolves in the manner of system S.**

On this treatment, each quantity contains an *intrinsic* measure of intensional "goodness" or "badness," assignable in advance of looking at any particular mechanical system. On EP's treatment of quantity, *the only inherent intensionality they are provided is the minimum needed to locate the "level surfaces" of the quantities within the phase spaces.* This localizing information is conveyed through EP's "f (p,q)." Whether a trait carries further intensional virtues relative to a particular system shall be determined by how the "level surfaces" intersect the trajectories inside the space. Traits must *earn* their further intensional characteristics.

Recall the concern among early mathematicians that a "rule"-based notion of function could not be abandoned: if a function were not associated with an expression to which the cookbook rules of the calculus apply, then there would be no basis for assigning a derivative to the function. When Cauchy began constructing "functions" as limits of broken lines, he gave them the freedom to assume derivatives or not, independently of whether or not they bore any specific sort of name. Cauchy taught mathematics to evaluate the smoothness of functions solely on the basis of the function's *behavior*; the "intensionalities" of smoothness no longer had to be inherited without lapse along the lineage of a well-bred family. Such an emancipation from cookbook considerations required that the notion of "derivative" be rearticulated in syntax-independent terms (as is provided in the familiar ε/δ construction).

As noted earlier, it is often unpredictable whether a function constructed as a limit will inherit a feature obtaining among its predecessors or not. It is wisest to define "function" in the most generous possible way and leave the acquisition of further desirable traits to *proof.* The wisdom of such a policy is doubly underscored as it turns out that "functions" have proved useful in many contexts where they lack one or another of the specific virtues that, *a priori,* one would presume that "good" functions needed to have. Nineteenth-century mathematicians doubted that a function with no derivatives whatsoever could serve as a "solution" within a plausible physical setting, yet Norbert Wiener's celebrated approach to Brownian motion provides a theory of exactly this sort. In fact, Harkness and Morley eventually dismiss the worries they had raised about Dirichlet's account of function by appeal to these sorts of consideration.

Returning to physics, consider the allegedly unsatisfactory quantity **evolves from t_0 to t_1 in the manner of system S,** which had posed difficulties for Lewis's definition of determinism in section 6. A physicist's attitude to this trait is completely different from Lewis's—she will immediately accept it as a well-determined property, but wonders, in the case of a particular system, whether its behavior will be smooth. In two dimensions, she will reason as follows: draw a line in the phase space to mark the current condition of a batch of possible systems at time t_0. Label this line with any arbitrary monotonic scale. From the t_0 line, track the system forward in time following the **evolves from . . .** trait. As one goes, deposit the number inherited along the path from the base line. Stop the process when a phase space point is encountered to which a number has already been assigned. If no trajectories cross, two basic eventualities are possible: case (i): the paths return to their origins or else wander off to unproblematic parts of the phase space (figure 6); case (ii): some paths recross the t_0 line in new places (see figure 7). In case (i), our physicist will say, the trait **evolves from the scale value n on the t_0 line** becomes well defined. The "level curves" of this quantity foliate the space in the sense of section 10; they carve it into neat layers according to the number inherited from the "time $= t_0$" line. In case (ii), the numbers deposited will jump discontinuously in spots, so the space is not foliated (which requires smoothness) by the construction. In higher dimensions, if one can obtain an initial foliation from **evolves from . . .** , one tries to construct a second trait that inscribes another foliation that slices transversally to the first set of leaves. As noted previously, the presence or absence of these kinds of dissection is crucial to the basic behavior of the system.

Our physicist does not doubt that **evolves from t_0 to t_1 in the manner of system S** is an acceptable quantity; the open question is what further characteristics it will earn as it unwraps itself within the phase space selected. The acquisition of smoothness is usually rather unpredictable and difficult to ascertain. The moral is that one should not try to ascertain the intensional virtues of a quantity, beyond its raw existence, in advance of an application to a particular mechanical system. The quasi-linguistic methodology of section 5 errs in trying to settle all questions of intensional worthiness *a priori,* somehow distilled from the *meaning* of a canonical name for the quantity.

On EP's view, two quantities relate to one another, not so much through preset ties of a quasi-semantical nature, but through the manner in which the trajectories lace through the "level surfaces" that each quantity carves in the space. In a particular space, the slices of **evolves from . . .** may close upon itself nearly in case (i) fashion and foliate the space in rings. Quantity *w* may then act as one of **evolves from . . .**'s partial derivatives. The addition of a new force to the system may perturb the paths of **evolves from . . .** so that they no longer join up; *w* will no longer relate to **evolves from . . .** in the derivative relationship.

Moral: the syntactic construction of a quantity name may not reveal its actual ties to other quantities adequately.

In discussions with other emancipationists, I have frequently encountered a persisting loyalty to language-based approaches to "property," although the detour through language seems problematic and, in light of EP, unnecessary. Suppose that the standard inch happens to be an unfortunate multiple *r* of the standard centimeter (assume the two measures were set up independer.tly). On a linguistic approach, **one inch long** may not count as a property relative to a physical theory formulated in CGS terms where *r* passes unnamed. The emancipationists to whom I have talked invariably repair this difficulty by allowing the base language

Figure 7

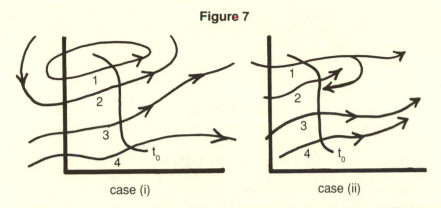

case (i)   case (ii)

to contain a name for every real number. *Mutatis mutandis,* **eccentric anomaly** type problems will need a name for every real valued *function.* This ploy grants that a new physical quantity will correspond to any expression "$f(w_o, \ldots, w_n)$," where $w_o, \ldots, w_n$ are quantities already known to exist. This principle, essentially, is EP. But now an awkward situation reminiscent of Russell's "no class" universe has arisen. We accept a collection of properties and quantities, some of which carry no language-based intensionality at all (those spawned by "$f(w_o, \ldots, w_n)$") and some which do (those engendered by more linguistic structures). The relationships (identity conditions, etc.) obtaining between these two groups seem unclear.

Why does this deep-seated attraction to syntax persist, even among declared emancipationists? On a traditional picture of universals, such as Russell's, "concepts" play two roles simultaneously: (i) they mark distinctions that actually differentiate the objects of the external world; (ii) they mark different conceptions or attitudes that *we* entertain as we attempt to decipher the structure of the distinctions under (i). The avowed purpose of emancipationism is to divide these tasks and to stop exporting characteristics natural to task (ii) onto the quantities wanted under (i). But, at the moment of divorce, a fear of separation sets in and we begin to worry that, unless we extract a dollop of intensionality from the fog of purpose (ii) considerations, we will retain no grip over the entities of purpose (i). In this respect, it is important to realize that nothing vital has been lost in treating quantities in EP's way. An arbitrary quantity, it is true, no longer owns any intrinsic intensionality beyond its basic location as a function within the phase spaces of mechanics. But this assignment alone is sufficient to fix the quantity's relationship to the system's behavior and allows it to earn whatever further intensionality it merits through proof. Quantities that deserve being intensionally rich become so through their own behavior. Accordingly, EP's treatment of a quantity as "$f(p,q)$" is not nearly as "thin" as it once seemed.

12

The basic reasonableness of EP's approach has been undercut by the common tendency to recast the history we have sketched as a manifestation of a more general "flight from intension." As described here, EP is motivated exclusively by an attempt to cover the world's bounty of traits accurately. On the "flight from intension" picture, approaches like EP whittle erstwhile robust attributes down to a skeleton for the sake of Ockham's Razor or some similar maxim (why "Science" should wish to mangle preexisting objects is never explained adequately). I have just argued that attributes are not "whittled down" under EP; the misconception otherwise arises because the phrase "flight from intension" jumbles together a variety of basically unrelated factors.

In its primary significance, the "intension-extension" distinction reflects the venerable debate in logic over the proper understanding of "if . . . then" and the quantifiers. Specifically, should an "all" range over *real world objects* only or incorporate some dependence upon a wider field of possibilities? Although George Boole probably could not have gotten his symbolic logic running without plumping for a "real world objects only" stance, we now recognize that many applications of logic require a mixture of the two elements. On this reading, the language of physics is clearly "intensional" because it relies heavily upon information about the behavior of possible systems unrealized in the actual world. A phase space, after all, is nothing but a geometrical coding of counterfactual data about physical possibilities. Some notions, to be sure, can be defined in a "real world only" manner—e.g., the time derivative of a quantity—but most cannot—e.g., a quantity defined by a partial derivative extending in another phase space direction. All of the basic existence theorems of mechanics rely heavily upon such counterfactual, "partial derivative" information.

What *is* lost, on EP's treatment, are "intensionalities" that depend upon considerations of non-mechanical possibility or possibilities which arise in theories rival to the form of classical mechanics for which EP is designed. The term "momentum," for example, pops up in many theories, but its properties tend to be different in each. In working within classical physics, we should pay no attention to these extra-theoretic possibilities. It would block our ability to define **momentum** classically as "$m\dot{x}$" if we needed to minister concurrently to Special Relativity's universe, where many classical definitional linkages fail. But this intensional blindness to trans-theoretic possibility is as it should be, for the world's quantities are surely indifferent to our sundry misconceptions of them. In framing a theory of quantities we do not want to paint them with all the colors of our species' struggle to understand them. In this manner, EP does flee from a limited group of intensions, viz., those allied with "human understanding" and "word meaning." On this reading, the "flight" metaphor turns out to be nothing but an extremely odd way of expressing the basic philosophy of emancipationism with which we began. Science's object is not to deprive quantities of intensional bounty that they rightfully deserve; it hopes to avoid misallocation of "mode of presentation" characteristics.

With a writer like Quine, the "flight from intension" is also displayed in mathematics' eventual adoption of Dirichlet's treatment of "function." We should be careful in making such an assumption. We have seen good reasons why classical physics will want to treat quantities in the "thin" manner of EP, but this argument does not show that mathematics, when it is *not* trying to model the quantities of physics, needs to approach "function" in a wholly extensional way. When we study algorithms, we are interested in the *rules* that lie behind the calculation of certain classes of function. The identity conditions of "algorithm" clearly reflect a rule-based sort of intensionality. As an intensionality, "algorithmic rule" is objectionable only insofar as we are tempted to paint it onto the worldly quantities we try to model with "functions." As the moon passes overhead, it ranges through successive values of the "eccentric anomaly" function ψ described previously, but it remains serenely indifferent in its passage to the sundry algorithmic schemes that astronomers have devised to calculate ψ. The desire to model physics' quantities with functions requires that mathematics expand the universe of "function" far beyond anything to which rules or names could be meaningfully assigned. It happens that there are types of "construction" (in the manner, say, of Baire) under which very large classes of function can be fruitfully studied. From such studies, one can extract generalized analogs of "built by rule." Once again, we would not want to paint such "constructive intensionalities" onto the quantities of physics.

Accordingly, it is not obvious that there is any well-defined "flight from intension" that applies to mathematical functions except insofar as "function" has been historically dragged along by a desire to model physical quantities adequately. To be sure, there are many areas of mathematics that are independently motivated to build objects through limit-taking operations and the like. As noted previously, this reliance has a tendency to push the objects nearer to "set," because of the general "intension destroying" quality of limit-taking operations. It is also true that, at present, set theory serves as the court of final appeal in settling existence claims, even in a discipline such as differential equations. This reliance often forces us to translate mathematical questions into set theoretic terms. It is a matter of some controversy whether set theory should permanently retain this status in all future mathematics; but even if its reign is inevitable, we are clearly dealing with issues quite independent of those raised in this essay.

Sometimes Quine understands the "thesis of extensionality" as meaning merely, "Everything one wants to do in science can be done in set theory." Leaving aside the problems of making this claim precise, it represents a very weak demand. Set theory supplies sufficient freedom of movement that information about virtually any class of object can be coded up in set theoretic form (*modulo* a few limitations on size). Can one model all "metaphysically possible worlds" as sets? Sure, why not? Quine's weak reading tolerates as "extensional" the coding of the most inappropriate meaning-based characteristics, as David Lewis, patron of disreputable intensionalities, duly notes.[16]

In sum, standard readings of "the flight from intension" are either absurdly strong (quantities can be distinguished only in terms of real world behavior) or absurdly weak (quantities are not asked to abjure unemancipated intensionalities). The real harm in cloaking physics' treatment of quantity in "flight from intension" garb is that it obscures the concrete reasons that actually motivate EP. Its approach is informed by two simple, albeit surprising, considerations: (1) collections of molecules, when they form into a system, often "lock together" in a manner that allows special quantities to serve as the best parameters to delineate the behavior of the collective system; (2) each system tends to favor its own special set of quantities, whose presence there can be easily overlooked. Such are the lessons that a long string of scientists — Chlandi, Euler, and the Bernoullis, Fourier, Rayleigh and Kelvin — have taught us. No sweeping trends operate here, but simply humble facts about the world's surprising diversity. If EP is viewed simply as classical mechanics' attempt to accommodate these facts adequately, then its treatment of "quantity," which starts "thin" and adds bulk as deserved, should seem well motivated and nondistorted. But when EP is misrepresented as the grinding of some anti-intensional wheel, without regard for the large amount of counterfactual information built into EP's arrangements, then its strictures will seem capricious and bizarre.

Several useful, albeit mildly technical, comments might be added that will align the history presented here with the standard accounts: First, the rise of "functions of a complex variable" played a major historical role in convincing mathematicians that "function" could safely abandon its original moorings in the notion of rule. Riemann particularly stressed that the "unity" of an analytic function was not revealed through any particular bit of syntax such as a power series expansion (whose range of validity was generally local), but through the singularities and topology of the

Riemann surface behind the function. Riemann's "transcendental" view supplied a striking geometrical portrait of how a function could be meaningfully credited with a robust "soul," completely divorced from considerations of linguistic rule. In EP, the phase space over which the quantity is defined performs a similar "soul"-sustaining function.

Intimately entangled with these concerns was the growing realization in the early nineteenth century that a function can be as robustly supplied by a differential equation as by an explicit formula. If a function (like "eccentric anomaly") solves a differential equation, it can be easier to calculate its values by a finite difference approximation—e.g., by marching through a discrete time approximation of a planetary motion—than by trying to utilize an explicit series expansion. This thesis—which can be recast in philosophical terms as "the soul of a function is completely given by a description of its developmental behavior; a proper name for the function adds nothing"—is undoubtedly the origin of Cauchy's "broken line" method of establishing functional existence (which was inspired by finite difference methods). Once again, physics' demands provided the chief motivation for this new attitude, for mathematicians otherwise had no reason to assume that an equation *has* a solution in the absence of explicit formulas (*vide* Poincare's well-known remark: "Without physics, we would not know differential equations").

These ideas were central to Riemann's outlook as well—he saw the "soul" of a complex function propagating outward from its "sources" following Laplace's equation, just as the electric potential spreads out along a charged body. Although EP reaches beyond the merely analytic in its postulation of quantities, the true prophet of the emancipationism it preaches is undoubtedly Riemann.

13

As noted earlier, many philosophers feel that the key to the "intensionality" of emancipated universals lies in *causal* considerations—thus Sydney Shoemaker's "The essential characteristics of emancipated universals derive from the way they contribute to the causal powers of things." EP instead conceptualizes quantities in terms of how they classify or decompose a system's *behavior* (= its phase space trajectories); the notion of "cause" does not play a critical role in EP's approach. Although "cause" has enjoyed a popularity akin to fadism in the philosophical analyses of recent years, it will not serve as a reliable Aeneas within the realms of physical properties. The misleading intuitions of the pendulum example represent a case in point. Such unreliability arises because the term "cause" carries a variety of meanings within popular use. Take an upright metal band and slowly add weights on top. Eventually the band sags under the weight. What "caused" the sagging? Answers: (i) the addition of excess weight; (ii) movements of the ambient atmosphere. Why (ii)? Without a kick from the air, the band would not know whether to sag to the left or the right; it would remain in a confused upright state forever. In the mathematics of the situation, the two notions of "cause" utilized here can be captured quite precisely. But they report upon rather different aspects of the situation (which are clearly demarcated in the appropriate mathematics).

Matters worsen with the phrase "property φ causally produces behavior . . .", upon which most emancipations heavily rely. Such talk of *causation by properties* should be sharply distinguished from more sober claims about *event* causation. Sometimes, it can be conceded, the intent of the "property causation" talk can be clear enough—"the appalling color of Miss Bassett's frock first caused my affections to waver," but this rather wuzzy locomotion is hardly the stuff upon which a metaphysics should be founded.

The awkwardness of relying upon "causation" rather than "classification of behavior" can be seen if we inspect more carefully the typical quantities that EP is designed to reach. We have seen the importance of finding, whenever possible, quantities under which the system's motion appears especially simple, as with the pendulum's polar Θ or the locked in "ordering" of ice. The "simpler" quantities often represent *global, cooperative* properties of the system. Consider Chlandi's metal plates. As each atom wiggles, it makes other atoms wiggle elsewhere in the plate. It is a nontrivial fact that these cooperative wigglings *en masse* can be usefully decomposed into distinct, basic patterns of global movement, which do not transfer energy to one another. This isolation allows us to claim that the plate exhibits various types of *cooperative order* that can be excited independently of one another.

Chlandi's modes are the most useful quantities for predicting, controlling, and otherwise understanding how the plate performs when struck. But do the modes "contribute to the causal powers" of the plate? The vagaries of "cause," it seems to me, permit both yes and no answers to this question.

Such matters become even vaguer when one looks at the global "ordering parameter" used to describe the subtle long-range cooperative effects in a liquid. Start with an analogy: It has recently been shown that seven good shuffles are needed to randomize a card deck. If the deck is shuffled the usual four or five times, a rarified order persists in the cards that magicians sometimes exploit in tricks of the "pick any card and replace it in the deck" variety. Write out, in the form of two monstrous disjunctions, the likely outcomes from four and seven times shuffled decks. Virtually no one, unless they run rather sensitive statistical tests on the data, will see any significant difference between the two disjunctions—they would both look equally random. But, in truth, the quadruply shuffled hands contain a hidden order, an order to which card player can respond, even if they have no conception of its presence. Experienced bridge players were unhappy when computerized shuffling was first introduced at tournaments—they believed that the computers did *not* supply genuinely random hands. In fact, their diagnosis was exactly backwards—they were lamenting the hidden order they had sensed in the under-shuffled decks of old.

The features that distinguish a *liquid* from a *gas* trace to long-range statistical orderings among the molecules akin to those found in the undershuffled card deck (the exact nature of the relevant ordering parameters is not fully understood). Can such abstract ordering properties be "causally responsible" for other events? Well, in one sense—the Bassett's gown sense—the answer is "yes," for it is reasonable to claim that the bridge players were "caused" to complain about the computer shuffling by the absence of the customary hidden order. But, in another way, it seems absurd to maintain that the hidden order has "caused" anything, for it merely represents a statistical distribution across many shuffles. A correlation, after all, is not "present" in any obvious sense within a particular hand. It is better to think of matters thus: the player employs a strategy, much of it unconscious, for bridge playing. One of the best *indices* for determining the likely success of that strategy is the **ordering parameter** of the cards. It is quite proper to claim that the quantity **ordering parameter** *governs* the strategy's success, but odd to contend that it "causally brings" about this success. In short, "a parameter useful for controlling X" may relate rather remotely to any causal processes occurring within and without X.[17]

I presume that no one would deny that its **ordering parameter** is a quantity genuinely pertaining to the card deck (or, *a fortiori,* that **liquid** is property of a swarm of molecules). It would seem that "causal power" is not the proper attorney to plead the case of emancipated universals; we should hew instead to the "classifier of behavior" utilized in EP, whose formulation was motivated by the need to stretch to abstract quantities of the "ordering parameter" ilk.

I believe that much of the great affection for "cause" among philosophers probably traces to the seemingly innocent toy theories we regularly teach in our "Introduction to Scientific Theory" courses—"All ravens are black" and all that. Such toy examples lead us to attend overly much to the logical aspects of the situation—what else is there to talk about in our "theories"? From our courses in *logic,* we sense that "in trying to prove something, one can safely stick with the vocabulary originally given in the problem"—there are a variety of famous theorems in pure logic that render this impression precise. Such theorems provide no basis for expecting that this feature persists in working with a formalization of scientific theory, but impressions linger. However, we have seen that the art of gaining control over a physical problem often reduces to finding new quantities far removed from the set of parameters with which we have begun, quantities that might not even be definable, in the usual logical sense, in terms of the original set.

In any event, excessive trafficking in toy theories seems to encourage the following reasoning: "The laws of a theory look like 'All R's are B'." We know that scientific laws support counterfactuals but other generalizations will not. The laws must therefore carry a 'causal thrust' that pushes objects from property R over to property B. Accordingly, the 'if . . . then' in the laws directly reports upon 'causal relations' between properties." It would take us too far afield to investigate this contention properly, but the basic claim made is simply wrong; legitimate appeals to "cause" (as revealed, say, through a Green's function) do *not* link to underlying laws in such a crude fashion.

14

The bulk of this essay has been concerned to document how physics has found ways to retain an "organizational soul" within its postulated range of quantities, yet also accommodate the vast variety of traits found in the world around us. Such, I believe, is the objective that most "causal" emancipationists have sought, although they have tried to achieve it by inadequate and outmoded tools.

Unfortunately, much of the current debate on "naturalism" issues has been framed through a reliance on exactly the kind of machinery, "causal" or "hierarchial", that I have criticized. In particular, it is commonly accepted that no "type/type" identity of the form "being in pain = physical property" is likely to be correct. Hilary Putnam, who originated much of the current orthodoxy in metaphysics, argued for this thesis on the grounds that, at best, **being in pain** could enter his property hierarchy only at a "functional" level, high above the proper traits of physics.[18] In my appraisal, such evaluations of "high" and "low" are physically unmotivated and appear only as artifacts of an unsatisfactory approach to "physical property."

Jerry Fodor has presented an influential development of Putnam's argument that pursues a theme he dubs "the methodological autonomy of the special sciences." He claims that each "special science" has its own "kind terms," complete with parochial methods for investigating their behavior. Fodor paints a picture where physicists all do more or less "the same thing" with their private stock of kind terms: "Physics develops the taxonomy of its subject matter which best suits its purposes."[19] Psychologists, presumably, work in different manners with their native set of tools.

But we have abundantly seen that physics, no matter how narrowly constrained, does *not* work with a limited set of terms — its potential range of properties is as wide as EP. By the same token, it is wrong to presume that any developed science follows a characteristic methodology or demonstrates a constant purpose. Mathematical considerations alone are usually sufficient to force considerable methodological variety upon a discipline. The slightest adjustment in the terms of a differential equation, for example, is apt to require completely new methodologies designed to unlock the specific secrets of the modified equation (as C. S. Peirce put it, "There is no perfect calculus enabling one to tilt at a differential equation like a knight in armor"). In fact, as much methodological variety probably exists among the standard set of approaches to the differential equations of celestial mechanics as can be found in any of Fodor's "special sciences" (which is not to deny the latter methodological variety!). As we have noted, the unraveling of different types of equation has a tendency to pull different kinds of properties out of the physical woodwork.

The net effect of Fodor's continual evocation of the phrase "kind predicate for the special science S" is to transfer a methodology for investigating a particular trait into the intensional character of the trait itself. We have seen ample reason to reject this sort of transfer. Of course, as a sociological fact, one can readily understand why the methodological autonomy thesis has proved so endearing to cognitive psychologists — there are many disheartening tales of sound psychological projects left unfunded because some supervisory board of neurophysiologists believed that the "unity of science" dictates that the human mind can only be studied with scalpel and electrode. But the erection of imaginary strongholds in the land of universals is not the only way to defend against intolerance.

In any event, Fodor forges an argument against "type/type" identities that trades heavily upon his picture of "kind terms." Following Putnam, he argues that if one tries to capture the extension of **money** in "physical kind terms," one can produce only a disjointed disjunction on the order of "(is a 2 cm disc of copper/zinc alloy minted in the Denver Mint) or (is a cowrie shell) or (is a 15.6 cm × 6.5 cm piece of inked fiber minted by the Denver Mint) or. . . ." But such a term, he claims, cannot have the true force of the **money** property it seeks to replace:

> [I]nteresting generalizations (e.g., counterfactual supporting generalizations) can often be made about events whose physical descriptions have nothing in common [and] it is often the case that *whether* the physical descriptions of the events subsumed by such generalizations have anything in common is, in an obvious sense, entirely irrelevant to the truth of the generalizations, or to their interestingness, or to their degree of confirmation, or indeed, to any of their epistemologically important properties.[20]

All of this rests upon the false presumption that physical properties bear a discernible intensionality, one that might be roughly characterized as "smelling like physics": "I kin tell one o' them varmints a mile away." But, we have seen that this assumption is false. Indeed, if one attempts to express any of Chlandi's modal quantities or the **ordering parameter** of a card deck in terms of the original *p/q* quantities for the system, the lengthy results would seem as opaque as Fodor's expression for *money.* But we have learned that we should not expect the counterfactual salience of a quantity (or the other virtues Fodor mentions) to be revealed simply within a canonical name for the quantity. Instead we must determine how the system's behavior — its trajectories — intersect with the level surfaces of the quantity in question. The mere fact that a physical quantity, when expressed Fodor style, *looks* hopelessly disunified gives one no reason to conclude that the quantity does not carry all of the counterfactual moxie of any selected "special science" predicate. To presume otherwise is to project an unwarranted "mode of presentation" intensionality onto the trait.

Such considerations leave me as an unreconstructed old physicalist of the "type/type" variety (and, insofar as I understand the term, I probably count as a "naturalist" also).[21] Nevertheless, I see physicalism as a comparatively unimportant issue within the philosophy of mind; it leaves all of the hard problems untouched. Physicalism, as defended here, provides no occasion for the kind of joy that some atheists derive from the tribulations of fallen television evangelists. The standard underestimation of the methodological and ontological resources of physics implicit in most anti-physicalist writings seems to me a more vital topic, because many important issues in philosophy of language ultimately turn upon a clear conception of what an emancipated trait might be and what sorts of intensionality they should enjoy.

In closing, I will stress that the argument of this essay, properly understood, does not spring from any form of "physics chauvinism." I have argued, to be sure, that the set of properties postulate within physical theory can adequately represent the *complete* range of emancipated universals. But in these pages this claim has not arisen as the raw rant of a physics jingoist. It seems, rather, that a strict accounting of the properties which arise within any discipline will eventually lead to the same list of traits as physics provides. I cannot see, if one hopes to unravel the biology of sea squirts, how the learning of a bit of hydrodynamics can be avoided.[22] Studying the latter leads, by insensible degrees, to the question of when such equations lose their validity, matters leading directly to considerations of molecular action, and so on down to the quarks. Although refined knowledge of ocean behavior at quark level may not benefit our understanding of the sea squirt greatly, I see no principled place to establish a cutoff. The backyard of every science, it seems, opens out onto all of the others. In this sense, a closure of the class "properties relevant to sea squirts" ought to lead to a representation of emancipated traits identical to that of physics.

The brute fact driving our entire discussion is simply that a lot of unsuspected properties lurk in the familiar objects around us, intertwined in a delicate and subtle web. So many traits roam the range of Nature that an elaborate collaboration between science and mathematics is needed to herd them all into a coherent corral. Left forever outside the fences are the intensionalities that derive from language, investigative methodologies, our epistemic histories and the like. Our study of EP has taught us how a quantity might keep a "soul" without wearing any of the forbidden characteristics.

Notes

I would like to thank Hilary Putnam, who started me down this road, Anil Gupta, George Wilson, Penny Maddy, and Geof Joseph.

1. Hilary Putnam, "On Properties," in *Collected Papers,* vol. 1 (Cambridge: Cambridge University Press, 1975); David Armstrong, *A Theory of Universals* (Cambridge: Cambridge University Press, 1980); Sydney Shoemaker, "Causality and Properties," in *Identity, Cause, and Mind* (Cambridge: Cambridge University Press, 1984); David Lewis, "New Work for a Theory of Universals," *Australasian Journal of Philosophy* 61, no. 4 (Dec. 1983).

2. Armstrong, *Theory of Universals,* vol. 2, p. 12.

3. Shoemaker, "Causality and Properties," 212.

4. Bertrand Russell, *The Problems of Philosophy* (London: Oxford University Press, 1959).

5. W. V. Quine, *From a Logical Point of View* (New York: Harper and Row, 1953) and *Theories and Things* (Cambridge, Mass.: Harvard University Press, 1981).

6. Elliott Sober, "Why Logically Equivalent Predicates May Pick Out Different Properties," *American Philosophical Quarterly* 19, no. 2 (April 1982).

7. This "law" is actually a linear approximation to the true pendulum law where the period is dependent upon the amplitude. For sake of example, we will

pretend that the principle is exact. Accordingly, the small angle approximation "sin $\Theta \simeq \Theta$" will be treated as a mathematical fact.

8. Lewis, "New Work." In truth, physics approaches determinism in a rather different manner, viz. a classical theory is deterministic if and only if no more than one trajectory leaves a phase point.

9. Ibid., 346. Lewis's terminology is different from mine, so I have introduced appropriate adjustments. His "sets," too, encompass objects drawn from all possible worlds; his claim would hold, *a fortiori,* for sets selected exclusively from the real world (I generally use "set" in the latter manner).

10. J. Harkness and F. Morley, *A Treatise on the Theory of Functions,* ed. G. E. Stechert (New York: 1925 reprint), 53.

11. Quoted in A. P. Youschkevitch, "The Concept of Function up to the Middle of the Nineteenth Century," *Archive for the History of the Exact Sciences* 16 (1976).

12. Walter Thirring, *Classical Dynamical Systems,* trans. E. M. Harrell (New York: Springer-Verlag, 1978), 5.

13. E. C. G. Sudarshan and N. Mukinda, *Classical Dynamics: A Modern Perspective* (New York: John Wiley and Sons, 1974), 524.

14. This treatment is appropriate only for classical particle physics (based upon ordinary differential equations). Continuum theories (utilizing partial differential equations) tend to require more subtle constructions.

15. Some writers hold that a nonsmooth u will be "unobservable" because, in any realistic measurement, a system is apt to be jostled from one phase space path to its neighbors. A measurement, it is argued, can only respond to an average over adjacent paths. These issues are too complicated to discuss here.

16. David Lewis, "Tensions," in *Philosophical Papers,* vol. 1 (New York: Oxford University Press, 1983).

17. Michael Liston, in a forthcoming work, has criticized the usual crude assumptions of the "causal theory of knowledge" from this point of view. The shuttling example came from a lecture by Persi Diacsnis.

18. Hilary Putnam, "The Nature of Mental States," in *Collected Papers,* vol. 2.

19. Jerry Fodor, "Special Sciences," in *RePresentations* (Cambridge, Mass.: MIT Press, 1978), 145.

20. Ibid., 133.

21. For a collaborative treatment, see my "What Is This Thing Called 'Pain'?" *Pacific Philosophical Quarterly* 66 (1985).

22. Marston Bates used to begin his lectures: "I think I'll start with a rabbit sitting under a raspberry bush and from this gradually go into the mechanics of the situation" (quoted in Stephen Vogel, *Life's Devices* [Princeton: Princeton University Press, 1988], ix).

Ethical Naturalism and the Explanatory Power of Moral Concepts

ROBERT AUDI

There are many kinds of naturalism, and several of them are important in ethics. The appeal of ethical naturalism, in any of its plausible forms, is strong: it promises ontological economy by construing normative phenomena as in some way natural; it provides for objectivity in ethics, at least assuming that there are objective methods for the study of natural phenomena; it sustains the hope that the rationality of scientific procedures can help in resolving moral issues; and it dispels the sense of mystery which, for many, beclouds other accounts of the ontology and epistemology of ethics. There are well-known obstacles to working out a naturalistic ethics. At least since Hume, many philosophers have been impressed with the argument that if moral judgments are factual, they cannot be practical in the motivational sense which full-blooded practicality is commonly felt to require; and at least since Moore, it has seemed to many philosophers that even if factual judgments can be full-bloodedly practical, moral judgments cannot be reduced to any kind of factual statement.

In the recent literature of ethics, the debate over the status of naturalism has taken a different turn. Most proponents of ethical naturalism are now above all concerned to show that moral properties have explanatory power and that moral statements are quite continuous with others that can explain concrete phenomena. Call this *explanationist naturalism*. Its guiding idea is, in part, that if moral properties can be shown to have such explanatory power, then naturalism need not accomplish a reduction of the kind Moore held impossible, and the way will be open to explicating the practicality of moral judgments without the burden of defending a naive reductionist account of them. This essay will assess explanationist naturalism in ethics and, in the final section, sketch a plausible alternative whose resources appear to have been underestimated.

95

1. The Supervenience of the Moral

It is instructive to compare ethical naturalism with materialism about the mind-body problem. Within each position, the main alternatives — each with its own variants — are reductionism and eliminativism. In ethics, the most far-reaching reductionist view would be to the effect that moral concepts, such as *rightness,* are analyzable in terms of naturalistic notions, such as those of *pleasure* and *pain.* Mill sometimes appears reductionistic,[1] though his main thrust is surely to establish a normative, not a conceptual, identification of rightness with hedonic optimality. The most important, though probably not the closest, ethical analogue of eliminativism is non-cognitivism, construed as denying that there *are* any moral properties or other real moral entities: rather, the function of distinctively moral terms is not assertive, but, in some way, expressive.[2] There is also a noteworthy intermediate strategy, which I shall call *substitutionism.* Unlike non-cognitivism, this view, most prominently represented by Brandt,[3] does not deny that moral terms have any "descriptive meaning," but proposes instead that we undertake to use them with a reconstructed sense that is elaborated within broadly naturalistic constraints.

If there is any framework currently shared by ethical naturalists outside the eliminativist camp, it is that of supervenience. It is widely held that moral properties — however they are in the end to be analyzed conceptually — supervene on natural ones. Supervenience has been characterized in many different ways,[4] and there is no need here to settle on a precise account. For my purposes it should be sufficient to conceive the notion of moral supervenience roughly as follows: first, no two things, whether acts or persons, can share all their natural properties and differ in their moral ones (if they have any); and second, any entity having moral properties possesses those properties *in virtue of* its natural properties (or certain of them), where 'in virtue of' expresses an asymmetric relation of dependence and is usually held to imply an explanatory connection as well, such that a thing's possession of a moral property is explainable, at least in part, by appeal to its possession of one or more of the natural properties on which the moral property supervenes.[5] There are differences of opinion over the modalities in question, and a similar supervenience view can be linguistically formulated for those who do not wish to countenance properties (we might, for example, speak of *terms* supervening on others and explicate this by appeal to relations among their uses). But it is commonly supposed that since the relation between the base properties and the supervening ones is in some sense explanatory, it is (for at least that reason) non-analytic, in the sense that there are no analytic propositions of the form of 'X is M because it is F', where 'M' ranges over moral properties and 'F' over the natural ones on which the former supervene.

This conception of supervenience allows that moral properties might *be* natural, and hence leaves a kind of *ontological reduction* open. What it is meant to rule out is analytic reduction of the kind Moore held to be impossible. But the supervenience relation is still *non*-reductive in the sense that it does not entail any kind of reducibility of the supervening property to some set of the base properties; indeed, it is usually understood in a way that rules out one kind of reduction — the strong kind implying property identity — since the relevant dependence relation is irreflexive and asymmetrical. Moreover, while I am thinking of supervenience as a relation between properties (or types of properties), I take this relation to be explicable (as above) in terms of relations between an individual's *having* a supervening property and its *having* one or more of the relevant base properties. We might thus speak of *general supervenience* between moral and natural properties or of *particular supervenience* between an individual thing's having a moral property, say (an action's) being a violation of a moral right, and its having a natural one, say (the action's) being a seizure of someone else's land.

Since the supervenience view leaves open the ontological reducibility of moral properties to natural ones (whether to the natural properties *in* the base or, more likely, others), and because it *grounds* moral properties in natural ones, one might be inclined to call it a (weak) form of naturalism. For instance, by leaving reducibility open, it contrasts with Moore's non-naturalism; for he held that goodness and rightness are irreducibly *non*-natural properties. On the other hand, he also maintained a supervenience doctrine apparently rather like the one sketched, and so provided moral properties with a *naturalistic anchor.* But this anchoring view by itself falls short of naturalism, because it leaves open the possibility that moral properties are in no way natural. They might have their feet firmly planted in the natural world and still, as Moore seems to have thought, rise above it.[6]

One might wonder how, as the supervenience view may be taken to allow, there could be an identity of moral with natural *properties* unless it *is* based on an analytic equivalence. To see how this might be, one could model a conception of ethical supervenience on a scientific analogue: supervenience as exhibited by, say, biological properties with respect to physicochemical properties as their base. Here one may plausibly claim that there are property identities, without positing analytic equivalence between predicates expressing them. This opens the way for a view of moral properties that is not merely naturalistic, but a *scientific* naturalism.[7]

The supervenience view of moral properties is also linked to the general issue of scientific realism. Insofar as one is inclined toward realism about scientific theories, and particularly insofar as one takes ontological questions to turn ultimately on what entities science will finally countenance, supervenience naturalism in ethics, especially the explanatory kind, will be appealing. There may indeed be some tendency for scientific realists to suppose that, for concrete entities, to be is to be a term in a causal relation, and, for properties, to be is to be instantiated by such terms *as* such, i.e., to figure predicatively (very roughly, in cause or effect position) in some lawlike generality linking cause to effect.[8] If moral properties can have causal efficacy — or, more liberally, at least explanatory power — which they apparently can if they are *reducible* to natural ones, then their reality is beyond serious question.[9] To be sure, if there are epiphenomena — items that have no causal power but appear only as effects — then being real is consistent with being inconsequential. But the supervenience naturalism that concerns us attributes both causal and explanatory power to moral properties. Section 2 will outline such a view.

2. Explanationist Moral Realism

Much recent discussion of moral realism, conceived naturalistically, has centered on a controversy that has been most prominently represented in a debate between Gilbert Harman and Nicholas Sturgeon.[10] The issues have engaged many other philosophers, and there is no hope of recounting all the major moves here. I shall simply try, in this section, to formulate some central issues and to assess the prospects for explanationist naturalism.

Moral Realism vs. Moral Epiphenomenalism

It is useful to start with a challenge to the moral realist. Consider a case in which Jan, who is a reliable moral judge, observes an action, such as one person's violently slapping another, and judges the action wrong. One might think that if its wrongness had no causal power, then Jan would not have judged it wrong. But as Harman points out, this causal impotence view would be held by a moral epiphenomenalist, one who "takes moral properties to be epiphenomenally supervenient on natural properties in the sense that the possession of moral properties is explained by possession of the relevant natural properties and nothing is influenced or explained by the possession of moral properties."[11] After all, the moral properties and what they *seem* to explain might be common effects of the same causes; and if so, then (other things being equal) the phenomena explained would not have occurred if the moral properties had not been instantiated. But this no more entails that the moral properties have explanatory power than the fact that (other things being equal) a car would not have moved if its shadow had not moved entails that the movement of the shadow caused the movement of the car.

The naturalistic moral realist can safely grant, however, that the truth of counterfactuals of the kind just cited is not sufficient to show that moral properties are explanatory. This concession leaves open a number of plausible arguments for the view. Three in particular are important here.[12] First, note similar cases in physics: Harry, seeing a vapor trail in a cloud chamber, may think, "There goes a proton." An instrumentalist colleague might hold that Harry's reaction is not produced (indirectly) by a proton, but is simply due to his sensibility and his observation of the "track," just as a moral judgment is produced, not by moral factors functioning causally, but by observations in the context of a certain sensibility. However, surely we need not take such instrumentalism as a serious objection to attributing explanatory power to protons. The second consideration concerns the observable impact of the moral. A morally sensitive person may be a "reliable detector" of moral wrongness, and observing such a person can change one's mind about a moral matter, as where one revises a moral view on hearing the person's differing account of the relevant action. Hence, there is a kind of moral observation — of persons and their moral judgments — that plainly affects one's views. Third, we must take seriously attributions of *causal* efficacy to moral facts, as where we cite injustice, along with poverty, as a cause of revolution. This is significant in itself; but it also suggests that the supervenience of the moral on the natural is like that of biological facts on physical ones — "a kind of 'causal constitution' of the supervening facts out of the more basic ones, which allows them a causal efficacy inherited from that of the facts out of which they are constituted."[13]

Moral Realism and Moral Naturalism

Each of the three considerations just cited seems to me plausible, yet inconclusive. Let us consider them in turn, with an eye to what metaethical view, other than epiphenomenalism — which (if mainly for different reasons) I join Sturgeon in rejecting — might account for them.

Since the instrumentalist case against realism is not peculiar to ethics and will in any case be discredited if the other lines of attack on moral realism are blocked, there is no need to discuss instrumentalism here. Indeed, my main interest is in the prior issue of whether moral statements are explanatory in the *way* causal and scientific ones are; if they are not, then moral realism must either be given up or reformulatęd in a way that is not vulnerable to instrumentalist criticism. Let us, then, consider how moral observation may bear on the status of moral realism.

It is certainly true that some people seem to be reliable moral observers, and if there are such people then moral realism gains support. But why need a *naturalistic* version in particular be supported? It is true that observations of such persons and their judgments may influence one; but this is not only compatible with epiphenomenalism, it is also consistent with a wholly different realism, such as the kind held by Kant (on one interpretation), which implies that moral properties are not causal in any sense: they figure non-causally in a priori principles as opposed to playing a causal role in empirically explanatory propositions. This kind of realism need not deny the causal impact of moral reliability. Consider a logical analogy. If we observe Jan proving theorems, we may obtain good grounds for concluding that she is logically reliable. Then, observing her pronounce a questionable proposition to be a theorem can influence (even change) our judgment. It does not follow that theoremhood, the property she reliably judges certain things to have, is causally efficacious. But suppose that the property is in some way causally efficacious. *This* kind of causal efficacy does not seem to be the sort the naturalist has in mind; for it is a kind possible for abstract entities whose fundamental place is in necessary truths, as opposed to testable causal or testable nomic truths.[14] Such efficacy is certainly possible for goodness and rightness as Moore construed them: namely, as *non*-natural properties. This reliability line of argument, then, may be useful in defending moral realism, but it does little if anything to support moral naturalism.

The Epistemic and Explanatory Dependence of Moral Properties on Natural Ones

The next defense of ethical naturalism to be considered here begins with an undeniable datum: we do *cite* what appear to be moral facts or moral states of affairs, such as a regime's injustice to its people, in explaining why certain events, such as a widespread revolt, have occurred. We also say things like 'It was because he was unjustly punished that his friends sought revenge against the authorities'. These locutions suggest that moral properties have both causal and (if it is different here) explanatory power. But this point does not follow from their having this use. For one thing, what we *cite* in giving an explanation need not be what, in the context, really *does* the explaining. I may say that I am taking an umbrella because it is going to rain; but the apparent fact I cite, that it will rain, is not what explains my behavior: my *belief* that it will rain does this work. I would take the umbrella if I believed it would rain, whether it will or not. For pragmatic reasons (such as my wanting to avoid suggesting doubt about the weather by *saying* 'I believe'), I *express* my belief by asserting the proposition believed, rather than by self-ascribing a belief of that proposition. But it is what I express in the context, and not what I cite as a causal factor, that does the explanatory work. We must distinguish, then, between cases in which a statement offered in order to explain something simply *provides an explanation* when conjoined with contextual information and cases in which, taken together with that information, it *constitutes an explanation,* in the sense that the purported explainer is what actually wields the explanatory power.

There is also a further issue. We have already noted that the supervenience of moral on natural properties reflects an *ontological dependence:* even if moral properties are not themselves natural, their possession presupposes that of certain natural properties as their basis. This is how, for any plausible moral realism, moral properties are anchored in the world. Now the moral epiphenomenalist, in effect, suggests that it is certain of the base properties which do the explaining that the moral properties seem to do. Explanationist moral realists may plausibly resist this move. For one thing, it leaves one wondering why we should *ever* attribute explanatory power to supervening properties, unless they can be plausibly claimed to be identical with sets of base properties not themselves supervenient on other properties. But is there good reason to think that any explanatory properties are *ultimately* irreducible or do not even supervene on others? And, supposing that some properties meet this condition, there are supervenient properties, such as temperature, solubility, and elasticity, which, in their own right, apparently do have explanatory, even causal, power.

This line of reply to moral epiphenomenalism has limited force, however, once we appreciate a difference between moral and scientific supervenience. Unlike, say, temperature and elasticity, moral properties are not only ontologically dependent, but also *epistemically dependent,* on their base properties: roughly, knowing a particular to have a moral property depends on knowing it to have one or more of a certain range of base properties, and justifiedly believing it to have a moral property depends on justifiedly believing it to have (or at least on being justified *in* believing it to have) one or more base properties in this range.[15] This is not to deny that one might, upon noticing a man severely beating a child, "just see" that he is wronging the child; there need be no process of inference (certainly no conscious one), and it may be that the moral belief formed here arises — given one's moral experience and cognitive ethical constitution — "directly" from what is perceived. But if the case is like ordinary perception of, say, color and shape, in a kind of directness of belief-formation —

and may to that extent be called moral "observation" — it differs from such ordinary perception in requiring an underlying belief ascribing relevant natural properties, or at least a perception of those properties sufficient to be at once a basis *for* justified ascription of them and a ground for attribution of the moral property "seen" to be present. If, for instance, I do not believe (or disbelieve), but "just see" that the man is hitting the child hard, my visual perception of his behavior justifies me in believing that and is thereby a ground for my believing (observationally) that he is wronging the child.

It might be more accurate to say that our descriptive and explanatory *uses* of moral properties exhibit this epistemic dependence, but nothing to be said here will turn on which formulation we use. My point is that if there is such a dependence, then *whenever* we explanatorily invoke a moral property, it will be in part on the basis of, or at least in the light of, some belief or presupposition to the effect that one or more natural properties is playing an explanatory role. We are thus in a position to rely — often unselfconsciously, to be sure — on those other properties to do the explanatory work, and it is arguable that they, and not any moral property, are in fact what does it. Let me illustrate.

Recall the possibility of citing governmental injustice in explaining a revolt by the people. One cannot know (and normally would not even believe) that there is such injustice except through some kind of awareness of, say, government seizure of land, arbitrary curfews, and police brutality, where these are construed behaviorally in terms of, e.g., soldiers occupying farmlands, clearing the streets at night, and clubbing non-violent protesters. But these are just the sorts of non-moral factors that, in their own right, we suppose (on the basis of our general knowledge of social forces) can perfectly well explain a revolt.[16] They also seem to have causal power in a quite intuitive sense. Perhaps it is on the basis of pragmatic reasons — for instance, out of a desire to combine explanation with moral assessment — that we *cite* the moral factor such as injustices as cause. Notice also that when we invoke a moral factor in giving an explanation, we are generally willing to say *how* it explains, and we always tend to do so in terms of the relevant base properties. We are indeed expected to be able to indicate, in this way, how the factor explains, on pain of being unjustified in our explanatory claim. Imagine John's claiming that injustice explains a revolt, but being unable to say, in terms of the sorts of factors I have cited, how it actually does so, or even how it might explain the revolt. If we thought his unwillingness came from inability to answer the question due to ignorance of the inferential relationships, as opposed to uncooperativeness, we would surely conclude not only that he is not entitled to accept the explanation, but probably also that he does not understand what injustice *is*. Nor, I think, would we be likely to cite moral factors in explanation of events if we could *not,* at least in a sketchy and general way, *see* causal connections between the base properties and the event to be explained.

There are, to be sure, several importantly different kinds of explanation that might be called moral. One might, for example, explain a revolt by simply saying that there is underlying injustice and it is a response to that. Call this kind of moral explanation *existential:* it represents the item to be explained as due to some causal factor or other belonging to an appropriate range. By contrast, one might explain a revolt by citing *the* injustice of the regime against which the people rebel. This kind of moral explanation is *referential.* To be warranted in the first kind, one needs justification for believing that *some* element in the base for injustice is operative in producing the revolt; to be warranted in the second, one needs justification for believing some element to be operative through its realization in the behavior of *the regime*. If, in addition, a referential explanation is *specific,* as where one cites the brutality of the regime as the injustice causing the revolt, one needs a justification for believing the *particular* base element in question to be operative.

One can of course give a *true* explanation without being justified in accepting it (truth here simply does not require justification). But what is of interest in these cases is how the epistemic dependence mirrors the ontological dependence: just as there cannot *be* an (actual, correct) explanation in terms of injustice unless some element in the base for injustice plays an appropriate causal role, one cannot be *justified* in believing that injustice explains something, such as a revolt, without being justified in believing that some such element, e.g., brutality, plays an appropriate causal role. One need not, of course, conceive the brutality or curfews or other crucial elements *as* part of the supervenience base of injustice; one need only grasp (in some appropriate way) how these elements figure in producing the item(s) one explanatorily attributes to injustice. [17]

Moral Explanations Naturalized

These points do not entail that moral properties *cannot* in their own right explain events; but there seems to be better reason to think that it is the base properties which do the real work when moral properties appear to provide explanations. Our understanding of how ascription of moral properties can explain (at least so far as causal explanation goes) seems wholly *derivative* from our understanding of how the relevant base properties can do so. [18] Indeed, *given* an explanation of (say) a revolt by appeal to such things as police brutality and seizure of lands, it is not clear what explanatory element one would *add* to the explanation of why the revolt occurred by pointing out that these things constituted governmental injustice. This is an appropriate moral comment, but does not seem to enhance the explanation of the event—unless it is taken to imply base variables *other* than those cited in giving the original explanation. If, in explaining why the revolt occurred, *all* the factors making the case one of injustice are cited, their constituting an injustice seems explanatorily, as opposed to morally, superfluous: at best it tells us something about why the revolt occurred which we should already know.

This view of explanations adducing moral properties might be said to *naturalize moral explanations* without *naturalizing moral properties* (or, at any rate, predicates). The idea is roughly that the empirical explanatory power of those explanations is natural and not due directly to any explanatory potential of the moral properties in question: explanations of empirical phenomena (above all of events) by appeal to moral properties are construed to be successful in virtue of implicitly exhibiting those phenomena as causally grounded in (or in some way due to) one or more of the relevant base properties. The view is, however, entirely consistent with granting that one's *citing* a moral property can succeed as an explanatory *act*. After all, it can call attention to the actual causes. There are, then, moral explanations in an *illocutionary* sense: explanatorily successful speech acts with a moral constituent playing the linguistically central role. Moreover, the appeal to injustice in explaining the occurrence of the revolt can also succeed in explaining why there *should* have been a revolt, in the sense that the revolt was a reasonable (or normatively appropriate) response. But this is an explanation of the rationality, not the occurrence, of the behavior: of why it is rational in the circumstances, not of why it happened. It seems doubtful that either kind of explanatory success is to be attributed to moral properties having, in their own right, either causal power or, more generally, the capacity to explain events. And that is what explanationist realism requires.

Causal vs. Conceptual Supervenience

This brings us to a further defense against moral epiphenomenalism: briefly, that moral properties inherit causal efficacy from the natural properties from which they are constituted. Here it is crucial to recall the scientific analogy. The parallel point is plausible for, say, a biological property like dark skin color and its physico-chemical base properties. There are, however, at least two cases here. First, if a subset of the latter properties can explain resistance to sunburn, and the former supervenes on that set, we would expect that dark skin color can also explain the resistance. Second, if the constitution relation represents not supervenience as usually understood, but property identity (a kind of identity some theorists posit in the case of certain scientific reductions), then, a fortiori, we would expect the same explanatory power in both cases. We are not, however, considering reductive naturalism; hence, only the first case — constitution without identity — is a relevant analogy here. How good is the analogy?

Notice that in the biological case the supervenience is causal, or at least nomic: it is a nomic, not a conceptual, truth that dark skin color depends on a certain biochemical constitution. In the moral case, however, the supervenience relation is surely not causal or nomic: it is some kind of conceptual truth, and not a causal or nomic truth, that government injustice depends on (indeed is in a way constituted by) such things as seizure of land or other property, police brutality, arbitrary restrictions of free movement, and the like.[19] These are the things one must point to in order to say what injustice *is;* they do not cause the injustice they underlie — though they may cause *further* injustice. Thus, the plausible assumption that the intermediate effect might be a cause of the distant one, by contrast with being epiphenomenal or with both events being common effects of the same causes, cannot be invoked to show that the moral properties must have at least some of the causal powers of their base properties. Hence, except on the strong — and reductionist — premise that the injustice simply *is,* or is at least necessarily equivalent to, a set of such natural properties, it is not evident why the causal heritability condition should hold.[20] If there is a weaker relation between the base properties and the supervenient one, why must the causal powers of the former accrue to the latter? So far as I can tell, no good answer to this question has been given in the literature.

One might reply that the strong assumption is probably true: moral properties are identical with sets of their base properties; it is simply hard, owing to vagueness and inadequacies in our moral theory, to spell out the equivalences. But it is surely not clear that the moral properties are identical with any set of their base properties, certainly not with any subset to which we might attribute the explanatory power of a moral property on every occasion of its plausible explanatory use. Indeed, if the relevant supervenience relation entails an *asymmetric* dependence between the moral and natural properties that are their base, the former presumably cannot be identical with the latter. It might be replied that the dependence is only epistemic: there is just one property, but we can know it to be present under a moral description only by virtue of knowing it to be present under a natural description. This is arguable; but it certainly appears that there is, as usually supposed, an (asymmetrical) ontic dependence. One might in fact take the apparent explanatory dependence of the moral on the natural to confirm this. A particular's having a moral property always seems explainable in terms of the relevant base properties; if it were identical to their conjunction one would not expect this. One might get an explanation of what the moral property *is,* but not of why the thing in question has it. The relation is apparently one of constitution; and in general indicating what constitutes a property does not explain why something has it, and indeed can leave open various alternative explanations of that fact.

There is further reason to doubt that moral properties explain in the way many ethical naturalists tend to believe they do (and here I speculate). On the face of it, one would think that moral terms are applied to events, including acts, on the basis of naturalistic criteria, either when the effects of these events — such as painful consequences for persons — meet those criteria, or when the events themselves have a certain intrinsic character, such as being the telling of a lie. The first case is illustrated by "That was wrong; it killed people." An example of the second is "Don't say that; it's a lie." If this suggestion is correct, then moral terms are apparently more classificatory than (directly) explanatory, at least if being explanatory is a matter of explaining the occurrence of natural phenomena as opposed to explaining the constitution of such moral facts as that a regime is unjust.

Moreover, we cite facts to explain the application of moral terms even more than we use moral terms in the course of explaining non-moral phenomena. Perhaps moral terms function primarily to describe what kind of act or person or situation is in question, and only secondarily in explaining, or paving the way for explaining, some (non-moral) event or situation. In saying, then, that the injustice of a regime caused an uprising, one may, from the moral point of view, be above all *morally describing the cause* — and perhaps thereby also condemning it — as opposed to *subsumptively explaining the phenomenon under a moral concept.* One need not, of course, be taking *only* the moral point of view in so speaking; it is indeed common that we have multiple purposes in making a single statement, and here one may also be trying to provide an explanation. One does put forward a *basis* for explaining the uprising in naturalistic terms, say by subsumption under a sociological generalization whose constituent concepts are "natural," above all, both non-moral and non-normative. One thereby at once provides an understanding of why the people rebelled, in terms of the presumed base properties that warrant the ascription of injustice, and an appraisal of the explanatory variables, in terms of the ethical implications of the moral term one implicitly applies to them, in this case 'injustice'.

3. An Alternative Moral Realism

It might seem that the difficulties which section 2 raises for ethical naturalism suggest that moral epiphenomenalism is correct after all. One merely softens the blow by allowing moral concepts to play a role in classifying natural phenomena, in expressing attitudes, and in contextually providing the materials for non-moral explanations. But this is a mistake.

First, I have simply been presenting an alternative to moral naturalism and do not claim that anything said above decisively shows that the view is wrong. Nothing said here decisively rules out a reductive form that gives moral properties all the explanatory power of the set of natural properties to which they are reducible, and so, on which they reductively supervene — if we may speak of supervenience at all here, where we would perhaps have a kind of degenerate case.

Second, if, as I have suggested, moral properties are conceptually rather than nomically connected with their naturalistic bases, then they are not *candidates* to be epiphenomenal: roughly, since they are not causally dependent variables, there is no reason to lament if they are not causal variables at all; they are apparently not the right sort of property to be in either category. In a sense, they do not belong to the causal order, though they are anchored in it. It might seem to follow that they play no role *at all* in explanations; but that, too, would be an unwarranted conclusion, as we shall see by considering a variety of explanations in which moral notions figure.

It is important to note that even if injustice by itself cannot explain events, *beliefs* that injustice is occurring can. This point might lead one to attribute explanatory power to moral properties by the following line of reasoning. Beliefs are what they are in part by virtue of their content. It is surely not *qua* neural state that a moral belief explains action. Even if beliefs turned out to be (by a synthetic identity) some kind of neural state, any explanation possible by appeal to such states will be quite different from those provided by appeal to the relevant beliefs. If moral beliefs (and other propositional attitudes essentially involving moral concepts and properties) are crucial in explaining action, and if moral concepts and properties are essential to those beliefs, then those concepts and properties are themselves explanatorily indispensable. They do not have *direct explanatory power,* in the sense that the ascription of moral properties by itself suffices to explain why some phenomena occur; but they might be said to have *contributory explanatory power,* in the sense that they can make an indispensable contribution to the direct explanatory power of propositional attitudes in which they figure. Even if the sheer possession of a belief, neurally characterized, could causally explain the occurrence of an action, it is only by virtue of the content of the belief that the agent's having this belief makes the action *intelligible* in the way appropriate to intentional human behavior: say as righting an injustice, taking revenge, or expressing gratitude. If there were no moral properties, then there would be no moral beliefs, such as the belief that one's government is unjust and one ought to fight it.

This case for the contributory explanatory power of moral properties is open to two objections. First, even beliefs that, say, something contains phlogiston can explain behavior, but we do not thereby want to claim for phlogiston any significant kind of explanatory power. Second, it might be objected that there are no moral properties, but only moral sentences and moral concepts, and we can give a non-cognitivist account of them and thereby do justice to moral discourse without granting any explanatory power to moral attributions.

The first objection is quite plausible, though it may be argued that the kind of explanatory power in question does have some significance, since not just any property can figure in people's action-explaining beliefs in the same way. Perhaps so, but the point is not obvious and I see no need to try to work out this line here. It would not affect any overall case if contributory explanatory power should turn out to be significant; for it is weaker than the sort required by explanationist naturalism. As for the non-cognivitist line, it seems open to a similar objection: one would still have to grant that the moral attitudes (or other non-truth-valued items they express) have contributory explanatory power, and just about any attitudes could apparently have it, too. The theoretically important point here (though I cannot argue it now) is that rejecting explanationist naturalism need not lead to non-cognitivism. Indeed, that rejection can be combined with recognizing a kind of explanatory power considerably stronger than non-cognitivism allows. Let me explain.

Again, let us start with the assumption that moral properties are not *directly explanatory,* in the sense that events can be explained by virtue of instantiating them and thereby being subsumed under some explanatory generalization, as where (to take an example from social psychology) an angry outburst is explained by calling it aggression and subsuming it under the generalization that frustration tends to produce aggression. This is quite consistent with moral properties' having a kind of explanatory power that goes beyond the contributory kind: they may be *collaterally explanatory,* in the sense that phenomena to which they apply — such as arbitrary curfews and rigging of elections — have direct explanatory power. The idea is that while a successful explanatory *use* of a moral term does not provide an explanation of the phenomenon *in terms of the causal or direct explanatory power of the moral property,* it does *contextually imply a direct explanation in terms of one or more base properties.* This is in a way to grant that there are moral explanations; what is denied is that they are causal or otherwise direct. More precisely, moral explanations are naturalized in the (indirect) sense that they point us to explanations in terms of the natural base properties whose presence is their ground; and *these* are the properties that do the direct explaining of events.

This view of the explanatory role of the moral is most naturally construed as realistic, at least regarding moral concepts and properties. For one thing, it allows them to figure predicatively in the propositional objects of beliefs to which truth and falsity apply, and it thus contrasts with non-cognitivism. A non-cognitivist, for instance, would tend to maintain that moral concepts and "properties" function solely in the expression of moral attitudes and have no ontological status beyond the minimal one implicit in that linguistic role. By contrast, on the most plausible realist interpretation of the collateral explanation view, concrete entities *have* moral properties and can be known to have them; and by attributing them to objects we are able both to understand those objects — in terms of certain of the base properties grounding the moral attribution — and to appraise the objects morally. Even taking the collateral explanation view as a modest version of moral realism, however, it is not naturalistic, but neutral with respect to whether moral concepts or properties are natural.

Are we now at the edge of a mysterious rationalist conception of moral truth and knowledge? How one answers this question depends heavily on one's position on what is traditionally considered a priori, for instance on the status of arithmetic truths. If one regards these as ultimately grounded in experience, and as testable in the way that the most general scientific theories are, then one is likely to find the view rather mysterious. But I doubt whether that conception of arithmetic truth is correct and am inclined to think that, whatever experience is required in order for one to *acquire* arithmetic and various other abstract concepts, *what* we grasp when we do acquire them, the object of our understanding of them, is abstract.[21] On this view, numbers are not numerals, propositions (or any other bearers of truth value) are not sentence tokens, and moral concepts and properties are not nouns or predicates.

In the case of moral concepts, experience is required for our acquisition of them — indeed even experience of the natural base properties on which they supervene. But it does not follow that they themselves are natural properties or have a direct causal or nomic connection with such properties. Indeed, it appears *necessary* that given certain base properties, a thing has a certain moral property. Consider, for instance, two convicted offenders receiving punishments of radically different severity for the same offense under the same conditions, say one versus five years for a first-offense gas station knifepoint robbery at the age of eighteen. Is it a contingent matter that an injustice has been done? It is surely not (it also does not seem analytic, though my purposes here do not require assuming that it is not); nor does the unequal sentencing *cause* injustice: it constitutes it, in a conceptual as opposed to causal sense of 'constitute'. Yet injustice so construed could hardly be more real. We need not suppose that its reality entails its having either causal power or direct explanatory power.

The view I am suggesting is one that seems to fit a broadly Kantian ethics, though the view implies neither the specific content of Kant's normative ethics nor the categorical imperative itself. A view of this sort need not be mysterious. Perhaps it can also be naturalistic, in one sense: that moral properties are not directly explanatory is neutral regarding the question whether moral concepts can be ultimately explicated in non-evaluative terms, say in terms of what will fulfill eudaemonistic desires purified of the effects of logical and factual error, and freed from the influence of egoism. Such a view would be *conceptually naturalistic,* since it would employ no irreducibly normative concepts. But this would not imply its being *substantively naturalistic,* i.e., empirical. It is the latter kind of view that is represented by a strong scientific naturalism, since this position holds out the hope of construing all truth, including all moral truth, as empirically confirmable. It thus aims at a naturalism of both sorts, since if moral notions are not reducible to naturalistically characterized ones, it is at best hard to see how all truth could be empirical. But to think that only the substantive naturalism genuinely deserves the name is to take naturalism to be the property of empiricism.

If a conceptually naturalistic analysis of moral properties can be carried through, then they have approximately the same explanatory powers as the properties to which they are conceptually equivalent. But if, as seems more likely, moral properties have only collateral rather than direct explanatory power, the rationalistic alternative I have been sketching is still as well off as the most plausible versions of empiricist ethical naturalism in accounting for moral explanation of concrete events. In both cases, these events are explained directly by nomically relevant properties. But the empiricist view, with its causal-explanatory conception of significance, must face the problem of how to show that moral properties are not epiphenomenal, whereas the rationalist view assigns them a kind of descriptive and evaluative role that makes the charge of epiphenomenalism inapplicable.

Both the rationalist and the empiricist views can account for the objectivity of moral judgments. On each account, they are ontologically objective because they attribute real properties; they are naturalistically anchored because they supervene on natural properties; and they are epistemically objective because there is an intersubjective way to know that an object possesses them: by appeal to the base properties on which they supervene. But whereas empiricist naturalism treats even general moral knowledge as empirical, the rationalist view construes it as a priori. Even if one thinks of the a priori as simply differing by degrees from what is directly testable, there is surely much plausibility in construing as a priori at least such simple moral knowledge as that it is unjust to give unequal sentences for equal crimes committed under the same circumstances.

There is much reason to think, then, that the issue of moral realism should not be cast wholly in terms of the comparison with scientific models. It simply may not be assumed that only causal or nomic properties are real, or that moral knowledge is possible only if it is causally or nomically grounded in the natural world.[22] Our moral beliefs often concern particular persons or acts; they are responsive to observations; and, together with our wants, they explain behavior. But this does not require that moral properties are natural, and it allows that general moral knowledge is a priori. It may be that, rather than naturalize moral properties and thereby take explanations by appeal to them to be in some sense causal, we should instead naturalize such moral explanations and construe their power to explain events as due to causal patterns to which we are already committed. The view sketched here is not the only plausible non-naturalist realism in ethics, but it provides as good an account of the epistemology of moral judgment as its empiricistic alternatives and a better account of our sense of the necessity of certain general moral principles.[23]

Notes

1. See, e.g., *Utilitarianism,* chap. 4, where he says that "to think of an object as desirable (unless for the sake of its consequences) and to think of it as pleasant are one and the same thing; and . . . to desire anything, except in proportion as the idea of it is pleasant is a physical and metaphysical impossibility." To be sure, even if Mill took the good (the intrinsically desirable) to be naturalistically analyzable, he may have been suggesting only a weaker equivalence between the rightness of acts and their hedonic optimality; but a case could be made that he took that equivalence, too, in a metaethical spirit.

2. If we think of an eliminativism that takes mental attributions to be cognitive but false, then non-cognitivism is not as close an analogue as an "error theory," such as J. L. Mackie proposes to account for what he takes to be the falsehood of standard, purportedly objective moral claims. See his *Ethics: Inventing Right and Wrong* (New York: Penguin Books, 1980).

3. See Richard B. Brandt, *A Theory of the Good and the Right* (Oxford: Oxford University Press, 1979). For a further indication of how the overall view

is naturalistic, with some detailed criticism of its central elements, see my "An Epistemic Conception of Rationality," *Social Theory and Practice* 9 (1983).

4. For discussion of many of these and a plausible general account of the notion, see Jaegwon Kim, "Supervenience as a Philosophical Concept," *Metaphilosophy* 21 (1990).

5. It may be adequately explainable by appeal to a proper subset; but I leave this open. On some views, a "full" explanation might require appeal to all of the base properties, assuming that this is a finite set. The sort of explanatory appeal important for this essay will be illustrated below.

6. Cf. Jaegwon Kim's case for the view that non-reductive physicalism based on the supervenience of the mental on the physical is an unstable position subject to pressures toward dualism on one side and eliminativism on the other. See "The Myth of Nonreductive Materialism," *Proceedings and Addresses of the American Philosophical Association* 63, supplement to no. 1 (1989).

7. There are powerful considerations supporting scientific naturalism, and the influence of the success of science and technology on recent philosophy is immense. In "Realism, Rationality, and Philosophical Method," *Proceedings and Addresses of the American Philosophical Association* 61 (1987), I describe and critically discuss this influence. I should add that while the formulation in this paragraph leaves open the possibility that moral properties are identical with their base properties or other natural properties, there is at least one difficulty with the former identification: the relevant in-virtue-of relation seems asymmetrical and hence not an identity relation. If we say that X is M in virtue of being N, it is at best unclear how these two properties can be identical and simply referred to under different descriptions.

8. A view not unlike this is criticized by Panayot Butchvarov in *Skepticism in Ethics* (Bloomington, Ind.: Indiana University Press, 1989). His focus, however, is more on explanatory than causal power as a standard of ontological commitment.

9. This is not to say that there *must* be an equivalence in explanatory power between a set of properties and any other set of them to which the former is reduced; but it is plausible to suppose that a set with *no* explanatory power cannot be reduced to a set that has it. More will said below about what it is for a property to have explanatory power.

10. See, e.g., Gilbert Harman, *The Nature of Morality* (New York: Oxford University Press, 1977) and Nicholas Sturgeon, "Moral Explanations," in David Copp and David Zimmerman, eds., *Morality, Reason, and Truth* (Totowa, N.J.: Rowman and Allanheld, 1985). Selections from the former and all of the latter are reprinted in Louis P. Pojman, ed., *Ethical Theory* (Belmont, Calif.: Wadsworth, 1988). That collection also contains relevant papers by (among others) David Brink and Bruce Russell. Other valuable sources are the *Southern Journal of Philosophy* 24, supplement (1985), which is devoted to moral realism, and David Brink, *Moral Realism and the Foundations of Ethics* (Cambridge and New York: Cambridge University Press, 1989).

11. Gilbert Harman, "Moral Explanations of Natural Facts—Can Moral Claims Be Tested Against Moral Reality?" *Southern Journal of Philosophy* 24, supplement (1985).

12. See Nicholas Sturgeon, "Harman on Moral Explanations of Natural Facts," *Southern Journal of Philosophy* 24, supplement (1985). Both the concession just described and the three considerations to follow are given in Sturgeon's paper. In the interest of brevity, I generally do not quote Sturgeon but simply try to keep fairly close to his wording.

13. Ibid. It should be noted that his speaking of facts being constituted from other facts is apparently not meant to suggest *propositional* equivalence, as one might think from the common treatment of facts as true propositions, but simply the equivalence of moral properties with the relevant natural base properties or other natural properties (though even this kind of equivalence has been thought to require a conceptually as opposed to nomically necessary equivalence). Compare Brink's apparently similar (and I think insufficiently explicated) use of 'constitute' in *Moral Realism* (e.g., 191–193).

14. Two clarifications are needed here. First, I leave unexplicated the idea that the fundamental place of abstract entities (or some of them) might be necessary truths; but in part the idea is that these abstract entities do not enter into causal relations and bear necessary, rather than causal, connections to certain other abstract entities. Second, a nomic truth is a lawlike one, hence one that supports counterfactuals and is confirmed by its instances; it may be that not all such truths are plausibly taken to express causal connections. Consider, for instance, the law relating the period of a pendulum to its length: is the length clearly a causal variable, as opposed to being suitably connected (causally) with gravity as the causal factor?

15. This concerns what might be called *primary knowledge* (and justification): I do not deny that one might know a thing to have a moral property on the basis of testimony, or that one might know there is an injustice from a pattern of events plausibly considered its effects. But surely no one can know of injustice in these ways except by virtue of *someone's* knowing of it through one or more of the base properties. It should also be said that knowledge may be like justified belief here in that its ground need not be actual belief, e.g., belief to the effect that the relevant base properties are present, but an appropriate justification for believing something to this effect.

16. Bernard Williams would, to be sure, call brutality a "thick" ethical concept to contrast it with the very general, "thin" ones like 'ought' and 'right'; but he does nothing to show that it is not simply a character trait *relevant* to moral assessment, and in any case there is certainly a behaviorally (and non-morally) specifiable narrow notion of brutality that would serve the limited purpose the notion must play here. See his *Ethics and the Limits of Philosophy* (Cambridge, Mass.: Harvard University Press, 1985), esp. chaps. 7 and 8.

17. Perhaps Brink took Harman to miss this point when, in reply to a claim of Harman's, he said, "I don't think we need know any of the naturalistic bases of the moral facts we offer in explanation, much less do we need a full-blown naturalistic reduction of all moral claims, in order for these moral explanations to be legitimate" (*Moral Realism,* 191n). In any case, if 'legitimate' here is used to mean 'true' I grant the point. But I think a stronger, epistemic claim is intended — and would be needed to block the line of argument I am developing. Perhaps Brink

has in mind that (as he nicely brings out) one can appeal to a moral notion like injustice in explanation without knowing what form the injustice takes, and one's explanation might remain sound even in circumstances where its form is different (see, e.g., 195–196). I grant this too, but it surely does nothing to undermine the point that one's warrant for such an appeal depends on justification for believing something to the effect that one or another of the base properties obtains. One need not be able to tell *a specific* story about how some base element operates; but if one is not warranted in positing *some* such story, the explanatory appeal to injustice is not legitimate. Thus, I am warranted in giving a purported moral explanation only if I am warranted in positing one or another naturalistic explanations by virtue of which the former can be true.

18. One might go further. As Warren Quinn puts it in explicating Harman's line of argument, "The better explanations that may always replace our moral explanations can . . . be fashioned from concepts that the intelligent moral explainer must already have because his own application of moral principles depends on them. Moral theory, in presupposing a rich supply of naturalistic concepts, contains the full-blown means by which its own explanations may be put aside." See "Truth in Ethics," *Ethics* 96 (1986): 531 (this essay as a whole is a helpful treatment of the controversy between Harman and Sturgeon). My point is that moral properties seem to be only indirectly explanatory of concrete events, and that moral explanations, spelled out, depend on appeal to natural properties. But the explanations are not put aside, or even replaceable, as somehow inadequate; indeed (as Harman would perhaps not deny), pragmatically, they may be indispensable.

19. It is perhaps noteworthy that Sturgeon himself speaks of a necessary connection in such a case; see, e.g., his "Moral Explanations," 69.

20. It is an interesting question whether Bernard Williams is committed to a premise of this sort for "thick" ethical concepts, e.g., those of cowardice, lying, brutality, and gratitude—the kind he countenances. See *Ethics and the Limits of Philosophy,* esp. chap. 8. One might of course question whether these are moral at all, as opposed to singling out elements which figure *in* moral principles, such as the prohibition of lying; but this is an issue I cannot pursue here. For a valuable critical discussion of Williams's treatment of these and the contrasting "thin" concepts such as that of rightness and obligation, see Warren Quinn, "Reflection and the Loss of Moral Knowledge: Williams on Objectivity," *Philosophy and Public Affairs* 16 (1987).

21. This is a large issue, and I am simply sketching one plausible alternative. For a brief discussion of this position in comparison with empiricist (including conventionalist) alternatives, see my *Belief, Justification, and Knowledge* (Belmont, Calif.: Wadsworth, 1988), chap. 4.

22. Bernard Williams's insistence on world-guidedness and action-guidingness seems to reflect such a view. A related, explanationist view of knowledge informs Alan H. Goldman's recent treatment of moral knowledge. See his *Moral Knowledge* (London and New York: Routledge, 1988). For a critical discussion of Williams's approach on this matter see Joseph Mendola, "Normative Realism, or Bernard Williams and Ethics at the Limit," *Australasian Journal of Philosophy* 67 (1989).

23. This essay has benefited from comments by Panayot Butchvarov, Joseph Mendola, and Louis Pojman, and Steven Wagner and from discussions with Jaegwon Kim, Nicholas Sturgeon, Mark Van Roojen, and a seminar I gave at the University of Nebraska in 1989.

Skepticism and
Naturalized Epistemology

David Shatz

When W. V. O. Quine, in his famous 1969 essay, urged that epistemology be "naturalized," he had in mind a quite radical proposal: that we abandon traditional epistemology and replace it with empirical psychology.[1] Quine arrived at this proposal by route of an argument we might term the argument from despair. The traditional project of validating common sense and scientific beliefs in the face of skeptical challenge has been, and is doomed to be, a failure; therefore, the project is best dropped; therefore, "epistemology, or something like it, simply falls into place as a chapter of psychology and hence of natural science" (*EN,* 82–83).[2] Or as Quine puts it elsewhere: "our liberated epistemologist ends up as an empirical psychologist, scientifically investigating man's acquisition of science."[3]

The term "naturalized epistemology" derives from Quine: yet few philosophers even among those who apply this label to their own theories, are prepared to embrace naturalism in its "replacement" version and abandon altogether the traditional issues of the theory of knowledge.[4] Two considerations underlie their reluctance. First, some aspects of traditional epistemology remain untouched by the argument from despair. For example, conceptual analysis (i.e., the explication of epistemic terms) and in addition the elucidation of epistemic norms can be carried on even by one who has given up on refuting skepticism. Since these projects ostensibly have no place in empirical psychology, pursuing them ensures that epistemology remains an autonomous discipline even if we despair over answering skepticism.[5] Second, Quine's pessimism about answering the skeptic, which led him to "replacement naturalism," is not shared by all philosophers. Few would quarrel with Quine that truths about the physical world cannot be *deduced from* or *reduced to* truths about sensory experience, but there are many different targets of skeptical attack (beliefs about the physical world, memory, other minds, induction), and many styles of both pro- and anti-skeptical argument. Why conclude that *all* anti-skeptical endeavors are doomed to fail? In Elliot Sober's words, ". . . Quine's advice, 'Since Carnap's foundationalism failed, why not settle for psychology' carries weight only to the degree that Carnapian epistemology exhausts the possibilities of epistemology."[6]

Convinced that there is still life in the traditional agenda — in the projects of conceptual analysis, the formulation of epistemic norms, and the justification of commonsense and scientific beliefs against skeptical challenges — and furthermore, that we can address these issues in a "naturalist" fashion, many contemporary writers attempt to integrate an allegiance to naturalism with preservation of some or all of the traditional agenda. In their view, naturalized epistemology, while incorporating — nay insisting upon — empirical inquiry into the formation of belief as part of the epistemological enterprise, somehow brings it all back to the traditional agenda in novel and interesting ways.[7] In this essay I should like to examine several attempts by self-proclaimed naturalists to carry out "integrative" naturalism in lieu of Quine's "replacement" naturalism. To keep the discussion manageable, my emphasis will be on the issue of skepticism and justification; however, our inquiry will also take us into the explication of epistemic terms and the formulation of norms.

1. Varieties of Naturalism in Epistemology

To begin let us distinguish between two versions of "naturalized epistemology": *conceptual* naturalism and *methodological* naturalism. Conceptual naturalism is the thesis that at least some key epistemic locutions (*S knows that p, S is justified in believing that p*) can be explicated by exclusively "naturalistic" conditions. What counts as a "naturalistic" condition for this purpose is not fixed or uniform among self-declared conceptual naturalists (a "naturalistic" account is variously understood as one that is non-normative, physicalistic, causal, nomic, or psychologistic[8]); nor is it always clear what is so naturalistic about the conditions these people think of as naturalistic, or what is so anti-naturalistic about the philosophers whom conceptual naturalists think they are correcting.[9] Resolve these issues as you will, conceptual naturalism has nothing to do, at least not immediately, with Quinean naturalism. Quine's naturalism is *methodological:* it is distinguished by the fact it utilizes empirical inquiry into belief as part of the epistemological enterprise. It is methodological naturalism, not conceptual naturalism, that will dominate our discussion, though we will have to deal with conceptual naturalism a bit as well.

What, more exactly, is methodological naturalism? Quine adheres to the following doctrines:

(1) the *mandatory use* doctrine: epistemology must make use of empirical data;[10]
(2) the *exclusive use* doctrine: no data other than empirical data may be used in epistemology—there is no first philosophy, no transcendent standpoint, no a priori truth;
(3) the *free use* doctrine: the free use of empirical data about the formation of belief is unproblematic.

The free use doctrine is especially important. Quine characterizes naturalism as "a readiness to see philosophy as natural science trained upon itself and permitted free use of scientific findings," and similarly tells us that "a conspicuous difference between old epistemology and the epistemological enterprise in this new psychological setting is that we can now make free use of empirical psychology" (*EN*, 83).

The mandatory use doctrine and the free use doctrine are the chief points of contact between Quine's replacement naturalism and the integrative naturalism espoused by others. Basically, integrative naturalism, we said, is an attempt to bring empirical inquiry to bear upon the traditional agenda, and that implies both a mandate and a permit. This having been noticed, we are in position to see why integrative methodological naturalism is *prima facie* implausible. Recall how Quine argued for free use in "Epistemology Naturalized." There, he grounded the free use doctrine in despair over solving the skeptical problem (as Quine conceived that problem). As a result, when Quine confronted the obvious objection to using empirical methods in epistemology—viz., that the use of such methods is inevitably circular—he responded thusly: because the enterprise is different, the rules of the game are different. We are not aiming at validation; hence, we need not worry about the problem of circularity which confronts the traditional epistemologist:

> Such a surrender of the epistemological burden to psychology is a move that was disallowed in earlier times as circular reasoning. If the epistemologist's goal is validation of the grounds of empirical science, he defeats his purpose by using psychology or other empirical science in the validation. However, such scruples against circularity have little point once we have stopped dreaming of deducing science from observations. If we are out simply to understand the link between science and evidence, we are well advised to use any available information, including that provided by the very science whose link with observation we are seeking to understand. (*EN*, 75–76)

Now, in contrast to Quine's replacement version of methodological naturalism, integrative methodological naturalists want to make free use of empirical data, but in the service of traditional problems. Clearly, if an integrative methodological naturalist wants to solve, in particular, the problem of skepticism by using empirical data in "free" fashion, he or she will need some justification for this free use other than Quine's despair argument.

What he will need is a thesis I call *dialectical naturalism.* Dialectical naturalism maintains that, in defending empirical claims against skeptical attacks, that is, in a dialectical context of debate with a skeptic, the use of empirical data can be shown to be unproblematic and perfectly defensible. In particular, you incur no vicious circularity by appealing to empirical data to validate the reliability of human faculties or to establish claims about the conditions in which beliefs are formed (viz., that they are formed in circumstances conducive to their being true); you do not fall into relativism; and you do not fall prey to specific skeptical challenges such as arguments based on the possibility of illusions. In short, dialectical naturalism maintains and shows (to the dialectical naturalist's satisfaction, at least) that naturalistic, i.e., empirical, arguments are dialectically effective against the skeptic. In essence, dialectical naturalism is the claim that the free use doctrine can be justified on a ground other than despair, even when one's interlocutor is a skeptic. In fact, dialectical naturalism is nothing less than an attempt to answer the traditional question of skepticism regarding empirical methods.

Dialectical naturalism, to my mind, is the most interesting form of naturalism because it is the most ambitious: it confronts the problem of skepticism and of circularity head on, and it offers a response. In essence, dialectical naturalism offers a kind of coherence approach to justifying common sense or science: we use empirical data to justify use of empirical data, and we offer a principled defense of our ostensibly viciously circular procedure.

Since a dialectical naturalist professes to have a reply to charges of circularity and relativism, as well as to other challenges that a skeptic might initiate, the Quine of "Epistemology Naturalized," who despairs over answering the skeptic in a dialectically effective way but then reasons, "so we may as well use empirical methods," does not count as a dialectical naturalist. In other essays, though, Quine referring to his earlier despair as "needless logical timidity" (*RR,* 3) provides a partial defense of dialectical naturalism. This defense rests on the claim that skeptical doubts presuppose science and that therefore we can make free use of science when we reply. It is science which tells us about the things the skeptic exploits in his argument: specifically, the contrast between the illusory and the veridical, and the gap between evidence and theory. "The skeptical challenge springs from science itself . . . in coping with it we are free to use scientific knowledge" (*RR,* 3); "Doubt prompts the theory of knowledge, yes; but knowledge, also, was what prompted the doubt. Scepticism is an offshoot of science."[11] This kind of response to skepticism is the very antithesis of the argument from despair. Here, the (dialectical) naturalist answers skepticism (to be more accurate: he or she answers certain forms of skepticism) instead of conceding it. But this response, too, serves Quine as a spur to replacement naturalism. The refutation of skepticism, no less than despair over refuting it, paves the way for doing psychology in lieu of traditional epistemology.

The bearing of dialectical naturalism on our present discussion is twofold. First, recognizing the difference between dialectical naturalism and the argument from despair helps clarify and sharpen the case for replacement naturalism. The real force of Quine's attack, we now see, is to place traditional epistemology in a dilemma. If skepticism cannot be answered (as Quine argued in 1969), traditional epistemology should not be pursued; if skepticism can be answered (as the later Quine asserts), then, once it is, we can leave this part of the traditional agenda—skepticism is finished business—and move on to empirical inquiry.

Second, it is clear that, for Quine—in both "Epistemology Naturalized" and later work—the skeptical problem is the problem of providing a dialectically effective argument against the skeptic. Given his conception of what the problem is, he rightly imposes a constraint on its solution. Specifically, if you utilize empirical methods in a dialectical context in which skeptics are participating, you should have to legitimate the use of such methods. If you do not, your use of empirical methods to deal with the skeptic becomes automatically suspect. The suspicion, specifically, is that either you are really committed to despair and are advancing a covert form of replacement naturalism; or you are dealing with some "skeptical" problem other than the traditional (dialectical) one, a problem that may be philosophically less interesting than the traditional one. This, I think, is precisely what we discover when we explore concrete applications of integrative methodological naturalism.

2. Hume and Strawson on the Idleness of Argument

My first example of an integrative methodological naturalist is Peter Strawson. In *Skepticism and Naturalism,*[12] Strawson asserts that a certain line of thought in Hume provides "a way of dealing with certain kinds of traditional skepticism" (52). Strawson paraphrases this Humean argument as follows:

> He [Hume] points out that all arguments in *support* of the skeptical position are totally inefficacious; and by the same token, all arguments *against*

it are idle. His point is really the very simple one that, whatever arguments may be produced on one side or the other of the question, we simply *cannot help* believing in the existence of body, and *cannot help* forming beliefs and expectations in general accordance with the basic canons of induction. He might have added, though he did not discuss this question, that the belief in the existence of other people (hence other minds) is equally inescapable. (Strawson, 11)

Strawson thinks that this is a "better, because more realistic, way [to deal with the skeptic] than any attempt to justify or validate by rational argument those very general beliefs which traditional skepticism seeks to put in doubt"(52). What his response amounts to is that "our commitment on these points is pre-rational, natural, and quite inescapable." This commitment "sets . . . the natural limits within which, and only within which, the serious operations of reason, whether by way of questioning or of justifying beliefs, can take place." In Hume's words:

> Whoever has taken the pains to refute the cavils of this total scepticism has really disputed without an antagonist and endeavored by arguments to establish a faculty which Nature has antecedently implanted in the mind and rendered unavoidable.

There are two distinct empirical claims in Strawson's response: (1) that argumentation cannot dislodge the belief in the existence of body or of the uniformity of nature or the existence of other minds; (2) that argumentation does not produce these beliefs. Proskeptical and antiskeptical arguments alike are idle, causally inert. We might call the line of thought which uses these claims to "deal with" the skeptic the argument from causal impotence. [13]

I confess to some uncertainty about how to interpret Strawson. On one reading, he is merely providing a reaction to skepticism from the vantage point of one who takes empirical data — claims about human psychology — as unproblematic; based on such data, he thinks that skeptical and anti-skeptical arguments have no causal bearing on everyday belief formation. Understood that way, Strawson is merely making descriptive-explanatory claims. His statement that his "response" "does not so much attempt to meet the challenge as to pass it by" (3) lends support to this reading. Some of Strawson's remarks suggest something stronger, however; namely, that he is providing a reply of some sort. After all, he says his response "deals with" the skeptic. Further, he expressly separates his position from Quine's, albeit without identifying the precise contrast (10). On a different reading of Strawson's view, what we are presented with is a version of integrative methodological naturalism. Using empirical data,

Strawson arrives at a particular picture of the cognitive makeup and disposi-
tions of human beings; then, armed with this picture and supporting data,
he "deals with" the skeptical problem (in the sense of replying, not react-
ing) by showing its irrelevance and the irrelevance of all reason-based solutions to it. The weaknesses of his view on this second reading are instructive; I will therefore press ahead with it, albeit with the caveat that the
"Strawson" I represent may be (but I do not think is) a strawman.

(1) Let us begin with the thesis that proskeptical arguments are causally impotent, i.e., commonsense beliefs are not dislodgable. One's first
instinct, perhaps, is to attack the truth of Strawson's empirical claim (What
about the ancient skeptics? What about Berkeley? Didn't they lose belief
in body as a result of skeptical arguments?[14]). But the more basic question
is about Strawson's methodology. For his argument falls afoul of my earlier warnings about "freely using" empirical data in the context of a debate with skepticism. The argument begins with an empirical claim about
the effects that certain arguments do or do not have (or: can or cannot
have) on people. But here is the problem: empirical claims are vulnerable
to skeptical doubt. How, then, can Strawson justify his empirical starting
point? Even if we would grant Strawson that undislodgable beliefs are immune from skeptical critique, his own empirical starting point would not
be immune by this standard for the belief that certain beliefs are not dislodgable is, itself, dislodgable. The ancient skeptics, as we noted, denied
Strawson's claim that commonsense beliefs are not dislodgable, and so did
Descartes when he attributed great power to the will in the sphere of belief. Hence Strawson cannot use even his own "undislodgability" (or "in-
escapability") criterion to entitle himself to use, against the skeptic, the
claim that commonsense beliefs are not dislodgable.

Absent a defense of dialectical naturalism, it seems that Strawson
is starting from the free use doctrine rather than arguing toward it. On
the other hand, if Strawson has a defense of dialectical naturalism, his
own "undislodgability" argument is superfluous.

Another difficulty lurks: some of the most prevalent forms of skepticism remain as hardy as ever when Strawson is finished. In particular,
Strawson fails to distinguish between first-order beliefs and second-order
beliefs. Suppose that belief in the uniformity of nature or the existence
of body or the existence of other minds is psychologically impervious to
skeptical refutation. This would not refute all versions of skepticism. Skeptics do not claim that there are no bodies, that nature is not uniform, or
that there are no other minds; indeed, by their own lights, they are not
entitled to *deny* commonsense beliefs, but only to attack their grounding.
Skeptics attempt to show that first-order commonsense (or scientific) beliefs are not well grounded, that these beliefs do not amount to knowledge

or rational belief. Now the second-order belief that our first-order beliefs constitute knowledge or are justified is not psychologically impervious to skeptical argument. Philosophers who claim we have no knowledge or no justified belief (Peter Unger, for example) might accept first-order common-sense beliefs while rejecting second-order ones. Since skepticism may be directed at beliefs which are dislodgable, namely second-order beliefs, Strawson's reply will be ineffective against skepticisms of this sort.

Strawson might respond that skeptics are in no position to make any claims of their own about which beliefs are dislodgable (for instance, the claim that second-order beliefs are dislodgable); if one is a skeptic, one would lapse into incoherence by making any assertions about human psychology. True enough. But all this shows is that the objections in the previous paragraph can be filed only by other naturalists; it does not show that empirical objections cannot be raised at all. Strawson cannot use just any old empirical assertion and then claim immunity from criticism merely by saying he is quarreling with a skeptic. He is accountable to both naturalists and skeptics.

(2) Let me now turn to the other half of the impotence argument, which says that commonsense beliefs are not produced by anti-skeptical arguments. I shall call this the argument from the lack of attributability, or, for short, the attributability argument. In part IV of the *Enquiry,* after having laid out the difficulties in proving the uniformity of nature, Hume adds the following:

> Even though we examine all the sources of our knowledge and conclude them unfit for such a subject, there may still remain a suspicion that the enumeration is not complete or the examination not accurate. But with regard to the present subject, there are some considerations which seem to remove all this accusation of arrogance or suspicion of mistake.
>
> It is certain that the most ignorant and stupid peasants, nay infants, nay even brute beasts, improve by experience and learn the qualities of natural objects by observing the effects which result from them. . . . If you assert, therefore, that the understanding of the child is led into this conclusion by any process of argument or ratiocination, I may justly require you to produce that argument, nor have you any pretense to refuse so equitable a demand. You cannot say that the argument is abstruse and may possibly escape your inquiry, since you confess that it is obvious to the capacity of a mere infant. If you hesitate, therefore, a moment, or if, after reflection, you produce an intricate or profound argument, you, in a manner, give up the question and confess that it is not reasoning which engages us to suppose the past resembling the future, and to expect similar effects from causes which are to appearance similar. This is the proposition which I intended

to enforce in the present section. If I be right, I pretend not to have made any mighty discovery. And if I be wrong, I must acknowledge myself to be a very backward scholar, since I cannot now discover an argument which, it seems, was perfectly familiar to me long before I was out of my cradle.

Hume's point is that, even if an "intricate or profound argument" for the uniformity of nature were produced, the argument would be irrelevant. But irrelevant to what? If Hume means that the argument would be irrelevant to the task of describing the psychological processes that produce inductively formed beliefs, his point is correct: the arguments would not be utilized in actual psychological processes. (To assert this presupposes free use, but let us leave that aside.) But this is to suppose that the only point of producing a philosophical argument for the uniformity of nature is to reconstruct human psychological processes. Why must a philosopher produce such an argument for this purpose in particular? Surely philosophers might produce such arguments because they want to validate inductive reasoning. And when the arguments are used for this purpose, it is neither here nor there whether anyone else actually utilizes them.

Despite this obvious weakness in the attributability argument, Strawson trots it out to discredit certain replies to the skeptic.[15] Thus, Strawson considers the view that hypotheses such as the existence of body, the existence of other minds, the uniformity of nature, etc., can be justified by the familiar argument pattern, "inference to the best explanation," used to construct theories within science. In opposition to this view Strawson writes:

> But the implicit comparison with scientific theory simply proclaims its own weakness. We accept (or believe) the scientific theories (when we do) just because we believe they supply the best available explanations of the phenomena they deal with. That is our reason for accepting them. But no one accepts the existence of the physical world *because* it supplies the best available explanation, etc. That is no one's reason for accepting it. (20)

Strawson quotes with approval Hume's remark: "'tis vain to ask Whether there be body or not? That is a point which we must take for granted in all our reasonings" (20–21). He also quotes with approval Wittgenstein's naturalism as it emerges in *On Certainty,* paraphrasing it as follows:

> To attempt to confront the professional skeptical doubt with arguments in support of these beliefs, with rational justification, is simply to show a total misunderstanding of the role they actually play in our belief-systems. The correct way with the professional skeptical doubt is not to attempt to rebut it with argument, but to point out that it is idle, unreal, a pretense; and then

the rebutting arguments will appear as equally idle . . . there is no such thing as *the reasons for which we hold* these beliefs. (19–20)

Here again, one wonders how Strawson would justify his beliefs about the place of certain beliefs in our conceptual scheme. Such meta-beliefs are, after all, empirical. However Strawson may address that problem, there is something initially peculiar about using the impotence of *anti*-skeptical (= pro-commonsense) arguments as a resource when one's ultimate aim is to reply to the skeptic. Strawson does nothing to remove this peculiarity; his statement is no defense of our beliefs against the skeptic's challenge. The skeptic can cheerfully grant — *arguendo,* that is; he will not believe any specific empirical claims — that the beliefs he attacks are foundational, central to our conceptual scheme, held without reason, etc. What he tries to show is that these foundational, central, or what-have-you beliefs are not justified. They are, by the naturalist's admission, held without good reason and cannot be defended with good reason; so, they *ought* not be held. Now, if we assume from the start that epistemology tries to provide a psychological map, if we assume replacement naturalism, Strawson's response is perfectly apt: anti-skeptical arguments translate into poor psychology. But why assume replacement naturalism? Why not assume the epistemologist is trying to justify and argue for beliefs? Given that project, a good line of argument would not be irrelevant if it were produced. Indeed, if produced, it would refute the despair argument that leads people to replacement naturalism in the first place.

A key error in Strawson lies in his statement: "that [i.e., the argument of the pattern inference-to-the-best-explanation, IBE] is no one's reason for accepting it [the commonsense view, CSV]." If he means by this that IBE is not the cause of anyone's believing CSV, or that IBE is not a necessary condition of anyone's believing CSV, he may well be right. But there is a clear sense in which a successful argument, if produced by a philosopher, would constitute a "reason" for the philosopher or someone else to hold the belief. There can be good reasons for believing that *p,* even if you would believe that *p* without having those reasons. If a good argument were produced, that argument might not serve as the reason *for which the philosopher holds CSV* (since he holds it because of his nature), but it would serve as a reason for him (or someone else) to hold it. Even a scientist or layperson, in Strawson's example, might accept a hypothesis because of subtle psychological influences, but that would not imply there is no reason for him to accept it. I would even go further: an argument for CSV could serve as a reason for which the person holds CSV, even if he would hold to CSV independently of the argument, and even if this independent commitment is a psychologically necessary condition for his accepting the argument. If a scientist learns of a good inductive argument for a conclusion, this can be a reason for which he believes it—even if he would believe the conclusion on unrespectable grounds were the argument not known to him, and even if this independent commitment is necessary for him to appreciate the argument's force.

At this juncture, Strawson might reply as follows. Even if a philosopher were to have a good justifying argument, this would not change the fact that, for ordinary people, that argument would be psychologically irrelevant. The argument could not be attributed to them, could not be their reason for believing common sense. Now I agree that most philosophical arguments for common sense do not mirror the beliefs of the ordinary person. For instance, a justificatory argument for common sense would have to rule out various skeptical hypotheses: imitations, illusions, brains-in-vats. "Ordinary" people do not rule these hypotheses out; they ignore them entirely unless there are contrary indications.[16] So the philosophical argument could not be a reason for which ordinary people hold their beliefs. But what of it? All that follows is that ordinary people are not justified in holding their commonsense beliefs. It would not follow that commonsense beliefs are not justifiable. Why can't there be a project of justification that will not reflect the causes, necessary conditions, or reasons which underlie the beliefs of the ordinary people which philosophers seek to justify? Arguments for commonsense beliefs are not irrelevant to the task of justification just because they are not psychologically common.

The only response I see remaining for Strawson is that the way in which people in fact arrive at their beliefs is normative, i.e., it dictates for us the way in which we *ought* to arrive at our beliefs.[17] If we do not use philosophical arguments to arrive at our beliefs, but instead accept them because we are born into them, then this fact about us generates a valid norm, and skepticism falls by the wayside. But a reply like this only brings Strawson back to square one. For how can he justify his beliefs about how people arrive at their beliefs? To what norms can he appeal to justify his beliefs that people form their beliefs in the way he says? He would need to make these procedures normative based on examining his own case alone; and even to determine his *own* reasoning processes he would require norms.

Deeper reflection on Hume's attributability argument suggests that Strawson may have stretched Hume beyond what Hume intended. In the context of Hume's aims, the attributability argument is very much in place. Hume wanted to show that, as a descriptive matter, human beings are not creatures of reason but, instead, creatures of feeling, sentiment, habit, and custom.[18] He achieves this in two steps: first, by showing that reason cannot validate common sense—in this way, Hume shows that human beings do not base their beliefs on good enough reasons, because there are no good enough reasons to be had; second, by arguing (in the animals passage) that, even if there is or were some argument good enough to validate commonsense beliefs, this argument would not be attributable to humans. Thus, Hume's attack is leveled at a thesis that itself purports to describe human beings and explain the origins of their beliefs; and a descriptive claim surely deserves an empirical refutation. It is entirely improper to convert Hume's attack, as Strawson does on the reading I am presuming, into a reply to the skeptic or an objection to the success of all future arguments on behalf of common sense. Similarly, Hume's other point, that skeptical arguments will not dislodge commonsense beliefs, is intended to rebut a descriptive claim made by the ancient skeptics and Descartes, namely, that the skeptic can live his skepticism or at least can actually suspend belief in CSV. In Hume, the undislodgability thesis in no way serves to "deal with," or reply to, the skeptic. It serves, rather, to characterize human psychology and bring out a fascinating aspect of the human predicament.

In sum, while Strawson may have furnished us with a reaction to skepticism from a naturalist perspective, i.e., a perspective that takes empirical data as unproblematic, a reaction is one thing, a reply another. As a reply to the skeptic, the argument from impotence is ineffective: skeptical and anti-skeptical arguments are not irrelevant to the epistemological enterprise. Strawson himself may not intend to provide more than a reaction, but this is by no means clear from his book. Alternatively, perhaps Strawson intends a reply, but means to say more than he actually says; perhaps he has some tacit thesis about meaning, for example (recall the Wittgenstein reference); perhaps he is an anti-realist; etc. Whatever Strawson's own intent, the relationship between naturalism and traditional epistemology remains, to this point, indiscernible.

3. Conceptual Naturalism and the Possibility Argument

The next exemplar of methodological naturalism I should like to take up is Alvin Goldman. However, in order properly to discuss Goldman's views on skepticism, we need to say a bit more about *conceptual* naturalism.

Conceptual naturalism, recall, is the thesis that at least some key epistemic locutions can be explicated by exclusively "naturalistic" conditions. It is common to take "reliabilism"—the view that knowledge and/or justified belief is belief formed or sustained by reliable processes and methods —as the paradigm of conceptual naturalism. Following this practice, let us consider how reliabilism relates—or does not relate—to skepticism.

A popular way of relating conceptual naturalism to skepticism is via the possibility argument. Reliabilists often argue as follows. Skeptics claim that we do not know what we think we know and are not justified in believing what we think we are justified in believing. Now, if, to know that p or be justified in believing that p, we need an argument that will be dialectically effective against the skeptic, then, alas, the skeptic is right. But suppose that knowledge and/or justified belief is defined as belief formed or sustained by reliable processes. We then have knowledge or justified belief just in case our beliefs are, in point of fact, formed or sustained by reliable processes. Skeptics have no proof that our beliefs are not formed by reliable processes. So skeptics have no right to assert that we do not have knowledge or justified belief. Possibly, we do have knowledge and justified belief.[19]

This is the basic reliabilist argument against skepticism; there are several variations on it. Some writers, such as Fred Dretske and Robert Nozick, try to capture a *tension* in our way of thinking about skepticism rather than reject skepticism outright. They want to preserve the thesis that we know ordinary commonsense propositions, but also want to cede to the skeptic that we do not know that the skeptic's bizarre hypotheses (e.g., demons, brains in vats, etc.) are false. To achieve this split in intuitions, they work out conditions of knowledge on which knowledge is not closed under known logical entailment, and on which if the world is as we think it is, we know commonsense propositions like "I am working at a desk," but do not know that brain-in-the-vat and other skeptical hypotheses are false. For present purposes only the anti-skeptical component of this position will be germane.

There is another variation on the basic reliabilist reply to the skeptic, this relating to the problem of how to justify belief in epistemic principles. Epistemic principles are principles stating which sorts of beliefs are justified. It would seem to be impossible to justify epistemic principles using empirical data, since in order to establish any particular datum, one would have to utilize epistemic principles as premises; if the principles justify belief in the data, and the data justify belief in the principles, we are caught in a vicious circle. But suppose a particular empirical belief can be justified by its having been formed or sustained in a certain manner. Then the belief is justified without appeal to an epistemic principle, and the principle can be established from the data without circularity; this, despite the fact that we have no dialectically effective argument for endorsing the data. This approach provides us with a view superficially like dialectical naturalism, but clearly not as potent as a version of dialectical naturalism that would find a dialectically adequate basis for endorsing the initial data.[20]

A great deal of criticism has been dumped on reliabilist accounts, and I quite agree that these accounts run into serious counterexamples.[21]

However, I am for the moment interested only in the move from reliabilism to anti-skepticism.

What is the skeptical challenge? The reliabilist response clearly takes the skeptic to be arguing for one form of skepticism, *epistemic* skepticism:

ES: We do not have knowledge or justified belief.

The skeptic argues for ES on the basis of *dialectical* skepticism:

DS: There is no dialectically effective argument for our first-level commonsense beliefs or our second-level commonsense beliefs.

But DS does not support ES, say reliabilists, because neither knowledge nor justified belief requires possession of a dialectically effective argument. Hence the skeptic's argument is a *non sequitur*.

What we really have in reliabilism's approach to skepticism, then, is a consistency argument: the thesis that we have knowledge and justified belief (i.e., the negation of skeptical thesis ES) is consistent with DS. Knowledge and justified belief are *possible*.

Against this reliabilist response I would argue that what is really important about the skeptical challenge is DS, not ES.[22] I say this for several reasons.[23] First, the same "reply" to the skeptic could be won even if knowledge were unpacked as true belief, period. On such an account, our beliefs would constitute knowledge *if* they are true. But this kind of reply to the skeptic is obviously of no real help; obviously we realized our beliefs *might* be true! Why should explicating knowledge as reliable true belief serve any better with respect to the skeptic's challenge? We have no more dialectically effective an argument for the reliability of the process by which the belief was formed, than we do for the truth of the belief.

A second way to see the significance of DS as compared to ES is to consider someone who endorses a hypothesis which is incompatible with the commonsense one (that physical objects produce veridical experiences in us), but which is equally compatible with the data. Suppose Joe actually believes that we are brains-in-vats. Whenever Joe has "table-like" experiences, he hypothesizes: the vat's caretakers are now stimulating me to have table-like experiences. (How Joe deals with what we would call "illusions" is more complex, but let us leave this aside; roughly, he can consider an experience "delusive" based simply on its incoherence with other experiences.) Suppose we object to Joe that he does not have enough warrant for this hypothesis. Paralleling the reliabilist's reply to the skeptic, Joe could fend off our "skeptical" objections to his envatment hypothesis. "That belief *may* be reliable," Joe will say. That is: if I really am a brain-in-the-vat, then (here I follow Nozick's account of knowledge, by way of example) I know that I am now being stimulated by the vat's caretakers to have table-like experiences provided that, if these fiends weren't stimulating me, I wouldn't be having the experiences. This reply would seem to be adequate given the possibility argument. And for that matter, we cannot be "skeptical" of any skeptical hypothesis Joe might endorse. Surely, however, a reply to the skeptic who puts common sense in doubt should make clear why those who endorse commonsense hypotheses are in a *better* epistemic position than those who endorse skeptical ones. The consistency argument of the reliabilist does not meet this demand.

If the example of a "skeptic's hypothesis" has failed to convince, look at various other *non-skeptical* hypotheses. Some of these would "refute" skepticism just as well as the particular nonskeptical hypotheses we endorse to explain our beliefs. It makes no difference whether you believe that perceptual processes implant your true beliefs or whether, instead, you believe you are perceptually impoverished but God, bent on your believing the truth on this-or-that occasion, implants an experience of X in you when X is in fact near you (this is a sort of epistemological occasionalism). To answer skepticism, on the reliabilist's argument, all you need is *some* hypothesis about how beliefs are formed such that, if that hypothesis is true, your beliefs are reliable; for, if the world is as you think, then you have knowledge and/or justified belief. It can be shown, I think, that, on many reliabilist accounts (Nozick's, for instance), your belief that God is stimulating you on this-or-that occasion is reliable given your metaphysics, just as, for adherents of the commonsense hypothesis, the belief that a physical object is directly causing a certain experience is reliable. Even the wildest hypothesis imaginable could be invoked to answer a skeptic. Of course, if the hypothesis is wild, then in fact the person who advocates it will not, given our metaphysics, have reliable beliefs in the way he imagines. But he will certainly be entitled to cook up the hypothesis and cite the possibility of its truth in the course of his anti-skeptical 'possibility' argument. What has gone wrong, obviously, is that we believe our commonsense "reliable belief" hypothesis is epistemically superior to the wild "reliable belief" hypothesis. But why should we think it is epistemically superior, if we do not have a dialectically effective argument for this claim?

For these reasons, I believe that skepticism is really a matter of DS, not ES; if skeptics ever framed their view as ES, this was because skeptics had few of our post-Gettier worries about defining epistemic terms, blithely assumed that knowing or being justified entails having a dialectically effective argument, and adopted ES as a *façon de parler*. Had skeptics realized that reliabilist accounts were available which would break the nexus between DS and ES, they never would have formulated their point in terms of ES.

In sum, the possibility argument leaves DS standing; and DS, not ES, represents the real core of the skeptical challenge.

With the possibility argument as background, I should like to turn to Alvin Goldman's naturalist treatment of skepticism. Superficially, his approach looks very different from the possibility argument. Yet, closer examination shows that, at a crucial point, he, too, falls back on the possibility argument.

4. Skepticism and Cognitive Psychology: Goldman's Approach

In *Epistemology and Cognition,*[24] Goldman suggests that "any adequate response to skepticism must involve or presuppose analyses (or 'accounts') of key epistemic terms like 'knowledge' and 'justification'" (36). Now suppose that our account of knowledge and/or justified belief — what Goldman calls a "criterion" — asserts that a belief constitutes knowledge/ is justified iff it results from reliable cognitive processes. By itself, this analysis does not tell us whether we have knowledge or justified belief, or even whether knowledge/justified belief are humanly possible (55). Also, the account, Goldman says, will have to be defended without use of empirical inquiry in the form of cognitive psychology; it will utilize, instead, appeals to intuitions about hypothetical cases. (Canvassing intuitions is arguably an empirical inquiry, but we may let this pass.) Nevertheless, once armed with the account, we could determine empirically whether skepticism is correct by inquiring (1) What cognitive processes do human beings actually use? (2) What is the reliability of these processes? "Hence this [reliabilist] account of justification would lead epistemology down a path that fosters collaboration with cognitive psychology" (37). The epistemologist, equipped with cognitive psychology, would be concerned not only with ascertaining whether there are reliable processes or methods, but with specifying what these are and evaluating them for their reliability. If the processes are reliable, we have justified belief; if not, we do not. In short, we determine whether skeptics are right by empirical inquiry.[25]

Goldman's conception of how reliabilism affects skepticism differs sharply from the "consistency" response (possibility argument) set out earlier. In the first place, Goldman is not content to point out that, with conceptual naturalism, knowledge/justified belief is now a *possibility;* he goes beyond this and tries to find out, through cognitive psychology, whether knowledge and justified belief are *actual.* Second, the possibility argument granted dialectical skepticism (DS); from DS, it concluded that non-reliabilist accounts of knowledge and justified belief lead to skepticism because they require possession of a dialectically effective argument, while reliabilism makes knowledge and justified belief possible. Goldman, in contrast, seems untroubled by DS; he has no qualms about finding out *empirically* whether human cognitive processes are reliable. He helps himself to free use of empirical data. That is what makes his approach naturalistic.

But this is precisely where the relevance of Goldman's approach to traditional concerns falls under suspicion. For he has no defense to offer of free use; and, when pressed, he falls back on the consistency approach. After articulating his reliabilist criterion, Goldman takes up the following problem, raised by Roderick Firth[26]: How one can determine whether a reliabilist criterion (or any truth-linked criterion) has been applied correctly; that is, how can one determine that one has identified a reliable (truth-conducive) set of rules? After all, a particular rule of inference has to be justified by its past successes and failures in leading to truth; but, besides presupposing that inductive inference is truth-preserving, a claim that may be under suspicion in the dialectical context at hand, how can we identify true beliefs except by assuming that some particular set of rules (the set we use in making the identifications of processes and the truth of the beliefs they yield) confers justification? Goldman's response is twofold. First:

> I offer no guarantee that (ARI) [Goldman's reliabilist criterion] (or any of the other truth-ratio criteria proposed here) can be correctly applied. But . . . no such guarantee can be offered for other criteria either. (119)

This part of Goldman's response is correct as far as it goes; no criterion, not even a non–truth-linked one, can carry its own guarantee of correct application. However, whereas for Goldman's purposes, a *tu quoque* of this sort is adequate, the concession that no criterion can carry a guarantee of its own correct application plays right into the hands of the skeptic. Hence this first response will not adequately rebut the skeptic, and in light of *our* purposes we will have to look at part two of Goldman's reply.

> We can certainly guarantee that it is logically possible for truth-ratio criteria to be correctly applied. It is logically possible that our native processes, together with our antecedently accepted scientific methods, should lead us to identify one or more rule systems that really do satisfy (ARI) or any other truth-ratio criteria. When it comes to factual possibility, though, the matter is open to doubt. It is conceivable that our actual cognitive resources are so poor, and our currently accepted scientific methods so weak, that they are incapable of correctly applying these criteria. I say that this is *conceivable,* but I am not inclined to think it is true. . . . (119)

> As long as we have some sufficiently reliable processes . . . and they are the sorts of processes needed for the question at hand, a right rule system would

permit the use of those processes. So we *could* arrive at a justified belief
about which particular rule system is right. (121)

Where does this reply leave Goldman with respect to skepticism? Ultimately,
Goldman is reduced to admitting that he must rely on the exercise of his
own empirical processes and methods to determine which empirical processes and methods are reliable, without having a guarantee that he has
applied the reliabilist criterion correctly. Ultimately, he has no way to defend his using some empirical claims to defend other empirical claims. An
analogy to Strawson is apt. Just as Strawson had to fall back on the claim
that, if his assertions about the role of certain beliefs in human belief-
structure are true, then skepticism is wrong, so, too, Goldman has to fall
back on the possibility that his procedures are reliable. He, like Strawson,
has no validation of his dialectical naturalism.

Goldman, to be sure, may not be alarmed. He thinks that traditional
epistemology has overemphasized skepticism anyway (39–41); hence he
might not be very disturbed by his own failure to defend his use of empirical processes and methods to determine what processes are reliable.
However, it is clear that Goldman sees his results as providing a response
of some type to some type of skepticism. If we reflect on just what this
response amounts to, we find it has very little connection to traditional
problems.

An investigator who wants to find out what processes people actually use in forming beliefs and who wants to ascertain the reliability of
these processes will come to one of two conclusions about each process
he or she studies: either the process is reliable relative to some particular
truth-ratio, or it is not. Goldman is decidedly open to the possibility that
many, most, or all of human belief-forming processes are unreliable; in
fact, when he studies specific processes — perception, memory, deductive
reasoning, probability judgments, etc. — his conclusions are not always favorable to the process under review. He insists that reliabilism gives us the
right criterion for justified belief; he does not insist that application of
the criterion shows humans to be reliable belief-formers. The right set of
substantive rules for justifiedness may not include anything "we" actually
utilize. This point becomes especially clear when Goldman distinguishes
a resource-relative criterion, which "fixes an acceptable truth-ratio as a function of the target cognitive system's resources," from a resource-independent
criterion, which "fixes an acceptable truth-ratio without regard to the (type
of) cognitive system in question" (104–105). He favors a resource-
independent criterion because "it makes the challenge of skepticism both
serious and credible," whereas a resource-relative criterion guarantees that
some human processes, viz., the best of the lot, can yield justified beliefs.

"Someone who wants to soften, or eliminate, the threat of global skepticism," will find resource-relative criteria congenial, but Goldman does not. It is quite clear that he is not loading the deck against skepticism, but, rather, begins empirical inquiry without preconceptions about the reliability of empirical methods (106).

Recall, however, that an inquirer who draws a conclusion, whether rosy or bleak, about the reliability of human belief-forming processes will have to trust the empirical methods and processes he utilizes in forming these conclusions. Now, once the inquirer is committed to this assumption, how will what he finds out about the general reliability of the processes be of significance to epistemology? If the inquirer undergoes processes and utilizes methods he trusts to identify processes and evaluate their reliability—perception, memory, inductive reasoning, statistical reasoning, deductive reasoning, attribution of propositional attitudes to others—the most the inquiry could tell him is whether these processes and methods are generally reliable, whether other people get true conclusions from their use. Granted this is the very stuff of cognitive psychology, or of some approaches to cog-sci, why should it matter for epistemology? If the inquirer did not already have trust in their reliability as he or she utilizes the processes, the inquirer could not trust the results of the inquiry. On the other hand, if the inquirer uses certain processes and methods because they are licensed according to his inquiry, he could not utilize those processes and methods before the inquiry is completed without falling into incoherence. Goldman's indifference to such problems emerges in a particular remark. He says that, even if empirical inquiry were to show that our cognitive processes are not sufficiently reliable, we might want to inquire into which processes are better than others, which ones come closer to a threshold of sufficient reliability (p. 40). That he would trust his inquiry to say which processes are better than others even though he would think the processes are not reliable enough—and that may include processes the inquirer uses—shows that Goldman simply trusts the methods and processes he is using in the course of his investigation. What we need to understand, in short, is the dialectical pattern here. What, precisely, is the relationship between the "conclusions" of the inquiry and the procedures by which the investigator reaches those conclusions? Dialectical naturalists have often sought to chart this relationship, but Goldman's remarks on Firth suggest he has no answer that would validate his procedure. He falls back on the *possibility* that the processes and methods of inquiry are reliable.[27]

Questions about the epistemological significance of Goldman's findings and the relation of his project to traditional skeptical questions arise with still greater force when we consider what it means, in Goldman's theory, to conclude that a particular process is or is not reliable. It is eminently clear that there is no *sans phrase* answer to the question, "Is process *P* reliable?" The answer will instead have to be relativized along several dimensions. First, we need to specify precisely what truth-ratio we regard as reliable enough for justifiedness. But no one truth-ratio is the "right" one to demand:

> For a belief to count as knowledge . . . it must be caused by a generally reliable process. Exactly *how* reliable I have not said. Nor do I think this can be answered with precision. The knowledge concept is vague on this dimension, and an analysis need not impose more precision than the common sense concept contains. (51)

> Since (ARI) does not designate any particular threshold, it is really a criterion-*schema*. A determinate criterion would be fixed by the choice of a threshold parameter. However, I am content to leave the theory with this degree of vagueness, since the ordinary concept of justifiedness is similarly vague. Before the theory could actually be applied, however, a specific threshold value would have to be chosen. (106)

So, we will not have a yes-no answer to "Is *P* a reliable enough process"; we will only have a string of claims of the following form: *P* is/not reliable given threshold *T;* beliefs formed by *P* are justified given threshold *T,* are not on *T',* are on *T",* etc. If this is the best we can hope for by way of results in our inquiry, why bother to get answers to the epistemological question? Why not just isolate the processes and figure out their degree of reliability? Why not, in other words, forget the philosophical, skeptical/anti-skeptical angle altogether, and just do straight cognitive psychology? In Quine's words: "Why not settle for psychology?"[28]

Goldman's account, as we have just seen, must be relativized to a truth-ratio threshold. A second dimension along which it must be relativized involves the way in which *P* is specified. Consider Goldman's discussion of probability judgments (chap. 14). Goldman cites the studies of Kahneman and Tversky, which claim that people, even those knowledgeable about probability theory and statistics, sin against probability theory by ignoring base-rate information, violating the conjunction rule, and being insensitive to sample size and regression toward the mean. In lieu of following probability theory, they make intuitive, incorrect judgments using a "representativeness heuristic." Should we conclude, therefore, that the representativeness (R-) routine, and with it probability judgments, are unreliable? Goldman says no: the use of representativeness is "a pervasive aspect of human cognition" and is reliable "for a large class of cases," which he identifies as "categorization" cases (322). So, the R-routine is highly reliable for categorization, not reliable for probability judgments. Goldman concludes his chapter by arguing that these two classes of cases are quite different and may actually involve "two different processes." After all this is said and done, what should we conclude about the reliability of probability judgments? Goldman's answer is a highly qualified one: we cannot conclude that the R-routine does yield justified beliefs in probability contexts; but "that possibility is not definitely precluded"; but "there are signs of trouble"; but "the gloomy diagnosis of the (local) skeptic is not vindicated" (323). With all this hedging; with all of the problems surrounding individuation of processes — it is well known that processes can be cut very finely or very coarsely; with all the problems involved with *counting* beliefs for the purposes of establishing a truth-ratio; with the further relativization that might be required for different historical periods, different geographic locales, as well as (more controversially) different genders or ethnic groupings; with the need to yet further relativize to a class of worlds in accordance with Goldman's full account of justified belief — with all that, why even try to settle the question of whether beliefs are or are not justified? Again, why not just catalogue the facts with as much precision as would interest a cognitive psychologist, and let the matter rest there?

Thus, whereas the first stage of Goldman's inquiry — the formulation of *criteria* for justified belief — is conducted in a standard philosophical way (examining intuitions about justifiedness and intuitions about specific cases in the hope of reaching "reflective equilibrium") and is empirical only to the extent that reports of others' intuitions are empirically based, the second stage — identifying human processes and determining their reliability — seems not philosophical at all. Goldman is hardly oblivious of this criticism; on the contrary, he formulates it squarely:

> Why shouldn't epistemology stop at the selection of a rightness *criterion?* Why should epistemology include the job of formulating the J-rules (or J-rule systems) that actually satisfy the criterion? (96)

He replies (1) that epistemology has traditionally been occupied with the endorsement of particular methods and procedures; (2) that stopping inquiry without trying to see which rule-systems are right is "unnatural"; (3) that "the prospects for this sort of skepticism [about the existence of justified belief and knowledge] stand or fall with the existence or nonexistence of J-rules satisfying the criterion" (97). By now my response to (3) should be clear: this is not an interesting form of skepticism; the interesting form would be directed at the empirical inquiry itself. Further, Goldman's relativizing of reliability to both thresholds and the way processes are specified precludes coming to a clear answer anyway. With respect to (1), Goldman is certainly right that epistemology has been occupied with

endorsing methods and procedures, but the methods and procedures epistemologists were after were methods and procedures that could be defended
against *dialectical* skepticism. To use empirical inquiry to formulate J-
rules, but not provide a defense of one's procedures against charges of circularity, is *not* to occupy oneself with "the endorsement of methods and
procedures" in the traditional sense. Finally, point (2) (that stopping after
formulation of a criterion is "unnatural") depends heavily on Goldman's
own predisposition; stopping, or at least moving to projects other than
Goldman's, is not unnatural for traditional epistemologists. The aim of
the traditional epistemologist is to see whether beliefs are justifi*able* in
dialectical contexts. The aim is not to determine whether, assuming we ignore problems posed by the dialectical context, particular people are justified by this-or-that reliabilist criterion given this-or-that description of
the process.

Goldman's conceptual analysis is fine as a piece of epistemology, and
his concern with it certainly prevents him from turning into a replacement
naturalist *à la* Quine. However, once we pass the stage of conceptual analysis, we are not doing anything Quine could not include in his replacement
naturalism. To do something distinctively epistemological would be to validate the processes and methods introduced in the inquiry into various processes and methods, without falling into circularity or incoherence — circularity if the inquiry is favorable, incoherence if it is not. This Goldman
does not do. As it stands, Goldman's procedure has the structure of Quine's
"Epistemology Naturalized": work from within science, stop dreaming of
validation, ignore circularity, describe human cognition. I do not see that
he has grappled with the problem of justification in any deeper sense.[29]

5. Summation: Despair or Dialectical Naturalism?

In contrast to the "replacement" version of methodological naturalism, integrative methodological naturalism utilizes empirical findings about
belief-formation to address traditional problems in the theory of knowledge. By reflecting on the approaches we have canvassed, we can discern
some of the unifying themes — and common problems — of integrative methodological naturalistic approaches to skepticism.

The most striking feature of integrative methodological naturalists'
writings on skepticism is their indifference to dialectical naturalism — to
the problems of circularity and relativism and to the force of specific skeptical attacks. Since skeptics claim we do *not* have dialectically effective
arguments for common sense or science, this indifference severely under-

cuts the ability of methodological naturalists to deal with skepticism in an effective way. Strawson freely uses claims about human belief structures; Goldman, claims about the processes and methods which people use and about the reliability of those processes and methods as used by the inquirer. For skeptics, this is like using biblical texts to verify the Bible's veracity against the doubts of agnostics. To redress their lack of a dialectically effective argument, integrative methodological naturalists would have to show that dialectical failure is irrelevant to "the skeptical problem"—this, by reconceptualizing what the problem of skepticism *is*. Attempts to do this have not been successful. In the case of Strawson, no such alternative conceptualization is forthcoming, and in fact part of his approach (the undislodgability argument) ignores a "second-order" construal of skepticism. In the case of conceptual naturalists, the problem of skepticism is reconceived as the following problem: showing that skeptics have not established that we do not have knowledge or justified belief (i.e., arguing for agnosticism on this issue is enough to rebut skepticism). I have argued that this construal of skepticism is much too weak and that conceptual naturalists' answers are of no use against more powerful forms. Finally, for Goldman, the problem of skepticism is determining whether methods and processes that people actually utilize to form beliefs are reliable—but only, I have argued, *assuming the reliability of the inquirer's methods*. It does not seem to me that the results of this inquiry will affect the skeptic in any serious way; a real skeptic would want to be shown by dialectically effective argument that empirical methods like those of the inquirer are reliable. In sum, try as they might, naturalists cannot find a construal of skepticism on which dialectical failure and dialectical success are irrelevant to the fate of the skeptical challenge.

Quine saw this clearly. He saw, that is, that the real project of traditional epistemology is to come up with a dialectically effective reply to the skeptic. In "Epistemology Naturalized," he despaired of achieving this goal. If he was right, and if, furthermore, I am right that many integrative methodological naturalist responses to skepticism are flawed, naturalists need to work hard if they want to avoid ending up in replacement naturalism.

Can replacement naturalism be avoided? One way of avoiding it is to retreat into conceptual analysis. Another (closely related) is to put a stress on normativity that is not found in Quine and develop a nonreductionist account of norms. But something more ambitious is possible, and that is to defend dialectical naturalism.

Easier said than done, of course, but there are at least two interesting routes to take. In closing, I should like to comment briefly on where these routes can take us.

First, Quine thought he could rebut skeptical arguments from illusion, for example, by showing that the skeptic presupposes science. Unfortunately, Quine's strategy suffers from several limitations. First, it works, at best, only against a subset of skeptical arguments, viz. those arguments which trade off of scientifically established modes of cognitive error.[30] Second, Quine's strategy offers no positive reason to endorse our nonskeptical view of the world; rather it merely rebuts skeptical arguments. And third, as critics like Barry Stroud and Ernest Sosa have pointed out, the skeptic's argument can be recast as a dilemma:[31] "Either science is true, or science is false. If science is false, we obviously are mistaken. But if science is true, then we cannot claim to have knowledge of the world." Once the skeptic's argument is formulated this way, the skeptic need not presuppose the truth of science in order to make his case. Now the crucial step in the skeptic's argument is that if science is true, then we cannot claim to have knowledge of the world. While I am not as convinced as Stroud that this premise is correct,[32] he certainly has lodged a *prima facie* challenge to Quine's assertion that skeptics start out with scientific claims.

A second route, one free of these limitations, is suggested by Michael Friedman in "Truth and Confirmation": we can use empirical methods to validate empirical methods because there is no antecedent guarantee that our inquiry will validate the methods and hence no circularity in our procedure. What we get in Friedman is a genuinely dialectical naturalism. Empirical data are relevant to epistemology and must be invoked if skepticism is to be met. But they are relevant and necessary only as part of a larger dialectical argument that seeks to nullify charges of circularity. A question we must ask about Friedman's pattern of argument is whether it can persuade someone who does not accept our methods — or, rather, can show us only why our procedures are good *on our own terms*.[33]

Despair, at any rate, is not the only note possible in reviewing skeptical arguments, as there may be ways to justify the free use of scientific data. Further examination of the prospects is beyond the scope of this essay. Nonetheless, whatever the ultimate fate of arguments like Quine's and Friedman's, I hope I have persuaded readers that the real choice we face is between despair and dialectical naturalism. And what about the point (made by Quine) that dialectical naturalism, precisely because it rebuts skepticism, gives us, no less than despair does, a license to move on to empirical inquiry and leave skepticism behind? I can only respond thus: no, epistemology will continue as long as philosophers debate, as they inevitably will, the cogency of specific arguments for dialectical naturalism.[34]

Notes

1. W. V. O. Quine, "Epistemology Naturalized," in *Ontological Relativity and Other Essays* (New York: Columbia University Press, 1969), 69–90, (henceforth referred to as *EN*). Quine actually speaks of the "reciprocal containment" of psychology and epistemology in this essay, but the simplistic formulation "replacement" is enough for my purposes.

2. This should not be construed as anything more than a generic statement of the argument, as my formulation prescinds from the details of Quine's critique: the particular projects of conceptual and doctrinal reduction he was attacking, the role of holism in his argument, the role of his opposition to analyticity and to "first philosophy," etc. In embracing the despair argument, Quine strongly resembles Hume, on one reasonable reading of Hume (see Barry Stroud, *Hume* [London: Routledge and Kegan Paul, 1977]). On this reading, Hume passes through two stages in his argument, a skeptical stage and a naturalistic one. Since our beliefs cannot be validated against skeptical attacks (skeptical stage) we must turn our attention to a task that is purely descriptive and explanatory (naturalistic stage). That Hume was studying the acquisition of commonsense beliefs rather than of science should not obscure this basic similarity in argumentation.

3. Quine, *The Roots of Reference* (LaSalle, Ill.: Open Court, 1974), 3. Henceforth referred to as *RR*. As explained below, Quine's route to replacement naturalism in *RR* is different from that taken in *EN*.

While Quine's favored replacement for traditional epistemology is psychology, and indeed psychology will remain the focus of naturalized epistemologies I will consider, replacement naturalists are not bound to follow this preference. Sociology, history, anthropology, neuroscience, and evolutionary biology will do just as well as psychology, as will any conjunction of these. For the heart of replacement naturalism is that empirical inquiry of *some* kind replaces traditional epistemology.

4. The term "replacement naturalism" is used by Hilary Kornblith in "What Is Naturalistic Epistemology?" in Kornblith, ed., *Naturalized Epistemology* (Cambridge, Mass.: MIT Press, 1985), 1–21.

5. The status of normativity in Quine's philosophy is a contested topic. Critics maintain that the kind of epistemology Quine is bent on has no room for the *evaluation* and *justification* of scientific claims, but only for description of their psychological origins. See, e.g., Harvey Siegel, "Justification, Discovery and the Naturalizing of Epistemology," *Philosophy of Science* 47 (1980): 297–321; Siegel, "Empirical Psychology, Naturalized Epistemology, and First Philosophy," *Philosophy of Science* 51 (1984): 667–676; Jaegwon Kim, "What Is 'Naturalized Epistemology'?" in James E. Tomberlin, ed., *Philosophical Perspectives, 2: Epistemology.* (Atascadero, Calif.: Ridgeview, 1988), 381–405. Quine might reply, "that isn't a *criticism* of my theory, that *is* my theory." However, Kim argues that Quine, contrary to his intention, cannot really avoid the normative, because (1) the "evidence-theory" relation he speaks about is normative, (2) the attribution of beliefs to human subjects, so central to replacement naturalism, cannot proceed without normative

considerations that will guide the attributions. In contrast to Siegel and Kim, other writers maintain that Quine does not want to reject normativity. See Roger Gibson, *Enlightened Empiricism: An Examination of W. V. O. Quine's Theory of Knowledge* (Tampa, Fla.: University of South Florida Press, 1988), 68, and Hilary Putnam, "Why Reason Can't Be Naturalized," *Synthese* 52 (1982): 3–23, p. 19.

6. Elliot Sober, "Psychologism," *Journal for the Theory of Social Behavior* 8 (1978): 165–191, p. 166.

7. A word is in order concerning the contrast between "naturalized" and "traditional" epistemology. Some naturalized epistemologists correctly insist that, "traditionally," epistemology *has* been naturalistic to the extent of seeking answers to *psychological* questions. The case of Hume needs no elaboration, but Alvin I. Goldman, *Epistemology and Cognition* (Cambridge, Mass.: Harvard University Press, 1986), 6–9, makes a strong case for a more general separation of "traditional" from "apsychological." In fact, some "traditional epistemologists" might think that some historically central figures, e.g., Locke, *confuse* epistemology and psychology. A historical division is not the important one, then, in distinguishing naturalized and non-naturalized epistemologists. Nevertheless, it is safe to characterize the refutation of skepticism and the formulation of norms as "traditional *issues,*" and then pursue the question of whether naturalism contributes to the fulfillment of the tasks on the "traditional" agenda. As for conceptual analysis, Mark Kaplan denies this has been a historically central project. See his "It's Not What You Know That Counts," *Journal of Philosophy* 82 (1985): 350–363.

8. A useful look at some possibilities is provided by Robert G. Meyers in "Naturalizing Epistemic Terms," in Newton Garver and Peter Hare, eds., *Naturalism and Rationality* (Buffalo, N.Y.: Prometheus Books, 1986), 141–154.

9. For elaboration on these difficulties of labeling, see William G. Lycan, *Judgment and Justification* (New York: Cambridge University Press, 1988), chap. 5.

10. What "may" and "must" would mean for Quine in these formulations, I do not profess to know.

11. Quine, "The Nature of Natural Knowledge," in Samuel L. Guttenplan, ed., *Mind and Language* (Oxford: Clarendon Press, 1975), 67–81, at p. 67. This sort of reply is found in ancient responses to skepticism. See the quotation from Aristocles in Julia Annas and Jonathan Barnes, *The Modes of Scepticism* (New York: Cambridge University Press, 1985), 44–45. For a cogent elaboration of Quine's approach (without explicit reference to Quine's statements) see James Bogen, "Traditional Epistemology and Naturalistic Replies to Its Skeptical Critics," *Synthese* 64 (1985): 195–224. Criticism of Quine may be found in Barry Stroud, *The Significance of Philosophical Scepticism* (New York: Oxford University Press, 1984), chap. 6, and in Ernest Sosa, "Nature Unmirrored, Epistemology Naturalized," *Synthese* 55 (1983): 49–72, pp. 64–70. A different version of dialectical naturalism is developed by Michael Friedman, "Truth and Confirmation," *Journal of Philosophy* 76 (1979): 361–382.

12. Peter Strawson, *Skepticism and Naturalism* (New York: Columbia University Press, 1985).

13. We should note here the view of Robert Fogelin in *Hume's Skepticism*

in the *Treatise of Human Nature* (London: Routledge-Kegan-Paul, 1985) that even for Hume, skeptical arguments serve a purpose: they induce a sense of modesty in inquiry and deter the inquirer from extending inquiry too far.

14. For this objection and another two paragraphs hence, I am indebted to Ernest Sosa, "Beyond Skepticism, to the Best of Our Knowledge," *Mind* 97 (1988): 153–188. (I am probably oversimplifying Berkeley.)

15. The idea that skepticism cannot be conquered by a dialectically effective argument unless that argument is attributable to ordinary believers is found in several writers. See, e.g., Sober, "Psychologism," 188–189; Anthony Quinton, *The Nature of Things* (London: Routledge-Kegan-Paul, 1973), 116. Quine makes clear that, since, if there is one rational reconstruction, there are many (*EN*, 75), therefore, naturalized epistemology is to be preferred to "fictitious history." It is this point that underlies his question, "Why not settle for psychology?" Sober seems to be playing off of this idea. Cf. my "Epistemic Terms and the Aims of Epistemology," in James H. Fetzer, David Shatz, and George N. Schlesinger, eds., *Definitions and Definability: Philosophical Perspectives* (Leiden: Kluwer, 1991), 187–202.

16. Cf. Alan Goldman, "Epistemology and the Psychology of Perception," *American Philosophical Quarterly* 18 (1981): 43–51.

17. This position is treated by Kornblith in his introduction to *Naturalized Epistemology*. There is a good deal of literature evaluating its tenability in light of recent empirical work demonstrating human irrationality. Important empirical work includes Robert Nisbet and Lee Ross, *Human Inference: Strategies and Shortcomings of Social Judgment* (Englewood Cliffs, N.J.: Prentice-Hall, 1980); Daniel Kahnemann, Paul Slovic, and Amos Tversky, eds., *Judgment Under Uncertainty: Heuristics and Biases* (Cambridge: Cambridge University Press, 1982). Jonathan L. Cohen argues for an a priori convergence between norms and actual human competence in "Can Human Irrationality Be Experimentally Demonstrated?" *Behavioral and Brain Sciences* 4 (1981): 317–331. The same issue of that journal and some subsequent issues contain discussions of Cohen's argument. For other important criticism, see the expanded version of Stephen Stich's comments: "Could Man Be An Irrational Animal?" *Synthese* 64 (1985): 115–135. Sober also defends the attribution of correct norms to human beings, but on empirical grounds: unlike Cohen, Sober does not argue that the norms and the actual practice *must* converge.

18. See Stroud, *Hume*, chap. 1.

19. See Robert Nozick, *Philosophical Explanations* (Cambridge: Harvard University Press, 1981), 167–288; Fred Dretske, "Conclusive Reasons," *Australasian Journal of Philosophy* 49 (1971): 1–22; and many others.

20. I evaluate this strategy in "Foundationalism, Coherentism, and the Levels Gambit," *Synthese* 55 (1983): 97–118. An outstanding treatment of circularity is William Alston, "Epistemic Circularity," in his *Epistemic Justification* (Ithaca, N.Y.: Cornell University Press, 1989).

21. These objections have been developed most fully and famously in Laurence BonJour, *The Structure of Empirical Knowledge* (Cambridge, Mass.: Harvard University Press, 1985).

22. In fairness to Nozick in particular, he says he is interested only in pro-

viding a "philosophical explanation" of how we can attribute knowledge to our-selves if we realize that we have no dialectically effective argument against skep-tical possibilities obtaining. Thus, his aim is to establish the coherence of our commonsense framework and not to reply to the skeptic. Note that Nozick would then surely not be answering the traditional problem. I develop criticisms of No-zick in "Nozick's Conception of Skepticism," in Steven Luper-Foy, ed., *The Possibility of Knowledge: Nozick and His Critics* (Totowa, N.J.: Rowman & Littlefield, 1987), 242-266.

23. Evaluations of the possibility argument may be found in Marjorie Clay and Keith Lehrer, eds., *Knowledge & Skepticism* (San Francisco, Westview Press, 1989). See especially the introduction by Clay and Lehrer, William Alston's "A 'Doxastic Practice' Approach to Epistemology," and Barry Stroud's "Understanding Human Knowledge in General," which is very much in the spirit of my objections. Cf. also my "Epistemic Terms and the Aims of Epistemology," sect. I.

24. Alvin Goldman, *Epistemology and Cognition* (Cambridge, Mass.: Harvard University Press, 1986).

25. Readers familiar with Goldman's work will note that I have ignored various nuances of his argument, including his concern with the power and speed of processes as well as their reliability and such distinctions as that between primary and secondary epistemics. These distinctions are important to an accurate exposition of Goldman's views, but the simplified exposition I have adopted, I believe, focuses the issues more clearly. I do not think that the material omitted from my summary affects my main argument.

26. Roderick Firth, "Epistemic Merit, Intrinsic and Instrumental," *Proceedings and Addresses of the American Philosophical Association* 55 (1981): 5-23.

27. Goldman has a brief reply to charges of circularity on pp. 393-394, note 21, when he discusses the topic of induction. For effective criticism of these remarks, see Douglas Winblad, "Skepticism and Natural Epistemology," *Philosophia* 19 (1989): 99-113, pp. 103-106. That Goldman deals with the problem only in a footnote underscores my claim that he is not worried about circularity. Cf. his remarks on p. 120, and also see note 29 below.

28. Fred Dretske expresses such worries in his review of Goldman in *Journal of Philosophy* 85 (1988): 265-270.

29. After writing this essay, I learned that Douglas Winblad raised to Goldman the question of whether we could discover that all our cognitive processes are unreliable (call this proposition *U*). Playing off the sort of incoherence I discuss, Winblad maintains that, for Goldman, we can never be justified in believing *U*. Goldman replies "that an analogous point holds for *any* account of justificational rightness, not just a reliability account." Goldman is right about this, but his response confirms rather than weakens my argument in this section: for my argument is a general argument to the effect that we cannot empirically discover anything about whether our beliefs are justified without already having what we regard as justified beliefs. I do *not* claim that only reliabilism will have trouble with using empirical inquiry for this purpose. The Winblad-Goldman exchange is in *Philosophia* 19 (1989): Winblad, "Skepticism and Naturalized Epistemology," 99-113, and Goldman, "Replies to the Commentators," 301-303.

More recent work by Goldman expresses a different conception of the relationships among various epistemological projects from the conception conveyed by *Epistemology and Cognition,* but this material appeared as this essay was in press. See "Epistemic Folkways and Scientific Epistemology," in Goldman, *Liaisons* (Cambridge, Mass.: MIT Press, 1992), 155–175.

30. See Goldman, *Epistemology and Cognition,* 57.

31. See the Stroud and Sosa critiques cited in note 11.

32. The crucial issue is exactly what feature of science the skeptic builds on. If he builds on the occurrence of illusions, it is *not* true that if science is right, we do not have knowledge; for if science is right, we *can* differentiate cases of illusions, hallucinations, etc., from veridical experiences. On the other hand, if the skeptic builds on the gap between sensory evidence and theory, then science may indeed turn out to be self-determining. See Stroud, *Significance of Philosophical Scepticism,* 228, and Sosa, "Nature Unmirrored," 67.

33. Friedman, himself, is therefore cautious about the utility of his argument against a skeptic. "The aim of confirmation theory is not to persuade someone who rejects our inductive methods to adopt them. Rather, it is to explain to ourselves what is so good about the methods we actually employ" (end of section 2 of his article). Despite this cautionary note, Friedman's point marks an advance in anti-skeptical argument.

34. I thank Steven Wagner and Hilary Kornblith for their comments.

What Am I to Believe?

Richard Foley

The central issue of Descartes's *Meditations* is an intensely personal one. Descartes asks a simple question of himself, one that each of us can also ask of ourselves, "What am I to believe?" One way of construing this question — indeed, the way Descartes himself construed it — is as a methodological one. The immediate aim is not so much to generate a specific list of propositions for me to believe. Rather, I want to formulate for myself some general advice about how to proceed intellectually.

If this is what I want, I am not likely to be content with telling myself that I am to use reliable methods of inquiry. Nor will I be content with telling myself to believe only that which is likely to be true given my evidence. It is not as if such advice is mistaken. It is just unhelpful. I knew all along that it is better for me to use reliable methods rather than unreliable ones, and I also knew that it is better for me to believe that which is likely to be true rather than that which is not. Besides, I cannot simply read off from the world what methods are reliable ones, nor can I read off when something is likely to be true given my evidence. These are just the sorts of things about which I want advice.

An appeal to the prevailing intellectual standards will not provide what I am looking for either. I will not be satisfied with a recommendation that tells me to conduct my inquiries in accordance with the standards of my community, or alternatively in accordance with the standards of those recognized in my community as experts. I will want to know whether these standards are desirable ones. The dominant standards in a community are not always to be trusted and those of the recognized experts are not either.

My question is a more fundamental one and also a more egocentric one. It is not that I think that the task of working out intellectual guidelines is one that is best conducted by myself in solitude. If I do think this, I am being foolish. A task of this sort is better done in full public view, with results being shared. This increases the chances of correction and

147

decreases the chances of self-deception. In the end, however, I must make up my own mind. I must make up my own mind about what is true and who is reliable and what is worth respecting in my intellectual tradition. It is this that prompts the question, what am I to believe? The question is one of how I am to go about making up my own mind.

Here is one way of answering this question: I am to make up my mind by marshalling my intellectual resources in a way that conforms to my own deepest epistemic standards. If I conduct my inquiries in such a way that I would not be critical of the resulting beliefs even if I were to be deeply reflective, then these beliefs are rational for me in an important sense, an egocentric sense. There are various ways of trying to spell out exactly what this amounts to, but for purposes here the details can be left open. The basic idea is that if I am to be egocentrically rational, I must not have internal reasons for retraction, ones whose force I myself would acknowledge were I to be sufficiently reflective.

An answer of this sort has the right egocentric flavor, but as advice it is not very satisfying. It seems misdirected. When I am trying to formulate some intellectual advice for myself, or more generally when I am deliberating about what to believe and how to proceed intellectually, my concern is not with my own standards. The point of my deliberations is not to find out what I think or would think on deep reflection about the reliability of various methods. My concern is with what methods are in fact reliable; it is with the objective realities, not my subjective perceptions.

Be this as it may, the recommendation that I conform to my own standards is an appropriate answer to the egocentric question, "What am I to believe?" More precisely, it is an appropriate answer if the question is interpreted as one about what I am to believe insofar as my ends are epistemic. Even more precisely, it is an appropriate philosophical answer to this question, the one that should be given if the question is pushed to its limit. The reflection prompted by the egocentric question initially has an outward focus. The object of my concern is the world. I wonder whether this or that is true. If pushed hard enough, however, the reflection ultimately curls back upon me. I become concerned with my place in the world, especially my place as an inquirer. I want to know what methods of inquiry are suitable for me insofar as I am trying to determine whether this or that is true. Should I trust the evidence of my senses? Should I use scientific methods? Should I rely on sacred texts? Should I have confidence in my intuitions?

These questions can lead to still others. They can make me wonder about the criteria that I am presupposing in evaluating various methods. Meta-issues thus begin to occupy me. My primary concern is no longer with whether it would be more reliable for me to use this method rather than that one. Nor is it with what each would have me believe. Rather, it is with my criteria for evaluating these various methods and in turn with the criteria for these criteria, and so on. This is the point at which the egocentric question can be appropriately answered by talking about me. What am I to believe? Ultimately, I am to believe that which is licensed by my own deepest epistemic standards. An answer of this sort is the appropriate one for epistemologists. It is the appropriate answer for those whose reflections on the egocentric question take them to this level.

Insofar as nonepistemologists raise the question of what they are to believe, they are principally interested in a different kind of answer. They want an answer that gives them marks of truth and reliability. Epistemologists also want such marks, but once their deliberations reach the meta-level that is characteristic of epistemology, they are forced to admit that regardless of how they marshal their intellectual resources, there are no non–question-begging guarantees that the way that they are marshalling them is reliable. Vulnerability to error cannot be avoided. It is built into us and our methods. However, vulnerability to self-condemnation is not, and it is essentially this that egocentric rationality demands. It demands that we have beliefs that we as truth-seekers would not condemn ourselves for having even if we were to be deeply reflective. This is the post-Cartesian answer to the Cartesian question.

It is also an answer that is bound to be disappointing to anyone who thinks that an essential part of the epistemologist's job is to provide intellectual guidance. Much of the attractiveness of the Cartesian method of doubt is that it purports to do just this. It purports to provide us with a way of proceeding intellectually, and a concrete one at that. The proposed method tends to strike the contemporary reader as overly demanding, but it would nonetheless seem to be to Descartes's credit, indeed part of his greatness, that he at least attempted to provide such guidance. Contemporary epistemology is apt to seem barren by comparison. Concrete intellectual advice has all but disappeared from it. Of course, no one expects epistemologists to provide advice about local intellectual concerns. The specialist is better placed to give us that—the physicist, the mathematician, the meteorologist, whoever the relevant expert happens to be. What we might like from epistemologists, however, is useful advice about the most basic matters of intellectual inquiry, but it is just this that contemporary epistemology fails to provide.

This is to be regretted only if epistemologists are in a privileged position to give such advice, but they are not. They may be in a privileged position to say something about the general conditions of rational belief. Likewise, they may be able to say interesting things about the conditions of knowledge and other related notions. The mistake is to assume that these conditions should provide us with useful guidelines for the most basic matters of intellectual inquiry. They cannot. The conditions will either be misdirected or not fundamental enough or both.

Consider the proposal that at least in one sense, being rational is essentially a matter of using methods that are reliable. Perhaps this is so, but if a proposal of this sort is meant to provide me with intellectual guidance, I must be able to distinguish reliable from unreliable methods. However, this is precisely one of the matters about which I will want advice. It is also a matter about which epistemologists are not in a privileged position to give advice, except indirectly. They may have useful and even surprising things to say about what reliability is, but once these things are said, it will be up to the rest of us to apply what they say. We will have to determine what methods and procedures are in fact reliable. So, no condition of this sort will be able to provide me with fundamental intellectual advice. On the contrary, if such conditions are to help guide inquiry, I must already be able to make the kind of determinations that they themselves imply are fundamental for me to make if I am to be rational. I reliably must be able to pick out which methods are reliable.

The same is true of other proposals. One proposal, for instance, is that I am rational only if I conform to the standards of the acknowledged experts.[1] If I am to use this to guide inquiry, I once again must be able to make determinations of just the sort that are said to be fundamental to my being rational. How am I to determine what the relevant expert standards are? Presumably by conducting an inquiry that itself conforms to the standards of the experts. But which standards are these, I want to know.

Suppose that the proposal is more inwardly looking. In particular, consider the proposal that it is rational in an important sense, an egocentric sense, for me to believe only that which I would not be motivated to retract even on deep reflection. If what I want is advice, this proposal is a non-starter. It is misdirected. Besides, I do not have the time to be deeply reflective about everything that I believe. So, even here I would be confronted with the problem of knowing how to apply the recommendation. How am I to determine whether my practices and my resulting beliefs conform with my own deep epistemic standards, the ones that I would approve of on reflection? Presumably by conforming to those very standards. But what I want to know, and what is often by no means obvious, is how I am to do this, short of being deeply reflective about all of these practices and beliefs?

The only way to avoid problems of this sort is to make the conditions of rationality ones to which we have immediate and unproblematic access. But this has a familiar and unpromising ring to it. Recall Bertrand Russell's epistemology, for example. He claimed that we are directly acquainted with certain truths and that these truths make various other propositions probable for us. If this kind of epistemology is to provide us with fundamental intellectual advice, we must be capable of determining immediately and unproblematically when we are directly acquainted with something and when we are not. Likewise, we must be capable of determining immediately and unproblematically what propositions are made probable by the truths with which we are directly acquainted. Otherwise we will want advice about how to make these kinds of determinations. Russell's epistemology leaves room for the possibility that we do have these capabilities. Being directly acquainted with something is itself the sort of phenomenon with which we can be directly acquainted. Similarly, according to Russell's epistemology, we can be directly acquainted with the truth that one thing makes another thing probable.[2]

An epistemology of direct acquaintance or something closely resembling it is our only alternative if we expect the conditions of rationality to give us useful advice about those matters that the conditions themselves imply are fundamental to our being rational. It is also the kind of epistemology that few are willing to take seriously anymore. But if not, we must give up the idea that epistemology is in the business of giving fundamental intellectual advice. For that matter, we must give up the whole idea that there is such advice to be had. There can be no general recipe for the conduct of our intellectual lives, if for no other reason than that questions can always arise about how to follow the recipe, questions to which the recipe itself can give no useful answer.

By contrast, consider the kind of advice that logic professors sometimes give their students. They sometimes tell them to try to solve difficult proofs from "both ends," working alternatively down from the premises and up from the desired conclusion. This is advice that is often useful for students, but it is also advice that has no pretenses of being about the most fundamental issues of inquiry. It is not even about the most fundamental matters of logical inference. This is no accident. It is useful precisely because it is embedded in a prior intellectual enterprise, one in which certain skills and abilities are taken for granted.

This is an obvious enough point once it is made explicit, but it is nonetheless a point that is easy enough to overlook. It is overlooked, for instance, by those internalists who argue against externalist conditions of rational belief on the grounds that they are unhelpful insofar as we are interested in advice about how to go about improving our belief systems. As a complaint against externalism, this will not do, but not because externalist conditions of rational belief provide us with useful advice. They do not. It is not especially useful to be told that we are to have beliefs that are products of reliable cognitive processes, for example. The problem, rather, is that internalist conditions of rational belief do not provide us with genuinely useful advice either.

Of course, internalists have often thought otherwise. One of Descartes's conceits, for example, was that the method of doubt provides advice to inquirers that is at once both useful and fundamental. By this I do not mean that Descartes intended his method to be used by everyone, even the fishmonger and the butcher. He did not. He intended it to be used only by philosopher-scientists, and he intended that even they use it only for a special purpose. It was not to be used in their everyday lives. It was to be used only for the purpose of conducting secure theoretical inquiry. However, the method was intended to provide advice at the most fundamental level about how to conduct such inquiry.

But, in fact, it fails to do this. It faces the same difficulties as other attempts to give intellectual advice that is both fundamental and useful. Either it presupposes that philosopher-scientists can make determinations of a sort that the recommendation itself says is fundamental or it is misdirected advice or perhaps both. Which of these difficulties Descartes's advice is subject to depends on how we understand it.

Suppose the advice is for philosopher-scientists to believe just those propositions whose truth they cannot doubt when they bring them clearly to mind. Then the advice faces both difficulties. First, it is not fundamental enough. It need not be immediately obvious to philosopher-scientists just what is indubitable for them in this sense and what is not. They thus can have questions about that which the advice says is fundamental to their being rational, and these will be questions that the advice cannot help them answer. Second, the advice is misdirected. It is advice that looks inward rather than outward. Insofar as the goal of philosopher-scientists is to conduct theoretical inquiry in an absolutely secure manner, their interest is to find propositions that cannot be false rather than ones that cannot be doubted. Of course, Descartes thought that there was a linkage between the two. He thought that what cannot be subjectively doubted cannot be objectively false, but there is no reason to think that he was right about this.

Suppose, then, that we interpret Descartes as offering more objective advice. He is telling philosopher-scientists to believe just those propositions that are clear and distinct for them, and he is stipulating from the very beginning that only truths can be genuinely clear and distinct. Then this exacerbates the first difficulty. If philosopher-scientists try to take the advice to heart, the question of whether something really is clear and distinct in this sense becomes one of the fundamental issues about which they will want advice.[3]

So, contrary to his hopes, Descartes did not succeed in providing advice that is both useful and fundamental. More precisely, he did not succeed in providing advice about the conduct of inquiry as opposed to its goals. For despite the above difficulties, we can still view Descartes as making a recommendation about what our intellectual goal should be. He is advising us to make certainty our goal, at least for theoretical purposes. We should try to believe as much as possible without encountering the risk of error. Of course, even this is advice that few of us would be willing to take seriously. The goal is far too demanding. Almost all of us are willing to put up with some risks of error in our theoretical pursuits.

But the important point here is that even if I did have this as my intellectual goal, Descartes has no good, substantive advice for me about how to achieve it. The advice he gives is either misdirected or not fundamental enough. If the advice is to believe what is clear and distinct, where by definition only truths are clear and distinct, it is not fundamental enough. If the advice is to believe what I cannot doubt, it is misdirected. At best, it is a piece of meta-advice. Indeed, when stripped of its spurious guarantees of truth, the advice amounts only to this: insofar as my goal is to believe as much as possible without risk, then from my perspective the way to go about trying to achieve this goal is to believe just that which strikes me as being risk-free and then hope for the best.

This is a sensible enough recommendation but also an altogether safe one. After all, someone can give me this kind of advice even if she has no convictions one way or the other about whether or not I am constituted in such a way that what I find impossible to doubt is in fact true. It is not much different from telling me to do what I think is best about the problem I have confided to her, even when she has no idea whether what I think best really is best.

Of course, if she were presumptuous enough, she could go on to advise me about what I myself deep-down really think is the best way to deal with the problem. Indeed, this would be the counterpart of Descartes's strategy. He first recommends that I believe just those propositions that I cannot doubt, and he then tries to tell me, albeit with a notorious lack of success, which propositions these are. On the other hand, if she is not in this way presumptuous, if she simply tells me to do what I think is best and then leave matters at that, this is not so much genuine advice as a substitute for it. She is not trying to tell me what is best for me. She leaves this to me to figure out for myself.

The recommendation that I have beliefs that I as a truth-seeker would not condemn myself for having, even if I were to be deeply reflective, has a similar status. This recommendation is internalistic in character, since it emphasizes matters of perspective. But insofar as it is conceived as a piece of advice, it is at best meta-advice. If it were interpreted as an attempt to provide me with something more than this — if it were interpreted, for example, as an attempt to provide me with serious, substantive intellectual guidance — it would be clearly inadequate. So, this cannot be the charitable way to interpret it. It must instead be conceived as a different kind of recommendation.

What kind of recommendation? It is a recommendation about the conditions of rational belief — more exactly, the conditions for a certain kind of rational belief, egocentrically rational belief. The goal is to provide a notion of rational belief that is both enlightening and recognizable: enlightening in that it helps us think more clearly about related notions — truth, knowledge, skepticism, dogmatism, and intellectual disagreement, to name a few; and recognizable in that it helps us to understand the ascriptions of rationality that we want to make, both the ones we are inclined to make in our everyday lives and also the ones we are inclined to make when doing epistemology.

This conception takes epistemology, even internalist epistemology, out of the business of giving intellectual advice. The primary epistemological project is to offer an account of the conditions of rational belief, and there is no reason why this project must generate useful advice. Indeed, epistemology is not even the part of philosophy that is most closely tied to the giving of intellectual advice. Studies in logic and probability are more likely to generate useful advice than is epistemology proper. But even here, expectations should not be too high. Nothing extensive in the way of advice will come out of these studies either.

In part, this is so because logic and probability theory do not tell how to react when we discover logical inconsistency and probabilistic incoherence. There will be any number of ways for us to restore consistency or coherency. Similarly, when inconsistency or incoherency threatens, there will be any number of ways for us to avoid them. In neither case does logic or probability theory have anything to tell us about which of these many ways is preferable.[4]

So, there will not be much in the way of concrete positive advice that can come out of either logic or probability theory. In addition, there are limits even to the usefulness of the negative advice they are able to generate. Part of this is because of a familiar problem. Insofar as the advice is always to avoid inconsistency and incoherency, this is often difficult advice to follow. To do so, we need to be able to determine whether or not a set of opinions is inconsistent or incoherent, but the original advice cannot help with this. For help with this problem, we will need new advice — in effect, advice about how to apply the original advice.

Moreover, there is an even more basic limitation on this advice. It is not always good advice. It is not always and everywhere desirable to avoid inconsistency and incoherency. Doing so might make my overall situation worse. It might even make it intellectually worse. If I recognize that my opinions are inconsistent or incoherent, I know that they cannot possibly all be accurate. So, I know that my opinions are less than ideal. But from this it does not immediately follow that it is irrational for me to have these opinions. What is rational for me in such situations depends upon what realistic alternatives I have.[5] In betting situations, it is often rational to adopt a strategy that I know in advance is less than ideal, one in which I am sure to lose at least some of my bets. Moreover, this can be rational even when there are available to me other strategies that hold out at least some possibility of a flawless outcome. These other strategies may be unduly daring or unduly cautious. The same is true of beliefs. Sometimes it is rational for me to have beliefs that I know cannot possibly all be accurate. Indeed, this is the real lesson of the lottery, the preface, and other such paradoxes.[6]

None of this is to say that logic and probability theory do not have a special role to play in intellectual guidance. They obviously do. Logical inconsistency and probabilistic incoherence indicate that my opinions are less than ideal. They thus put me on guard about these opinions. What they do not tell me is how to react to this situation. From the fact that my opinions are less than ideal, it does not automatically follow that I must on pains of irrationality change any of these opinions. And even in those cases where I do have to change something, nothing in logic or probability theory tells me which opinions to change. They give me no concrete advice about this.[7]

Of course, things are different when it is issues of logic and probability theory that are themselves being debated. Similarly, they are different when other specifically philosophical issues are being debated. The relevant philosophical experts will then be in a special position to give me substantive advice. But when it is not philosophical matters that are at issue, advice will have to come from other sources. Fortunately, there is no shortage of such sources. Most are relatively specific in nature. I am confronted with an intellectual problem. So, I go to an expert on the topic in question or consult a reference work or perhaps simply ask a knowledgeable friend.

There are also sources that hold out the hope of more general advice, and it is no accident that among the richest of these are ones in which philosophers have become more and more interested — cognitive science and the history of science. Of course, there are other philosophical motives for interest in these fields. Nevertheless, there is a story to be told here, one whose rough outlines are that as it became increasingly obvious that epistemology could not be expected to give fundamental intellectual advice, philosophers became increasingly interested in empirical disciplines that had human intellectual inquiry as part of their subject matter.

It is not as if these disciplines can be expected to provide the kind of fundamental advice that epistemology fails to provide. If this were their aim, they would encounter all the familiar problems. There would be problems of how to apply the advice, for example. But with these disciplines, unlike epistemology, there is not even a pretense of their being able to provide fundamental advice. This is so not just because we can have questions about the way inquiry is conducted within these disciplines themselves, although this is true enough. It is also because the kind of information that these disciplines are in a position to provide will itself call for interpretation. The fact that scientists have historically used procedures of a certain kind or the fact that we are disposed to make inferences of a certain kind are themselves facts that need to be evaluated before they can provide us with intellectual advice. We will especially want to know whether these procedures and inferences are reliable ones. But to answer this question, we will need to appeal to something more than the history of science and cognitive science.

On the other hand, if what we seek is not advice about the most fundamental matters of inquiry but rather some useful rules of thumb, these disciplines can be of help. At their best, they are able to provide a rich supply of data from which, with persistence and with the help of still other disciplines, we may be able to tease out some useful advice.

Sometimes it may not even take much teasing, especially for negative advice. Recent cognitive science is filled with studies that purport to show recurrent patterns of error in the way that we make inferences. The errors arise, for example, from an insensitivity to sample size or an underutilization of known prior probabilities in making predictions or an inclination in certain kinds of situations to assign a higher probability to a conjunction than one of its conjuncts.[8] These are data from which we can fashion intellectual advice for ourselves — advice that alerts us about our tendency to make these kinds of errors.

Extracting intellectual advice from the history of science is seldom so straightforward a matter, but it, too, can provide us with useful data. It does so in part because historical examples are less easily manipulable than purely hypothetical ones. This is not to say that dreamed-up examples cannot instruct. They obviously can, and indeed they are often more convenient, since they are more neat than real life examples. They can be designed to our purposes, with extraneous features deleted. But, of course, this is just the danger as well. It is sometimes all too easy to tailor them to suit our purposes. Actual cases in all of their detail are not so malleable.[9]

Suppose, then, that I have looked at the history of science and at the findings of cognitive science and at various other studies that provide data about human inquiry. So, I now have all this data. How am I to go about using the data to generate some rules of thumb for the conduct of inquiry? Sometimes it will be obvious, since sometimes the data will reveal that I have a tendency to make what I myself readily concede to be errors. But matters will not always be so obvious, and besides, I want positive as well negative advice. Is there any general advice to be had about this, the process of using the available data to generate intellectual advice?

Those who have been influenced by contemporary moral theory might advise me to employ something akin to the method of wide reflective equilibrium. The rough idea would be that I am to begin with my initial intuitions about what constitute sound methods of inquiry. Then I am to test these intuitions against all the data and all the cases that strike me as relevant — data from cognitive science about characteristic patterns of inference, cases from the history of science, imaginary cases, and anything else that I take to be relevant. Finally, I am to use my best judgment to resolve any conflicts among these intuitions, data, and cases. Sometimes I will judge that my original intuitions are sound. Other times the data or the cases will convince me to alter the original intuitions, and still other times I will be disposed to alter both by a process of give-and-take.[10]

The problem with this recommendation is the familiar one. It is not so much mistaken as unhelpful. At best, it is meta-advice. Indeed, it is essentially the same meta-advice that is implicit in the notion of egocentric rationality. It tells me essentially this: take into account all the data that I think to be relevant and then reflect on the data, solving conflicts in the way that I judge best. On the other hand, it does not tell me what kinds of data are relevant, nor does it tell me what is the best way to resolve conflicts among the data. It leaves me to muck about on these questions as best I can.

And muck I must, for this is part of the human intellectual predicament. It is not that there is no useful intellectual advice to be had. There obviously is. It is just that philosophy is not in a particularly privileged position to provide it. The kind of intellectual advice that philosophy has been sometimes thought to be in a privileged position to give — viz., general advice about the most fundamental issues of intellectual inquiry — is precisely the kind of advice that cannot be usefully given. Attempts to provide this kind of advice are inevitably misdirected or not sufficiently fundamental.

On the other hand, philosophy in general and epistemology in particular has no special claim on more modest kinds of advice — e.g., specific advice on local intellectual concerns or general rules of thumb about the conduct of inquiry. The relevant expert is better positioned for the former, while the latter is best produced by reflection upon all of the available data. We can potentially use anything to fashion intellectual rules of thumb, from the findings of cognitive science to studies in the history of science to mnemonic devices and other intellectual tricks, even relatively trivial ones, such as carrying nines, for example.

This is a project to which philosophers can make important and diverse contributions. They can help us to appreciate that there are various ends at which inquiry might be aimed, for example. Some of these ends are epistemic in nature, in that they are concerned with the accuracy and comprehensiveness of our belief systems. Others are more pragmatic. Moreover, there are distinctions to be made even among those ends that are epistemic. Some are synchronic (roughly, getting things as right as we can for the moment), while others are diachronic (roughly, getting things right eventually). Such distinctions can be important when we are trying to provide ourselves with intellectual advice, since certain kinds of recommendations — for example, the recommendation that we prefer the simplest of otherwise equal hypotheses — will seem plausible relative to some of these aims and not so plausible relative to others.

There is much else of relevance that philosophers can tell us. They can tell us what it is to have an explanation of something, or what it is to have a merely verbal disagreement as opposed to a substantive one. They can distinguish different sorts of arguments for us, emphasizing that different criteria are appropriate for evaluating these arguments. More generally, they can act as intellectual gadflies, examining and criticizing the developments in other intellectual disciplines. And of course, they can also try to describe the conditions under which inquiry is conducted rationally, only these conditions will not be of a sort that provides us with much useful intellectual guidance.

There are those who will insist that this will not do. They will insist that one of our most important intellectual projects is that of generating sound intellectual advice and that we need guidance about how to conduct this project. There are better and worse ways of doing so, and it is epistemology's special role to instruct us about this. Nothing else is positioned to do so. Science, for example, cannot do so, since what we need is advice that is prior to inquiry rather than the result of inquiry. It is only epistemology that can provide us with this kind of fundamental guidance.

This is a view that sees epistemology as the arbiter of intellectual procedures. The presupposition is that epistemology can be prior to other inquiries and that as such it is capable of providing us with a non–question-begging rationale for using one set of intellectual procedures rather than another. Just the reverse is true. Epistemology begins at a late stage of inquiry. It builds on preexisting inquiry and without that inquiry it would be subjectless. One consequence of this is that there is no alternative to using antecedent opinion and methods in thinking about our intellectual procedures. There is no way of doing epistemology *ex nihilo,* and hence it is no more capable of giving us non–question-begging advice about basic issues of intellectual procedure than is anything else.

There is deeper presupposition that also must be abandoned, the presupposition that it is important for us to have such advice. Descartes and the Enlightenment figures who followed him — Locke, for example — thought that this was important, since they thought that the alternative was intellectual anarchy, and perhaps as a result religious and political anarchy as well. Their assumptions seemed to be that there are countless ways of proceeding intellectually, that we are pretty much free to choose among them as we please, and that there must be a non–question-begging rationale for preferring one of these ways over the others if intellectual chaos is to be avoided. Descartes and Locke saw it as their task, the task of the epistemologist, to provide such a rationale.

If this were an accurate description of our intellectual situation, they might have been right. But in fact, this is not our situation. It is not as if we are each given a menu of basic intellectual procedures and that our task is either to find a non–question-begging way of choosing among these procedures or to face intellectual anarchy. Our problem tends to be the opposite one. By the time we reach the point at which it occurs to us that there might be fundamentally different kinds of intellectual procedures, we are largely shaped intellectually. We come to this point equipped not only with a battery of assumptions about the world but also a battery of intellectual skills and habits. All of our intellectual inquiries are grounded in these resources, and the bulk of our intellectual lives must be conducted using them in largely automatic fashion. We have no choice about this. Fundamental rules for the direction of the mind would do us little good even if we had them. We would not have the time or resources to make proper use of them. Insofar as our goal is intellectual improvement, the emphasis is better placed on the development of skills and habits that we think will help make us more reliable inquirers.

The project of building up such skills and habits lacks the drama of the Cartesian project. It is inevitably a piecemeal project. To engage in it, we must draw upon an enormous number of background assumptions, skills, and habits, ones that for the time being we are content to use rather than reform. Questions can still arise about this background. We may realize that had we been born with significantly different cognitive equipment or into a significantly different environment, these assumptions, skills, and habits might have been considerably different. These possibilities are mainly of theoretical interest, however. They are of interest for epistemology. They can be used to discuss skeptical worries, for instance. On the other hand, they normally will not be of much interest insofar as our purpose is epistemic improvement. After all, most of these fundamentally different ways of proceeding will not be real options for us. It is not as if we are radically free to reconstitute ourselves intellectually in any way that we see fit and that we need some guidance about whether to do so or how to do so.

Of course, we are not entirely without options. We cannot alter our fundamental intellectual procedures by a simple act of will, but by making incremental changes over a long enough period of time, we perhaps could train ourselves to use procedures that are very different from those that we currently employ. Perhaps there are even ways of bringing about the changes more immediately. Drugs might do the trick, for instance. There are those who have recommended peyote or LSD as a way to truth. But even here, insofar as our worry is intellectual chaos, the search need not be for a non–question-begging way of deciding which procedures, our present ones or the drug-induced ones, are the more reliable. It is enough to point out that from our present undrugged perspective, most of us have no reason to think that the drugged perspective is the more reliable one. Quite the contrary, from our current perspective it seems far less reliable. Thus, insofar as our ends are epistemic, we have no motivation to drug ourselves.

Descartes and Locke notwithstanding, our primary intellectual threat is not that of chaos, and our primary intellectual need is not for advice about the most fundamental matters of intellectual outlook. We cannot help but be largely guided by our intellectual inheritance on these matters. The primary threat is rather that of intellectual conformity, and our primary need is for intellectual autonomy. Little in life is more difficult than resisting domination by one's intellectual environment. It is all too easy for us to be intellectual lemmings. We do not have the ability to cast off wholesale the effects of our environment and adopt a radically new intellectual outlook, so this cannot be the basis of our intellectual autonomy. It is instead based upon our ability to use our existing opinions and existing methods to examine our opinions and methods. It resides in our ability to make ourselves into an object of study, to evaluate and monitor ourselves, and moreover to do so not so much in terms of the prevailing standards but rather in terms of our own standards. This ability creates a space for intellectual autonomy.

But it is only a space. Self-monitoring in terms of our own personal standards does not altogether eliminate the threat of intellectual domination. As Foucault emphasized recently and as Marx had argued earlier, the most effective kind of control is that which is internalized.[11] We accept as our own the very norms by which we are controlled. Be this as it may, our only alternative is to monitor ourselves for this as well, to try as best we can to make ourselves aware of this possibility and thus prevent it. Of course, there is no guarantee that we will be successful. If the domination is thorough enough, leaving no trace of its influence, then no amount of self-monitoring will do much good.

But in this respect, the possibility of complete and utter domination is not much different from the possibility of complete and utter deception. Just as a powerful enough demon could use our own experiences to deceive us thoroughly without our being aware of it, so too a powerful enough dominating force could use our own standards to control us thoroughly without our being aware of it. But neither of these gives us a rationale to be dismissive of our intellectual projects. The possibility of radical error does not mean that knowledge is altogether impossible for us, and the possibility of radical domination does not mean that intellectual autonomy is altogether impossible for us.

Our intellectual standards cannot help but show the effects of our intellectual environment, but they need not be swallowed up by it. My standards can and presumably sometimes do differ from the standards of the people who surround me. When they do, intellectual autonomy as well as egocentric rationality requires that I conform to my standards rather than the prevailing ones.

Notes

1. "[W]hen we judge someone's inference to be normatively inappropriate, we are comparing it to (what we take to be) the applicable principles of inference sanctioned by expert reflective equilibrium" (Stephen Stich, "Could Man be an Irrational Animal?" *Synthese* 64 [1985]: 115–135).

2. Bertrand Russell, *The Problems of Philosophy* (Oxford: Oxford University Press, 1959). See also Richard Fumerton, *Metaphysical and Epistemological Problems of Perception* (Lincoln, Neb.: University of Nebraska Press, 1985), especially 57–58.

3. Roderick Chisholm's epistemology faces analogous problems. Like Descartes, Chisholm thinks that our "purpose in raising [epistemological] questions is to correct and improve our own epistemic situation; . . . we want to do our best to improve our set of beliefs — to replace those that are unjustified by others that are justified and to replace those that have a lesser degree of justification with others that have a greater degree of justification." See Chisholm, *Theory of Knowledge,* 3d ed. (Englewood Cliffs, N.J.: Prentice-Hall, 1989), 1. He takes this to show that the notion of epistemic justification cannot be explicated in an externalist manner. Instead, the conditions of epistemic justification must be both "*internal* and *immediate* in that one can find out directly, by reflection, what one is justified in believing at any time" (p. 7). However, the conditions that Chisholm himself defends,

as expressed in his principles of epistemic justification, are often very complicated. They are difficult enough to understand and even more difficult to apply, especially since many of them make reference to the believer's total evidence and total set of beliefs. Thus, even if I thoroughly understand Chisholm's principles, it is unlikely that I will always be able to determine by reflection on my state of mind whether or not a belief is justified according to them. Moreover, even if this always were at least theoretically possible, it need not always be obvious to me how I am to go about making these determinations. I will not always be able to look inward and simply read off whether Chisholm's conditions are met. So, not just any kind of reflection will do. But if not, I will want to know how to conduct these reflections, and Chisholm's principles do not provide me with any helpful advice about this.

4. Points of this sort have been especially emphasized by Gilbert Harman. See his *Change of View* (Cambridge, Mass.: MIT Press, 1986).

5. Again, see Harman, *Change of View.* Also see Christopher Cherniak, *Minimal Rationality* (Cambridge, Mass.: MIT Press, 1988).

6. Similarly, it can be rational for me to have a degree of confidence in a proposition that cannot possibly be an accurate reflection of its objective probability. Suppose I am presented with a logically complex claim and told by an utterly reliable source that either it or its negation is a tautology. I thus know that its objective probability is either 1 or 0. After much effort, I construct a complicated proof that it is a tautology, but I am unsure of the proof. Moreover, it may be reasonable for me to be unsure. After all, the proof is a complicated one. But if so, it can be rational for me to believe the claim with something less than full confidence.

7. This is one of the reasons why treatises on informal logic and critical reasoning tend to be either unhelpful or theoretically unsatisfying. Insofar as the project is seen to be one of deriving useful advice for our everyday intellectual lives from the rules of logic and the axioms of the probability calculus, there simply is not a lot of useful advice to be had. On the other hand, insofar as the treatise does contain useful rules of thumb, these rules must have extralogical sources. But then, we will want to have information about these sources, information that we are rarely given.

8. See, e.g., Richard Nisbet and Lee Ross, *Human Inference: Strategies and Shortcomings of Social Judgement* (Englewood Cliffs, N.J.: Prentice-Hall, 1980).

9. The detail is important, however. Without it, real cases and real arguments can be manipulated just as easily as hypothetical ones. Witness textbook examples of the so-called 'informal fallacies'. Often enough, the examples are arguments from real sources that have been taken out of context and then uncharitably interpreted as deductive.

10. Compare with Nelson Goodman, *Fact, Fiction and Forecast* (Indianapolis: Bobbs-Merrill, 1965).

11. Karl Marx, *The German Ideology* (London: Lawrence and Wishart, 1938); Michel Foucault, *The History of Sexuality,* trans. R. Hurley (New York: Vintage Books, 1980). See also Gary Gutting's discussion of Foucault's views on these matters in his *Michel Foucault's Archaeology of Scientific Reason* (Cambridge: Cambridge University Press, 1989).

The Incoherence of Empiricism

George Bealer

A person's experiences and/or observations comprise the person's *prima facie* evidence.[1] This is the first dogma of empiricism. This principle, together with two others, forms the core of W. V. O. Quine's empiricism.

The principle of empiricism:

> (i) A person's experiences and/or observations comprise the person's *prima facie* evidence.[2]

The principle of holism:

> (ii) A theory is justified (acceptable, more reasonable than its competitors, legitimate, warranted) for a person if and only if it is, or belongs to, the simplest comprehensive theory that explains all, or most, of the person's *prima facie* evidence.[3]

The principle of naturalism:

> (iii) The natural sciences (plus the logic and mathematics needed by them) constitute the simplest comprehensive theory that explains all, or most, of a person's experiences and/or observations.[4]

This sort of view has a remarkable hold over philosophers and scientists today, as it has in centuries past. Indeed, it yields a veritable *Weltanschauung*. The aim of the present essay is to try to refute this view by arguing that it is at bottom incoherent. We will give three such arguments: one concerning starting points, one concerning epistemic norms, and one concerning terms of epistemic appraisal. Unlike the standard anti-empiricist arguments, which usually strike empiricists as question-begging, these arguments are designed to lay bare difficulties internal to their view. The purpose is to present arguments that have persuasive force even for people under the spell of empiricism.

Reprinted by courtesy of the Editor of the Aristotelian Society: © 1992

The Standard Justificatory Procedure

We begin by reviewing some plain truths about the procedure we standardly use to justify our beliefs and theories.

First, we standardly use various items — for example, experiences, observations, testimony — as *prima facie* evidence for other things, such as beliefs and theories.

At one time many people accepted the traditional doctrine that knowledge is justified true belief. But now we have good evidence that this is mistaken. Suppose someone has been driving for miles past what look like herds of sheep. At various points along the journey, our person *believes* that a sheep is in the pasture. Since the situation appears to be perfectly normal in all relevant respects, certainly the person would be *justified* in believing that there is a sheep in the pasture. Suppose that it is indeed *true* that there is a sheep in the pasture. Is this enough for knowledge? No. For suppose that the thousands of sheep-looking things the person has been seeing are a breed of white poodle that from a distance look just like sheep and that, by pure chance, there happens to be a solitary sheep hidden in the middle of the acres of poodles. Clearly, the person does not know that there is a sheep in the pasture.[5] Examples like this provide good *prima facie* evidence that the traditional theory is mistaken. We find it intuitively obvious that there could be a situation like that described and in such a situation the person would not know that there is a sheep in the pasture despite having a justified true belief. This intuition — that there could be such a situation and in it the person would not know — and other intuitions like it are our evidence that the traditional theory is mistaken.

So, according to our standard justificatory procedure, *intuitions* count as *prima facie* evidence. Now sometimes in using intuitions to justify various conclusions, it is somewhat more natural to call them *reasons* rather than *evidence*. For example, my reasons for accepting that a certain statement is logically true are that it follows intuitively from certain more elementary statements that intuitively are logically true. I have clear intuitions that it follows, and I have clear intuitions that these more elementary statements are logically true. Standardly, we say that intuitions like these are *evident* (at least *prima facie*).

For convenience of exposition let us extend the term '*prima facie* evidence' to include reasons that are *prima facie* evident in this way. So in this terminology, the standard justificatory procedure counts, not only experiences, observations, memory, and testimony as *prima facie* evidence, but intuitions as well. It shall be clear that this terminological extension does not bias our discussion.[6] Readers who object to this practice should hereafter read '*prima facie* evidence' as 'reasons that are *prima facie* evident'.

Now an important step in the standard justificatory procedure is *criticism*. A special form of criticism deserves mention here. The standard justificatory procedure incorporates a mechanism for self-criticism by means of which any component of the procedure can be subjected to critical assessment that might lead to an adjustment somewhere in the procedure itself. Specifically, this mechanism permits one to challenge the legitimacy of any standing source of *prima facie* evidence (experience, observation, intuition, memory, testimony). The presence of this mechanism in the standard justificatory procedure keeps the procedure from being either obviously empiricist or obviously non-empiricist. It all depends on which sources of *prima facie* evidence survive the process of criticism. So in saying that the standard procedure counts intuitions as *prima facie* evidence, we do not preclude using the mechanism of self-criticism to eliminate intuition as a source of *prima facie* evidence.

By intuition, we do not mean a supernatural power or a magical inner voice or anything of the sort. When you have an intuition that *A*, it *seems* to you that *A*. Here 'seems' is understood, not in its use as a cautionary or "hedging" term, but in its use as a term for a genuine kind of conscious episode. For example, when you first consider one of de Morgan's laws, often you draw a blank; after a moment's reflection, however, something happens: it now really *seems* obvious. You suddenly "just see" it. It presents itself as how things must be. Of course, this kind of seeming is *intellectual*, not sensory or introspective. For example, suppose it seems to you that, if *P* or *Q*, then it is not the case that both not *P* and not *Q*. When this occurs, it is a purely intellectual episode; not a sensation or a reflection. There is, accordingly, a sharp distinction between intuition and imagination. Typically, if it is possible for someone to have the intuition that *A* (i.e., if it is possible for it to seem intellectually to someone that *A*), then it is possible for someone (perhaps the same person) to have the intuition that *A* in the absence of any particular sensory (imaginative) or introspective experiences that are relevant to the truth or falsity of the proposition that *A*. For this reason, intuitions are counted as "data of reason" not "data of experience."[7]

When we speak of intuition, we mean "*a priori* intuition." This is distinguished from what physicists call 'physical intuition'. We have a physical intuition that, when a house is undermined, it will fall. This does not count as an *a priori* intuition, for it does not present itself as necessary: it does not seem that a house undermined *must* fall; plainly, it is *possible* for a house undermined to remain in its original position or, indeed, to rise up. By contrast, when we have an *a priori* intuition, say, that if *P* then not not *P*, this presents itself as necessary: it does not seem to us that things could be otherwise; it must be that if *P* then not not *P*.

Intuition should also be distinguished from belief: belief is not a seeming; intuition is. For example, there are many mathematical theorems that I believe (because I have seen the proofs) but that do not *seem* to me to be true and that do not *seem* to me to be false; I do not have intuitions about them either way. Conversely, I have an intuition—it still *seems* to me—that the naive comprehension axiom of set theory is true; this is so despite the fact that I do not believe that it is true (because I know of the set-theoretical paradoxes).[8] There is a rather similar phenomenon in sense perception. In the Müller-Lyar illusion, it still *seems* to me that one of the two arrows is longer than the other; this is so despite the fact that I do not believe that one of the two arrows is longer (because I have measured them). In each case, the seeming persists in spite of the countervailing belief. Of course, one must not confuse intuition with sense perception. Intuition is an *intellectual* seeming; sense perception is a *sensory* seeming (an *appearing*). By and large, the two cannot overlap: most things that can seem intellectually to be so cannot seem sensorily to be so, and conversely.[9]

Intuitions are also quite distinct from judgments, guesses, and hunches. As just indicated, there are significant restrictions on the propositions concerning which one can have intuitions; by contrast, there are virtually no restrictions on the propositions concerning which one can make a judgment or a guess or have a hunch. Judgments are a kind of occurrent belief; as such, they are not seemings. Guesses are phenomenologically rather more like choices; they are plainly not seemings. And hunches are akin to merely caused, ungrounded convictions or noninferential beliefs; they, too, are not seemings. For example, suppose that I ask you whether the coin is in my right hand or whether it is in my left. You might have a hunch that it is in my left hand, but it does not *seem* to you that it is. You have no intellectual episode in which it seems to you that I have a coin in my left hand. When I show you that it is in my right hand, you no longer have a hunch that it is in my left. Your merely caused, ungrounded conviction (noninferential belief) is automatically overridden by the grounded belief that it is in my right hand, and it is thereby displaced. Not so for seemings, intellectual or sensory; they are not automatically displaced by your grounded contrary beliefs. (Recall the naive comprehension axiom and the Müller-Lyar arrows.)

Many items that are, somewhat carelessly, called intuitions in casual discourse in logic, mathematics, linguistics, or philosophy are really only a certain sort of memory. For example, it does not *seem* to me that $5^3 = 125$; this is something I learned from a teacher's testimony or from calculation. Note how this differs, phenomenologically, from what happens when one has an intuition. After a moment's reflection on the question, you "just see" that, if P or Q, then it is not the case that both not P and not Q. Or, upon considering the example described earlier, you "just see" that the person in the example does not know that there is a sheep in the pasture. Nothing comparable happens in the case of the proposition that $5^3 = 125$.

Intuitions must also be distinguished from common sense. True, most elementary intuitions are commonsensical. However, a great many intuitions do not qualify as commonsensical just because they are nonelementary, for example, intuitions about mathematical limits, the infinite divisibility of space and time, the axiom of choice, and so forth. Conversely, we often lack intuitions (i.e., a priori intuitions) about matters that are highly commonsensical. For example, the following are just common sense; if you undermine your house, it will fall; items priced substantially below market value are likely to be defective; it is unwise to build houses in flood plains; and so forth. But *a priori* intuition is silent about these matters. Such considerations suggest something like this: common sense is an amalgamation of various widely shared, more or less useful empirical beliefs, practical wisdom, *a priori* intuitions, and physical intuitions. Common sense certainly cannot be *identified* with *a priori* intuition.

The foregoing distinctions are obvious once they are pointed out. However, in many philosophical discussions the term 'intuition' is often used quite indiscriminately. Indeed, some philosophers use it more or less interchangeably with 'uncritical belief' or even with 'belief' *simpliciter*.[10] When we said earlier that, according to the standard justificatory procedure, intuitions are counted as *prima facie* evidence, we were not using 'intuition' in this indiscriminate way but rather in the above quite restricted way as a term for intellectual seeming. The distinction is of utmost importance.

Like sense perceptions, intuitions can (at least occasionally) be mistaken; for example, our intuition regarding the naive comprehension axiom is evidently mistaken. Thus, the infallibilist theory of intuition is evidently incorrect. There is a further analogy between intuition and sense perception: the standard justificatory procedure directs us to give greatest evidential weight to intuitions about specific concrete cases. By comparison, "theoretical" intuitions have relatively less evidential weight.

Two final points. Intuitions play a significant role in our belief-formation processes. First, at any given time, there are a number of novel questions about which one has no belief one way or the other but about which one would have a clear-cut intuition. In cases like this, one will typically form the belief associated with the intuition as soon as the intuition occurs. Second, intuition plays a crucial role in following rules and procedures — for example, rules of inference.

The Starting Points Argument

A special case of our last point arises in connection with justificatory procedures, for typically we rely on our intuitions whenever we follow such procedures. (This fact is not required for our argument. See the close of this section.) This evident use of intuitions leads to a serious problem for empiricists who would have us follow their procedure (i.e., the procedure associated with principles (i) and (ii)). Indeed, there is a special irony here, for in their actual practice empiricists typically make use of a wide range of intuitions. For example, what does and does not count as an observation or experience? Why count sense perception as observation? Why not count memory as observation? Or why not count certain high-level theoretical judgments as sense experiences? Indeed, why not count intuitions as sense experiences? Likewise for each of the other key notions that play a role in the empiricist principles (i) and (ii). What does and does not count as a theory, as justified (or acceptable), as an explanation, as simple? The fact is that empiricists arrive at answers to these questions by using as *prima facie* evidence their intuitions about what does and does not count as experience, observation, theory, justified, explanation, simple. In their actual practice, empiricists use such intuitions as evidence to support their theories and to persuade others of them. However, such use of intuitions contradicts the principle of empiricism, which includes only experiences and/or observations as *prima facie* evidence. So in their actual practice, empiricists are not faithful to their principles.

To avoid this inconsistency, empiricists could fall back on the traditional distinction between discovery and justification. Accordingly, they would hold that, although they use intuition as a guide in formulating their theories, they do not invoke intuitions as *prima facie* evidence when they actually get down to justifying their theories. Let us use the term *starting points* for basic epistemic classifications (i.e., what does and does not count as an experience, an observation, a theory, an explanation, a simple explanation, a law of nature, a deductively valid argument, a logical truth, a theoretical virtue, etc.). In this terminology, the empiricists would hold that, although they use their intuitions about starting points as a guide in formulating their theories, they do not, strictly speaking, use them as *prima facie* evidence.

Even with the aid of this distinction, however, empiricists are caught in a fatal dilemma over the issue of their starting points. Either a person's intuitions regarding starting points are reliable or they are not.

If starting-points intuitions are *not* reliable, then empiricists are in big trouble. For their starting-points judgments (like everyone else's) are in fact determined by their intuitions (e.g., intuitions about what counts as experience, observation, theory, explanation, simplicity, logical truth, etc.). Therefore, if these intuitions regarding starting points are prone to error, the error will be reflected in the comprehensive theory that results from them, making that theory highly unreliable. It is true that errors in one's ordinary pretheoretical judgments about matters other than starting points can often be spotted and eliminated by a "bootstrapping."[11] For example, suppose that someone has a disposition to make errors when thinking unreflectively about race or gender. Nevertheless, upon formulating a systematic and comprehensive theory, the person will often be able to spot and eliminate these errors. Or suppose that a person suffers from an astigmatism, making his visual observations of shape and length prone to error. Again, it is plausible that, upon formulating a comprehensive and systematic theory on the basis of all his observations, including the largely reliable observations provided by his other senses and by his largely reliable visual observations of color, continuity, contiguity, and other topological properties, the person will be able to spot and eliminate these errors about shape and length. By contrast, this "bootstrap" method of error detection would break down if a person's observations generally (not just visual observations of shape and length) were unreliable. As long as the person's observations happened, by luck, to permit theoretical systematization (surely this is logically possible), the person's overall empirical theory would be quite unreliable, and the person would have no way to detect the errors. Now the situation would be just that much worse if, instead, the person's pretheoretic judgments about the very question of what counted as an observation were unreliable; and it would be worse still if the person's pretheoretic judgments about what counted as a theory, an explanation, as simple, as logically valid, as logically consistent, and so forth were unreliable. The effect of these errors on one's overall theory is of an order of magnitude greater than that of ordinary errors. Bootstrapping would be powerless to repair the situation.

On the other hand, suppose that intuitions about starting points *are* reliable. That is, suppose our intuitions regarding what does and does not count as an experience, as an observation, as a theory, as an explanation, as simple, as logically true, as logically consistent, and so forth are reliable. Then, certainly whatever it is that makes such intuitions reliable would also make our intuitions about what does and does not count as *prima facie* evidence (or as reasons) reliable. However, we have a wealth of concrete-case intuitions to the effect that intuitions are *prima facie* evidence (reasons). Because these intuitions about the evidential status of intuitions would be reliable, it would follow that intuitions are in fact *prima facie* evidence and, hence, that empiricism is false. Moreover, if intuitions are *prima facie* evidence, then the sort of overall theory that empiricists would formulate (after excluding intuitions as *prima facie* evidence) would be highly unreliable (notably, on such matters as modality, definition, property identity, evidence, and justification).

Therefore, on both prongs of the dilemma, empiricism leads one to formulate a comprehensive theory that is highly unreliable. But, given that we can now see this, we certainly would not be justified in accepting this comprehensive theory. However, empiricism implies that we would. So empiricism is false.

This is the starting-point argument. A response to this argument is to deny that a person's pretheoretic starting-points judgments are really determined by intuitions and to hold instead that they are a kind of non-inferential judgment determined by some other mechanism.

Phenomenological considerations along the lines of those mentioned at the close of the previous section show that this reply is not faithful to the psychological facts. This should put an end to the reply. But even if it does not, the reply would not help to save empiricism, for much the same type of dilemma would still exist. On the one hand, if our pretheoretic starting-points judgments are unreliable, the resulting comprehensive theory would also be unreliable. The earlier considerations show that, because starting points are involved, bootstrapping would be powerless to correct the problem. On the other hand, if our pretheoretic starting-points judgments are reliable, then whatever it is that makes them reliable should also make reliable our pretheoretic judgments about what is and is not *prima facie* evidence. But, just as we have intuitions to the effect that intuitions are *prima facie* evidence, we have pretheoretic judgments to the effect that intuitions are *prima facie* evidence. Because these pretheoretic judgments would be reliable, it would follow that intuitions are *prima facie* evidence, contrary to what empiricism implies. Moreover, given this conclusion that intuitions are in fact *prima facie* evidence, we would have good reason to conclude that the empiricists' comprehensive theory, which excludes intuitions as *prima facie* evidence, would be highly unreliable (in connection with modality, property identity, definition, evidence, justification, etc.). So on both prongs of the dilemma, empiricism would lead to an unreliable comprehensive theory. Seeing this, one would not be justified in accepting this theory. Since empiricism implies that one would, empiricism is false.

The Argument from Epistemic Norms

We now move on to a "hermeneutical" problem produced by the empiricists' departure from our epistemic norms. We have seen that the standard justificatory procedure admits as *prima facie* evidence not only experience and observation but also intuition. Empiricism would have us circumscribe our *prima facie* evidence by just excluding intuition. But consider some other exclusionary views. For example, *visualism,* the view that only visual experience provides *prima facie* evidence; tactile, auditory, olfactory experiences are just arbitrarily excluded. Or consider a theory that excludes as *prima facie* evidence all standard items that do not fit in neatly with some antecedently held political, religious, or metaphysical view. Plainly, we would not be justified in accepting these departures from the standard procedure. How is empiricism relevantly different?

Some empiricists might try to answer as follows. Suppose that the comprehensive theory that results from following the empiricist procedure is "self-approving"; that is, suppose that this theory deems itself — and the procedure that produces it — to be justified and that it deems as unjustified all other comprehensive theories and procedures that yield them, including, in particular, the competing deviant procedures (e.g., visualism, etc.).[12] In this case, the empiricsts might invoke their comprehensive theory hoping to mark a relevant difference between their procedure and the other deviant procedures. However, this strategy merely yields a stalemate, for at least some of the other deviant procedures might themselves yield comprehensive theories that are "self-approving" in this sense. (With the use of logicians' tricks we can easily construct deviant procedures that yield "self-approving" comprehensive theories in this way.) If the above strategy were legitimate, advocates of one of these competing procedures would also be entitled to appeal to the comprehensive theory yielded by their procedure to show that the empiricists' comprehensive theory and the empiricist procedure are not justified. Hence a stalemate.

To avoid this kind of stalemate, empiricists have no choice but to try to reach their conclusion *from within* the standard justificatory procedure. Specifically, they must employ the standard justificatory procedure *critically:* they must employ the standard procedure's mechanism of self-criticism in an effort to show that a component of it (namely, the admission of intuitions as *prima facie* evidence) is defective. Suppose that the empiricists' attempt to employ the standard procedure critically succeeds, and suppose that analogous efforts on behalf of the competing deviant procedures (visualism, etc.) are not successful. Then, a relevant difference between empiricism and its competitors will have been found. Unlike its competitors, empiricism would not be an *arbitrary* departure from our epistemic norms. The question to consider, therefore, is this: when we implement the standard justificatory procedure's mechanism of self-criticism, does intuition get excluded as a source of *prima facie* evidence? (In our discussion we will confine ourselves to concrete-case intuitions, for, as we have seen, it is to these intuitions that the standard justificatory procedure assigns primary evidential weight.)

Consider an example of how a candidate source of *prima facie* evidence would be thrown out. Take tea leaves (or tarot, oracles, the stars, birds, or what have you). They are thrown out as a legitimate source of *prima facie* evidence (roughly) because they fail to satisfy the "three *cs*" — *consistency, corroboration,* and *confirmation.* First, to the extent that we have looked, we find no particular consistency among the tea-leaf readings made by a single person. Second, a person's readings are not corroborated by other people. Third, there is no pattern of confirmation of the tea-leaf predictions or other tea-leaf claims by our experiences, observations, and intuitions. Indeed, there is a pattern of disconfirmation by these sources of *prima facie* evidence.

Intuition, however, is not at all like this. (Recall that we are discussing concrete-case intuitions here.) First, a person's intuitions are largely consistent with one another. To be sure, a given person's intuitions occasionally appear to be contradictory, but so do our observations, our memories, and even our pure sense experiences. This is hardly enough to throw out observation, memory, and sense experience as sources of evidence. Moreover, most of these apparent conflicts (including apparent conflicts among one's intuitions) can be reconciled by standard techniques (see below). The occasional inconsistencies among a person's intuitions are nothing like the inconsistencies we would expect to find in a collection of someone's tea-leaf readings.[13] Second, although different people do have conflicting intuitions from time to time, there is an impressive corroboration by others of one's elementary logical, mathematical, conceptual, and modal intuitions.[14] The situation is much the same with observation: different people have conflicting observations from time to time, but this is hardly enough to throw out observation as a source of evidence. On the contrary, there is, despite the occasional conflict, an impressive corroboration by others of one's observations. Third, unlike tea-leaf reading, intuition is seldom, if ever, disconfirmed by our experiences and observations. The primary reason is that the contents of our intuitions — whether conceptual, logical, mathematical, or modal — are by and large independent of the contents of our observations and experiences (in much the same way that, say, the contents of our sense experiences and the contents of our emotional experiences are independent of one another). The one potential exception involves our modal intuitions. But virtually no conflicts arise here because our intuitions about what experiences and observations are logically (or metaphysically) possible are so liberal. The conclusion is that the opportunity for disconfirmation by experience and/or observation seldom, if ever, arises.

Let us consider more carefully the matter of inconsistencies among a given person's intuitions. The pattern of inconsistencies among one's intuitions—and the standard ways of dealing with them—are quite like what we find in the case of the other sources of *prima facie* evidence. Evidently, there are some rare cases of irreconcilable inconsistencies among a person's intuitions. For example, Russell's paradox and the liar paradox evidently show that intuitions about the naive comprehension axiom from set theory and the naive truth schema are irreconcilably in conflict with intuitions about classical logic. But there are analogous, apparently irreconcilable conflicts among a person's observations. For example, upon putting my right hand (which was just warmed) into the water, I report that the water is cool; and upon putting my left hand (which was just cooled) into the same water, I report that the water is warm. The two observation reports are inconsistent, and there seems to be no reasonable way to reconcile them; one is forced to retreat from the "objective" observational level to the "subjective" phenomenological level: the water *feels* warm to my left hand and *feels* cool to my right hand. There also seem to be inconsistencies on the subjective phenomenological level. Russell cites the example of an expanse of phenomenal color in which locally there seems to be no variation in hue but whose extreme left and right nevertheless seem plainly different in hue.[15] But these rare, irreconcilable inconsistencies hardly call into question the legitimacy of observation or of phenomenal experience. The same holds for the rare irreconcilable inconsistencies among a person's intuitions.

In any event, most apparent conflicts are reconcilable by standard techniques. For example, suppose that, upon watching Smith's efforts at the shooting range, I report that he hit a bull's-eye. But when I walk over to Smith, I see that he is not even holding a gun but rather an electronic toy wired to the bull's-eye bell; and when I walk over to the target, I see that it has not been hit at all. I report that Smith did not hit the bull's-eye. Now, in the face of this conflict between my observations—my earlier observation that Smith hit the bull's-eye and my later observation that he did not—we certainly do not throw out observation as a legitimate source of evidence about the episode and retreat to the subjective phenomenal level. On the contrary, we *redescribe* what I observed using relevant units and distinctions. Redescribed, what I observed in the earlier episode was this: Smith was pointing a black, shiny gun-shaped object in the direction of the target; there was a loud crack; then the bull's-eye bell went off. These observations are consistent with my later ones. By using these more specific units and distinctions, we are thus able to reconcile my earlier observations with the later ones, and we are able to do so while remaining on the "objective" observational level. This is the standard practice. It would be mad to discard observation altogether because of this sort of apparent conflict and to hold instead that I have no legitimate observational evidence. I did have observational evidence and at most it needed to be reported more cautiously.

We do exactly the same sort of thing with intuitions that are apparently in conflict. Consider three examples. (1) In the Galileo paradox of infinity, I have an intuition that there are fewer *odd* numbers than there are *natural* numbers (odd numbers plus even numbers). But I also have an intuition that the odd numbers are in one-to-one correspondence with the natural numbers and a collection that is in one-to-one correspondence with another does not have fewer things in it. These two intuitions can be reconciled by invoking a distinction between fewer-than in the proper-subset sense and fewer-than in the no-one-to-one-correspondence sense. My first intuition was that the odds are fewer than the naturals in the former sense, and my second intuition was that they are not fewer in the latter sense. Properly reported, both intuitions stand as *prima facie* evidence. It would be absurd to throw them out as illegitimate without even trying to reconcile them by means of redescription in terms of relevant distinctions. (2) The scientific-essentialist literature (Kripke et al.) provides a second illustration of how redescription can be used to reconcile intuitions that initially appear to be in conflict. Initially, there appears to be a conflict between old-fashion anti–scientific-essentialist intuitions (e.g., the intuition that there might be some water with no hydrogen in it) and the new pro–scientific-essentialist intuitions. Such conflicts would result in a mere stalemate between the old view and the new view. However, by redescribing these intuitions in terms of the distinction between epistemic possibility and metaphysical possibility, scientific-essentialists are able to resolve the apparent conflict in favor of their view. Evidently, anti–scientific-essentialists are unable to do the analogous thing for their view. So the stalemate is evidently broken in favor of scientific-essentialism. (3) The Gricean distinction between genuine semantical implication and mere conversational implicature also yields redescriptions that serve to reconcile a great many intuitions that initially appear to be in conflict.

Another type of apparent conflict among our intuitions arises in connection with cases that are *incompletely specified*. Consider the following specification similar to that which was given earlier: one day in normal observation conditions someone drives past a pasture in which there are animals that look to him exactly like sheep and, indeed, there are sheep in the pasture; as a result of his observations the person comes to believe that there is a sheep in the pasture. Does the person know that there is a sheep in the pasture? Before learning of the Gettier-style examples, perhaps you would have had the intuition that the person would know that there is a sheep in the pasture. However, as soon as we add the further detail that virtually all of the sheep-looking animals are poodles and that the only sheep there are completely hidden from view by thousands of poodles, you have the intuition that the person does not know that there is a sheep in the pasture. This apparent conflict between intuitions is readily explained. Upon hearing the initial specification, you supposed that *all* the sheep-looking animals were normal sheep. Once we address this detail explicitly, it becomes clear to you that there are really two distinct cases — one with normal sheep, the other with sheep-looking poodles. Your two apparently conflicting intuitions turn out to be consistent with one another, for they are not even about the same case! The point is that, when using intuitions as *prima facie* evidence, we must carefully attend to all relevant details. This requirement hardly calls into question the evidential status of intuitions. Indeed, when we use experiences and observations as *prima facie* evidence, somewhat similar requirements are in force.

In summary, just as with observation and experience, so with intuition: our standard procedure is to try to reconcile apparent conflicts by more complete description and/or redescription. When we try to do this, we succeed in a *very* large extent.[16] For this reason, neither observation, experience, nor intuition is eliminated as a legitimate source of *prima facie* evidence on grounds of inconsistency. The overall conclusion, therefore, is that intuition does not get called into question on grounds of inconsistency, lack of corroboration, or conflicts with experience or with observation.

There is another kind of conflict we must consider, namely, conflicts between certain *theories* and certain intuitions (e.g., intuitions about simultaneity and Euclidean geometry[17]). Do such conflicts call intuition into question as a source of *prima facie* evidence? No. For there are analogous conflicts between certain theories and certain observations (e.g., observations that the sun is about the same size as the moon and that it moves across the sky). Likewise, experience, memory, and testimony come into conflict with certain theories. None of these conflicts suffice to overturn observation, experience, memory, or testimony as a source of *prima facie* evidence. The same holds for intuition. Like the deliverances of these other standard sources, most of our intuitions are consistent with our empirical theories. Indeed, most of our elementary conceptual, logical, and numerical intuitions are actually affirmed by our empirical theories. And modal and higher mathematical intuitions, while not affirmed by our empirical theories, are for the most part not inconsistent with them. Moreover, our best comprehensive theory based on *all* standard sources of *prima facie* evidence, *including intuition,* affirms most of our modal and higher mathematical intuitions. The reason is twofold: first, these intuitions are largely consistent with one another and with our empirical theories (at least, our intuitions can be made largely consistent with one another when carefully reported); second, they admit of theoretical systematization to a significant degree. So it is no surprise that a comprehensive theory that begins by including intuitions as *prima facie* evidence should affirm most of them.

If empiricists are to try to overthrow intuition by means of the standard justificatory procedure's mechanism for self-criticism, they have only one alternative. They must invoke the comprehensive theory that one would formulate if one admitted only those sources of *prima facie* evidence *other than* intuition. Characterized more abstractly, this method of challenging a standard source of *prima facie* evidence goes as follows. One formulates one's best comprehensive theory on the basis of the standard sources of *prima facie* evidence that one is not challenging. If the resulting theory deems the omitted source(s) not to be reliable, then it is (they are) seriously discounted as a source(s) of *prima facie* evidence.

This method is appropriate in some cases. Consider a hypothetical example. Suppose the pronouncements of a certain political authority (reminiscent of the Wizard of Oz) have acquired the status of *prima facie* evidence, and suppose that these pronouncements do not fail the three *c*s. (That is, they are consistent with one another. They do not go against the pronouncements of others. And they are not disconfirmed by other sources of *prima facie* evidence because they are carefully contrived to avoid such disconfirmation.) Nevertheless, we could legitimately challenge the *prima facie* evidential status of these pronouncements as follows. First, we should formulate the best overall theory based on all *other* sources of *prima facie* evidence. If this theory were not to deem the pronouncements of the political authority to be (largely) reliable, then we would be justified in rejecting the political authority as a special source of *prima facie* evidence.

However, there are cases in which this method does not work. Recall the example of visualism, discussed at the outset of this section. Suppose that a visualist tried to use visual experience to eliminate other modes of experience (tactile, auditory, etc.) as sources of *prima facie* evidence. Suppose that this effort happened to yield a formally neat comprehensive theory that denied the reliability of these other sorts of experiences.[18] Would the standard justificatory procedure direct us to reject these other modes of experience as sources of *prima facie* evidence? This suggestion is preposterous. Neither vision nor touch can override the other as a source of *prima facie* evidence. To be admitted as a source of *prima facie* evidence, neither requires auxiliary confirmation from other sources of *prima facie* evidence, nor do they require affirmation by the best comprehensive theory based on other sources of evidence. Those who would deny this have lost their grip on the standard justificatory procedure and, indeed, on what evidence is. (This assessment conforms to principle (i) of empiricism, which admits all experience — visual, tactile, etc. — as *prima facie* evidence.)

What is the difference between the political-authority case and the visualism case? The answer is plain. The political authority is intuitively not as basic a source of *prima facie* evidence as the sources of *prima facie* evidence that are being used to eliminate it (i.e., experience, observation, etc.). By contrast, vision and touch are intuitively equally basic sources of *prima facie* evidence. The standard justificatory procedure permits us to apply the present method against a currently accepted source of *prima facie* evidence if and only if *intuitively* that source is not as basic as the sources of *prima facie* evidence being used to challenge it. That is, according to the standard procedure, we are to consult our intuitions regarding the relative basicness of a given source of *prima facie* evidence. If and only if intuition declares that source not to be as basic as the sources that are being used to challenge it are we to proceed. Someone might think that, rather than consulting intuition on the question of relative basicness, one should consult the simplest overall theory that takes as its evidence the deliverances of one's currently accepted sources of *prima facie* evidence. But this approach yields the wrong results. For example, according to it, the political authority, with just a bit of cleverness, would be as immune to challenge as, say, sense experience. (E.g., the political authority could carefully restrict itself to empirically untestable pronouncements that suggest that it has a special new cognitive power; it could deem itself to be a maximally basic source of evidence; etc.) But despite this, it would be appropriate to reject the political authority as a special source of evidence. The way we would do this, according to the standard procedure, would be to fall back on our intuitions about relative basicness: intuitively, a political authority's pronouncements are not as basic as, say, one's sense experiences. The overall theory one would formulate on the basis of the sources of evidence that are intuitively more basic would not deem the political authority to be reliable.

Now let us return to the empiricists' effort to eliminate intuition as a source of *prima facie* evidence. Their idea is that the standard justificatory procedure warrants this because the overall theory that admits only experience and/or observation as *prima facie* evidence does not deem intuition to be reliable. The mistake is now plain. The standard justificatory procedure would warrant this move only if we had intuitions to the effect that intuition is a less basic source of *prima facie* evidence than experience and/or observation, one requiring auxiliary support from the best comprehensive theory that is based exclusively on other sources of *prima facie* evidence that are intuitively more basic. But when we consider relevant cases, we see that we do not have such intuitions. For example, suppose a person has an intuition, say, that if P or $Q,$ then not both not P and not $Q;$ or that the person in our sheep-looking–poodle example would not know that there is a sheep there; or that a good theory must take into account *all* the *prima facie* evidence; and so forth. Nothing more is needed. Intuitively, these intuitions are evidentially as basic as a person's experiences. In rather the same way one's visual experiences are intuitively as basic as one's tactile experience, and conversely. In consequence, the present method for challenging a source of *prima facie* evidence cannot be used against intuition, any more than it can be used against, say, touch or vision.[19]

The conclusion is this: intuition survives as a genuine source of *prima facie* evidence when one applies the standard justificatory procedure's mechanism for self-criticism. We have not been able to find a relevant difference between empiricism, which excludes intuition as a source of *prima facie* evidence, and various preposterous theories (e.g., visualism) that arbitrarily exclude standard sources of *prima facie* evidence (e.g., touch). But, surely, these preposterous theories are not justified. So empiricism is not justified, either.

There is a way to strengthen this argument. Suppose that in our justificatory practices we were to make an arbitrary departure from our epistemic norms. In this case there would be *prima facie* reason to doubt that the theories we would be led to formulate by following the non-standard procedure are justified. Given that empiricists make an arbitrary departure from our epistemic norms, what can they do to overcome this reasonable doubt in their own case? They are caught in a fatal dilemma. On the one hand, they could invoke theories arrived at by following the standard justificatory procedure, with its inclusion of intuitions as *prima facie* evidence. But, by the empiricists' own standards, these theories are not justified. So this avenue is of no help to our empiricists. On the other hand, they could invoke theories arrived at by following their empiricist procedure.[20] But this would be of no help, either. For, as we have seen, there is reasonable doubt that, by following the empiricist procedure, one obtains justified theories. To overcome that reasonable doubt, one may not invoke the very theories about whose justification there is already reasonable doubt. That would only beg the question.[21] Either way, therefore, empiricists are unable to overcome the reasonable doubt that their procedure leads to justified theories. So the reasonable doubt stands.

Our epistemic situation is in this sense "hermeneutical": when one makes an arbitrary departure from it, reasonable doubts are generated, and there is in principle no way to overcome them. This is the fate of empiricism. Only the standard justificatory procedure escapes this problem: because it conforms to — and, indeed, constitutes — the epistemic norm, there is no *prima facie* reason to doubt that the theories it yields are justified; so the problem never arises.

Terms of Epistemic Appraisal

We have seen how empiricism is cut adrift when it rejects the special authority of intuitions in connection with starting points, and we have just seen how empiricism is caught in a general hermeneutical dilemma triggered by its arbitrary departure from our epistemic norms. Our third argument concerns a more specific hermeneutical difficulty that arises in connection with our standard terms of epistemic appraisal. Our argument builds upon George Myro's important and elegant paper "Aspects of Acceptability."[22]

The setting is the version of empiricism articulated by Quine. As noted at the outset, this position consists of three principles: (i) the principle of empiricism, (ii) the principle of holism, and (iii) the principle of naturalism. Quineans use these principles to obtain a number of strong negative conclusions. The following is an illustration. From principles (i) and (ii) — the principle of empiricism and the principle of holism — it follows that a theory is justified for a person if and only if it is, or belongs to, the simplest comprehensive theory that explains all, or most, of the person's experiences and/or observations. From this conclusion and principle (iii) — the principle of naturalism — it follows that a theory is justified for a person if and only if it is, or belongs to, the natural sciences (plus the logic and mathematics needed by them). It is understood that this is to be the *simplest regimented formulation* of the natural sciences. By implementing various ingenious techniques of regimentation, Quineans give arguments showing that the underlying logic needed for this formulation of the natural sciences is just elementary extensional logic and, in turn, that no modal propositions (sentences) are found in this formulation of the natural sciences. If these arguments are sound, it follows that no modal proposition (sentence) is justified. Indeed, (the sentence expressing) the proposition that modal truths exist does not belong to the simplest regimented formulation of the natural sciences. Given this, it follows that it is unjustified even to assert the existence of modal truths. This, then, is how empiricism joins forces with naturalism to attack the modalities and modal knowledge.

Quineans mount much the same style of argument to attack definitions, definitional truths, analyticities, synonymies, intensional meanings, property identities, property reductions, and the associated ontology of intensional entities (concepts, ideas, properties, propositions, etc.). For, just as no modal propositions (sentences) belong to the simplest regimented formulation of the natural sciences, neither do propositions (sentences) to the effect that such and such is a definition (definitional truth, analytic, etc.). According to Quineans, the natural sciences on their simplest regimented formulation have no need to include definitions and the special apparatus from intensional logic and/or intensional semantics needed to state them. Likewise for propositions (sentences) about definitional truth, analyticity, synonymity, intensional meaning, property identity, property reduction, and so forth: to explain one's experiences and/or observations, one always has a simpler formulation of the natural sciences that avoids these things.[23] Therefore, given principles (i)–(iii), any theory that includes these things is unjustified.

With this summary before us, we are now ready for our argument that empiricism, as formulated, is epistemically self-defeating.

Let us suppose that principles (i)–(iii) are true. (Principles (ii) and (iii) are very plausible. It is principle (i), the principle of empiricism, that is questionable. Thus, our argument may be thought of as a *reductio ad absurdum* of principle (i). We will return to this point at the close.) And let us suppose that the Quinean arguments from principles (i)–(iii) to the above negative conclusions are correct, at least by empiricist standards. (This supposition is extremely plausible when one comes to appreciate the full power of Quinean regimentation techniques and when one realizes that, for empiricists, those techniques need not be constrained by intuitions.) Given these suppositions, what is the justificatory status of principles (i)–(iii) themselves?

Notice that these principles contain the familiar terms 'justified', 'simplest', 'theory', 'explain', and '*prima facie* evidence'. These terms do not belong to the primitive vocabulary of the simplest regimented formulation of the natural sciences.[24] Moreover, given the correctness of the Quinean negative arguments, these terms cannot be defined within this formulation of the natural sciences (likewise they cannot be stated to be translations of other expressions; nor can they be stated to express the same properties as, or to be synonyms of, or abbreviations for, other expressions; etc.). The reason is that this formulation of the natural sciences does not contain an apparatus for indicating definitional relationships (or relationships of translation, synonymy, abbreviation, property identity, property reduction, or anything relevantly like them).[25] (See below for a discussion of what is needed to show that a new notion is *relevantly like* a standard notion.) It follows that the radical empiricists' principles (i)–(iii) do not belong to this formulation of the natural sciences and, therefore, that principles (i)–(iii) do not count as justified according to principles (i)–(iii). Hence, this version of empiricism is epistemically self-defeating.[26] This is the first step in our argument.

The problem results from the fact that the simplest formulation of the natural sciences does not contain our standard epistemic terms 'justified', 'simplest', and so forth, nor does it contain an apparatus for defining them (or for translating them; or for stating that they express properties that are identical to those expressed by other terms; or that they express properties that reduce to those expressed by other terms; or that they are synonyms of, or abbreviations for, other terms; or anything relevantly like this). If any of these items were adjoined to or included in a formulation of the natural sciences, that would exceed the essentially simpler resources required for the simplest regimented formulation of the natural sciences and, therefore, would (according to principles (i)–(iii)) be unjustified.

The most promising empiricist response to this self-defeat argument goes as follows. It is acknowledged at the outset that the simplest regimented formulation of the natural sciences does not include either the terminology of principles (i)–(iii) or a standard apparatus for defining that terminology (or for stating relations of translation, synonymy, abbreviation, property identity, property reduction, etc.). It is nevertheless maintained that this formulation of the natural sciences does contain scientifically acceptable "counterparts" of these terms, that "counterparts" of principles (i)–(iii) can be stated in this terminology, and that, unlike principles (i)–(iii), these "counterpart" principles are consequences of the natural sciences on their simplest regimented formulation. Therefore, unlike the original (unscientific) statement of empiricism, the new (scientific) statement of it is not epistemically self-defeating. So goes the empiricists' response. This is the "best-case scenario" for saving empiricism from epistemic self-defeat.[27]

To illustrate how this response would go in detail, let J, S, P, and E be complex predicates from the simplest regimented formulation of the natural sciences. For example, J, S, P, and E might be complex behavioral-*cum*-physiological predicates. These predicates are supposed to be the scientifically acceptable "counterparts" of 'justified', 'simplest explanation', '*prima facie* evidence', and 'experience', respectively. Let N be the simplest regimented formulation of the natural sciences. And let us suppose that the following are derivable from N:

(1) $E(z,y)$ iff $P(z,y)$.
(2) $J(x,y)$ iff $(\exists w)(\exists z)(x \in w)$ & $S(w,z)$ & $(P(z,y))$.
(3) If $E(z,y)$, then $S(N,z)$.

These principles are supposed to be "counterparts" of the empiricists' original principles (i)–(iii).[28]

The problem with this empiricist response is that, if the standard idiom for epistemic appraisal (justification, acceptability, etc.) is abandoned in favor of this new idiom of "counterparts," empiricists must show (or do something relevantly like showing) that this new idiom is *relevantly like* the standard idiom, for otherwise there would be no reason to think that principles such as (1)–(3), which use the new idiom, have any bearing on epistemic appraisal. After all, epistemic appraisal, or something relevantly like it, is what is at issue. There can be many similarities between a standard idiom and a new idiom (e.g., length or sound of constituent expressions, etc.), but only some of them are *relevant*. Therefore, it is incumbent on the empiricists to show that the new idiom is relevantly like the standard one. If they cannot do this, their talk is, for all we know, irrelevant verbiage.[29]

How might the empiricists try to show that their idiom is relevantly like the standard idiom? Well, they could try to show that the standard idiom can be *defined* in terms of the new idiom. (Or they could try to show that the *meaning* of expressions in the new idiom are relevantly like the meaning of expressions in the standard idiom.[30] Or they could try to show that the *reason, purpose,* or *function* of the new idiom is relevantly like that of the standard idiom.[31] Or they might try to show that the two idioms share something that is relevantly like a definitional relation, meaning, reason, purpose, or function.[32]) But we have already seen that, according to principles (i)–(iii), the use of a standard apparatus for indicating definitional relationships does not belong to the simplest regimented formulation of the natural sciences and, hence, is unjustified. (Likewise for other intensional idioms dealing with meaning, reason, purpose, function, and so forth.) To avoid this problem, empiricists have no choice but to drop the standard apparatus for treating definitions (meaning, reason, purpose, function, etc.) and to put in its place some "counterpart" that does belong to the natural sciences on their simplest regimented formulation.

There are a number of ways in which empiricists could try to implement this maneuver. The following is perhaps the most elegant; in other respects it is typical. Suppose that D is a complex predicate that belongs to N and that the following are theorems of N:

(4) $D(\ulcorner A \text{ iff}_{\text{def}} B \urcorner, \ulcorner D(\ulcorner A \urcorner, \ulcorner B \urcorner) \urcorner)$.

(5) $D(\ulcorner \alpha \text{ is justified for } \beta \urcorner, \ulcorner J(\alpha,\beta) \urcorner)$.

(6) $D(\ulcorner \alpha \text{ is, or is part of, the simplest explanation of } \beta \urcorner, \ulcorner S(\alpha,\beta) \urcorner)$.

(7) $D(\ulcorner \alpha \text{ is } \beta \text{'s } \textit{prima facie} \text{ evidence} \urcorner, \ulcorner P(\alpha,\beta) \urcorner)$.

(8) $D(\ulcorner \alpha \text{ are } \beta \text{'s experiences} \urcorner, \ulcorner E(\alpha,\beta) \urcorner)$.

(9) $D(\ulcorner \ldots \text{ that } A \ldots \urcorner, \ulcorner \ldots \ulcorner A \urcorner \ldots \urcorner)$.

(10) $(S(u,z) \& u \vdash \ulcorner \ldots A \ldots \urcorner \& D(\ulcorner B \urcorner, \ulcorner A \urcorner)) \to S(u \cup \{\ulcorner \ldots B \ldots \urcorner\}, z)$.

Items (4)–(9) are supposed to be "counterparts" of definitions of 'iff$_{def}$', 'justified', 'simplest explanation', '*prima facie* evidence', 'experience', and 'that'-clauses, respectively. And item (10) is supposed to be the "counterpart" of the (debatable) thesis that a definitional extension of a theory is as simple as the original theory.

The empiricists' idea is that items (1)–(10) are supposed to be an "image," in the language of scientifically approved "counterparts," of the sorts of thing one would need in order to get a self-justifying epistemology of natural science.

However, a moment's reflection shows that no progress has been made at all. The predicate D could, for all we know, be irrelevant to definitions. So, in turn, for all we know, items (1)–(10) are just irrelevant to epistemic appraisal. Indeed, "images" of the sort of thing one would need to have a self-justifying theory are a dime a dozen. For example, using Gödelian techniques of self-reference, we can construct infinitely many complex predicates D, J, S, P, and E such that these ten items can be derived from N (assuming that N is rich enough to describe its own syntax). Are there any predicates like this that express "natural properties"? It seems doubtful. But even if there were, their "naturalness" would count for nothing according to empiricists, for statements about the naturalness of properties fall outside the domain of the simplest regimented formulation of the natural sciences and so are unjustified according to principles (i)–(iii). As far as epistemic appraisal is concerned, (1)–(10) are, for all we know, just so much irrelevant verbiage.[33]

There is only one way out of this problem of establishing a relevant connection between (1)–(10) and the standard idiom of epistemic appraisal: at least one *bridge principle* stated in the standard idiom is needed.

To illustrate how this would go, let us consider the simplest and most elegant bridge principle of the requisite sort, namely, a "definition of definition." Let N^+ be the enlarged theory that consists of N plus the following:

(11) $(A \text{ iff}_{def} B) \text{ iff}_{def} D(\ulcorner A \urcorner, \ulcorner B \urcorner)$.

By *using*, not just mentioning, the standard idiom 'iff$_{def}$' this principle explicitly affirms the requisite connection between the standard idiom 'iff$_{def}$' and the "counterpart" idiom D. In N^+ one can derive consequences such as the following:[34]

> N is justified.
> (11) is justified.
> N^+ is justified.
> (i)–(iii) are justified.

Moreover, in N^+ one can derive the 'that'-clause formulations of these statements about justification. Thus, with (11) adjoined, we can show that (1)–(10) are relevantly like principles of epistemic appraisal stated in the standard idiom. Indeed, we can show that they are definitionally equivalent to them and, hence, that the empiricists' original principles (i)–(iii) are justified. Therefore, if empiricists could justify (11) by their own standards, they would avoid epistemic self-defeat. Such, then, is the "best-case scenario" for saving empiricism from epistemic self-defeat. However, if empiricists cannot by their own standards justify (11) — or some comparable "self-applicable" intensional principle — their effort to avoid epistemic self-defeat would be doomed. So, can (11) — or some comparable "self-applicable" intensional principle — be justified by empiricist standards?

Not at all. On the one hand, suppose that one admits one's intuitions as *prima facie* evidence, and suppose that the simplest explanation of one's experiences and intuitions, taken together, is provided by the enlarged theory N^+. (This supposition is almost certainly false. For example, when intuitions are admitted as *prima facie* evidence, we end up with the conclusion that it is justified that intuitions are *prima facie* evidence. However, N^+ implies that it is justified that only experiences are *prima facie* evidence.) Would our supposition imply that (11) is justified according to empiricist standards? No, for according to empiricism, intuition does not count as *prima facie* evidence. So this supposed outcome would do nothing whatsoever to justify (11). On the other hand, suppose — as the empiricists' principle (i) requires — that one admits only one's experiences and/or observations as *prima facie* evidence. Then, by principle (ii), it follows that a theory is justified if and only if it is, or belongs to, the simplest explanation of one's experiences and/or observations. Hence, by principle (iii), a theory is justified if and only if it is, or belongs to, the simplest regimented formulation of the natural sciences (i.e., N). However, by Quinean arguments the simplest regimented formulation of the natural sciences (i.e., N) does not include 'iff$_{def}$' and, hence, (11) is not derivable as a theorem from this formulation of the natural sciences. Is there any further *prima facie* evidence (reason, etc.) recognized by empiricists that would justify adjoining (11) to N (i.e., that would justify the enlarged theory consisting of N^+)? No. The theory N, which is justified according to empiricism, already takes into account *all* the *prima facie* evidence recognized by empiricism. Adjoining (11) to N is a gratuitous complication based on no *prima facie* evidence. According to empiricist standards, adjoining (11) would be nothing but a blind, irrational leap.[35]

The same conclusion holds for every bridge principle that, like (11), *uses,* not just mentions, one of the standard idioms we have been discussing (i.e., a standard idiom for dealing with definition, definitional truth,

analyticity, meaning, translation, synonymy, abbreviation, property identity, property reduction, reason, purpose, function, etc.). Because each of
these standard idioms exceeds the resources of the simplest regimented formulation of the natural sciences, adjoining one of these bridge principles
would be a wholly unjustified leap according to empiricist standards. However, according to the "best-case scenario" for saving empiricism from
epistemic self-defeat, at least one of these bridge principles must be adjoined. So even on the "best-case scenario" epistemic self-defeat is inevitable. The conclusion, therefore, is that empiricism is *essentially* self-
defeating.[36]

Moderate Rationalism

Principle (i) — the principle of empiricism — is evidently to blame for
this epistemic self-defeat. After all, principle (ii) — the principle of holism —
is very plausible. Something like it is surely embedded in our standard justificatory procedure. Although there might be reasonable alternatives to
principle (ii), none of them is sufficiently different to enable empiricists
to escape the self-defeat. Principle (iii) — the principle of naturalism — has
good empirical support (in the form of the ongoing success of the natural
sciences).[37] Furthermore, it is supported by arguments based on considerations of ontological economy. So there is good provisional reason for accepting the principle of naturalism. Moreover, even if the principle of naturalism should happen to be mistaken, it is rather likely that we could still
mount an epistemic self-defeat argument against empiricism. The reason
is this. Suppose that, to explain our experiences and/or observations, we
are led provisionally to accept various empirical theories above and beyond those belonging to the natural sciences. The principle of holism then
obliges us to find the simplest regimented formulation of these theories.
However, when we apply all the clever Quinean regimentation techniques
to these theories, it is plausible that, just as in the case of the natural sciences, terms of epistemic appraisal ('*prima facie* evidence', 'justified', 'simplest', 'theory', 'explanation', etc.) would prove inessential and would
therefore not occur in the resulting regimented theories. Furthermore, it
is plausible that the apparatus for indicating definitional relationships
(meaning, property identity, etc.) would likewise prove inessential and so
would not occur in the resulting theories. These two claims become even
more plausible when one appreciates the full power of Quinean regimentation techniques and when one realizes that, for empiricists, those techniques need not be constrained by intuition in any way. Given this, it is
quite plausible that our epistemic self-defeat argument against empiricism

would go through just as before even if some of our empirical theories were non-naturalistic. The conclusion, then, is that principle (i) — the principle of empiricism — is mistaken.

The failure of empiricism raises the question of whether epistemic self-defeat is not a general problem for any theory of evidence. Is there an alternative to the principle of empiricism that escapes this problem? Yes there is.

The principle of moderate rationalism:

> (i′) A person's experiences and intuitions comprise the person's *prima facie* evidence.[38]

True enough, principles (i′), (ii), and (iii) do not belong to the natural sciences on their simplest regimented formulation. But this fact does not lead to epistemic self-defeat. The reason is that, given principles (i′) and (ii), it follows that a theory is justified for a person if and only if it is, or belongs to, the simplest overall theory that explains all, or most of, the person's experiences and intuitions. The natural sciences do not constitute this theory. For, even though (by principle (iii)) the natural sciences explain all, or most, of a person's experiences, they do not even begin to explain all, or most of, a person's intuitions (for example, a person's intuitions about higher mathematics, metaphysical necessity and possibility, definitional relationships, etc.). So the remainder of the epistemic self-defeat argument does not go through.

Do principles (i′) and (ii) lead to a comprehensive theory that is epistemically self-approving, that is, a theory that includes these principles and deems itself to be justified? Yes. Consider the following plausible principle:

> (iv) The traditional theoretical disciplines — including philosophy, logic, mathematics, and the empirical sciences — provide the simplest explanation of a person's intuitions and experiences.

Philosophy, logic, and mathematics explain (or at least have the potential to explain) most of a person's intuitions. For example, logic — in particular, intensional logic — provides an apparatus for stating definitions, and it includes general laws governing definitional relationships — for example, $(A \text{ iff}_{\text{def}} B) \rightarrow (A \text{ iff } B)$. And philosophy — in particular, epistemology — provides (or has the potential for providing) theories of evidence, justification, simplicity, theoretical explanation, theoretical definition, and so forth. These philosophical theories would yield as consequences — and in that sense would explain — most of our intuitions about evidence, justification, simplicity, theoretical explanation, theoretical definition and so forth. Prin-

ciples (i′) and (ii) — or something like them — would be among these philosophical theories. Indeed, principle (ii) — or something like it — might even
be identified as a definitional truth. Principle (iv) is also a philosophical
theory. However, unlike principles (i′) and (ii), principle (iv) does not respond just to intuitions; it has a significant empirical content concerning
the actual theoretical activities of scientists, mathematicians, logicians, and
philosophers. Accordingly, it is best viewed as an example of applied epistemology — the result of applying pure epistemology to our actual theoretical activities as documented by relevant empirical theories. Now because
principles (i′), (ii), and (iv) — or something like them — may be expected to
belong to philosophy, they will count as justified according to the epistemic standards that they affirm. For this reason, these principles may be
expected to be epistemically self-approving.[39]

Summing up, we have found that empiricism is incoherent three times
over — once in relation to starting points, once in relation to epistemic norms,
and once in relation to terms of epistemic appraisal. By contrast, moderate rationalism, which is already embedded in our standard justificatory
practices, is in the clear on all three counts.

To its credit, empiricism has often served as an antidote to intellectual radicalism. On final analysis, however, empiricism is a member of that
same colorful company. Like Thales, Parmenides, Berkeley, and the others,
the adherent succumbs to the lure of a simplistic monolithic answer even
in the face of the obvious.

Notes

This essay is the first step in the argument of a book in progress on the philosophical limits of science. The overall thesis of the book is the autonomy of philosophy.
This is the thesis that, among the central questions of philosophy that can be answered at all, most can be answered by philosophical investigation and argument
without relying evidentially on the empirical sciences. Earlier versions of the essay
were presented at the George Myro Memorial Conference in March 1989, at the
Pacific Division Meeting of the American Philosophical Association in March 1990,
and at the *Discipuli* Conference at the University of Southern California in March
1991. This material was also presented as a talk at Reed College, University of Notre
Dame, and University of Washington. I am grateful for helpful comments I received at these gatherings. I am particularly indebted to George Myro and to Carol
Voeller for lengthy discussions of these topics.

1. More precisely, a person's *prima facie* evidence includes a given item
if and only if that item is (a report of) the contents of one of the person's experiences and/or observations. Traditionally, experience includes not only sensation,

but reflection (or introspection): feeling pain, experiencing emotions, and so forth. Certain philosophers (e.g., Brentano, Russell) would also include introspection of current conscious intentional states. Our discussion will apply to liberal versions of empiricism that include this kind of introspection as a kind of experience. However, we do not intend our discussion to apply to versions of empiricism that posit forms of experience above and beyond sensation and reflection (e.g., religious experience). A narrow version of empiricism would include only a person's sensations as *prima facie* evidence. Another narrow version includes only a person's observations (i.e., perceptions of the "external world") as *prima facie* evidence; for example, Bas van Fraassen and, at times, Quine appear to accept this version. As formulated in the text, empiricism does not admit memory or testimony as sources of *prima facie* evidence; however, much of our discussion would apply to a formulation of empiricism that did admit them.

Numerous philosophers have been attracted to one or another such formulation of empiricism, for example: John Stuart Mill, William James, W. V. O. Quine, Wilfrid Sellars, Nelson Goodman, Hilary Putnam, Bas van Fraassen, Hartry Field, Paul and Patricia Churchland, and others. It is not clear whether David Hume and various twentieth-century logical positivists should be classed with these philosophers; the reason is that Hume and these positivists seem to accord a special epistemic status to "relations of ideas" and "analytic truths."

2. There are passages in Quine's writings that seem at odds with this principle, for example, passages in which Quine appeals to intuition to help to justify his set theories NF and ML and passages in which Quine appeals to intuitions to defend various logico-linguistic claims (e.g., claims about the logic of mass terms, the intensionality of modal and belief contexts, etc.). However, for the purpose of the present essay, it would be best to sidestep issues of Quinean scholarship. Hereafter, when we speak of Quine's (formulation of) empiricism, we will mean the formulation given in the text. Certainly this formulation is accepted by a number of philosophers who consider themselves to be followers of Quine.

3. I.e., the simplest comprehensive theory that explains why (all or most of) the various items that are *prima facie* evident to the person do in fact hold.

4. These principles appear to be pretty close to Bas van Fraassen's version of empiricism (*The Scientific Image,* Oxford: Oxford University Press, 1980) except that he would replace 'justified theory' with 'good theory' and 'experience and/or observation' with simply 'observation'; moreover, van Fraassen makes a further claim about what should and should not be believed. The arguments we will give against Quine's empiricism, as formulated in the text, apply *mutatis mutandis* against van Fraassen's empiricism.

5. This example is adapted from Alvin Goldman, "Discrimination and Perceptual Knowledge," *Journal of Philosophy* 73 (1976): 771–791.

6. After all, if something counts as *prima facie* evidence, it also counts as a reason that is *prima facie* evident. And empiricists believe that all and only experiences and/or observations qualify as reasons that are *prima facie* evident, and they believe that a person is justified only if the person has taken into account the *prima facie* evident reasons.

7. When we say that an intuition counts as *prima facie* evidence, we of

course mean that the *content* of the intuition counts as *prima facie* evidence. When one has an intuition, however, often one is introspectively aware that one is having that intuition. On such an occasion, one would then have a bit of introspective evidence as well, namely, that one is having that intuition.

8. I am indebted to George Myro for this example and for the point it illustrates, namely, that it is possible to have an intuition without having the corresponding belief.

9. For example, it cannot seem to you sensorily that the naive comprehension axiom holds. Nor can it seem to you intellectually (i.e., without any relevant sensations and without any attendant beliefs) that there exist billions of brain cells; intuition is silent about this essentially empirical question. There are, however, certain special cases in which intellectual seeming and sensory seeming can evidently overlap. For example, it can seem sensorily that shades s_1 and s_2 are different, and it can seem intellectually that s_1 and s_2 are different.

10. For example, in philosophical discussions of the empirical findings of cognitive psychologists such as Wason, Johnson-Laird, Eleanor Rosh, Richard Nisbett, D. Kahneman, and A. Tversky, many philosophers use 'intuition' in this indiscriminate way. As a result, those discussions have little bearing on the topic under discussion in the text. The fact is that empirical investigators have seldom been concerned with intuitions *per se,* as we intend the term. Empirical investigators have not attempted to test empirically for the occurrence of genuine intuitions; they certainly have not employed anything like the criteria we have been listing in the text. Therefore, their results do not in a straightforward way yield philosophical conclusions about the nature of intuitions.

11. I thank Elizabeth Lloyd for the suggestion that bootstrapping be explicitly discussed here.

12. In the next section we will see that empiricism is not even self-approving and that this fact leads to a further kind of incoherence in empiricism.

13. Is it *possible* for contradictory concrete-case intuitions to become the norm? This is a highly theoretical question whose answer I think is negative. I certainly do not have concrete-case intuitions that support an affirmative answer. In any case this question is not relevant to the question in the text. The question we are examining there is whether intuition should *now* be thrown out as a source of *prima facie* evidence because of *actual* widespread inconsistencies. The answer to that question is negative.

14. Andrew Jeffrey has pointed out to me that, if our attribution of mental contents to others is guided by a principle of charity, we shall inevitably find a significant degree of corroboration between our intuitions and those of others.

15. This example is cited by Russell in *The Problems of Philosophy* (1912; reprint, Oxford: Oxford University Press, 1959), 138.

16. It is often claimed that there are widespread conflicts among moral intuitions and among aesthetic intuitions. Two comments are in order. First, people making this claim usually make no effort to distinguish between genuine intuitions and other cognitive states. It is far from clear that there is widespread conflict among genuine intuitions about moral and aesthetic matters. For example, I have a vivid intuition that, if I should never lie, then it is not the case that I should sometimes

lie. It is less clear that we truly have intuitions about categorical evaluative propositions. (Recall that we are only discussing *a priori* intuitions.) But the supposed conflict is almost always traceable to "evaluative intuitions" that are categorical. So it is not clear that there really are widespread conflicts among genuine intuitions about evaluative matters. Second, suppose, however, that there really are such conflicts. This would not call into question the evidential status of intuitions generally, for there is not widespread conflict among non-evaluative intuitions. At most "evaluative intuitions" would lose their evidential status.

17. These examples are still matters of controversy.

18. For simplicity, assume that empiricists have already eliminated intuition as a source of *prima facie* evidence.

19. There is an intuitive explanation of why intuitions should qualify as basic *prima facie* evidence: having largely reliable intuitions concerning the application of a concept is a logically necessary condition for having the concept in the first place; and the deliverances of a given cognitive faculty (e.g., intuition) qualify as basic *prima facie* evidence iff it is necessary that the deliverances of that faculty are largely reliable. This theory is developed in detail in the book mentioned in note 1.

20. Specifically, they would need to invoke theories about the justificatory status of theories that would result when one follows the empiricist procedure. In the next section we will see that, by following the empiricist procedure, one does *not* arrive at the requisite sort of theory about justification.

21. The following preposterous theory — let it be called 'Jack' — gives rise to the extreme case of this kind of question-begging.

> Jack is the one and only theory anyone is justified in accepting.

Suppose that out of the blue someone boldly asserts Jack. Because this would be an arbitrary departure from our epistemic norms, there would be *prima facie* reason to doubt that the assertion is justified. Our person certainly would not succeed in overcoming this reasonable doubt by invoking the theory that Jack guides one to accept (i.e., Jack itself).

22. George Myro, "Aspects of Acceptability," *Pacific Philosophical Quarterly* 62 (1981): 107–117, reprinted in this volume.

23. According to principle (i), a person's observations and/or experiences comprise the person's *prima facie* evidence. Quineans assume that a person's observations and experiences can all be reported in extensional language. This is relatively uncontroversial in the case of observation and *sense experience*. According to the most popular versions of empiricism, only observation and/or sense experience are recognized as sources of *prima facie* evidence; this is the position that Quineans accept. However, certain traditional empiricists hold that *introspection* (*reflection*) is a kind of experience and, accordingly, that one can experience one's own conscious intentional states. For example, Brentano, Russell, and perhaps Locke accepted this position. Such "reflective empiricists" would then hold that one's experiences of one's conscious intentional states qualify as *prima facie* evidence. Since the standard idiom for reporting such states is intensional (e.g., 'I am thinking that Cicero ≠ Tully'), perhaps, unlike Quinean empiricists, these reflec-

tive empiricists would not be led to reject intensionality. For this reason, one might conclude that the argument that we are about to give in the text will not work against reflective empiricists. (Of course, the other two arguments we have given would work against them.) However, this conclusion would be a mistake. The reason is that simplicity demands that reflective empiricists try to avoid the indicated intensionality. The most promising way for them to do this would be to try to abandon the standard intensional idiom for reporting conscious intentional states and, instead, to use some new extensional idiom. For example, instead of using the intensional sentence 'I am thinking that Cicero ≠ Tully', our reflective empiricists might (following Quine) use an extensional sentence such as the atomic monadic sentence 'I-am-thinking-Cicero-≠-Tully' or the metalinguistic sentence 'I am thinking "Cicero ≠ Tully".' There are, I believe, sound *intuitive* arguments to show that these new extensional idioms do not successfully report conscious intentional states unless they make at least implicit commitment to intensionality. However, empiricists do not honor arguments like these which rely on intuitions as evidence, so they would feel free to disregard them and to use the indicated extensional idioms. Accordingly, our reflective empiricists would be led to accept the full Quinean position embodied in principles (i)–(iii) and, in turn, the Quinean rejection of intensionality. Consequently, despite initial doubts to the contrary, reflective empiricists do not escape the argument we are about to give in the text. The moral will be that "data of reason" are needed to appreciate the ontological significance of one's "data of experience."

24. In "Aspects of Acceptability," George Myro concludes from this fact that Quine's philosophy is epistemically self-defeating. Our argument differs from Myro's in three respects. First, we consider the prospect that empiricists might try to avoid this self-defeat by introducing the standard terms of epistemic appraisal by means of definition, translation, synonymy, abbreviation, property identity, property reduction, etc. Second, we consider the prospect that empiricists might try to avoid self-defeat by relying on scientifically acceptable "counterparts" of the standard terms of epistemic appraisal. Third, we summarize Quine's empiricism in a more fine-grained fashion, isolating three distinct principles (i)–(iii). Because the latter two principles are so plausible, this permits us to identify principle (i) — the principle of empiricism — as the source of epistemic self-defeat. This makes it possible to reach a positive conclusion, namely, that some form of moderate rationalism is inevitable. The main aim of Myro's essay is metaphysical, rather than epistemological: he was primarily interested in legitimizing intensionality and intentionality. I do not know whether he was aware of this epistemological implication.

25. Quine tells us, "There does, however, remain still an extreme sort of definition which does not hark back to prior synonymies at all: namely, the explicitly conventional introduction of novel notations for purposes of sheer abbreviation. Here the definiendum becomes synonymous with the definiens simply because it has been created expressly for the purpose of being synonymous with the definiens. Here we have a really transparent case of synonymy created by definition; would that all species of synonymy were as intelligible" ("Two Dogmas of Empiricism," *From a Logical Point of View* [New York: Harper and Row, 1953], 26). Quine is mistaken. In view of the critique of intensionality sketched above, he cannot con-

sistently maintain this sanguine attitude toward stipulative definitions and abbreviation. But even if he could, that would not help to avoid the problem in the text. To avoid that problem, Quine needs an apparatus for giving definitions of terms that are *already* in use ('evidence', 'justify', etc.). Stipulative definitions do not fulfill this function.

26. Someone might object that we are requiring too much, for any comprehensive theory that deems itself to be justified runs into a paradox akin to the Montague-Kaplan paradox. See David Kaplan and Richard Montague, "A Paradox Regained," *Notre Dame Journal of Formal Logic* 1 (1960): 79–90; Richard Montague, "Syntactical Treatments of Modality, with Corollaries on Reflexion Principles and Finite Axiomatizability," *Acta Philosophica Fennica* 16 (1963): 153–167; Richmond Thomason, "A Note on Syntactical Treatments of Modality," *Synthese* 44 (1980): 391–395; Rob Koons, *Analogues of the Liar Paradox in Epistemic Logic,* Ph.D. Dissertation, U.C.L.A., 1987. However, the inevitability of a genuine self-justification paradox can be reasonably disputed. See, for example, the work of Nicholas Asher and Hans Kamp for suggestive ideas on how this sort of paradox might be avoided in a suitable type-free setting ("Self-reference, Attitudes and Paradox," in *Properties, Types, and Meaning, Volume I: Foundational Issues,* ed. G. Chierchia, B. Partee, and R. Turner [Dordrecht: Kluwer, 1989] 85–158). But even if it is accepted that such a paradox is inevitable, empiricism is still caught in a fatal epistemic self-defeat that does not arise for an epistemology that accepts intuitions as *prima facie* evidence. (See the final section in the text.) At worst, advocates of the latter type of epistemology would need to introduce some form of hierarchy of terms of epistemic appraisal like that found in a ramified type theory; for example, an infinite hierarchy of primitive predicates $\ulcorner$justified$_\alpha\urcorner$, one for each ordinal α. The problem for empiricists is that *no* terms of epistemic appraisal (e.g., $\ulcorner$justified$_1\urcorner$, $\ulcorner$justified$_2\urcorner$, etc.) belong to the simplest regimented formulation of the natural sciences. Therefore, *no* version of principles (i)–(iii), including the contemplated typically ambiguous versions, would be justified, or justified$_\alpha$ according to the contemplated versions of (i)–(iii).

27. Although this view has, to my knowledge, never been explicitly developed in the philosophical literature, it seems inevitable that Paul and Patricia Churchland would be forced to advocate something like it in an attempt to save their naturalistic account of property reduction from epistemic self-defeat. See Paul Churchland, *Scientific Realism and the Plasticity of Mind* (Cambridge: Cambridge University Press, 1979); Patricia Churchland, *Neurophilosophy* (Cambridge, Mass.: MIT Press, 1986). In our opinion, therefore, the argument given in the text applies *mutatis mutandis* to the Churchlands' empiricist philosophy.

28. Of course, the term 'counterpart' does not belong to *N*. Nevertheless, we may suppose that the following is a theorem of *N:* (1)–(3) are theorems of *N,* and (1)–(3) are syntactically isomorphic to (i)–(iii). For the sake of argument, let us suppose that this is enough to get the empiricists' response started.

29. Given that empiricists actually eschew various systematic positive relationships between their new terms and our standard terms of epistemic appraisal (e.g., $P(z,y)$ iff z is y's *prima facie* evidence; $J(x,y)$ iff x is justified for y; etc.),

there is *prima facie* reason to doubt that the new terms are relevant to epistemic appraisal.

30. To show that the meaning of an expression in a new idiom is *relevantly like* the meaning of an expression in the standard idiom, one has a cluster of similar options. First, one can show an actual meaning identity. But statements of meaning identities have the following systematic relation to statements of intensional identities: the meaning of $\ulcorner A \urcorner$ = the meaning of $\ulcorner B \urcorner$ if and only if that A = that B. So intensionality enters in here. Second, one can show that the two expressions are synonymous. But statements of synonymy have the following systematic relationships to statements of meaning identity: $\ulcorner A \urcorner$ and $\ulcorner B \urcorner$ are synonymous if and only if the meaning of $\ulcorner A \urcorner$ = the meaning of $\ulcorner B \urcorner$ if and only if that A = that B. So this is no advance over the previous option. Third, one can show that the two expressions are definitionally related. However, the standard devices for indicating definitional relationships are intensional, for example: 'iff$_{def}$', '=$_{def}$', 'It is definitionally true that', and so forth. So this option does not lead to the elimination of intensionality. Fourth, one can show that one expression is an abbreviation of the other. But such statements about abbreviation have the following systematic relationship to definitional statements: $\ulcorner A \urcorner$ is an abbreviation for $\ulcorner B \urcorner$ only if A iff$_{def}$ B. So this is no advance over the previous option. Fifth, one can show that the (Gricean) intentions that a speaker would have for uttering the two expressions are the same. However, the standard idiom for reporting speaker's intentions is intensional. Sixth, one can show that the purpose or function served by (the meanings of) the two expressions is the same. However, our standard idiom for discussing purpose and function is also intensional. For example, $\ulcorner$The purpose of F-ing is to $G\urcorner$, $\ulcorner$The function of F-ing is to $G\urcorner$, etc., contain gerundive and infinitive phrases, which like 'that'-clauses, generate intensional contexts. Seventh, one can show that the two meanings are inherently similar. (The expressions $\ulcorner A \urcorner$ and $\ulcorner B \urcorner$ are, of course, not inherently similar.) But the meaning of $\ulcorner A \urcorner$ and the meaning of $\ulcorner B \urcorner$ are inherently similar iff that A and that B are inherently similar. So the intensionality remains. Moreover, to show that two items are inherently similar, one must show that they share fundamental qualities and relations. But a general theory of fundamental qualities and relations is already a property theory; indeed, such a theory is, on its own, sufficient for the construction of intensional logic. (See chapter 8 of my *Quality and Concept* [Oxford: Oxford University Press, 1982] for an elaboration of this argument. See also David Lewis, "New Work for a Theory of Universals," *Australasian Journal of Philosophy,* 61 [1983]: 343–377). On all these options, therefore, intensionality—or a framework that implies it—plays a central role. Of course, our empiricists could attempt to replace one or more of these standard intensional idioms with an extensional idiom. However, given that our empiricists would have to eschew systematic positive relationships between the extensional idiom and the standard intensional idioms, there would be a *prima facie* reason for doubting that the extensional idiom is truly relevant to meaning, synonymy, definition, abbreviation, intentionality, purpose, function, or inherent similarity. To overcome this reasonable doubt, our empiricists would need to show that the extensional idiom, as they are using it, has a meaning,

reason, purpose, or function (or something relevantly like meaning, reason, purpose, or function) that is relevantly like that of our standard idioms. This is precisely the sort of challenge empiricists are facing in the text.

31. An important kind of function that two idioms might have in common is their *explanatory role*. The standard idiom for discussing explanatory role is doubly intensional. First, the standard idiom for talking about explanation is intensional; for example, ⌜That A explains why it is the case that B⌝. Second, as we mentioned in the previous note, our standard idiom for discussing function is intensional; for example, ⌜The function of F-ing is to G⌝. Of course, our empiricists might try to use some extensional idiom to talk about explanatory role. However, if this extensional idiom does not bear obvious systematic positive relationships to our standard intensional idioms, there would be *prima facie* reason to doubt that the extensional idiom, as our empiricists are using it, is truly relevant to explanatory role. To overcome this reasonable doubt, our empiricists would need to show that this extensional idiom has a meaning, purpose, function, or explanatory role (or something relevantly like meaning, reason, purpose, function, or explanatory role) that is relevantly like that of the standard idioms. But this is once again just the sort of challenge empiricists are facing in the text. Incidentally, the theory of property reduction espoused in Paul and Patricia Churchland is, in our opinion, caught in the same sort of trap.

32. Our empiricists might instead try to show that the two idioms have a common *reference* (or something relevantly like reference). Two observations are in order. First, the mere fact that two idioms have a common reference does not imply that they are *relevantly* like one another (e.g., the fact that 'electron' and some complex predicate that enumerates all the actual electrons in the universe are co-referential does not make these expressions *relevantly* alike). This is just the old point about intensionality and co-reference: to be relevantly alike, two idioms must be intensionally alike (or something relevantly like intensionally alike). Second, any plausible theory of reference is committed to some form of intensionality. Consider, for example, a direct reference theory. According to such a theory, the expression 'justified' was introduced by a speech act akin to a baptism. In this speech act a special sort of relation, call it R, held among the expression 'justified', the person or persons who introduced the expression, and a certain set S of propositions or sentences (namely, those that are in fact justified). What is this relation R? Well, it might be a relation of causation; S caused the person or person who introduced the expression 'justified' to introduce it. Or it might be a relation of historical explanation: S was the item that best explains why the person or persons performed the relevant speech act. Or it might be a relation of salience: S was the item that was salient for the person or persons in the context. Or it might be intentional: S was the item of which the person or persons were thinking at the time. However, the standard idioms we use to talk about causation, explanation, salience, and intentionality are intensional (e.g., ⌜It is causally necessary that, if A, then B⌝, ⌜That A explains why it is the case that B⌝, etc.). As before, there are also standard extensional ways of talking about causation, explanation, salience, and intentionality. However, these extensional idioms bear systematic positive relations to the standard intensional idioms. If our empiricists assert these systematic posi-

tive relationships, they are caught in self-defeat. If they deny them, that creates a *prima facie* reason for doubting that their extensional idiom, as they are using it, is relevant to causation, explanation, salience, or intentionality. How can our empiricists overcome this reasonable doubt? They must show that their extensional idiom, as they are using it, has a meaning, reason, purpose, function, or reference (or something relevantly like meaning, reason, purpose, function, or reference) that is relevantly like that of the standard idiom. But this is, once again, precisely the sort of challenge facing empiricists in the text.

33. Indeed, given that empiricists do not accept that D serves to define definition—i.e., given that empiricists do not accept that (A iff$_{def}$ B) iff$_{def}$ $D(\ulcorner A \urcorner, \ulcorner B \urcorner)$—there is *prima facie* reason to doubt that the empiricists' new term D is relevant to definition.

34. These derivations require the auxiliary premise that everyone has a body of experiences.

35. To dramatize the point, we could produce, by using standard Gödelian techniques of self-reference, infinitely many alternatives to (11) having the form: (A iff$_{def}$ B) iff$_{def}$ $Q(\ulcorner A \urcorner, \ulcorner B \urcorner)$. Like (11), each of these alternatives would yield a self-justifying theory when it is adjoined to N. However, each of these alternatives is inconsistent with (11) in the sense that, when any of them is adjoined to N^+, the resulting theory is inconsistent. Indeed, for absolutely *any* sentence A, no matter how crazy, we can construct an alternative to (11) such that, when it is adjoined to N, the resulting theory yields the following as a theorem: A is justified. Using empiricist standards, one has no way to justify choosing (11) over these alternatives (and conversely); the choice among them would be utterly arbitrary. So clearly none of these definitions of definition—including (11)—can be justified by empiricist standards.

36. Another response to this epistemic self-defeat is to try to modify the principle of holism in such a way that empiricism is no longer epistemically self-defeating. Consider two ways in which this might be done. The first, which was discussed by George Myro in "Aspects of Acceptability," is this: a theory is justified for a person iff it is, or belongs to, the simplest overall theory that explains all, or most, of the person's *prima facie* evidence and that deems itself to be justified. Ironically, this revised principle does not save empiricism, for the simplest theories like this are ones constructed by means of logicians' tricks. Such theories do not deem the principle of empiricism to be justified. For example, perhaps Bob is such a theory, where Bob is the following: N and Bob is justified. Bob does not deem empiricism to be justified.

The following is a second way in which the principle of holism might be revised: a theory is justified for a person iff it is, or belongs to, the simplest comprehensive theory that explains all, or most, of the person's *prima facie* evidence, or it is, or belongs to an extension of that simplest comprehensive theory by means of the person's old terminology. A theory T' extends theory T by means of a person's old terminology iff the primitive terms β belonging to the person's previously held theory can be paired with (primitive or complex) terms d in T in such a way that T' is the result adjoining all the biconditionals. $\ulcorner \beta$ iff $\delta \urcorner$ to T, and T' yields as theorems most of the sentences in the person's previously held theory. (This way of revising the principle of holism came up in conversation with Stephen Leeds. It bears some resemblance to an idea implicit in Paul and Patricia Churchland's views on property reduction.) The problem is that there are clear-cut counter-examples. Here is an illustration. Suppose that a person's previously held theory consists of N plus the following: For all x, x is a physical object iff x is inhabited by an animal spirit. Then, since the old term 'inhabited by an animal spirit' can be paired with the term 'physical object' in N, the previously held theory would itself qualify as an extension of N by means of the person's old terminology. Accordingly, the theory that every physical object is inhabited by an animal spirit would count as justified according to the revised principle. For another counter-example, suppose that the person's previous theory is just like N except that it contains more empirically insignificant, wholly speculative metaphysics. The problem, of course, arises from the fact that the revised principle of holism does not restrict a person's previously held theories to those that were really justified at that time. How can this restriction be imposed without triggering a vicious regress? Evidently, the only plausible way would be to require that, at some earlier stage or other, the person held a theory that satisfied (something like) the original, unrevised principle of holism. But if this requirement is imposed, then nothing resembling the empiricists' principles (i)–(iii) would at any stage get admitted as justified. The result, then, would be that empiricism would still be epistemically self-defeating.

37. This principle is roughly equivalent to the Kantian thesis that occurrences in the phenomenal world are causally explainable only in terms of other occurrences in the phenomenal world.

38. As it stands, principle (i′) is plainly too strict. For example, observation and testimony also count as *prima facie* evidence. To correct this problem we should replace '*prima facie* evidence' with 'basic *prima facie* evidence'. This modification would in turn require us either to replace '*prima facie* evidence' with 'basic *prima facie* evidence' in principle (ii) or to keep principle (ii) as it stands but to adjoin a further principle defining the relation between '*prima facie* evidence' and 'basic *prima facie* evidence'. (Given principle (iv), which we are about to state in the text, and some relevant empirical facts about the overall reliability of human observation and testimony, it is plausible that these two alternatives can be shown to be equivalent.) For simplicity of presentation, these complexities will be suppressed in the text.

39. It is understood that the sophistications mentioned at the end of note 26 might need to be incorporated into principles (i′), (ii), (iii), and (iv).

Aspects of Acceptability

GEORGE MYRO

I find myself in a state of philosophical Dr. Jekyll and Mr. Hyde. Surmising that my predicament is not entirely idiosyncratic — not to say: idiotic — I parade it before you in the hope of provoking, ultimately, a more single vision. My division into Dr. Jekyll and Mr. Hyde arises out of being bothered by the following question. What makes a theory — particularly, a *philosophical one — acceptable:* that is, *such* that, as far as we can tell, it is true?

Merely by way of illustration, let me cite a particular philosophical view which I find appealing and ruminate on the question of its acceptability. So let me split myself into Dr. Jekyll and Mr. Hyde.

Jekyll believes that, along with various other things, there are, first, such abstract entities as "propositions", "attributes", and the like, and second, states of consciousness, such as experiences, thoughts, desires, intentions, and the like. Items of the second sort he regards as cases of standing in one or another, specially "mental", relation to one or another item of the first sort. This is, of course, very vague and, perhaps, implausible. But my concern is not to articulate or defend a precise ontological view. Rather, it is to consider how such a view *might* be defended: what does or *would* make it *acceptable* or not.

Jekyll thinks that his view (about propositions, etc.) is acceptable, ultimately, in part because of its being incorporated in an acceptable theory of language, or in what one may make bold to call its Frege-Grice-Schiffer fragment, a part of which may be sketched with summary crudeness as follows.

Sentences "express" propositions. This is to be explicated in terms of there being a general expectation ("convention"?) that speakers generally utter a sentence intending (in a certain manner) to get the audience to have in mind a certain proposition — the one (or one of those) said to be "expressed" by the sentence, most often with the intention that the audience take up an attitude (e.g., belief) towards that proposition or another suitably related one (which is "implicated", perhaps "conversationally").

If something like this is to be part of the acceptable theory of language, then we shall have propositions and "propositional attitudes", which provide us with an opening towards states of consciousness (an opening which I will not attempt to widen at present).

Among various objections that one may raise against Jekyll's line of defense, there is one that is particularly pertinent to my predicament. This is that there are plenty of good looking theories dealing with language which, on the one hand, do not postulate propositions or do not have recourse to propositional attitudes, or both, and which, on the other, seem to compete well with the so-called Frege-Grice-Schiffer fragment.

Jekyll's reply to this objection begins by raising an issue which gives rise to my predicament. There is indeed, Jekyll would say, a welter of variously competing and sometimes unconnected theories dealing with language—a sort of creative chaos. And this is in part because of a lack of clarity about what makes a given theory (or thesis) dealing with language *acceptable* or not.

This is meant to be an epistemological question. So the answer "being true" is ruled out. In other fields, particularly the natural sciences, we seem to be able to give epistemological answers, such as—for example, being (part of) the simplest theory which explains the data.

Jekyll himself is strongly attracted to the view that the epistemological answer given by way of illustration for the case of the natural sciences is to be accepted and generalized across the board. Indeed, with a vengeance: it is to be applied, in the first instance, to our "total theory" of the world. What is acceptable as the total theory of the world is the simplest theory which explains the "totality" of the data (I should say that I use "theory" throughout somewhat misleadingly to include both law-like generalizations and plain fact statements such as that there is a black hole in such and such locus in the sky). Particular theories of this or that, such as theory of language, and even isolated statements, are acceptable just in case they are "part" of the acceptable total theory. This is, of course, a view which is or is rather like Quine's.

No doubt, further elucidation is welcome. But one point should be made here. The condition being adumbrated is intended as the condition of "*serious*" acceptability: acceptability of theory as "limning the true and ultimate structure of reality" (in Quine's words). It does not preclude other forms of "acceptability", which I shall, by way of chiaroscuro, label summarily: pretended, for practical purposes, acceptability. An illustration of this might be a case in which, for certain practical purposes, it is useful, perhaps even indispensable, to treat atoms as elastic spheres. Another illustration of this might be a case in which talk of the average American, Swede, etc., is used to abbreviate certain seriously acceptable talk.

Well, then, Jekyll asks: how do the various competing theories dealing with language fare when assessed for acceptability? Almost always, it is not clear what the theories are supposed to do. Is it to explain, perhaps with the assistance of a further theory, some body of data? What further theory? Which data? What manner of explanation? Often when one of these questions is answered, another recedes further into obscurity. For instance, Quine tells us what the data for "radical translations" are and what theories we may wish to come up with. But what is the relationship between the theories and the data? Is it one of explanation? Are "translation-manuals" and "analytical hypotheses" supposed to predict/ postdict verbal behavior, perhaps with assistance of further theory? Is Davidsonian "theory of truth" similarly supposed to predict/postdict displays of "linguistic competence"? Similar questions can be asked about the other competitors.

To be sure, I am harping on a rather narrow notion of "explaining" (within an arguably narrow notion of acceptability as being simplest data-explaining). But what are the alternatives? What is it (not necessarily one and the same thing) which makes generative grammar, logical theory, semantical theory, speech act theory acceptable?

As we have already seen, Jekyll is inclined to cleave to the narrow notion of acceptability and, with misgivings, to something like the narrow notion of explaining. In his view, the data are sayings, writings, and doings—and, on another level, ultimately thinkings, wantings, and sensings, and certain features of them. These are to be explained in some manner closely related to predicting/postdicting. The simplest theory which will do this, he thinks, is one that incorporates some compound of theory of language together with *psychological theory.*

In line with this, he favors the Frege-Grice-Schiffer fragment. For is it not almost ready to be plugged into psychological theory in order to explain linguistic behavior and other human functioning by the intentions, beliefs, desires, and experiences of human beings?

Such, then, are (some of) Jekyll's views. But the entrance cue for Mr. Hyde has sounded.

II

Hyde agrees with Jekyll that a theory is (seriously) acceptable just in case it is the simplest theory which explains the data. He is quite willing to go along with applying this, in the first instance, to determine what the acceptable total theory is and with assessing subtheories or isolated theses by whether they are part of the acceptable total theory. He is willing to go along with Jekyll's view of explaining as something rather like predicting/postdicting. He demurs at something Jekyll slipped in toward the end about "data".

If by 'sayings, writings, and doings' is meant human behavior properly described, Hyde would say, I certainly count these among the data. Of course, we must not leave out from among the data the doings of non-human material objects. However, let us not pause for a precise delimitation of data. What I demur at is the inclusion among data of whatever is supposed to be represented by the phrase 'thinkings, sensings, and wantings, and certain features of them'.

For, insofar as I understand the phrase, the items supposed to be covered by it are surely "theoretical", postulated by a psychological theory supposed to explain human behavior. You yourself, Jekyll, said as much, when you defended propositional attitudes, by maintaining that they will show up in the acceptable theory of language cum psychological theory. So, on your own view, they are not data. (*Obiter dictum:* we see here a lineament of the "other minds" problem.)

But, Hyde would continue, I shall go further and say that propositional attitudes and the like, and, along with them, propositions and the like, are not (seriously) acceptable as postulated "theoretical" items either. For we have every reason to think that the simplest theory which explains the behavior of human and non-human material objects — which is all the data there are — is *physical theory,* assisted, to be sure, by set theory. And we have every reason to think that, whatever advances it may undergo, physical theory *cum* set theory will talk — at least, in its primitive notation — about such things as particles, fields, or what-nots, and sets of these, etc., but certainly not of propositional attitudes or anything of the sort.

Surely, material objects, including human beings, are assemblages of particles or what-nots, and "sayings, writings, and doings" are vibrations of the air produced by these, ink-tracks left by these, movements of parts of these, and effects of this upon further assemblages of particles or what-nots. And surely, all this is most simply explained by interactions among the particles or what-nots, and there is no room for anything of the sort of propositional attitudes, etc., to play any explanatory role. So I say that nothing outside physical theory *cum* set theory is required to explain all the data there are, and *no* theory outside of physical theory *cum* set theory is seriously acceptable.

Consequently, I view with amusement and amazement your efforts to defend the "theory of language" you favor against its so-called competitors and the squabbles among those competitors. For there is *no* seriously acceptable "theory of grammar", "logical theory", "semantical theory", or "speech act theory". There is no seriously acceptable theory other than physical theory and set theory.

Of course, I don't deny, Hyde might continue, that such theories might be acceptable *in a way*. You yourself, Jekyll, have used the example of a theory according to which atoms are elastic spheres, which might be useful and even indispensable for certain practical purposes. And you used an example of talk of the average American, Swede, etc., used to abbreviate certain seriously acceptable talk. And you introduced the notion of "pretended acceptability for practical purposes". I have no quarrel with this. If psychological theories and theories of language are needed in some such way, have them. Call them "pretend-acceptable for practical purposes". But, for God's sake, don't squabble about them. It doesn't matter whether such theories postulate sentences, propositions, or Olympian gods. All that matters is that these theories do whatever job they are supposed to do and do it as commodiously as possible. After all, they are not supposed to be "limning the true and ultimate structure of reality". Physical theory and set theory have pre-empted this job. The job(s) of your pretend-theories must be quite different. And can it matter to the performance of that job (those jobs) whether a theory postulates "sentences" — which, as sets constructed in a certain way out of ink-marks, are "real", as attested by set theory cum physical theory — or "propositions", which are not, or engages in (merely apparent!) ontological excess and postulates both? Can it matter whether it talks of "propositional attitudes" or "sentential attitudes", neither of which are to be found in the world? Remember that your atoms-as-elastic-spheres theory would be no worse off if it postulated little springs attached to the atoms, as long as it did its job. And your talk of the average American would be no worse off if it assigned to him, along with his three and a half children, a soul with a post-mortem survival of 15.2 years, if that did a useful abbreviatory job.

So, I say to you, Jekyll: there are no propositions, there are sentences. But for theory of language this is of no importance. In it you might ("pretend"-) postulate propositions as well as anything else. I myself don't see that you should have in it even sentences (though I suppose that's "natural"). And that is, because, in a way, I agree with you: It's quite unclear what job theory of language is supposed to perform, what *practical purpose(s)* it's supposed to serve. If we became clear about that, then, perhaps, we could see what sort of theory would do the job commodiously. And it might be one with propositions. But that would tell us nothing about what's "really" the case.

Such, then, is what Hyde thinks.

III

One serious difficulty with Hyde's view is — as the reflective listener may have noticed — that apparently, Hyde cannot, in all consistency, hold and propound it as seriously acceptable, as "limning the true and ultimate structure of reality", but at most for some "practical purpose". That is, he cannot consistently maintain his view and further hold that what he thus maintains is seriously acceptable.

To make the matter clearer I shall outline a line of reasoning:

Premise 1: Physical theory *cum* set theory is the simplest theory which explains the data.

Premise 2: A given thesis *t* is seriously acceptable (if and) only if *t* is "part" of the simplest theory which explains the data. We must infer: Thesis *t* is seriously acceptable only if it is "part" of physical theory *cum* set theory.

Premise 3: Neither Premise 1 or 2 is "part" of physical theory *cum* set theory. We must infer: neither Premise 1 nor Premise 2 is seriously acceptable.

Let us, first, observe that the line of reasoning demonstrates that Premises 1, 2, and 3 are such that if all three are true, then not all three are seriously acceptable, and by contraposition and a triviality, if all three are seriously acceptable then not all three are true.

So, insofar as Hyde's view boils down to the combination of Premises 1, 2, and 3, it cannot both be true and seriously acceptable.

I wish to say that any combination of theses like this — namely, demonstrably incapable of being (in all consistency regarded as) all true if (supposed to be) all seriously acceptable — is *"epistemologically self-defeating"*.

And I wish to propose (call this Proposal A) that no combination of theses which is epistemologically self-defeating is seriously acceptable.

So if Proposal A is true, the combination of Premises 1, 2, and 3 is not seriously acceptable.

I further wish to propose (with certain qualifications that I am unable to spell out but which seem irrelevant to the present discussion) (call this Proposal B) that a combination of theses which is not seriously acceptable is — as far as we can tell — not true.

So, if Proposal B is also true, the combination of Premises 1, 2, and 3 is — as far as we can tell — not true.

To summarize: I am proposing that since the combination of Premises 1, 2, and 3 could not be *both* seriously acceptable and true, it is *neither* seriously acceptable nor, consequently — as far as we can tell — true.

But then, insofar as Hyde's view boils down to the combination of Premises 1, 2, and 3, it is neither seriously acceptable, nor — as far as we can tell — true. It is not "limning the true and ultimate structure of reality", but at most promoting some "practical purpose".

But does Hyde's view boil down to this?

IV[2]

Well *of course* Hyde's view boils down to the combination of Premises 1, 2, and 3. I invented Hyde to represent a half of my thinking which eventuates in that combination. But you are rightly not interested in autobiography, or the idiosyncrasy of my thinking. I meant to present a view which might have a big tug of appeal for you too.

I shall discuss Premise 3 first.

It is clear that if we concentrate on the *notation,* the words and phrases of Premises 1 and 2, then obviously neither of them is "part" of physical theory *cum* set theory in any reasonable primitive notation. So, clearly, Premises 1 and 2 are not *primitive-notationally* "part" of physical theory *cum* set theory. It seems pretty clear that they are notationally part of theory of language *cum* psychological theory, which is, in turn, *not* primitive-notationally part of physical theory *cum* set theory.

But one may feel that does not matter too much: perhaps Premises 1 and 2 are part of physical theory *cum* set theory in some more recondite way.

They had better not be part in a way analogous to that in which talk of the average American, Swede, etc., are part of demography. Jekyll and Hyde, both, have agreed that such talk, being abbreviatory for other talk, is not seriously acceptable as "limning the true and ultimate structure of reality" but at most pretend-acceptable for practical purposes. And this seems to me to be the correct view of such talk. And if so, and the analogy holds, we can argue as before that Premises 1 and 2 are not both seriously acceptable and are not both ("really") true, so that Hyde's view faces the same difficulty.

But, perhaps, the two premises are "part" of physical theory *cum* set theory in still another way. I think the intuitive idea in such a proposal must be that Premises 1 and 2 somehow "say the same thing as", "express the same facts as", somehow "amount to", certain remarks in the primitive notation of physical theory *cum* set theory.

Now, it seems to me that notions such as these are in a particularly unclear state nowadays, because, as I suggested earlier, of the creative chaos in theorizing about language and unclarity about what makes a theory of language acceptable. But let us explore the idea.

Some options occur to one concerning the putative relationship between Premises 1 and 2, on the one hand, and certain imagined statements in the (primitive) notation of physical theory *cum* set theory, on the other:

(1) The former result from the latter by substitution of expressions (regarded as) introduced by stipulative/abbreviatory definitions. (Perhaps in the way that number theory is supposed to arise out of set theory.)

(2) The former are analytically synonymous with the latter.

(3) The former do something like "expressing the same facts" as the latter, in some way explicated by, for example, a "causal" theory of language.

(4) The former somehow "amount to" the latter in some way to be elucidated by future inquiries.

The suggestion is that Hyde could reasonably maintain that Premise 3 is false if he could reasonably maintain something like one or another of these options. But does this help him?

Let us observe that, apart from the other difficulties, each of the options, when more fully articulated, is, at least notationally "part" of theory of language *cum* psychological theory and, at least, primitive-notationally *not* "part" of physical theory *cum* set theory.

So it looks as if Hyde could reasonably deny Premise 3 only at the cost of maintaining a thesis — say, X — with respect to which we could form an analogous Premise — say, 3* — and argue as before. It looks as if Hyde's position must continue to be epistemologically self-defeating.

I observe in passing that similar considerations apply should Hyde wish to use with serious acceptability ordinary material object expressions such as 'chair' or 'hand', and want to hold that these somehow "amount to" primitive notation of physical theory *cum* set theory. Or wished to maintain that language-theoretic and/or psychological terminology "amounted to" behavioral (and, therefore, "material-object") terminology. In both cases, he would have to be maintaining a thesis to this effect. And this thesis would be at least notationally part of theory of language *cum* psychological theory and, at least, primitive-notationally, *not* part of physical theory *cum* set theory. And then we could form a suitable Premise — say 3** — and argue as before.

What it looks like is this: Hyde can reasonably maintain that certain remarks of his (which he intends to be seriously acceptable) which *appear* not to be part of physical theory *cum* set theory "really" *are* "part" only at the cost of making a further remark which, in turn, appears *not* to be "part" of physical theory *cum* set theory.

Is this perhaps a harmless infinite regress? (The following idea on behalf of Hyde was crystallized for me by George Bealer.)

Well, I am supposing that we can get Hyde to settle down on a definite set (or perhaps several, perhaps infinitely many, sets) of remarks which he wishes to regard as seriously acceptable. Perhaps each such remark will be either itself in the primitive notation of physical theory *cum* set theory or will be "accompanied" by a remark to the effect that the former amounts to some other remark in such primitive notation. Is Hyde home free?

No. For, by hypothesis, a *proper* (and deductively closed) subset (perhaps, an infinity of such proper subsets) of his remarks is sufficient to explain the data he allows — namely a multitude of remarks in (whatever he regards as) primitive notation sufficient for describing the data he allows and formulating physical theory *cum* set theory. This multitude of remarks is (we may suppose) the simplest theory which explains the data and so is seriously acceptable. The remainder of the remarks, being devoid of explanatory power, is (on Hyde's own view) *not* seriously acceptable.

But it is pretty clear that (on Hyde's view) Premises 1 and 2 will be in that remainder, and we can draw the conclusions, as before, that Hyde's position is epistemologically self-defeating, not seriously acceptable, and not — as far as we can tell — true.

(I observe, by way of concessionary caution that I have assumed, first, that, in assessing the serious acceptability of a theory, what is to be taken into account is at least, in the first instance, its "*notational*" simplicity — whatever, exactly, that might mean, and, second, that data *need not* be described in terminology which has been declared to "amount to" some other terminology.)

V

But, now, how does Jekyll deal with this problem? How does he avoid epistemological self-defeat?

Well, in the first place, he is inclined to deny *Premise 1*. For he thinks there are more data than Hyde allows. He thinks that the data include "thinkings, wantings, and sensings, and certain features of them". (Indeed, he is inclined to think that, ultimately, these are the only data, and, in all ultimateness, just one's own are, for each one of us.) And he thinks that the simplest theory required for the explanation of the data *so* conceived is something like a compound of a theory of propositions, attributes, and the like, physical theory, psychological theory, and theory of language (the latter being, perhaps, "reducible" to the others).

And he thinks that if one articulated his view into an analogue of Premise 1 — say, 1' — then Premise 1' and Premise 2 *would* be "part" of the compound theory he favors as seriously acceptable, and so the analogue of Premise 3 — say, 3' — would be false, thus freeing him from epistemological self-defeat.

He thinks, incidentally, that considerations such as these might be helpful in deciding in a reasonable manner what sorts of items are in fact the data.

But he wants to alter Premise 2 as well. For he thinks that the aim to be "limning the true and ultimate structure of reality" includes the aim to be able to discern that one is (succeeding in) doing this. That is, the ability to arrive at seriously acceptable theories should involve the ability to find seriously acceptable that the former are seriously acceptable.

In line with this, he thinks that in order to be a seriously acceptable "total" theory of the world (at a given time t, perhaps, for a given individual x) a theory must be what I shall call "*epistemologically self-approving*". That is, it is to

(1) contain a specification of conditions under which a theory is seriously acceptable,
(2) contain an assertion to the effect that it itself fulfills these conditions,
(3) in fact fulfill these conditions (discernibly to x at t).

So Jekyll is inclined to propose a revision of the account of serious acceptability — call this Proposal C:

The seriously acceptable "total" theory of the world is the simplest theory which both explains the data and is epistemologically self-approving. (And if what the data are is chosen properly, this may be just the simplest theory which explains the data.)

In line with this, Jekyll thinks that the theory of the world he favors *is* the simplest epistemologically self-approving data-explaining theory, and so the seriously acceptable one.

(But Jekyll's Proposal C seems to open another round for Hyde. For he could now maintain that, according to the proposal, what is seriously acceptable as the "total" theory is physical theory *cum* set theory *cum* thesis X and that a consequence of this [notationally] larger theory is that it itself "amounts to" just physical theory *cum* set theory. The question now would be whether Hyde's [notationally] larger theory is [notationally?] *simpler* than the theory Jekyll favors as the seriously acceptable "total" theory. This reflection arises, in part, out of a point of George Bealer's earlier alluded to.)

VI

I shall conclude by sketching a somewhat different line of reasoning which appears to head for the conclusion that theory of language *cum* psychological theory must be seriously acceptable in its own right. This is based on considerations of what I shall call "epistemology of language-use" and starts with reflecting on what the use of language accomplishes and how.

Even very cursory such reflection reveals that one of the main accomplishments of the use of language, if not *the* main one, is the conveying of information (or misinformation) from person to person. Now, it is not merely that on suitable occasions noises or inscriptions made by a speaker or writer get (cause?) the audience or readership to accept certain theses. It is that on suitable occasions noises or inscriptions made by a speaker or writer render certain theses *acceptable* to the audience. If I am told with suitable authoritativeness that such and such tracks have been observed in a bubble-chamber, then not merely do I in fact accept the thesis that such-and-such tracks have been observed in a bubble-chamber, but also this thesis becomes *acceptable* for me.

This phenomenon is not a luxury or a convenience; it is an epistemological necessity. For, being the limited creatures that we are, if what others report on suitable occasions did not become acceptable to us in the audience, precious little would be acceptable for us individually.

For, presumably, that is the real issue of acceptability: under what conditions is a theory (or thesis) acceptable to an individual (at a time)? My earlier talk about *the* best total theory of the world, acceptable because of being the simplest theory explaining "*the* totality of the data", if not taken as an over-simplification and idealization, amounts to a Hegelian theory of "objective knowledge" not known to anyone in particular. The over-simplification and idealization was advantageous for getting a glimpse of certain truths without getting bogged down in a mass of details and qualifications. But one must not lose sight of the fact that acceptability is primarily: for an individual (at a time). Unfortunately, I am quite unclear about the relationship between the idealized notion of "the acceptable total theory of the world" and the theories acceptable to individuals (at times). None of the schemes for this that I have considered seems to work very well. So I make the transition to acceptability for individuals (at times) with a bump and a thud.

And do we not want to retain the main idea that acceptability — for individuals, too — is a matter of being ("part of") the simplest theory which explains the data "accessible to one"? (I am leaving out "epistemological self-approval", since it is not our present concern.) I say 'data accessible to one' to call attention, without fuss, to a somewhat complicated point. What renders a theory acceptable to an individual is its being the simplest theory which explains not only his own data, say, what he himself has observed, but also the data of others, what *they* have observed, when it is acceptable to him that there are such further data. (I think this is compatible with holding that, in some way, ultimately the theory acceptable to him is the simplest which explains just his own data.) Let us consider a physicist. What makes physical theory acceptable to him is that it is the simplest theory which explains not only his own observations and experimental results but also observations and experimental results of others which have been in one way or another reported to him. If he were not entitled to accept the reports of others, the data accessible to him would be so slim as *not* to render acceptable to him any physical theory at all elaborate.

The point I am trying to make is that a physical theory of any interesting degree of elaborateness is acceptable for a physicist only if various noises and inscriptions made by fellow physicists render it acceptable for him that various observations and experimental results have occurred which he himself has not made or witnessed. So it is an absolute epistemological necessity that noises and inscriptions people make should render various theses acceptable for us.

Now, how can noises and inscriptions make such theses acceptable?

I suggest that we aim for a unitary view. Confrontation with a certain sort of rock in certain circumstances renders acceptable for a geologist the thesis that certain kinds of stress and temperature existed in this or a neighboring location in the distant past. This comes about because a geological theory is already acceptable to the geologist such that the thesis in question — about stress and temperature in the distant past — together with the geological theory explain the features of the rock he is confronting in those circumstances. In a quite parallel fashion, witnessing noises or inscriptions in certain circumstances renders acceptable to a language-using being the thesis that, for example, such-and-such tracks occurred in a bubble-chamber. In quite parallel fashion, I suggest, this happens because a theory of language *cum* a psychological theory is already acceptable to the language-using being such that the thesis in question — about the tracks in the bubble-chamber — together with the theory of language and psychological theory explain, in the circumstances, the occurrence of the noises or inscriptions he is witnessing. In both cases, a phenomenon observed makes a new thesis, *not* primarily about the phenomenon, acceptable because a sort of "background" theory explains the phenomenon observed.

If what I am saying is right, the acceptability of what others report depends on the possession of an independently acceptable theory. Let us, for brevity's sake, call such an independently acceptable theory which renders what others report acceptable a "decoding theory". In the normal case, the "decoding theory" is a theory of language *cum* a psychological theory.

Could another theory—for example, physical theory or physiological theory—play the role of a "decoding theory"?

I think two points may be made by way of suggesting why neither physical theory nor physiological theory could play this role.

First, as we are now, we simply do not have acceptable for us enough physical or physiological information which together with, for example, the thesis that such-and-such tracks occurred in a bubble-chamber could explain the production of such-and-such noises or inscriptions.

Second, hopes of increase of our physical or physiological information don't help. For such increase can occur only with the aid of reports of others. And this new information will be acceptable for us only if these reports are acceptable for us. But these reports are acceptable for us only if our present "decoding theory" is acceptable for us. Thus the acceptability of future scientific discoveries depends on the acceptability of our present "decoding theory". And our present "decoding theory" is theory of language *cum* psychology.

Thus, I am suggesting, we have a sketch of an argument for the conclusion that a theory of the world of any interesting degree of elaborateness is acceptable for us only if theory of language *cum* psychological theory is antecedently acceptable for us in its own right.

By this I mean something like the following. If acceptability of thesis t_1 is required for acceptability of thesis t_2, but not *vice versa,* then the acceptability of thesis t_1 is *antecedent* to acceptability of t_2. And in such a case t_1 is not to be regarded as merely "amounting to" t_2.

But since we are discussing conditions of acceptability of a "total" theory of the world, the foregoing is about the *serious* acceptability of theory of language *cum* psychological theory.

Notes

1. Many of the ideas of this paper go back to some even more inchoate formulations in my largely unreadable Ph.D. dissertation, Harvard 1969. A trial run of an earlier version of this paper at Reed College was made possible by George

Bealer. A discussion with Dick Grandy, at Paul Grice's house, was made possible by Paul Grice toward whom I feel, and hereby express, deep gratitude for immeasurable and not easily specified help which he has extended to me in connection with this paper (as well as in numerous other connections) and which I regard as (with respect in one way or another to this paper) greater than any which I have received, with the possible exception of (though unbeknownst to him) Quine's. I'd better not trace any ideas in this paper (other than those known to be and expressly said in the paper to be his) to Grice, because during the discussion just mentioned Paul told me that he disliked both Jekyll and Hyde in so not uncertain terms, that had I not been used to his disliking what I think, I would have abandoned the project on the spot. Thanks to many others including particularly Nancy Watson and Neil Thomason.

2. The need for this section was made clear to me by the comments of Professors Stephen Schiffer, David Reeve, George Bealer, and Richard Grandy.

Why Realism Can't Be Naturalized

STEVEN J. WAGNER

> Do not use a philosophical truth in the place of a physi-
> cal truth, or vice versa.
> — *Black Belt*, August 1988

Well over a decade ago, Hilary Putnam rejected standard, "realistic"
views of reference on the grounds of the so-called model-theoretic argument (MTA).[1] Thereby hangs a curious tale: Putnam continues to uphold
the MTA,[2] while his opponents still advance an objection that appeared
immediately. Each side accuses the other of question-begging. One sus-
pects a failure to communicate.

I believe neither side has understood the argument. Resolving the im-
passe depends on giving the MTA the right target: not realism, as Putnam
thinks, but a complex view within which realism standardly appears. For
realists have, all along, been right to regard the attack on realism as a non-
starter. Properly — albeit radically — recast, however, it refutes the position
they actually hold.

The typical realist is at the same time a naturalist, indeed typically
feeling that both positions are obviously right. My point will be that these
positions are *inconsistent*. Since Putnam himself directs the MTA just
against "moderate" realists, that is, realists who take reference to be a natural relation (e.g., MR 1–2), my view of the MTA seems to echo his. Yet
our apparent agreement is deceptive. Naturalism and realism are terms
loosely employed; my version of the MTA requires a particular interpretation of each. We will then find, contrary to Putnam, that the problem lies
strictly with naturalism.

Nor does the difficulty turn on points about reference as such. The
key will be that naturalism must assume the very concepts it calls into doubt.
Naturalism opposes the uncritical use of semantic and intentional terms.[3]
Yet these appear, explicitly or implicitly, in naturalism itself. If the MTA
is best read as an attempt to exploit this tension, then it has little to do
with models or the connection of word to object. It is, rather, a variation

211

on the self-refutation charges that have shadowed empiricism since Hume. Although Putnam might find this outcome congenial, it will not serve his own further ends.

1. What Is Naturalism?

This section will address some of the ambiguities and difficulties in the notion of naturalism. One might expect definitional problems about naturalism to have received special attention in the literature, but in fact we are largely on our own here. For while professed naturalists abound, they tend hardly to explain themselves.[4] Naturalism is widely taken to be understood and accepted from the start. This, however, is an illusion, as any attempt to state the position carefully will show.

One question concerns the most general character of the naturalist thesis. Naturalism in its epistemological form takes natural science as a paradigm of justified belief. The idea, roughly, is that only scientific beliefs are legitimate or that these have more legitimacy than any others. Ontological naturalism asserts, in one way or another, that only natural things exist. Thus a restriction of our ontology to concrete aggregates of elementary particles would be a form of ontological naturalism. Of course the ontological thesis has epistemological implications since it will let us believe only in natural objects, but it does not seem to limit us to scientific belief. If Saturn is a natural object, then ontological naturalism apparently permits the quite unscientific belief that its rings are sublime. Epistemological naturalism, on the other hand, seems to imply its ontological counterpart. If only scientific belief is acceptable, then we can believe in nothing but the objects of science. Yet there are questions about whether mathematical objects, which science is widely taken to recognize, are "natural." Some related complications will be dealt with below. Suffice it to say for the moment that epistemological and ontological naturalism are distinct views, of which the former seems more committal.

A second division occurs over the status of physics. Physics has often been viewed as a paradigm of natural science, so that the naturalist preference for science can amount to a philosophical elevation of physics specifically. Yet many naturalists reject this orientation, regarding chemistry, geology, and genetics as full-fledged natural sciences regardless of whether they reduce to physics in any sense. This division cuts across the first. One can assert either the epistemological or the ontological primacy of natural science and can do so whether science is broadly or narrowly construed.

The difference between epistemological and ontological formulations will be important for us. Quite arbitrarily, I will call the former 'naturalism' and the latter 'physicalism'. (There is no standard usage.) We will be less concerned with the status of physics within the natural sciences. What matters in the discussions of naturalism that form the background for this essay is the contrast between the natural and the social or human sciences. From that viewpoint, physiology is as natural, or physical, as physics.

Subsection A offers brief remarks on physicalism. My claim will be that physicalism cannot stand apart from naturalism — the attempt to restrict oneself to a purely ontological thesis is ill conceived. Subsection B therefore undertakes the search for a reasonable formulation of naturalism. That will be the preliminary for an antinaturalist argument in the spirit of the MTA. The point will not just be to define a specific target but to block escapes: if the argument works, naturalists will have no alternative position.[5]

A

Physicalism is not easily formulated.[6] The claim that everything is an object of physics (or natural science more generally) requires a notion of physics that covers future theories as well as our own. No one believes that every real entity is an object of *present* physics. The requisite notion may be hopelessly vague,[7] but naturalists will reply that our admittedly vague and inexplicit notion of physics is not at all trivial. There are possible (as well as actual) theories radically unlike physics, and if any of these should replace physics, then physicalism will be falsified. According to physicalism, then, everything is an object of a theory reasonably similar to our physics. But such a retrenched physicalism faces two difficulties, aside from the (perhaps tolerable) increase in vagueness.

Most obviously, the retrenchment may still not be credible. The fundamental objects of a Grand Unified Theory will not closely resemble anything from mid-nineteenth–century physics. Why then suppose that the ontology of science a few centuries hence should resemble our own to any reasonable degree? If the answer depends on rather subjective judgments of similarity, then the interest of a physicalism built on such judgments becomes unclear.

A less familiar difficulty arises from the fact that physicalists must decide whether the quantifier in 'everything is physical' covers something like concrete objects only or also extends to abstract ones. Each option brings trouble.

To hold that everything concrete is physical has an air of circularity. Intended, however, is that the only nonphysical objects are sets or properties of physical objects, sets or properties of these, and so on. It is widely agreed that at least this much of an abstract ontology must be affirmed.[8]

But the physicalist's opponent will ask: if we are already willing to make two exceptions to the physicality requirement, why not one for, say, Cartesian minds? Either everything is physical, or it is not.

One may defend the introduction of sets by claiming that these will aid theorizing on any subject at all. (An analogous claim would involve properties.) Thus it is taken for granted that we will posit abstract objects over any domain of discourse. The point of physicalism would be that only physical objects enter at the lowest level. But this still does not solve the problem of motivation. If admittedly nonphysical sets are countenanced because of their theoretical utility, why not souls, should these prove to be useful? Perhaps sets are unlike souls in being useful no matter what we are theorizing about, but still, if utility is grounds for admitting one exception, why not for another?[9] The attempt to let in some but not other nonphysical objects still looks inconsistent.

The reply will be that the sets and properties do not count as exceptions. There is no question about the need for objects of higher type; the idea is simply that everything else is physical. But this continues to miss the difficulty. The physicalist is now positing a fundamental division of reality into two categories, entities of higher type and the rest, and claiming that physical objects must exhaust the latter. Her opponent will now repeat the charge of arbitrariness.

First, the physicalist's way of sorting objects into types can appear as a dodge aimed at shielding sets from the condemnation reserved for, say, Cartesian minds. Sets are exempt from the physicality requirement for not being "individuals," or objects of type zero, but this classification is not at all mandatory. In a broadly Fregean treatment, sets are "objects" along with tables and chairs. The entities of higher type are (something like) properties. This scheme leaves us with nonphysical individuals. Moreover, it violates no clear intuition about how to sort objects, insofar as intuitions are even available in this area. Suppose, for example, that the distinction between objects of type zero and of higher type is modeled on a traditional particulars-universals distinction. Then sets come out looking more like particulars: they are not "repeatable" or "common to many things." (It is true that a given set may contain many particulars, but any particular bears all sorts of relations to other particulars. Why can't the range of the membership relation contain particulars?) Of course the segregation of objects into types can be quite unrelated to any more traditional distinction, but then there is likely to be even less intuitive resistance to a classification of sets as individuals.

Similarly, properties can be counted as individuals. The selection of individuals is, *prima facie* at least, accomplished within a theory, not given absolutely. So ontological physicalists wishing to found their position on a nonarbitrary sorting of objects into types have their work cut out for them.

Further, such a sorting would not suffice. Permit physicalists to divide objects into types, then to claim that all the individuals, and just these, must be physical. Or suppose, perhaps, that the concept of an abstract object is clear and not scheme-relative, and let the physicalist claim that all nonabstract objects are physical. Thus one carries out a fundamental partition of reality and restricts the thesis of physicalism to one of the sectors. The physicalist's opponent can then easily counter with an alternative: why not further partition the individuals or nonabstract objects into mental and nonmental ones, then hold that physical objects exhaust the latter class only? Each way of dividing things up seems acceptable. But if the choice is arbitrary or dependent on passing interests, then physicalism has not been motivated.

The general problem is this. If physicalists want to leave the possibility of nonphysical objects open, then a specific way of dividing reality is needed. Some concept C must include all the candidate objects physicalism intends to rule out while extending to none of the permitted exceptions. (In one of our illustrations above, *individual* played the role of C.) The physicalist then claims that, in fact, every C-thing is physical. To the charge that non-C things are simply counterexamples to physicalism, one replies that a principle of physical exhaustion is appropriate only for the category C.[10] The physicalist's opponent will then ask why, if exceptions are allowed at all, it is precisely C to which the physicalist principle applies. For the sake of illustration, let us continue to suppose that physicalism is directed against souls and that these fall under C. Then the opponent's counterproposal will be that physical exhaustion should really apply (if at all) only to some subcategory C' of C which excludes souls. In short, physicalism in this form requires a boundary distinguishing legitimate exceptions from counterexamples. The opponent is apparently free to object that it is being drawn in an arbitrary way.

Some physicalists have, in any case, held that the physical-nonphysical distinction makes sense for abstract objects, yet asserted the physical character of absolutely everything. For they have feared that blocking nonphysical concreta does not go far enough; that one must also ensure the physical character of everything abstract.[11] But the notion of a *physical abstract* object is problematic on its face, and while it can no doubt be made consistent, motivation remains a problem. What kind of ontological intuition is it that says first that everything is physical, then that what seem to be blatantly nonphysical objects are "physical" in an extended sense appropriate to them? In any case, the usual idea is that the physical abstract objects are just those recognized by physics. But to mention just one problem, physics is mathematical, and mathematics is exceedingly generous with abstract objects. It is unclear what a restriction of abstract objects to physical ones in this sense will leave out.[12]

That aside, the physicalist will typically advance a claim about properties: properties mentioned in nonphysical theories that we wish to retain are real because they are *identical* to physical ones. Yet no satisfactory way to establish such identity claims has been found. There is little agreement on when to identify properties posited by theories from different domains (typically, a reduced and a reducing theory). Although the problem continues to be investigated, the investigations are driven primarily by reductionist faith. If we do not assume in advance that a viable statement of physicalism must be possible, then the motivation for establishing intertheoretic property identities useful for physicalists falls away. We might stop trying to square this particular philosophical circle.

The problem here is substantially independent of the details of physicalist reduction. Physicalists might agree that the relation of psychology to biology is not "textbook" reduction. There may, for example, be no bridge principles that permit the formal derivation of psychological laws within the biological theory; looser and more limited explanatory relations may suffice. This does not remove the problem of when to identify psychological with biological properties. Indeed, the obstacles to positive identifications will now be greater. Speaking generally, it is hard to see why a psychological property should be *identical* to a biological property that seems to underlie it in some loose or partial way.[13]

But suppose that some statement of physicalism may avoid such difficulties. At best it will still look arbitrary in the absence of reasons to think that natural science exclusively should tell us what there is. Why should only the objects of natural science exist, unless only natural science merits belief? If one does hold that, it is likely to be on the grounds that only natural science exhibits the epistemic features appropriate to legitimate belief in general. Thus one's ontological views would after all derive from an epistemological form of naturalism. So physicalism seems to lack independent motivation. Let us therefore explore naturalism proper.

B

Naturalism holds that the only legitimate doctrine is natural science.[14] I will use 'legitimate' as a most general term of epistemic approbation, one roughly synonymous with 'acceptable' or 'justifiedly employed'. Any broad philosophical viewpoint distinguishes correct, or legitimate, doctrines and concepts from the rest. According to empiricism, for example, all legitimate concepts and doctrines derive (in senses to be specified) from experience. Other viewpoints will delineate the legitimate along other lines, perhaps by recognizing a priori or pragmatic justifications that empiricism cannot accommodate. Whatever epistemology we end up with, we must begin with a sense of the distinction we would like to draw. That distinction may resist elucidation, unless we count as elucidations particular accounts, such as the empiricist's, of how to draw it. In any case the issue of legitimacy appears intuitive enough for our purposes.

A next step might be to define natural science. Yet that would considerably delay us, for in this context we can take for granted neither the notion of science nor any approach to delineating specifically *natural* science. It is, for example, unclear whether an area of inquiry is "natural" in virtue of its subject matter, its methods, or both. But trying to settle all such questions now would be inefficient. What matters, if we are to see which further issues need to be resolved and which are secondary, is a working grasp of naturalism and its aims. Let us therefore proceed informally, relying heavily on ostension.

Physics, chemistry, meteorology, population biology, physiology, and the like are paradigmatic natural sciences. Mathematics is not, but since the paradigms require it, we will include it without further ado. Possible doubts about its status lie far from our present concerns. Similarly for mundane views on tables, rocks, and such. The lore of medium-sized dry goods is not properly science at all, yet naturalists universally accept it. And we may go along with them: not because their attitude is free from difficulties, but in order to focus on the central cases of what I will call unnatural doctrine. Such are, for example, anthropology, economics, intentional ("folk") psychology, and ethics. Overlaps and family resemblances among the paradigms on both sides will be evident.

I take the main point of naturalism to be a skeptical stance (whose exact nature is yet undetermined) toward the intentional and semantic notions that pervade the unnatural disciplines. One can hardly discuss distinctively human activities without representing us as believing, feeling, perceiving, wanting, and reasoning; without regarding us as language-users; without regarding the language we use as a vehicle for meaning, reference, and truth. Any attempt to understand human life will begin from this viewpoint — which is just what the naturalist calls into question. Naturalism invidiously contrasts our talk of belief, meaning, and truth with natural science.

Here the grounds for this stance will only briefly be indicated. On the one hand, natural science is widely regarded as an epistemic paradigm. Scientific language is clear; scientific doctrines are supported by reason and correctible by evidence readily agreed on. Of course there are exceptions, but if such claims on behalf of natural science seem too strong, one need only compare it to history or psychology, not to mention anthropology, philosophy, or the criticism of the arts. The methodological ills of such disciplines dwarf any that science exhibits.

Typical of the unnatural disciplines is the heavy influence of personal prejudice or cultural viewpoints on inquiry. In contrast, the relative precision and testability of scientific questions promotes an ideal of objectivity: we hope for answers that meet independent and impartial criteria, that can be verified to the satisfaction of investigators with diverse backgrounds and points of view.[15] Although the ideal of scientific objectivity may well be open to challenge, we will not pursue this larger argument here. It suffices to observe that the naturalist's high epistemic regard for science is readily understood.

Now there is no question that intentional and semantic doctrines suffer by comparison to science. Although eliminative materialism is highly controversial, the empirical critique that encourages it is not. The terms of folk psychology are ambiguous and vague. Folk predictions of action are, although indispensable, frequently chancy even given ideal knowledge of an agent's mental states; and in practice these are often inscrutable to boot. Intentional interpretation seems to depend far less on the application of general laws than on the projection, onto a subject, of the interpreter's point of view. These criticisms have been convincingly elaborated elsewhere.[16] Serious disagreement arises primarily over their implications. The invidious epistemic contrast between natural and unnatural doctrine is clear enough.

This contrast motivates but does not establish naturalism. One may find chemistry epistemically superior to anthropology while according the latter equal legitimacy as an object of belief. Agreement on the merits of science does not *per se* entail dismissal of doctrines that fail to measure up. This is why naturalism is such a radical step beyond the empirical critique of folk psychology and semantics.

Here the naturalist's defense may be rather pragmatic. Granted that science does establish an ideal of inquiry, naturalists may ask why we should tolerate lower standards of belief. If we can get away with accepting only the best, why not do so? Of course this is hardly a decisive argument. Yet our reflections so far may make the attractions of naturalism clear. Many philosophers would readily accept naturalism — if the position should turn out to be tenable. The question is whether we can afford the naturalist's high standards of doxastic legitimacy. Specifically, naturalism as developed so far invites two fundamental challenges.

First, our naturalism is immediately self-defeating. It is an epistemic view, and epistemology is clearly unnatural, hence not naturalistically legitimate. So naturalism disqualifies itself.[17] The difficulty is particularly obvious for forms of naturalism that stress the goal of "naturalizing" semantic and intentional terms.[18] A naturalization *defines* the concept under investigation using the language of natural science, yet definition is a paradigmatically nonnatural concept.

Any detailed account of naturalization will in fact use a variety of suspect terms. We might, for example, limit acceptable definitions to certain finite biconditionals, thus introducing the circle of notions associated with logical form (negation, predication, quantification, etc.). Naturalizations are also required to be lawlike — an obscure notion that apparently involves restrictions on, among other things, the *contents* of predicates suitable for inclusion in laws. And we will of course have to characterize natural science itself, thus introducing such concepts as explanation and evidence.

The logico-semantic or epistemic concepts used to state naturalization will also be transcendent in Quine's sense. That is, the naturalist will assume their application not just to her present language but to languages in general. For one cannot afford to explicate 'naturalization' (and such) merely for one's language of the moment. The naturalizations one envisages or predicts may be possible only within far more advanced scientific frameworks. Stating a naturalist program at all therefore commits one to saying what makes a statement in any language a naturalization of reference. With that, one takes on the notorious task of explicating translation naturalistically — and it is hard enough to say anything illuminating about translation *without* heeding naturalistic constraints. In short, naturalism is utterly enmeshed in unnatural concepts. Naturalists must deal with the self-application of their own standards.[19]

Second, the naturalism articulated so far is not discriminating enough. Calling everything outside of natural science illegitimate is just too crude, since unnatural doctrines may be quite unequal. Parapsychology and semantics, for example, are both unnatural, but there is presumably a significant epistemic difference between them. Just one has fatal conceptual and empirical problems quite apart from its failure to be natural science. A blanket condemnation of unnatural doctrine erases crucial epistemic distinctions.

Thus we are led to a fundamental modification. Our original binary classification gives way to a threefold division that recognizes something between natural science and the flatly unacceptable. This is Quine's idea of the double standard which, as applied to unreduced intentional terms, rules them out of serious science yet allows their use as needed.[20] Analogous views, of course, pervade the philosophical tradition, notably within empiricism. Phenomenalists, for example, found it reasonable — up to a point — to speak of material objects even in the absence of the reduction they thought necessary. Descartes, too, accepted the practical employment of doctrines not up to his standards. Quite generally, advocates of radical epistemic reform will feel the pressure to compromise. Naturalism involves a critical stance toward unnatural doctrine, yet one cannot easily avoid granting some legitimacy to what seemed reasonable, naturalism aside.

Borrowing terms from Quine, I will speak of a distinction between serious theory (serious acceptability, etc.) and grade B doctrine. Any reasonable naturalism needs such a distinction: simply rejecting grade B doctrine is extreme, but simply accepting it collapses naturalism into a straightforward empiricism or pragmatism. Grade B doctrine needs warrant, in an ordinary sense, to earn its status. Its superior relation to the data is just what distinguishes it from such things as astrology or demonology, which are not even grade B. Thus, grade B doctrines are the unnatural ones that ordinary empiricists (say) would simply accept. (The relation of acceptance comes in degrees, but for our purposes that will not matter.) It is, then, just the qualification of ordinary acceptance, based on recognition of higher standards, that distinguishes naturalism.

Naturalism's modified, tripartite classification of doctrines raises deep questions. A distinction between the acceptable (justified) and the unacceptable (unjustified) seems obvious. But just what are the content, force, and motivation of the naturalist's further distinction? A full understanding of naturalism will require an answer. For the moment, however, it suffices for the distinction to be familiar, as Quine has made it, and needed in some form. Observe now that it seems to provide a reply to the first as well as the second of the objections to our initial formulation of naturalism.

We may, with Quine, regard ordinary semantic and intentional doctrines as paradigms of grade B lore. Although not scientific, they are indispensable for the discussion of language and action. Further, their use is empirically well-behaved: attributions of beliefs to agents, for example, or of denotations and truth values to linguistic items can be grounded in publicly accessible evidence. Thus are semantics and psychology distinguished from the likes of astrology. But then naturalism seems to avoid self-rejection. Since it is formulated in the everyday language of belief, evidence, and so forth, naturalism may be just as acceptable. Given suitable reasons, we may accept this methodological doctrine in the same way that we accept the intentional vocabulary it depends on.

We will later ask whether naturalism might not still, by rating itself lower than natural science, more subtly undercut itself. An immediate task is the delineation of two important species of naturalism, which divide over a question of upward mobility.

What I will call hard naturalism makes no provision for redeeming inferior doctrines. Soft naturalists, in contrast, may extend the rights and privileges of serious acceptability to qualified applicants. According to a soft naturalist, semantics might rise from grade B status to serious theory, but not by itself becoming natural science. Although we have left the characteristics of natural science open, it seems highly unlikely that semantics could ever take them on. (If natural science is, for example, generally experimental and quantitative, then semantics seems to have little chance of being included.) The soft naturalist hopes rather to *naturalize* semantics: to find definitions reducing semantic terms to natural-scientific ones (or to intermediate terms already reduced).[21] The reduction transfers legitimacy from natural science to the reduced domain. Thus one might hope to explicate reference via a definition of the form

(*) x refers to $y \leftrightarrow C(x, y)$,

where C is an open sentence in naturalistic language, presumably mentioning causal relations between naturalistically described speakers and things. The claim, then, is that finding an appropriate (*) would give semantics the status of serious theory.

As remarked, the detailed conditions on reduction are not germane here. Let us instead consider the motivation and commitments of soft naturalism.

Soft naturalism arises from the unpalatability of its hard counterpart. We may grant that many of our fundamental beliefs are not serious theory in any reasonable sense, yet feel unhappy about a permanent, irremediable grade B status. Psychology is the obvious example: whether intentional discourse can be made very scientific — rigorous, systematic, and clear — is doubtful, but we can hardly live without it. Thus intentional concepts roughly as they stand may always be indispensable. Under the circumstances, denying them any prospect of serious acceptability may seem unreasonable. We may agree, in a naturalistic vein, that some betterment is necessary: even assuming its indispensability, psychology is not seriously to be accepted on the spot. Yet we soften this judgment through the promise of redemption by reduction.

Such considerations are by no means decisive. Hard naturalists may regard our need for inferior doctrines as a sign of human inadequacy, nothing more.[22] Standards of acceptability need not be relaxed just because seriously acceptable accounts are hard to find. Still, the attractions of the soft naturalist's program are evident: naturalism on the one hand, a way to save our familiar, attractive image of ourselves as believers and speakers on the other.

Thus soft naturalism is the generally preferred variety. But I may already seem to have made naturalists out to be unduly contentious. Although eliminative materialists have reflected on the threatened self-rejection of their own position, naturalists in general have not. And few writers besides Quine have puzzled over the meaning of grade B status — as I claim we are led to do, once we take naturalism seriously. Naturalism is, it seems, widely taken to be a more tolerant view, one that fosters the naturalizing urge without taking any committal view of unnatural doctrine. Such a naturalism would be more concerned to tout the merits of natural science than to denigrate everything else. It would, in particular, avoid the self-referential tension that afflicts (even if not fatally) Quine's position. I believe, however, that this gentler naturalism is a mirage. There is no naturalism apart from (something like) Quine's trichotomy of serious, grade B, and unacceptable statements; and the grade B label must count as a significant condemnation. Naturalism involves a strong epistemic commitment, and the issue of self-denigration cannot be ducked.

I will argue this by showing that the likely milder interpretations of naturalism are unsatisfactory. Of course, we have Humpty Dumpty's freedom to use 'naturalism' as we please, but I assume that a serious candidate for the label must satisfy two constraints. First, it must have critical and methodological import. It must somehow guide inquiry and place restrictions on our theories and attitudes. Second, it must be a distinctive position. As indicated above, naturalism will demote doctrines that pass ordinary empirical or pragmatic muster when these are not, in spite of their empirical (say) credentials, suitably grounded in natural science. In just this way naturalism goes beyond competing views, as it must in order to have independent interest. If a position amounts, instead, simply to a form of respect for science, its claim to being naturalism vanishes. Consider in this light the plausible alternatives to our account of naturalism.

(1) The point or content of naturalism cannot be to reject, say, vitalism or natural theology. Although such theories are not naturalizable, they do not call for a naturalist critique since they fail anyway. They explain such data as they have badly if at all. Hume showed how to refute natural theology on its own terms. The same job is easier for, say, astrology. One need not ask for a reduction to natural science to explain why you should not trust your horoscope; it suffices to ask the astrologers for their evidence. Further — and importantly — where a bad theory violates natural science, it does not take a naturalist to protest. Suppose that the parapsychologist posits telepathic powers based on transmission of certain "brain waves." Since none of our organs seems able either to send or to receive such signals, this hypothesis conflicts with well-confirmed science. Anyone with normal respect for established empirical doctrine will therefore regard the parapsychologist's claim most skeptically. Since naturalism must, in order to be interesting, amount to more than respect for empirical theory, there is no work for naturalism to do here.

The same holds, incidentally, for the ontological physicalism of sub-section A. The attempt to deploy it against scientifically suspect doctrines encounters a dilemma. If the physicalism is empirically established, there is nothing distinctive about this line of attack. Insofar as science tells us that all things, or perhaps all perceptible things, are made of atoms, a belief in ghosts will run afoul of ordinary scientific rationality, not natural-ism.[23] Yet if the physicalism is not empirically founded, then its critical value is dubious. Naturalism can only be useful for the critique of empiri-cally supported doctrines, as I am emphasizing. The rest can be rejected without invoking naturalism. But why should a good empiricist reject a use-ful view on the strength of a physicalism that is not empirically confirmed?

Naturalism more or less by definition challenges intentional and semantic doctrines. (Perhaps the challenge can be met, but it must be real.) Yet these look immune to the charges brought against astrology. Nor do they reject an ontology of physical things. So we must look elsewhere for a formulation of naturalism.

(2) Naturalists typically welcome or seek naturalizations. But this, too, fails to define a satisfactory naturalism.[24] Again, our two constraints are violated, as may be seen by considering the program of naturalizing reference. Finding an acceptable instance of (*) would be a deep achieve-ment, hence of interest to everyone, regardless of epistemological persua-sion. One need not be a naturalist of any kind to think naturalizations worth looking for. Success in the search adds explanations and unifies the-ory; failure shows equally important limits. Thus, anyone desiring scien-tific insight has full reason to aim at or explore the possibilities of natural-ization. Naturalism does not consist in promoting reductionist efforts.

The search for naturalizations is not guaranteed to be fruitful—in some possible worlds, it would be hopeless or offer insufficient rewards. But we have inductive reasons (which may sometimes be overridden) to pursue reductionist projects, given the advances they have brought in the past—by succeeding or by failing. Recognizing these reasons does not call for naturalism. Again, ordinary appreciation of empirical evidence and scientific practice suffices. So the soft naturalist will neither desire nor ex-pect naturalizations more than anyone else. She cannot promise to do bet-ter science than her nonnaturalist colleague.

The recurring point is that naturalism is not simply respect for the results and methods of science. Any reasonable epistemology gives science authority within its own domain and encourages its progress. Thus alter-native views account for various results or advantages that naturalists claim. So far then, we must still identify naturalism with the view that natural scientific status—or, for soft naturalists, naturalization—is necessary for serious acceptability. No better construal has emerged.

(3) Naturalism is also independent of "naturalistic" expectations, such as the expectation that belief can be naturalized. It is not a form of confidence in scientific progress.

To identify naturalism with this kind of confidence would be to abandon the naturalist's critical stance. Expecting naturalizations does not mean passing negative judgment on concepts that fail to measure up, yet that seems to be among the naturalist's commitments. Moreover, naturalistic optimism about semantic and intentional concepts is unfounded, as we will see in a moment. A well-founded naturalism had therefore best avoid it.

What would make it rational to *demand* naturalizations is a difficult question. Deep problems arise when we ask about the rationality of what is already a broad normative framework, such as pragmatism, rationalism, or naturalism. But if naturalism means expecting, not demanding, naturalizations, the question becomes straightforward. The expectation is irrational if no evidence supports it. And this seems to be the case. The naturalists' *track record* certainly provides no grounds for optimism. What semantic or intentional concept has been naturalized? Or seems close to naturalization? We can reject any inductive justification of naturalist hopes without reviewing the relevant history, which speaks for itself.[25] Reductionist faith is not sustained by confirmation to date.

If there is any other reason to expect naturalizations, it would presumably lie in considerations of materialism, supervenience, or the like. (I pass over the fact that these notions should seem rather metaphysical to naturalists.[26]) To evaluate this idea, let us suppose that some version of functionalist materialism is correct and guarantees naturalistic equivalents for psychological facts—in some appropriate sense of equivalence. Still we have not the least guarantee that naturalizations will be found; no support, that is, for naturalism as interpreted under (3).

First, the dependence of semantic on physical facts is known to entail no reducibility even in principle.[27] Reductions are finite definitions in our vocabulary. Why must the natural correlates of psychological facts be finitely expressible in any human vocabulary? Second, if finding a naturalization means being in a position to *recognize* it as such, we face a further difficulty. No plausible thesis of materialism or supervenience ensures the *knowability* of naturalistic reductions.[28] Even if our functional language lets us state the right definitions, we might be unable to identify them. Thus our materialist or functionalist faith, however well grounded, encourages no naturalist expectations. But then it is pointless to identify naturalism with the holding of such expectations—all the more so since that reading was strained anyway.

Expecting naturalizations will also not affect the practice of inquiry.

Whatever our expectations, we should try to naturalize for the reasons given in (2). Naturalism, however, is supposed to make a difference.

A philosopher introducing naturalism and the serious grade B distinction might find an irremediable grade B status for our semantic and intentional concepts unpalatable. A step towards reducing the discomfort is to make one's naturalism soft; to allow science ultimately to reclaim notions of mind and meaning. But if the discomfort was real, then the possibility of reconciliation *in principle* is likely to seem insufficient. One wants to believe that naturalizations really will appear. Thus is optimism about reductions incorporated into the naturalist package. But the optimism is not the naturalism, nor even part of it properly speaking. It is, rather, an attitude held by naturalists who might otherwise shrink from the implications of their stance.

(4) Naturalism might be identified with the rejection of views that *rule out* future naturalizations. A naturalist would then be willing to (seriously) accept unnaturalized views for which the possibility of naturalization remains open. Only the irreducible is rejected — not the merely unreduced. I will interpret this as a form of soft naturalism, since the idea must be that the mere epistemic possibility of reduction validates unnatural doctrines. The hard naturalist policy of accepting only science cannot accommodate such a tolerant attitude. But this attempt at a modest soft naturalism is too weak. If a doctrine is not unacceptable anyway, its irreducibility will generally be hard to show.

Our latest form of naturalism is typically a reaction to certain (alleged) paradigms of disreputable theory: doctrines of Cartesian souls, Moorean ethical properties, or of propositions or Fregean *Gedanken* as the objects of thought. Let us examine the first of these, which seems most important (broadly similar remarks would apply to the other two).[29]

For reasons already anticipated, naturalism is not as readily applicable to dualism as one might expect. We need, first, a dualism that survives ordinary nonnaturalist scrutiny. Yet dualism faces serious difficulties over the obscure notion of an immaterial soul and over the description of psychophysical interaction. So naturalism can enter the argument only given a logically tenable form of dualism. That is already more than many critics would allow. This dualism must also not violate known science, for again, one need not be a naturalist to reject conflicts with established biology or physics. Further, dualism seems to offer no help with any problem in the philosophy of mind — qualia, for example, and the nature of representation are every bit as puzzling for dualists as for anyone else. This suggests that positive reasons to believe dualism may be lacking. That, too, would provide sufficient reason to abandon it, in view of the difficulties it undoubtedly brings. In short, most of the common reasons for opposing dualism fall outside of naturalism. A form of dualism open to a specifically naturalist critique would be a more robust and successful theory than is widely thought possible.

Naturalists would still reject such a dualism, but they cannot do so on grounds of anything like irreducibility. Exactly what naturalizing the soul would mean is unclear, but I see no bar in principle to stating naturalistically the conditions for having or even being an immaterial soul. Descartes himself more or less envisioned that: possession of a soul was held necessary for language use, and sufficient in the presence of a suitable interface (e.g., the pineal gland). Thus, a satisfactory naturalistic rendering of 'language use' — which naturalists generally posit anyway — would lead to naturalistic conditions on ensoulment. This would, to be sure, still leave souls as entities outside the spatiotemporal order. But that should not offend any naturalist who accepts abstract mathematical objects. (Recall Quine's use of sets to explain the empirical data.) Cartesian souls are at least as legitimate naturalistically, if Descartes is right, since they aid the explanation of language use. Indeed, a main naturalistic reservation about sets will have no counterpart, since Cartesian souls, unlike sets, interact causally with matter.

Positing nonphysical souls does not in itself rule out a naturalistic movitation and interpretation for discourse about them — assuming that such discourse is sensible at all. In general, placing a class of objects outside the natural order as we presently understand it does not block all possible connections to natural things. Future inquiry may permit naturalistic accounts of these connections, hence something in the nature of "reductions." At that juncture one might hold that our conception of the natural order had expanded to include a new kind of objects, but in a way that is the point. Well-motivated concepts that are demonstrably irreducible to naturalistic language are hard to come by. A naturalist who opposes just these will find little employment. So (4) is not an adequate rendering of naturalism.

Naturalists must avoid the pitfall of saying too little, either by merely rejecting what everyone else rejects anyway (as in (1)) or by failing to reach their intended targets (as in (4)). Similarly, they must go beyond generally accessible methodological stances (see (2)), without embracing doubtful views about the future of inquiry (see (3)). The space of possible naturalist positions is thereby restricted. Hence the naturalist's best course is most likely the one I have defined.[30] Naturalism should denigrate doctrines that lie outside of natural science. Since this view threatens self-refutation, it presupposes (some form of) the serious grade B distinction; naturalist theorizing must be rated grade B acceptable. The naturalist then has a choice concerning the status in principle of nonnatural views, notably of semantic and intentional ones. The hard naturalist will never seriously accept anything but natural science. The alternative is to countenance a kind of scientific definition or interpretation — "naturalization" — that would seriously legitimize suspect concepts. Among the candidates for such legitimation, one hopes, would be naturalist epistemology itself. This is the soft naturalist vision. One tries to maintain naturalist tough-mindedness while holding out a promise of grace.

Section 4 will present an argument against both forms of naturalism. It will, however, leave the soft naturalist with a highly theoretical possibility of escape. I will then try to close that, too, arguing that the soft naturalist's attempted intermediate position is necessarily unstable. I will at the same time try to show that the MTA contains a similar suggestion. On a reasonable, although free and selective construal, Putnam's argument points up a subtle inconsistency in soft naturalism. Of course the critique of soft naturalism should hold interest independently of its relation to Putnam, but the interpretive question is also important.

2. The Model-theoretic Argument

A

The MTA ostensibly concerns realism and the relation of an empirical theory to its possible models. Although I will set out its essential points, I assume familiarity with Putnam's presentations of the argument and with their broader philosophical context.

I will take realism to be a thesis about reference. At least three claims concerning reference may be at issue in the MTA:

  (i) Reference is determinate.
  (ii) The objects of reference are mind-independent.
  (iii) Reference is a legitimate notion.

The MTA explicitly addresses (i) and (ii). Putnam argues that on these realist principles, any language will admit infinitely many correct, incompatible *schemes of reference* — assignments of denotations or extensions to words. Since that indeterminacy seems absurd, Putnam thinks we must abandon (ii) (e.g., *MMS*, 123–130; *RR*, viii–xi). Thus, (i) is something to be upheld if at all possible; its denial constitutes an antinomy. The MTA is supposed to show that (ii), the characteristically realist element, generates this antinomy and is therefore untenable.

Although the claims in question (particularly (ii)) are hardly clear as they stand, requiring realists to maintain determinacy without giving up mind-independence seems right. I will, however, further represent the realist as being concerned with (iii). The realist's commitments include (iii) in any case. Realists, paradigmatically, accept talk of truth and reference — often in ways others find uncritical. And if their task, on our account, is to defend (i) (while keeping (ii)), then a defense of (iii) will suffice. Legitimacy seems to imply determinacy: if there is no fact of the matter about what a word refers to, then ordinary semantic talk is thoroughly confused.[31]

A few remarks on this well-worn topic may suffice. Putnam saddles realists with the view that 'cat' does not simply refer to cats: while it so refers on one acceptable scheme, it denotes cows, say, or neutrinos on others. Since the schemes are incompatible, all claims of reference (e.g., "cat' refers to cats') must be relativized to them. This is not reference as we know it. In fact, the indeterminacy to which Putnam finds realism committed radically violates common understanding, for he allows only weak constraints on reference-in-a-scheme. Roughly speaking, any two schemes yielding the same assignments of truth values to sentences would be equally correct for Putnam. Hence anything refers to anything within some correct scheme. Putnam rightly finds this bizarre. His view is that since (ii) carries this consequence, upholding the legitimacy of reference entails renouncing mind-independence. This is his antirealist result.

It will be convenient for us to identify realism just with (iii) (and, by implication, (ii)). The departure from Putnam's usage is harmless: although my realism does not definitionally include mind-independence, I will ask whether realists are forced to reject (ii) on pain of abandoning (i), for I agree that we want to preserve a notion of reference and that radical indeterminacy is unacceptable. But it will turn out that mind-independence (in any reasonable sense) has nothing to do with (any reasonable version of) the MTA. Putnam's alleged connections are imaginary. Thus, if realism in the limited sense of (iii) is not vulnerable to the MTA, then neither is its conjunction with (ii).[32] Realists may continue to believe in mind-independence until further notice.[33] The question then will be whether Putnam's argument has any other use.

B

To approach the argument proper, let us naively assume the notion of an empirically ideal theory (*MMS*, 125–126). For any such theory T, we may ask whether T is true and what its words refer to. Putnam holds that T cannot be false. For T is empirically ideal, hence consistent, and thus it has models — infinitely many. Any model includes a scheme of reference, and Putnam claims that its scheme specifies actual referents for the words in $L(T)$. Hence referential indeterminacy: infinitely many distinct, incompatible schemes of reference for $L(T)$ are correct. But since this is absurd, the argument must, for Putnam, be a reductio of the notion of reference it employs.

Why assert that a scheme is correct if it appears in some model of T? Putnam invites critics to add any constraint they please, say, an instance of (*) above. Their objection would be that for w to refer to a, it does not suffice for some model of T to assign w to a. Rather, a causal relation $C(w, a)$ must obtain. But if (*) is reasonable, it must be compatible with the empirically ideal T.[34] Hence, $T \cup \{*\}$ has a model M, which we can evidently choose so that it assigns w to a. Indeed, under plausible conditions, M can be the same model originally chosen for T, or an expansion of it. For example, if T is empirically ideal, one may well suppose that it already contains (*). In any case, however, Putnam concludes that additional constraints do not reduce the indeterminacy. For any w and any a, some model of T assigns w to a and also makes any reasonable constraints on reference come out true.[35]

On this basis Putnam asserts a complex set of conclusions. He holds that the indeterminacy problem arises only for a realism, 'external' or 'metaphysical', that asserts mind-independence. The weaker thesis of internal, 'empirical' realism is safe. Hence mind-independence must be a suppressed assumption in the above argument for indeterminacy. He also holds that internal and external realism differ *only* over whether an empirically ideal theory could be false; that in virtue of this difference, external realism alone is concerned with how our whole system of language and thought can refer (represent); and that the distinctive element of external realism arises from overlooking the procedural character of language understanding.

One may well marvel at this potency of the belief in empirically ideal but false theories. Indeed, while the full unraveling of Putnam's position lies outside the scope of this essay, it is clear that a lot has gone awry by the time he is done. Apart from his puzzling attribution of certain commitments to realism, there are the difficulties besetting his statement of an alternative. The key idea is supposed to be the truth of any empirically ideal theory. Yet the identification of empirical ideality with genuine truth faces strong counterexamples: imagined cases in which our best efforts at observation fall short or in which even an ideally rational inference from our observations to the unobserved is wrong. Such objections are likely to be met only by strengthening the notion of empirical ideality to the point where it guarantees truth in an uninteresting way.[36]

Further, Putnam's concept of mind-dependent, agent-relative truth presupposes an absolute notion he rejects. His empirically ideal theories are consistent with (and take into account) all possible observations—but

just which observations are these? The question is not just which propositions to count as observational, or which observations to count as "possible." Rather, the observations on which an empirically ideal theory is
based must, intuitively, be *true*. For the identification of truth with empirical ideality to have any plausibility at all, no empirically ideal theory
should contain the (false) observation statement that there is now a pink
elephant in front of me. Yet that is a perfectly possible observation, one
I might well be inclined to make had I spent the past few hours a bit differently. If the example seems too crude, far more subtle and plausible
observational errors can be substituted. The point will always be that no
empirically ideal theory need be consistent with these. Although Putnam
can of course try various responses here, the basic difficulty seems too clear
to permit much chance of escape.

An analogous problem concerns the logical properties of empirically
ideal theories. These are crucial: an ideal theory is presumably the deductive closure of an ideally rational set of beliefs and is required to be logically consistent. But Putnam's account of mind-dependent truth runs into
difficulty when applied to metalogical descriptions. Consider, say, the claim

(i) T is empirically ideal.

Hence,

(ii) T is consistent.

According to Putnam, this is equivalent to

(iii) The consistency of T ($\text{Con}(T)$) is asserted by an empirically
ideal theory T'.

The equivalence of (ii) and (iii) is one form of Putnam's mind-
dependence thesis. He has on occasion remarked that this equivalence is
not supposed to imply a reductive analysis of truth in terms of empirical
ideality.[37] It is simply equivalence. But whatever exactly may be at issue
here, Putnam is committed to the possibility of explaining (ii) as (iii). A
statement for which such an explanation would not be possible would be
a case of mind-independent truth, an inadmissible exception to the mind-
dependence thesis.

The explication of (ii) as (iii), however, raises familiar problems. If
T and T' are the same theory, then we are equating the consistency of T
with T''s assertion of $\text{Con}(T)$. Since T is assumed to contain arithmetic,
T would then be inconsistent by Gödel's Second Theorem. Therefore, T'
must be stronger than or independent of T. Now a plurality of empirically
ideal theories is in itself no problem. A progression of increasingly strong
theories, each asserting the consistency of its predecessor, would be one

natural way to generate the plurality, but Putnam also (and plausibly) leaves open the possibility of ideal theories that are independent of or even contradict each other.[38] These correspond to points where ideally rational inquirers might reasonably have diverged in their interpretations of or inferences from the data. Our question, however, is whether the consistency of T can amount to the assertion of $Con(T)$ by any ideal T'.

An appropriate T' can clearly not be stronger than T. For in that case the assertion of $Con(T)$ would have value only if T' were consistent, which presupposes the consistency of T. The explanation of (ii) as (iii) would therefore be circular. So T' must be independent of T. One question then is why the consistency of T should amount to the assertion of $Con(T)$ in some ideal T', when for all we know another T'' denies $Con(T)$. In the absence of guarantees that no ideal theory will deny the consistency of another, this is unsatisfactory. Apart from that, our previous problem will recur with respect to the consistency of T'. If T' is inconsistent, then its assertion of $Con(T)$ is useless. If T' is consistent, then what does that amount to? Since the consistency of T' must also be mind-dependent, it amounts to the assertion of $Con(T')$ by some independent T'', whose consistency in turn amounts to. . . . In the place of a circle we now have an equally unacceptable regress. So the logical properties of ideal theories must instead be absolute, and mind-dependence fails.

The difficulties here follow a known pattern. Recall the positivist attempt to avoid "metaphysics" by reducing problems of meaning and truth to the special cases of observational and logical language. The content of a theory, for example, was supposed to be fixed by its logical relations to observation sentences. One step toward the rejection of positivist semantics was the realization that displacing the problems did not diminish them. No unproblematic account of what it is for an observation sentence or a logical relation to hold was available.[39] Similarly, Putnam's attempt to avoid an excessively metaphysical (as he sees it) view of truth might work if a truth concept for observational and metalogical statements were given in advance. But none is. Putnam has retraced the path that already led to the downfall of an earlier antirealism.

Mind-dependence was supposed to be the alternative to the position attacked by the MTA. If it fails, then either the MTA itself is unsound, or we are without any tenable position at all. So we have strong reason to scrutinize the MTA.

C

Let us examine four curious junctures in Putnam's reasoning.
(1) Discussion of the MTA has centered on Putnam's treatment of

(*). Realists protest that for M to satisfy (*), *in the relevant sense,* is not for M so to interpret $L(T)$ that (*) comes out true. Rather, M must assign any w a referent to which w bears C — the relation *now* denoted by '$C(x, y)$'. We are not allowed to put '$C(x, y)$' itself up for interpretation and point out that on a suitable *re*interpretation, pairs of words and their "referents" in M satisfy it. To this Putnam replies that reference cannot be fixed by identifying it with C. In trying to do so, he says, we assume determinate referential properties for our causal language — which 'was just the question at issue' (*RR*, xi).[40]

But why *shouldn't* realists assume that? Putnam writes as though proving referential determinacy were up to the realist, but the dialectical situation only requires the realist's position to be consistent. As Devitt remarks: "Putnam claims to be offering an argument against metaphysical realism. At no point is he entitled to *assume* this doctrine false."[41] Devitt, a causal theorist, offers what he regards as a fully adequate reply to Putnam: if we allow that causal relations can determine the referents of terms, then they can also determine the referents of any terms — e.g., 'causes' — appearing in our theory of reference. Thus, 'refers' will be as determinate as anything else. Devitt has of course not proven determinacy, but his position seems entirely consistent. On his own terms, his answer stands up. Hence Devitt's charge of question-begging. Yet Putnam, long familiar with the charge, rejects it and counters with one of his own.[42]

(2) Putnam asserts this moral for the philosophy of language:

> On any view, the understanding of the language must determine the reference of the terms, or, rather, must determine the reference given the context of use. . . . To adopt a theory of meaning according to which a language whose whole use is specified still lacks something — namely its 'interpretation' — is to accept a problem which *can* only have crazy solutions. . . . Either the use *already* fixes the 'interpretation' or *nothing* can. (MR, 24)

The problem is that realists will accept every word of this. Similarly for the remark that we need a standpoint linking use and reference (ibid.), or that ". . . from the viewpoint of non-realist semantics, the metalanguage is completely understood, and so is the object language. So we can say and understand, "'cat' refers to cats'" (MR, 24–25). Realists will applaud, noting that causal theories, for example, are simply attempts to say *how* certain aspects of use and context determine reference. Such theories may be wrong, but their goal seems coherent and identical to Putnam's own. No one thinks that fixing the causal relations leaves the interpretation of the language open. Thus it is hard to understand what Putnam thinks he has shown, and against whom.

By way of offering a sympathetic answer, David Lewis takes Putnam to have refuted a "purely voluntaristic" view of reference.[43] That is, referential relations are not in general created by our decisions or intentions. We can decide to have 'cat' refer to cats, but such decisions cannot account for the referents of all our words, nor can they establish how reference works. We cannot *decide* to speak so that a causal theory of reference, or any other, is true of our language, since any such decision or stipulation must take place in an already determinate language. Now making this the point of the MTA does at least produce a coherent reading. The voluntarist appears as someone who tries to use words to fix the referents of words, overlooking the problem of indeterminacy, or irreferentiality, for the very words employed to this end; that sounds like the kind of error Putnam is trying to expose. The trouble is that no one has ever taken pure voluntarism seriously. It would be peculiar for Putnam to give so much emphasis to refuting a phantom opponent, and such a foolish one.

Yet the fact remains that Lewis makes some sense of the MTA. At least it is clear how the argument would be directed against a voluntarist. In contrast, the MTA does not look like a proof that use determines reference, or that objects depend on mind. The problem, then, is how Lewis's interpretation can look right even though the voluntaristic premise is not a plausible target for Putnam and certainly not one his actual opposition would accept. It would also be satisfying to find *some* useful lesson in the MTA.

(3) Besides, the MTA may not even hit what seems to be its ideal voluntarist (or constructivist) target. Someone who thinks, for whatever reason, that reference can be created by linguistic acts will believe that language can be meaningful, and have creative power, prior to being referential. But then I see no contradiction in supposing that some meaningful statement might create determinate referential properties for a class of expressions that includes itself. Of course I am assuming that the constructivist idea here makes some kind of sense, but that does not seem to be the issue.

Putnam in a way addresses this very point. Given that reference is possible at all, he finds it absurd to suppose that referential properties could remain open once meaning is fixed. If this is correct, semantic constructivism fails; and I do think Putnam is right. The MTA, however, was supposed to *demonstrate* the absurdity by deriving an antinomy from the constructivist assumption. That assumption was not simply offered as its own refutation. What is the intended absurdity? Evidently, the fact that (*) is supposed to construct its own referential properties. But if we allow that language can be meaningful before being referential—which is precisely the question—then no contradiction has been shown. The constructive power of (*) may simply be taken to be independent of its referential properties. If this is hard to believe (or even understand), it is not on grounds of the MTA.

(4) A main point for Putnam is that the MTA tells against "moderate," "naturalistic" forms of realism only (e.g., MR, 2, 4). A philosopher who thinks mind is linked to the world by direct grasping, noetic rays, or something of that sort is said to be safe from the MTA (however otherwise misguided). But as Lewis[44] and others have noted, this exemption is odd. If the causal condition (*) does not fix reference, why should a constraint involving supernatural grasping work any better? Indeed, the MTA is plainly independent of the particular content, causal or noncausal, of (*). The point is that *any* constraint consistent with T can be disinterpreted, then satisfied. So mystical theories of reference cannot escape the difficulty Putnam sets the naturalist. But this oversight of Putnam's is obvious enough to need explanation.

These and similar reflections make it unlikely that the MTA serves just one aim or that any sound reconstruction will much resemble the original. Thus we may interpret freely in order to bring out at least one cogent line of thought.

3. Definition and Legitimation

Let us focus on a main point of Putnam's discussion. The realist's task is, he believes, to *fix* the reference relation (*RR,* ix). The following questions are apparently taken to be equivalent (*RR,* viii–xi):

(a) Whether there is a determinate correspondence between words and things.
(b) Whether such a correspondence can be fixed.
(c) Whether such a correspondence can be singled out.

Putnam treats (b) and (c) as requests to *define* a correspondence. "Fixing" reference means giving a two-place open sentence satisfied just by the pairs < a, b > such that *a* refers to *b*. This leads at once to the mutual charges of question-begging. Realists are happy to comply by producing, say, $C(x, y)$. Putnam objects that this predicate only fixes reference if the terms of the metalanguage in which it appears have determinate satisfaction conditions. Realists reply that they may so assume as long as Putnam's project is to demonstrate an incoherence—an antinomy—in realism.[45]

So the question is what is supposed to come first—the determinacy or the singling out. The realist holds that given determinacy, reference can evidently be singled out. Putnam, however, thinks the singling out should *bring about determinacy,* which is impossible if singling out requires reference. But who is Putnam's target here? As noted, no one really expects reference in general to be created by definitional acts. We need to find a realist for whom definition has something distinct from, but resembling, this creative function.

Definition cannot create semantic relations if none already exist, but one might consider it as a way to introduce semantic terms into our language. The idea would not be to create a relation but to extend our expressive resources: the definition would let us speak of a referential relation we could not previously discuss. This, too, seems paradoxical. Anyone *intending* to define *reference* must already have that concept; the definition cannot yield new expressive power. But this difficulty is avoided if the definition is not supposed to provide a further concept but to show something about an existing one.[46] And of course, section 1 has already offered such a view of definition. The soft naturalist has but does not yet seriously accept a concept of reference. Serious acceptance requires naturalization — a form of definition. Naturalizations, then, are not literally creative but are in a manner of speaking supposed to create seriously acceptable concepts. I suggest that this idea, which echoes voluntarism and its kin without being obviously incredible, will make a proper target for the MTA.

Substituting naturalism for constructivism would give Putnam a more serious opponent and eliminate puzzles (2) and (3) of section 2.C. It would also explain his refusal to allow his opponent realist assumptions. Roughly speaking, soft naturalists may hope to *end up* realist but must place semantic notions in question pending naturalization. More accurately, their hope is to make realism (here in the sense of (iii)) part of serious theory. Although realism may already belong to their grade B scheme, its serious acceptability cannot be a starting point. And naturalization is not just a matter of showing that realism can be maintained without inconsistency; so the consistency of realism is no answer to Putnam. *Pace* Devitt, Putnam (under our present reformulation) nowhere assumes that realism is false. Putnam's opponent is rather prevented, on her own terms, from even provisionally assuming the truth of realism.

Putnam's claim to refute a naturalist — "moderate" — realism seems to be in line with my reading. But my soft naturalist is not at all Putnam's moderate realist. The latter is, by Putnam's own account, someone who takes reference to be legitimate, while also believing in naturalization; a realist for whom semantic terms are naturalizable. The soft naturalist, in contrast, is first of all a naturalist in the sense of section 1: she needs a naturalization, or convincing evidence of naturalization to come, before accepting realism. Given one, she will (at least seemingly — see section 5) fit Putnam's description of the moderate realist. But while she may already suspect, for whatever reason, that a naturalization should be possible, seriously affirming realism requires evidence. So the soft naturalist wants a naturalization of what the realist accepts from the start. It is this difference, plus the mystery of how the MTA could possibly impugn realism, that suggests a way out of our interpretive quandary. Since soft naturalism and naturalist realism are superficially similar, a critic might readily confuse his targets, advancing an objection to one that has force only against the other. I suspect that Putnam committed this oversight. Although the MTA cannot touch realism, naturalist or otherwise, it contains a genuine challenge to soft naturalism.

At this point, the MTA might look like a version of the standard self-defeat argument against naturalism. Soft naturalists hope to legitimize reference via a naturalization; Putnam replies that their framework already assumes that language is referential. This reading is suggested not just by Putnam's remarks on circularity, but by his explicit use of a self-defeat objection in subsequent, thematically related, writings.[47] I believe, however, that the situation is more complicated. First, the serious-grade B distinction blocks the usual self-defeat objection. If the MTA amounted to no more, it would hold no further interest. Second, the *effective* self-defeat argument against naturalism is quite different and has nothing to do with the MTA. I will sketch it below, both in order to propose a verdict on naturalism and to make the contrast clear. But third, that argument leaves open the tenability of soft naturalism under certain theoretically ideal conditions. The antinaturalist argument on this point turns out to be analogous to the MTA. So a less obvious reading of the MTA will also turn out to be deeper and more effective.

Before proceeding, let me stress an implicit generality. Any successful version of the MTA, or of any self-defeat argument of the kind considered here, tells not just against naturalism but against any view requiring semantics to be legitimized via definition. Whether the envisioned definitions involve physics, theology, souls, neurocomputation, or noetic rays is irrelevant. The question will always be whether we can demand legitimizing definitions when definition itself is regarded as a suspect concept. Since naturalistic reductionism is the only version of this idea now taken seriously, I will continue to focus on the tension between realism and naturalism. But we are asking quite generally what a legitimation of semantics could be.

4. Self-defeat and a Theoretical Escape

With the serious grade B distinction in place, the meaning of the grade B label is crucial to the possibility of continued self-defeat. Whether a theory survives its self-demotion to grade B status depends on just what that status is. Although this is a complex issue, reflection on Quine's double standard may suggest roughly the following account.

I model grade B acceptance on an attitude common in science: our attitude toward hypotheses that are clearly wrong yet the best we can now manage. We will often suspect a certain theory T of being substantially wrong (not just incomplete), without knowing just where or how to improve it. T might be a fair-sized body of propositions, of which some may be true but which on the whole, we think, must be shot through with error and inaccuracy. (Talk of truth and rightness in these lines need not be very "realist." One might gloss it in various ways, say in terms of empirical utility in the long run.) Under the circumstances, it might seem logical to reject T, holding out, perhaps indefinitely, for something better. If we have any epistemic standards at all, T is not the kind of thing we will happily believe. Yet believe it we may, for having even a bad theory in the domain of T may seem better than having none.

I emphasize that T is really *believed,* not just held to be instrumentally useful. Belief in this case is indeed problematic, but possible and not necessarily irrational. Belief, even in a rather poor theory, seems to hold pragmatic rewards. Certainly, scientists often do believe theories that are quite visibly off the mark — theoretical physics is a rich source of examples — and I assume that in this they are not irrational. But in such cases, our attitude is complex. We believe but regard our belief as a concession to our epistemic limits and to our need for a theory. Entering into it *faute de mieux,* we expect it not to survive the transition to a more satisfactory view — should we ever reach one.

These remarks may, in spite of their difficulties, roughly characterize a familiar attitude, one important for such epistemically limited creatures as ourselves.[48] They also agree with Quine's hints. (Indeed, the pragmatic view of belief suggested here is congenial to both Quine and Putnam.) Our question then is whether naturalists can take this attitude toward naturalism.

It appears not. The naturalist's ideal is to hold only seriously acceptable views: since the rest are patently deficient, no one would hold them by choice. But sometimes one has no choice. We reluctantly accept intentional psychology, whatever its ills, because it is (and may remain) indispensable. Here and elsewhere, grade B acceptance has the pragmatic component already mentioned. Our needs override epistemic scruples, leading us to espouse views we would prefer not to hold. The general point is that each violation of standards of serious acceptability requires pragmatic justification. And this has not been done for naturalism (hard or soft). *No practical gains have been shown to accrue from taking the naturalist's critical view of unnatural doctrine.* But if there are none, then the particular bit of unnatural doctrine that is naturalism is best not asserted, so that naturalism really is self-defeating.[49]

Certain observations from section 1 are crucial here. Only one pragmatic reason for being a naturalist suggests itself: that naturalists, more than others, will advance inquiry by seeking naturalizations and by regarding suspect doctrine with proper suspicion.[50] But this we have already rejected. Any successful naturalization will advance science, hence be universally desired. Something like (*), for example, can be fully appreciated without supposing that it is needed to rescue reference from grade B status. And the inductive reasons to hope for naturalizations are, where they exist, accessible at all. As for suspect doctrine, naturalists have no superior vantage point from which to criticize poor explanations or bad data. Nor does inconsistency with established natural science *particularly* weigh with them, for it already weighs as heavily as it should with everyone else. So the naturalist's science will not be empirically superior. What the naturalist uniquely has is a tempered view of theory falling below naturalist standards. But that is just naturalism, so offering it as a reason to go naturalist begs the question.

This kind of self-defeat argument (the "pragmatic argument") is not found in Putnam. Since it tells against both hard and soft naturalism it also seems to supercede potential antinaturalist uses of any form of the MTA. Yet that is not entirely correct.

The soft naturalist might hope to escape self-defeat objections by actually finding a naturalization of reference (and related terms). For (*) would lead to naturalization of the concept of reference itself, thus making soft naturalism seriously acceptable by its own lights. Once naturalized, naturalism would count as serious theory. (Only soft naturalists can try this line. Because hard naturalists will always regard their naturalism as being grade B, the pragmatic argument will always defeat them.) Now this seems a curious hope. Since reference has not been naturalized, our proper attitude toward soft naturalism now is rejection. Having rejected it with good reason, why hope for its rehabilitation? But for a philosopher receptive to the charms of natural science, the possibility of using only scientifically legitimate terms might define an ideal state of knowledge.[51] The soft naturalist might advance her ideology not as something to be espoused now, but rather as part of the total view we should aim to hold in the limit of inquiry. Once we know enough science, the idea runs, we can be soft naturalists; and we should want to be, since restricting oneself to scientifically respectable discourse is preferable. If this stance is attractive, then it would still be important to know whether soft naturalism is tenable in the presence of (*). Since the pragmatic argument exploits our present lack of a naturalization, this question is beyond its reach.

What, if anything, an ultimate system of belief would be, and how (or even whether) to dispute about its elements, is obscure. But philosophers have long asked not just what we should believe and do in our present circumstances, with the needs and abilities we happen to have, but about the nature of ideal human conduct and thought. We explore the ideal as a way of regulating our present life: it seems characteristic of human beings that our ideals help to define what we are. Since a closer investigation of this point would, obviously, take us far afield, I will here simply assume that something of this kind is reasonable.

In that case it is worth asking whether soft naturalism could be held under any circumstances. Given a naturalization of semantics, is it coherent to seriously accept naturalistic statements only? Of course only an actual reduction, to which we now have no clue, could make this stance possible. A soft naturalist might, however, find this consistent. In the ideal state, one would exploit one's naturalization to observe otherwise unaffordable epistemic scruples. An ultimate goal of inquiry, then, would be the luxury of holding only scientifically validated beliefs.

More accurately, the goal would be to hold natural scientific beliefs plus appropriate normative beliefs. A naturalized formulation of soft naturalism would use reduced concepts (or analogs) of belief, evidence, and so forth, but it would still not be part of science. It would *recommend* certain attitudes to us rather than explaining the empirical data. This leads to no immediate difficulty. Since an ideally advanced science would not eliminate our need for epistemic (or moral or aesthetic) recommendations, the soft naturalist's vision of advanced inquiry should be able to accommodate these. Seriously acceptable norms would, of course, require naturalistic descriptive language, but that would be available. Yet one still needs to know why soft naturalism would be a reasonable normative stance for ideal inquirers.

This question is important, since the pragmatic argument has already shown that naturalists cannot reasonably assert a grade B naturalist thesis. The problem is whether soft naturalists would have any better reason to maintain a naturalized version of their view. Now the pragmatic argument seems to carry over at least this far: soft naturalism would have no more heuristic value in an ideal state of knowledge than it does now. The reasons why soft naturalist standards would not lead to better theories seem to apply as well to ideal inquirers as to ourselves. The objection to holding soft naturalism, however, may not carry over. A grade B naturalist thesis uses unreduced terms that the naturalist would rather avoid but will employ for the sake of empirical gains. Thus our earlier argument was that if these gains are lacking, naturalism should be abandoned. Since ideal inquirers could express naturalism naturalistically, this criticism is blocked. Still, with what reason would they hold a naturalist epistemology that has no empirical point?

This seems to be a genuine difficulty. Soft naturalists must, at least, explain why the pragmatic argument should not apply to ideal inquirers. Because the question concerns the permissible epistemic standards for such inquirers, a general account of rationality seems to be called for. On this question naturalists have been rather silent. Just for that reason, it is hard to tell whether the pragmatic argument will apply under all conditions of knowledge. I believe another objection, closer to the MTA, will have more force. Thus a line of thought somewhat like Putnam's will retain independent interest.

Putnam takes the MTA to apply regardless of whether we actually have a naturalization of reference: possession of a causal theory is supposed to do his realist opponent no good (e.g., MR, 17–18). Thus the MTA does seem intended to show that realism is untenable in any possible state of scientific knowledge. If soft naturalism is to be our substitute target for realism, then the MTA should bear on whether ultimate inquirers could be soft naturalists. Yet Putnam gives his argument a temporal element. He charges his opponent with aiming to construct a reference relation through (*) and claims that this could be done only if our words already referred. That is, the difficulty is supposed to lie in a construction that cannot get started. Ideal theorists who can naturalistically validate their naturalism appear to have no such problem. An argument for legitimation can apply to its own terms without evident paradox. This makes it questionable whether Putnam's argument can serve our purposes.

The underlying issue here is whether a soft naturalist validation of referential concepts could have force against genuine doubts. The naturalist begins with a genuinely critical view of semantics; soft naturalists hope to meet the criticism through naturalization. We have seen that this position collapses in the absence of a naturalization. Would the naturalization allow naturalists to combine their critical attitude and nonskeptical resolution?

Perhaps not. Establishing the internal consistency of a realist position should not satisfy the skeptical element in naturalism. But how could a soft naturalist's appeal to an existing causal theory do more? A genuine skeptic about reference should also reject as question-begging the soft naturalist's idea of conferring legitimacy by naturalistic definition. To this the soft naturalist (with a causal theory in hand) might reply that pressing such doubts cannot, at any rate, be a point of the MTA. The MTA is supposed to uncover an inconsistency. Soft naturalism without a causal theory may be inconsistent or self-defeating, but if a causal theory restores consistency, no version of the MTA can work against soft naturalists fortunate enough to possess one. If the fortunate soft naturalist still has problems, they are not exposed by the MTA. Or so it may seem. I will resolve this issue in the naturalist's disfavor.

5. The Escape Closed

Let us more carefully consider just when a causal theory might legitimize semantic concepts. The possibilities are easily seen to be quite limited, and I will argue that in fact they cannot obtain. Even under the most favorable conditions for naturalism, the attempted justification of semantic concepts via (*) is incoherent. Thus the naturalist view of semantics is a total misconception.

It is just for naturalists that can (*) even aspire to a legitimizing role. If the legitimacy of semantics turns merely on considerations of empirical or pragmatic value, then causal theories are irrelevant. For example, a causal reduction would not help to show a practical value for semantic concepts. Reducibility establishes no utility at all. Nor is it necessary for utility, since an unreduced concept can be as useful as you please. For analogous reasons, reduction is essentially irrelevant to empirical value. Putnam has a similar view of the significance of causal theories, claiming that despite their potential interest, they would not advance realism: they would not yield additional warrant for semantic discourse. I think this is the right idea, but soft naturalism raises a special problem. If (serious) legitimacy in general depends on naturalizations, then the legitimacy of reference in particular seems to require one. (*) might, then, seem to support realism just from this viewpoint. That is exactly the soft naturalist position.

Of course this naturalist viewpoint would be tenable only given a naturalization of reference, as the pragmatic argument shows. This restriction is not to be underestimated. We must now reject soft naturalism; if we want reference to be legitimate now, we cannot appeal to a naturalization. Many soft naturalists are confident of naturalizability, at least in principle, but that *assumes* the legitimacy of semantic concepts. If these concepts are illegitimate, then no naturalization is in the cards. So naturalists have no right to assume that naturalization can be achieved; no right to take naturalizability for granted. And a hypothesized naturalization cannot help the defense of realism. Whether an existent naturalization could serve any better is of considerable theoretical interest but irrelevant to the present status of realism. Hence the remarks to follow bear on our acceptance neither of realism nor of soft naturalism, but concern the significance causal theories could *possibly* have; the reasons for which realism could possibly be held.

Suppose reference has been naturalized, making soft naturalism assertible. Does (*) then support (the serious acceptability of) realism? The positive argument is that soft naturalism requires a naturalization for the legitimacy of reference; but (*) is one; so (*) is here part of the support for realism. Against this, note that the coherence of the theory requiring a naturalization of reference depends on one. If the naturalization (which, being held on empirical grounds, might be overthrown) were rejected, soft naturalism would go too, and with it the threat to semantic concpets. The challenge (*) was supposed to meet arose just within soft naturalism. Under the circumstances, (*) supports realism in appearance only. It is presupposed in the viewpoint from which support appears necessary.

A certain soft naturalist (still under conditions of ideal knowledge) might take this stance: some form of naturalism is right; possession of (*) makes soft naturalism tenable; but if (*) were to be given up, one would have to revert to hard naturalism, thus rejecting semantic concepts (for serious purposes). Thus might realism be tied to naturalization. One would, with a naturalization, maintain both realism and soft naturalism, yet prefer hard naturalism over realism given a forced choice. One's realism would then depend on keeping (*), which would hence seem to give realism a kind of support. The naturalization would, in contrast, not support the realism of a theorist preferring realism to hard naturalism in case the soft line fails.

Yet the position just described is untenable. Since hard naturalism fails its own test for serious acceptability (whether a naturalization is given or not), it falls to the pragmatic argument. It cannot reasonably be maintained at all, let alone chosen over realism. So we have not yet found an acceptable position on which (*) legitimizes reference.

Further, the position seems to involve incoherent preferences quite apart from the weakness of its hard naturalist fallback. We are imagining a theorist who

(i) would choose soft naturalism over hard naturalism. Observe that hard naturalism is — *if* we set the pragmatic argument aside — perfectly tenable in the presence of (*). One simply prefers to seriously accept propositions of natural science only. Thus a genuine choice between hard and soft naturalism is possible.

(ii) Would choose hard naturalism over realism. Since removing (*) leaves realism perfectly tenable, hard naturalism is not mandatory if soft naturalism fails. So again this is a genuine choice.

(iii) Hence would choose soft naturalism over realism. But holding soft naturalism presupposes holding realism. The former is tenable only when its semantic terms are seriously legitimized. Thus, soft naturalism is pragmatically, although not logically, stronger than realism: although the two positions may be combined, no rational choice of soft naturalism over realism is possible, since the former without the latter is irrational. So either preference (i) or preference (ii) must be given up. The result will be a position in which (*) does even seem to support realism.

To bring out the intuitions here, note that a desire to hold *some* form of naturalism, either hard or soft, is itself odd. Since one form lets *only* natural science be seriously acceptable, while the other admits natural science and more, the two are mutually inconsistent. In this way they are like hard and soft determinism, of which one denies while the other affirms free action.[52] But the two determinists share a basic thesis — determinism — while differing on the further question of freedom. Useful common ground for the two naturalists is hard to find. Although they agree on the serious acceptability of natural science, so does everyone else. Although both reject unreduced unnatural doctrine, even this is not entirely a point of agreement. Given (*), the soft naturalist seriously accepts the claim that unreduced doctrine is seriously unacceptable. But since this claim is semantic, the hard naturalist's attitude is grade B acceptance instead. So their attitudes are distinct. It is, then, unclear whether one can view these positions as alternative versions of a single naturalist idea. Opting for either already involves a commitment on the fundamental question of the status of semantic concepts. The basic problem is that we are comparing a position that lets *only* natural science be seriously accepted with one that denies this restriction. This leaves little room for significant agreement. It is almost as though our theorist were to announce a desire to take *some* view of semantic concepts: either acceptance or rejection. In contrast, there is nothing odd about the desire to be some kind of determinist: to assert determination while leaving open the question of freedom.

The decisive fact is still that soft naturalism cannot reasonably demand a legitimation of a realism it presupposes. That presupposition was what made the preference in (iii) irrational. We tried to construct a complex position in which (*) somehow legitimizes realism, but an incoherent view is not usually repaired by embedding it in something further. And indeed, the difficulty reappears. At the end, we have one more variation on the theme of self-defeat.

A modest soft naturalism, consisting in the serious acceptance of any doctrines that do not seem irreducible, was found uselessly weak in section 1. It would probably have avoided the pragmatic argument, but our present reflections would in any case also have defeated it. The modest naturalist who believes semantic notions to be reducible is in the same position as our soft naturalist with a reduction in hand. In neither case can the reduction — actual or possible — help to *support* the realism, as a naturalist would require.

One must decide for either realism or naturalism. If one chooses realism, one cannot try, in soft naturalist fashion, to add on naturalism. If one takes naturalism, one cannot try, in soft naturalist fashion, to get the realism back. That is the lesson: realism can't be naturalized, nor naturalism realized.

6. Putnam Revisited

Putnam had argued that a causal theory could not construct ("fix") the reference relation for realists. While allowing that a suitable version of (*) would reduce or naturalize reference, Putnam denied that it could have the significance realists intended. Substituting soft naturalism for realism and legitimation for construction in this position yields our own conclusion. These changes are logical, since soft naturalists are Putnam's de facto opponents, and his talk of construction or fixing invites metaphorical construal. And while Putnam's circularity charge against realism is notoriously unclear, our representation of soft naturalism as presupposing semantic doctrines it tries to question seems as close as a clear substitute is likely to get. Thus we have preserved key elements of the MTA's structure. Yet we have also diverged considerably. Let us attempt a final assessment of the MTA.

My account of the MTA shows how Putnam's debate with the realists could end in mutual charges of question-begging. Putnam, as I represent him, sees that the soft naturalists he opposes should begin with agnosticism toward semantics. Yet soft naturalism presupposes realism. The opposition officially forgoes semantics, yet begs the question in its favor. Realists, on the other hand, see that Putnam's argument works only against an opponent who starts without the realist premise. Unaware that he is holding up a mirror, they rightly object that a consistent realism cannot thus be threatened. So they miss Putnam's point; he misses his own. The key is to separate the failed attack on realism from the refutation of soft naturalism. Both sides neglect this distinction; both have now gotten their due.

We also explain the appearance of argument against a voluntarism no one takes seriously. The naturalist and Putnam's voluntarist (who may be a caricature) both assume that their words already refer. Since that is the element Putnam attacks in voluntarism, his fundamental idea can be recast to apply to soft naturalism, as I have done.

My construal makes no use of mind-independence. The soft naturalist does not assume it in any sense, and the refutation proceeds without it.

This divergence from Putnam points up an error in his development of the MTA, one which may arise as follows.

Putnam sets realists the problem of nonverbally specifying the objects of reference. The idea is that words cannot (in general) attach words to things, since the words used to do the attaching need their own attachment. Thus he thinks realists need a prior, nonverbal mode of attachment, an ability to specify (identify, grasp, represent) objects without using descriptions. Now a realist who believes in that contrasts with Putnam's antirealist: crucial to antirealism, for Putnam, is the belief that objects *are given through descriptions*' (MR, 21). And this in turn, for Putnam, amounts to belief in mind-dependence, or a form of idealism: a claim that talk of objects is just talk of what we can establish in certain ways.

Realists will deny that mind-dependence in any interesting sense follows from the fact that objects are given by descriptions (conceptual representations) only. I would agree. This view of Putnam's is mysterious, and denying it is enough to make mind-independence irrelevant to the MTA.[53] But Putnam goes wrong at the start by positing an opponent who might invoke a faculty of nonconceptual grasping. Who could that be? Obviously not the soft naturalist, who cannot escape her circularity problem by knowing how to do things without words. Yet I made Putnam's opponent a soft naturalist just to find some plausible rejection of the constructivist he seems to imagine. Certainly, it is incredible that realism as such should require nonconceptual grasping. The legitimacy of reference cannot possibly entail that; nor can realism conjoined with a belief in naturalizability ("moderate realism"). But if nonconceptual grasping would help no opponent of Putnam's, then none will suspect that objects can be given without descriptions. So the alleged link between the MTA and questions of mind-dependence is broken at once.

We also noted that realists can find no refuge in a mystical theory of reference. Reading the MTA as an attack on soft naturalism explains Putnam's error here as well. For a realist could expect to escape the MTA by adopting a nonnaturalist realism. And that would be correct, but the way to do it is not to replace naturalism by a copy in which supernatural theories of reference take over the role of causal ones. Credibility aside, *that* cannot work. The naturalist's problem lies in the demand for legitimizing definitions, not in the specific content of definitions like (*). Hence the MTA provides no motive at all for mysticism. The point is to go *non*-naturalist, not *super*naturalist. That is, we keep both realism and the view that reference consists in a nonsemantic relation. But we keep these claims sharply distinct, rather than following the naturalist in tying the first to the second.

Putnam erred by confusing naturalism with the belief in naturalizations. Thus he inferred both that the supernaturalist could escape the naturalist's difficulty and that nonnaturalist realism must be mystical. The confusion was understandable: since Field and others have tied realism to naturalization, the only articulated forms of nonnaturalist realism *were* mystical. Realists should, however, reject naturalism while agreeing that reference is as physical as any relation can be.[54]

In short, the metaphysical purposes for which Putnam employed the MTA, and which have been prominent in his subsequent thinking, are lost. Nothing follows about "metaphysical realism," the relation of truth to confirmation, or the dependence of objects on mind.[55] And while our reconstruction of the argument retains both a core structure and the polemic against naturalists, we have not only changed the subject but also thrown out Putnam's machinery. The essential idea — the one that works — is circularity or self-defeat. There is no role for model-theoretic considerations of any kind. We have neither assumed a formalized language, nor used Skolemization, constructibility, permutations of individuals, or any other technical devices. Of course, that might just be a peculiarity, even a defect, of our reconstruction. But we have found a powerful application that avoids the difficulties and obscurities besetting Putnam's own version. It has been necessary to destroy the MTA in order to save it.

7. Naturalism and Realism

The distinction between naturalism and the belief in naturalizations has been crucial. One can think that certain definitions are forthcoming, yet not demand them for purposes of legitimacy. Our argument was, therefore, directed against naturalist epistemology, not against the definitional enterprise itself. Yet that enterprise also needs reconsideration. We observed that neither metaphysical principles nor past successes provide reason to expect naturalizations of semantic concepts. I suspect that most philosophers who believe in naturalizations are committed to doing so by their combination of naturalism and belief in the legitimacy of semantic (or intentional) terms. But giving up naturalism removes such reasons for expecting naturalizations.

These reflections do not preempt all naturalist efforts. I have not shown that significant naturalizations are impossible; besides, the search may well be fruitful even if its objects are out of reach. But a more skeptical attitude toward many of the naturalist efforts now in the field is recommended. An approach to naturalizing reference (say) that seems promising in the light of naturalist faith will often look grossly implausible under revised

expectations. And certainly, the search for naturalizations should not pre-
occupy philosophers of language and mind. Its prospects are too unclear,
and there are too many other good questions to ask.

Realism has held up better than naturalism. But how is realism to
be supported, if not through a naturalist validation?

One answer would exploit the utility of semantic concepts, which
are inextricably involved in our discourse about ourselves.[56] Thus one might
propose a kind of transcendental argument for realism, an argument for
legitimacy from indispensability. But this might legitimize only weakened
(perhaps "epistemic" or "disquotational") surrogates for genuine semantic
notions.[57] Also, we may obtain no more than grade B acceptability. If
semantic doctrines are useful, even essential, only for such limited beings
as ourselves, we might still not seriously accept them.

Of course the distinction between serious and grade B acceptability
was introduced as part of a now rejected naturalism. But as noted in section 4, something like it seems to be an essential part of scientific thought
anyway. If so, and if even indispensable concepts can be grade B, then an
argument from utility may not show that semantics is seriously acceptable.
Yet surely, serious acceptability is what we want. Thus the realist would
need an entirely different line.

Note that we have found no objections to realism—no positive case
for antirealism.[57] Even the dispensability of semantic concepts need not
force us to give them up. We might choose to employ them. If antirealism
is also not refutable, both positions might be open. Yet we presumably
want to choose one, and on rational grounds, for the decision seems real
and important. More subjective considerations might then come into play.
If we want to end up realist, it might, for example, suffice to find that realism leads to an attractive view of inquiry, perhaps because it alone permits
a significant notion of theoretical progress and truth. Such appeals to a
kind of metatheoretic taste might seem to support realism only weakly but
may look better if other realist strategies fail. Besides, denials of realism
would require equally subjective grounds.

I am sympathetic to this line of thought. Perhaps there is no good
route to realism: not because it is incoherent, as Putnam claimed, but because it is a position one must start with, or occupy by sheer choice, not
try to reach from neutral ground. I think that result would generally be
unwelcome, for realists do not wish to be naive. Empiricism and pragmatism have conditioned us not to enter into realism lightly. Quine studied
semantic concepts from a sophisticated, critical viewpoint in *Word and Object* and found them wanting. The realist ideal has been to adopt roughly
his perspective while avoiding his outcome. One tries, for example, to argue that realist assumptions are necessary for linguistic behavior or the

practice of science. Such a project may succeed, but it may also fail: realism may be attainable only through rigorous naivete. If so, and if realism is the right choice, then in metaphysics, the least sophistication brings decadence.[59]

Notes

1. Originally in "Realism and Reason," in *Meaning and the Moral Sciences* (London, Henly, and Boston: Routledge and Kegan Paul, 1978), henceforth *MMS*. Other abbreviations: *RR* is the Introduction to Putnam's *Realism and Reason* (Cambridge: Cambridge University Press, 1983); MR is "Models and Reality," in the same volume.

2. As in *Reason, Truth, and History* (Cambridge: Cambridge University Press, 1981) or "Model Theory and the Factuality of Semantics," in *Reflections on Chomsky,* ed. Alexander George (Oxford: Blackwell, 1990).

3. 'Semantic' will be used in its "transcendent," language-general sense unless otherwise noted. Similarly for particular semantic terms. (In contrast, "immanent" notions of truth, reference, and so forth are defined only for a fixed language. See W. V. Quine, *Philosophy of Logic* (Englewood Cliffs, N.J.: Prentice-Hall, 1970), chap. 2. Incidentally, my talk below of defining reference and truth must, of course, be modified to avoid paradox.

4. What pass as explanations tend to be laced with such *vatic dicta* as "According to naturalists, thinkers are squarely in the only world there is" (Ruth Millikan, "Metaphysical Anti-Realism?" *Mind* 95 [1986]: 423). Of course such formulations promote the image of naturalism as a position (which is laden with implications yet) which no sensible person could deny.

5. My interpretation of naturalism draws heavily on Quine's writings, notably *Word and Object* (Cambridge, Mass.: MIT Press, 1960), chap. 1 and *passim.* For more discussion, see the Introduction to the present volume as well as my "Truth, Physicalism, and Ultimate Theory," in *Objections to Physicalism,* ed. Howard Robinson (Oxford: Oxford University Press, 1992). Of course 'naturalism' has meanings quite distinct from any at issue here, e.g., the idea that epistemology can use empirical results.

6. For an extended investigation of ontological physicalism, see John Post, *The Faces of Existence* (Ithaca, N.Y.: Cornell University Press, 1987). Post himself, incidentally, defends a "physicalism" virtually devoid of ontological restrictions. Thus, for all the interest of his position, its claim to be called physicalism is doubtful. The critical discussion below is not intended to apply to him in any simple way.

7. Roughly this had long been one of Chomsky's complaints against physicalism.

8. The sets vs. properties issue aside, serious disagreement of course centers on the interpretation of the 'and so on'.

9. One would, besides, have to meet the argument that any self-conscious

theorist will use irreducibly mental language. For this kind of line (which I am not now endorsing), see the contributions of George Bealer, George Myro, and Richard Warner to *Objections to Physicalism.*

10. I take 'principle of physical exhuastion' from Geoffrey Hellman and Frank Thompson. See their "Physicalism," *Journal of Philosophy* 72 (1975): 551–564, and "Physicalist Materialism," *Nous* 11 (1977): 309–435. One response is Richard Healy's "Physicalist Imperialism," in *Proceedings of the Aristotelian Society* 79 (1978–79): 191–211.

11. E.g., Hartry Field in "Mental Representation," *Erkenntnis* 13 (1978): 9–61.

12. See Mark Wilson's contribution to this volume.

13. For a systematic and very good, although in my view unsuccessful, attack on the issues of this subsection, see David Lewis, "New Work for a Theory of Universals," *Australasian Journal of Philosophy* 61 (1983): 343–377. Lewis gives an excellent sense of the metaphysical contortions a satisfactory formulation of physicalism would require. Not surprisingly, certain ways of denying physicalism replicate the contortions. See, e.g., George Bealer, *Quality and Concept* (Oxford: Oxford University Press, 1982), chap. 8, and his "Materialism and the Logical Structure of Intentionality," in *Objections to Physicalism.* Implicit in my present text is a critique of metaphysical pretensions on both sides. More on this on another occasion.

14. The naturalist will probably want to recognize legitimate normative beliefs in addition to the propositions of natural science. Such a position will be considered later. But for the moment, this issue is unimportant.

15. I take the phrase 'independent and impartial criteria' from Israel Scheffler's classic portrait of scientific objectivity in *Science and Subjectivity* (Indianapolis: Bobbs-Merrill, 1967), 1.

16. Some main sources: Quine's *Word and Object;* Daniel Dennett, *Brainstorms* (Cambridge, Mass.: MIT Press, 1978); Stephen Stich, *From Folk Psychology to Cognitive Science* (Cambridge, Mass.: MIT Press, 1983); Patricia Churchland, *Neurophilosophy* (Cambridge, Mass.: MIT Press, 1986).

17. Note that ontological physicalism faces no obvious threat of self-defeat. Saying that everything is physical does not restrict us to scientific beliefs. This would be one attraction of a purely ontological physicalism.

18. See, e.g., Hartry Field, "Tarski's Theory of Truth," *Journal of Philosophy* 69 (1972): 347–375.

19. A problem taken to be fatal by various antinaturalists, including Lynne Rudder Baker in *Saving Belief: A Critique of Physicalism* (Princeton: Princeton University Press, 1987) and Putnam in *The Many Faces of Realism* (La Salle, Ill.: Open Court, 1987).

20. *Word and Object,* 216–221. My "Truth, Physicalism, and Ultimate Theory" explores the ideas of the next few paragraphs at greater length.

21. I find it implausible to say that naturalization would actually make semantics (e.g.) part of natural science, but for present purposes that is largely a verbal issue. Note also that the actual definitions might be loose or approximate in various ways. My text will assume an idealization.

22. This seems to be Quine's view. Field's "Tarski's Theory of Truth" is a

classic exposition of soft naturalism and a main source for my remarks below on the soft naturalist's motives.

23. Of course the simple atomic theory is wrong, but not in a way that affects the present point.

24. "Truth, Physicalism, and Ultimate Theory" develops this point at greater length.

25. Among the landmark efforts that have generated waves of counterexamples are Fred Dretske's *Knowledge and the Flow of Information* (Cambridge, Mass.: MIT Press, 1981) and Jerry Fodor's *Psychosemantics* (Cambridge, Mass.: MIT Press, 1988). Representatives of the teleological wing include Ruth Garrett Millikan, *Language, Thought, and Other Biological Categories* (Cambridge, Mass.: MIT Press, 1984) and William Lycan, *Consciousness* (Cambridge, Mass.: MIT Press, 1987). There is irony in naturalists' finding themselves driven to positing *natural purposes* in order to naturalize intentional concepts; such purposes are just what naturalists were once supposed to avoid. For some criticism, see Mark Bedau's contribution to this volume and my "Teleosemantics" (ms.).

26. For difficulties with supervenience versions of materialism, see Jaegwon Kim "'Strong' and 'Global' Supervenience Revisited," *Philosophy and Phenomenological Research* 48 (1987): 315-326 and "The Myth of Nonreductive Materialism," *Proceedings of the American Philosophical Association* 63 (1989): 59-79; Terence Horgan's essay in this volume; and Richard B. Miller, "Supervenience is a Two-way Street," *Journal of Philosophy* 87 (1990): 695-701.

27. As noted by Hellman and Thompson in "Physicalism."

28. Functional definitions of psychological terms must perhaps be knowable if they are analytic, as David Lewis holds. Indeed, he claims that the defining conditions are "platitudes" ("Psychophysical and Theoretical Identifications," *Australasian Journal of Philosophy* 50 (1972): 249-258). But that seems implausible. For one approach to the idea that a true naturalization of the mental might not be recognizable, see my "A Philosopher Looks at Artificial Intelligence," in D. L. Farwell, S. C. Helmreich, and W. D. Wallace, eds., *Perspectives in Cognitive Science* (Urbana, Ill.: University of Illinois Linguistics Students' Organization, 1983). Cf. Thomas Nagel, "What Is It Like to Be a Bat?" and "Panpsychism," in *Mortal Questions* (Cambridge: Cambridge University Press, 1979).

29. For a naturalist's use of propositions, see Brian Loar, *Mind and Meaning* (Cambridge: Cambridge University Press, 1981).

30. A form of naturalism we have not directly considered holds that all phenomena admit physical explanation *in principle*. Considerations much like those given in the text show that this form, too, lacks distinctive methodological force. It alters neither our conduct of inquiry nor our attitudes toward various theories. Further, defining an appropriate sense of 'physical explanation' requires delicate footwork; and whether the end result will aptly be called naturalism (physicalism, materialism) is unclear.

31. I have Putnam's kind of indeterminacy in mind. Lesser cases of indeterminacy, such as those generated by vagueness, are genuine but not so threatening.

32. I am granting that there *is* a significant mind-independence principle. But the evolution of Putnam's own attempts to state one (in his case, for the pur-

pose of denying it) suggests the obscurity of the issue. (Compare, e.g., "Realism and Reason" with *The Many Faces of Realism,* chaps. 1–2.)

33. In Putnam's terms, roughly, one can be an external as well as an internal realist (*MMS,* 129–130). But I will avoid the complexities of that distinction.

34. Maybe this sheds light on why Putnam chooses *T* to be ideal. (The problem is why the indeterminacy argument does not apply to any confirmed, or consistent, or perhaps even inconsistent theory, which would commit Putnam to the Protagorean view that no theory at all can be false.)

35. It would be interesting to compare Putnam's indeterminacy argument with the more familiar ones of Quine and Davidson. These are notable for giving the issue of behaviorial evidence for schemes of reference center stage, a matter at least suppressed in Putnam. On the other hand, there is the common idea that interpretation aims just to assign the right truth values, or holophrastic truth conditions, to sentences; that interpretations of words are otherwise arbitrary. I suspect that the various indeterminacy arguments are at bottom quite similar, but making that case would require investigation of Putnam's use of "operational and theoretical constraints" (e.g., *MMS,* 126).

36. As Donald Davidson remarks in "The Structure and Content of Truth," *Journal of Philosophy* 87 (1990): 307.

37. E.g., in *Representation and Reality* (Cambridge, Mass.: MIT Press, 1988), 115.

38. See Putnam's "A Defense of Internal Realism" in his *Realism with a Human Face* (Cambridge, Mass.: Harvard University Press, 1990).

39. To Quine's immense credit, this difficulty is confronted in chapter 1 of *Word and Object.*

40. I first heard the objection of this paragraph from David Lewis in a symposium with Putnam at Princeton in the spring of 1977. See Clark Glymour, "Conceptual Scheming, or Confessions of a Metaphysical Realist," *Synthese* 51 (1982): 169–180; Michael Devitt, *Realism and Truth* (Princeton: Princeton University Press, 1984), chap. 11.

41. Devitt, *Realism and Truth,* 191.

42. Putnam's recent elucidation (he acknowledges that "some readers have found [the MTA] unclear") is that the causal theorist makes the causal relation *C* (but not any "nonstandard" *C', C'',* . . .) intrinsically capable of fixing reference; that causation is credited with a built-in dignity or intentionality that enables it to choose its own name. This he finds unintelligible (*Realism with a Human Face,* 85, 328). The charge of unintelligibility is beyond doubt, but where are Devitt and Glymour (e.g.) supposed to have taken on this bizarre commitment? Putnam is apparently saddling causal theorists with an obligation to explain *why* reference is *C* and not some other relation. Of course this will appear nonsensical — as though one were to demand reasons why water is H_2O or why first order semantic entailment is first order derivability and not some other property. One can show that these identities obtain, just as the causal theorist thinks reference can (say, by a method of intuition and counterexample) be identified with *C.* But the analog of Putnam's demand within logic would be to ask for a demonstration that "the derivability relation is capable of fixing the consequence relation (while other rela-

tions are not)" (compare *Realism with a Human Face,* 328). What could that possibly be?

These recent passages are exactly what would be expected from a philosopher who assumes reference cannot be treated as one more natural relation and proceeds to charge others with violating this principle. This is substantially identical to the position discussed in the text and has no dialectical value against causal results.

43. Davis Lewis, "Putnam's Paradox," *Australasian Journal of Philosophy* 62 (1984): 221–236. Putnam makes the same point in "Why There Isn't a Ready-made World," in *Realism and Reason.*

44. Ibid., 232–233.

45. Hence the causal predicate *C* is a distraction. If Putnam's challenge to the realist can be met at all, 'refers' will serve as well as any other predicate.

46. The difficulty is serious for anyone who makes linguistic or conceptual activity genuinely creative. See my "Frege's Definition of Number," *Notre Dame Journal of Formal Logic* 24 (1983): 1–21.

47. E.g., *The Many Faces of Realism.*

48. On this view, natural science may be full of grade B doctrine. The naturalist's claim would be that seriously acceptable material is also found there and not (barring naturalization) elsewhere.

49. Again, see "Truth, Physicalism, and Ultimate Theory" for more details, including a longer version of the argument now to follow.

50. This seems to be Hartry Field's view in "Mental Representation" and "Tarski's Theory of Truth" and in conversation.

51. In this context I use 'ideal' and 'ultimate' to characterize a state of knowledge so advanced that, e.g., neurocomputational predictions of behavior are feasible. There is no suggestion of our knowing absolutely everything; indeed, ideality in this sense is compatible with considerable ignorance.

52. Analogy proposed by Frederick Schmitt.

53. Putnam may, like Davidson, hold that we must be mostly right about our objects of reference. But even if that were granted, the step to mind-dependence in any sense of Putnam's would be problematic.

54. This phrasing is deliberate. Section 1 already suggested that any attempt to segregate relations into the physical and the nonphysical is an error. Rejecting naturalism may be a step toward freedom from such discriminatory impulses.

55. Contrary to Putnam in *Reason, Truth, and History, Realism and Reason, The Many Faces of Realism,* and *Representation and Reality.* For the technical machinery alluded to a few lines on, see esp. "Realism and Reason," *Reason, Truth, and History,* and "Models and Reality."

56. E.g., Donald Davidson, *Inquiries into Truth and Interpretation* (Oxford: Oxford University Press, 1984) and "The Structure and Content of Truth." See also Putnam, "Reference and Understanding" in *MMS.*

57. I explore this idea, reaching an intermediate conclusion in "On Some Concepts of Truth" (ms.). For a version of the envisioned transcendental argument (more or less) see Hartry Field's "The Deflationary Conception of Truth," in *Fact,*

Science, and Morality: Essays on A. J. Ayer's Language, Truth, and Logic, ed. G. MacDonald and C. Wright (Oxford: Blackwell, 1986.)

58. I leave it open whether the antirealist simply rejects semantic concepts or instead makes them grade B. The following remarks hold either way.

59. For responses to a late draft I thank Hugh Chandler and particularly Frederick Schmitt. I have also followed James Janowski's editorial advice.

Is the Body a Physical Object?

Richard Warner

You are floating weightlessly in a completely dark room; your right arm extends from your body at roughly a right angle. Can you, without touching it, know the position of your arm? Of course; you can feel where your arm is. You know, let us say, by "inner feeling."[1] It follows that the human body is not a physical object. This may seem mad. How could the *body* not be physical? I do not, of course, really deny that it is — in *some* sense. My point is that — on the prevailing philosophical conception of the physical — the body is not physical. The conception is, I will argue, that the physical is the exemplar *par excellence* of the mind-independent; so, a less tendentious way to put my claim is that the body is not mind-independent, at least not fully. Of course, the relevant sense of mind-independent needs explanation; indeed, part of my point — a point I urge against the prevailing and complacent naturalism of the day — is that we lack an adequate understanding of the body, the physical, and the mind-independent.

These claims rest on one crucial claim. Suppose, in the dark room example, you have the unimpaired ability to recognize by inner feeling the position of your limbs; as a result of exercising this ability, you believe your arm is extended at a right angle. Given that your ability is unimpaired, your belief *must* be true — roughly speaking, that is. Impairment is just one of three possible ways in which you could end up with a false belief, but, for now, talk of impairment captures the intuitive idea. It follows that the body differs in a crucial way from objects such as foxes, chairs, and mountains. Thus: suppose your ability to recognize foxes is unimpaired, and that, as a result of using this ability, you believe an animal to be a fox. The difference is that your belief could be false — the "animal" might be a hologram, for example. This means that the body — unlike foxes, chairs, and mountains — is not mind-independent. An item is mind-independent just in case its being the way it is does not, in any essential way, depend either on our beliefs about it or on the way in which we form those beliefs.[2] Therefore: F's (things, properties, events, whatever) are mind-independent only if there is *no* necessary connection of the sort just described between the exercise of the ability to recognize F's and the truth of the resulting belief that a given item is (an) F. Such a connection makes being (an) F depend, in an essential way, on beliefs about whether something is (an) F. The body is not mind-independent in this sense. In what follows, I will take the non-existence of the sort of necessary connection just illustrated as a necessary *and sufficient* condition for mind-independence. This is stipulative; it captures one — important — sense of 'mind-independence' to the exclusion of other legitimate senses.

As a last preliminary, a few general remarks about recognitional abilities are in order. The ability to recognize F's is the capacity reliably to form true beliefs as to whether or not a given item is an F. I will, because it is natural and convenient, talk of the exercise of a recognitional ability; however, I do not mean to imply that the activation of the ability is always or even usually under one's voluntary control. An ability, e.g., to recognize foxes by sight may be causally and non-voluntarily activated by a fox's coming into view. Such a non-voluntary activation counts as an exercise.

1. The Prevailing Conception

I claim that, on the prevailing conception, the physical is mind-independent. My first step is to say what the prevailing conception is. It is true but uninformative to say that, according to the conception, physical things are the sorts of things that the predicate expressions of the physical sciences are true of; and physical properties are the sorts of properties denoted by such predicates.[3] Four additional points yield a more informative characterization.

(1) We may take the physical sciences to include just physics and the theories reducible (in some sense of 'reducible') to physics, or we may take them to include more — e.g., chemistry and biology whether or not these reduce to physics. By 'physics' I do not mean just *current* physics but also any future theory that would count as a theory of physics. Merely for ease of exposition, I will focus on physics, and I will take the physical sciences to include just physics and the theories reducible to physics; everything I say remains true on the broader construal of what belongs on the list of sciences.

It is worth noting that the list of sciences could be more liberal. We could add psychology and sociology, for example. Some will exclude them on the ground that they are not physical sciences; others will include them on the ground that, even if they are not physical sciences, they are *natural* sciences. In the latter case, we shift from defining what it is to be a physical thing to defining what it is to be a *natural* thing. I intend everything I say to apply to the "natural" as well as the physical.

(2) The key to seeing that the physical is mind-independent lies in the fact that physics is objective. Israel Scheffler captures the relevant sense of 'objective':

> A fundamental feature of science is its ideal of objectivity, an ideal that subjects all scientific statements to the test of independent and impartial criteria, recognizing no authority of persons in the realm of cognition. The claimant to scientific knowledge is responsible for what he says, acknowledging the relevance of considerations beyond his wish or advocacy to the judgment of his assertions. In assertion . . . he is trying to meet independent standards, to satisfy factual requirements whose fulfillment cannot be guaranteed in advance.[4]

A theory merits the title 'physics' only if it is put forward as (an approximation to) scientific knowledge. As such, the statements of the theory are subject to the test of "independent and impartial criteria, recognizing no authority of persons in the realm of cognition." I do not, of course, suggest that there are precisely formulable "criteria"; the "criteria" may range from explicit methodological injunctions to vague and unformulated problem-solving procedures.

(3) We can give some content to this talk of independent and impartial criteria by first noting that there are degrees of objectivity. Thomas Nagel makes this point:

> At one end is the point of view of a particular individual, having a specific constitution, situation, and relation to the rest of the world. From here the direction of movement toward greater objectivity involves first, abstraction from the individual's specific spatial, temporal, and personal position in the world, then from the features that distinguish him from other humans, then gradually from the forms of perception and action characteristic of humans, then gradually away from the narrow range of a human scale in space, time, and quantity, toward a conception of the world which as far as possible is not the view from anywhere within it.[5]

Physics is — or aims to be — objective in the highest degree; it abstracts "from the forms of perception and action characteristic of humans, then gradually away from the narrow range of a human scale in space, time, and quantity." The relevant independent and impartial criteria are the source of this abstraction; that they effect such an abstraction is part of what makes them independent and impartial. To take a simple example, suppose that I assert that apples are red — i.e., not just red *for humans,* but red *simpliciter.* My sole reason is that apples appear red to humans. The relevant criteria prohibit accepting the statement on this ground since we would be recognizing the authority of certain persons — humans — in the realm of cognition. We would be violating the requirement of impartiality; apples, after all, might normally appear green to the people from Alpha Centauri, and the criteria prohibit us from favoring the human perspective over the Alpha Centaurian.

(4) There is another, similar — and for us far more important — consequence. Suppose '*F*' is a predicate of physics. It follows that physics cannot countenance necessary connections between the exercise of the ability to recognize *F*'s and the truth of the resulting belief that a given item is (an) *F.* To countenance such a connection is to hold that we are *guaranteed* that something is (an) *F* whenever our properly employed and unimpaired *human* recognitional ability leads us to believe that it is. This would be to recognize the authority of persons in the realm of cognition — with a vengeance. We would be saying that the world *has to be* the way it appears to those humans who properly employ the unimpaired recognitional ability. But this is like accepting that apples are red solely on the ground that they appear red to humans. To subject statements to the test of independent and impartial criteria, recognizing no authority of persons in the realm of cognition, is in part to acknowledge that what appears a certain way may not be that way — even when those to whom it so appears properly employ the relevant unimpaired recognitional ability. To abstract "from the forms of perception and action characteristic of humans" is to recognize that our particular, human recognitional abilities are not infallible guides to truth, even when properly employed and unimpaired.

Thus, physics, by virtue of its aspiration to objectivity, is the study of the mind-independent. It follows that the physical is mind-independent; for, to return to our starting point, physical things are the sorts of things that the predicate expressions of the physical sciences are true of and physical properties are the sorts of properties denoted by such predicates. This is the prevailing conception. It is false and misleading; nothing shows this as dramatically as the fact that, on this conception, the body is not physical. Let us see why this is so.

2. Recognitional Abilities

The key to seeing that the body is not mind-independent lies in distinguishing two ways in which one may fail to know: failures due to lack, impairment, or misuse of a recognitional ability; and, failures that arise from other sources.[6] My claim is that, where one's belief results from exercising the ability to recognize by inner feeling the position of one's limbs, failures to know that one's limb is in a certain position can arise only from the first source.[7] To distinguish the two ways in which one may fail to know, let us focus initially on a belief, not about the position of one's limbs, but about an ordinary physical object. Suppose that you see—or, at least, think you see—that the animal in the field is a fox; and so you claim to know, by sight, that it is a fox. Now, it really is a fox, a paradigm fox, in plain view in good light. Even in such conditions, you may fail to know. There are three cases to distinguish.

(1) *Lack of ability.* Ignorant of the color, size, and shape of a fox, you do not have the ability to recognize a fox by sight; so, since it is by sight that you claim to know, you do not know that the animal is a fox. You believe the animal is a fox because you mistakenly believe you have the ability to recognize foxes by sight. For a joke, we told you that the only small, pointy-eared animals around were foxes, when in fact the area is full of small, pointy-eared dogs.

(2) *Impaired ability.* In this case, you have the ability to recognize foxes by sight; however, the ability is impaired. It is important to distinguish two sub-cases.

Distortions: You do not have your glasses on or you have been drugged so that your vision is blurred and so on. In these cases, the item in your visual field, the item you take to be the fox, does not determinately look like a fox; at best, it looks like a blurry fox; at worst, it looks like a blurry indeterminate something. If your ability is sufficiently impaired in this way, you do not know that the animal is a fox.

Illusions: In this sort of case—which, for want of better, I have called "illusions"—the item in your visual field determinately looks like something other than what it in fact is. For example, suppose you are a subject in a double blind experiment in which you may be given a drug that makes foxes look exactly like dogs to you. Such a drug would impair your ability to recognize foxes by sight; for, to have that ability is to be a reliable detector of foxes and, if dogs look exactly like foxes to you, you are not reliable. This point bears emphasis: illusions—in the sense intended here—are impairments of recognitional abilities. This means that, even though a hologram of a fox may quite properly be called an illusion in the colloquial sense of the word, it is not, in the sense intended here, an "illusion," for it is not an impairment of a recognitional ability.

There is, of course, no sharp distinction between illusions and distortions. Is this an illusion or a distortion? I am looking at a fox, but the fox as presented in my visual field looks more like a blurry dog than anything else. It is pointless to look for a non-arbitrary answer here; rather, there is a continuum of cases, and we are merely labeling one end 'distortions' and the other end 'illusions'. Nonetheless, the distinction is important. The reason is that in some cases there is nothing that could count as an illusion; the only possible impairments are distortions. Pain is an example. Provided that the ability to recognize pain is unaffected by distortions, a sensation that seems exactly like pain is pain, or so I have argued elsewhere.[8] In contrast, it can feel exactly as if your arm is at a right angle even when it is not. Imagine that there is a little person—a mini-evil-demon—inside your arm just above the elbow. The demon stimulates your nerves to make it feel *exactly* as if your arm were extended at a right angle when it is in fact hanging by your side. There is nothing "blurry" or indeterminate here; this is an illusion, not a distortion. This contrast between pain and the body will be important later.

A final point about impairments: in discussing impairments, we have focused on cases in which there is an actual item perceived, the fox in the examples. If we remove this restriction, we can think of dreams as impairments of recognitional abilities. In my dream it may seem to me exactly as if I see a fox; this is an impairment of my ability to recognize foxes, for when I am dreaming in this way, I am not a reliable detector of foxes.

(3) *Improperly used ability.* In this case you have the unimpaired ability to recognize foxes by sight, but you do not employ it properly. You merely glance for a second at the animal—not nearly long enough to see what you need to see to determine if it is a fox; nonetheless, because you are being careless, you form the belief that it is a fox. Given the way in which you employed (or tried to employ) your recognitional ability, you do not know that the animal is a fox.

The distinction between impairment and improper use needs clarification. Improper uses arise from various forms of lack of careful attention —carelessness, over-hastiness, distraction, and so on. One can avoid these pitfalls simply by paying careful attention to the matter at hand. Impairments are not avoidable in this way. For example, if a drug makes foxes look exactly like dogs to you, careful attention to the dog-like item in your visual field will not reveal it to be a fox.[9] This difference in avoidability provides a rationale for distinguishing between improper uses and impairments.

(1)–(3) are exhaustive of the ways in which failures to know can be laid at the door of recognitional abilities. If you have the unimpaired and properly employed ability to recognize foxes by sight, how could you fail to know because of something wrong with the recognitional ability? By hypothesis there is nothing wrong.

The fox case also illustrates the distinction—crucial for our purposes

— between failures to know due to lack, impairment, or misuse of a recognitional ability and failures that arise from other sources. As an example of the latter sort of failure, suppose you exercise your unimpaired, properly employed ability to recognize foxes by sight; as a result, you form the belief that a certain item is a fox. In response, I tell you that earlier, as a practical joke, I placed holograms of foxes in various spots; the holograms are indistinguishable by sight from real foxes. I ask you how you know that the apparent fox is not just a hologram. You are at a loss to answer, revealing that you do not know that the object is a fox.[10] Here your recognitional ability is entirely in order. It is unimpaired — you are not drunk, drugged, hypnotized, fatigued, or any such thing — and it is properly employed — you have not been inattentive, careless, or any such thing. The problem is not your ability; it is the holograms.

Some may object that all the example shows is that you lack the ability to recognize foxes: if you really had it, you would be able to tell a fox from a hologram. This objection overlooks the fact that one can have the ability to recognize F's without having the ability to recognize F's in all circumstances. Suppose, as we are about to go out fox hunting, I ask you, "Can you recognize a fox when you see one?" Your "yes" answer means that — in normal circumstances — you are a reliable detector of foxes. Your inability to distinguish the real foxes from the holograms does not show that you lack the ability you attribute to yourself. Lack, after all, is a relative notion, relative to some conception of completeness. The relevant conception of completeness in the example is "reliable detection in normal circumstances." This is the ability that human beings typically have, and (part of) the explanation of your failure to know is that the object of perception has an aspect — its being a hologram — that even a subject of perception in complete possession of the relevant recognitional ability may fail to detect.

Now let us return to the body. We can state the crucial claim more precisely:

> (*) Necessarily if, as a result of the proper exercise of the unimpaired ability to recognize by inner feeling the position of one's limbs, one believes that one's limb is in a certain position; then, one's limb is in that position.

Is (*) true? Before we turn to this question, there are three points to note.

First, (*) does not mention *knowledge;* it merely asserts that the belief must be true. This may seem odd, for in formulating (*) we have relied on a distinction between two ways in which one may fail to *know:* failures due to lack, impairment, or misuse of a recognitional ability and failures that arise from other sources. Shouldn't (*) be formulated in terms of knowledge? But this is not necessary. Ordinarily, when you satisfy the conditions of (*) you do know that your limb is in the relevant position; you qualify as knowing whenever you are sufficiently justified in thinking that your belief results from the properly employed, unimpaired ability, for you are justified in thinking things that, if true, mean your belief cannot be false. So, by focusing on true belief in (*), we have not really abandoned our original focus on knowledge.

The second point also concerns knowledge. Recall the dark room example with which we began. We said you knew by *inner feeling; feeling* where your arm was gave you knowledge. This idea seems not to have made its way into (*), for (*) mentions feeling only obliquely in the context of the ability to recognize by inner feeling. (*) focuses on belief, not feeling — or so it seems. It seems this way because it is natural to think that there are, as it were, two sides to recognition by inner feeling: the feeling of one's limb being in a certain position and the belief that arises in the presence of the feeling, the belief that one's limb is in that position. But to think this way presupposes far too sharp a distinction between feeling and believing. When I feel my arm extended at a right angle to my body, the sensory and the cognitive are mixed together in the state of "feeling my arm." There is a single state of feeling my arm that has both sensory and cognitive content. So (*) does not really focus on belief to the exclusion of feeling. It focuses on the single state of belief-feeling.

The third point concerns the degree of mind-*de*pendence that (*) secures for the body. The issue arises because, as I have argued elsewhere, a necessity like (*) holds for pain — thus: necessarily, if one believes that one is in pain, and that belief results from properly exercising one's unimpaired ability to recognize pain, then one is in pain.[11] Pain therefore lacks mind-independence — like the body. And this would seem to be a problem, for surely the body cannot be mind-dependent in *exactly* the way pain is. After all, pain is a mental event while the body is not. To see the way out of this difficulty, consider the antecedent of the necessity claim in the case of pain: "if one believes that one is in pain, and that belief results from properly exercising one's unimpaired ability to recognize pain . . ." Here 'unimpaired' need only be understood to exclude distortions, not illusions, since the latter are impossible in the case of pain. In the case of the body, we must understand 'unimpaired' to include both. What this shows is that, while the body is mind-dependent, it is not *as* mind-dependent as pain; for, degree of mind-dependence is a function of the number of kinds of ways in which the relevant belief may turn out to be false. Or so I suggest; I will not develop this idea further here.

With these points out of the way, let us turn to the question of whether (*) is true.

3. An Argument for (*)

(*) is true provided that there are only three ways — lack, impairment, or misuse — in which my belief can turn out false. To evaluate this claim, it helps to have a more detailed picture of what it is like for a belief about the position of a limb to be false because of lack, impairment, or misuse of a recognitional ability. So let us consider each case in turn.

(1) Lack of ability. Consider the case of Charles D., who suffered from syphilis. As the disease progressed, Charles gradually lost the ability to recognize by inner feeling the position of his feet. Instead, he suffered from

> a flutter of ever-changing positional illusions — suddenly the floor seemed further, then suddenly nearer, it pitched, it jerked, it tilted — in his own words 'like a ship in heavy seas'. In consequence he found himself lurching and pitching, *unless he looked down at his feet.* Vision was necessary to show him the true position of his feet and the floor — feel had become grossly unstable and misleading — but sometimes even vision was overwhelmed by feel, so that the floor and his feet *looked* frightening and shifting.[12]

Imagine Charles after he has lost the ability to recognize by inner feeling the position of his feet, but suppose also that he does not realize yet that he has lost the ability. When asked where his feet are, it seems to him as if he feels them in a certain position, and he believes, falsely, that they are where he feels them to be.

Charles D. recalls Descartes's obscure, if compelling remark that we are not in our bodies as a pilot is in a ship. Charles *is* in his body like a pilot in a ship. He has to navigate by visual cues, inferring the position of his body from what he sees. We do not have to rely on such an exterior perspective. We have the ability to recognize by *inner* feeling the position of our limbs.

(2) Impaired ability. Charles D. provides an example here as well. Imagine an earlier stage in the disease when he still has the ability to recognize by inner feeling the position of his feet. The "ever-changing positional illusions" impair his ability. Are they, in our terms, distortions or illusions? There need not be any clear answer to this question; some may be more like distortions, some more like illusions. To get a pure illusion case, recall the mini-evil-demon in your elbow who makes it seem exactly as if your arm were extended at a right angle when, in fact, it is hanging by your side.

To switch to a non-clinical, ordinary life example, suppose you have (as you no doubt do) the ability to tell by inner feeling when you are standing straight as opposed to slouching. Someone is about to take your picture. You very much want to stand straight, but you are so anxious about doing so that your anxiety impairs your ability. Your shoulders do not seem level; the left one seems too high; so you lower it, but then the right one seems too high. You raise your left shoulder, and believe that your shoulders are now level. The picture reveals that your left shoulder was too high. (Again, there is no reason to worry about whether this is a case of distortion or illusion.)[13]

(3) Improperly used ability. In this case, the exercise of your ability to tell by inner feeling when you are standing straight as opposed to slouching is unimpaired, but you still do not know. You have reluctantly packed yourself up against others for a group picture. When the photographer says, "Now stand straight everyone," you think, "I am," attending fleetingly to your bodily sensations. The picture shows you slouching terribly. You did not attend long enough to your sensations.[14]

Now, suppose that, under the circumstances specified in (*), I believe that my limb is in a certain position. My claim is that the three possibilities just illustrated exhaust the possible ways in which the belief can be false. We can convincingly describe any case in which your belief is false as a case of lack, impairment, or improper use.

The following general considerations support this claim. Any case in which your belief is false will be one in which you feel as if your limb is in a certain position even though it is not. The feeling must be explained somehow, and any adequate explanation will refer to something that prevents the formation of a true belief. This "something" will have to be the lack, impairment, or misuse of a recognitional ability. What other possibilities are there? Try to imagine one. It would have to feel to you as if your limb is in a certain position when it is not — where this delusive feeling would not be the result of lack, impairment, or misuse of the recognitional ability. Compare a delusive visual appearance — the hologram of a fox. Here the delusive appearance is not the result of the lack, impairment, or misuse of the recognitional ability. But note: nothing has to go wrong with your mind or body to create the delusive appearance; the fox hologram occurs outside your mind and body, as do the events that explain its occurrence. However, we cannot locate the delusive *feeling* outside the mind or body, nor can we explain its occurrence without some reference to a malfunction of the mind or body. But this "malfunction" will always turn out to be the lack, impairment, or misuse of a recognitional ability.

3. A Principled Distinction

Some may be skeptical that (*) is true because (*) relies so heavily on a distinction between failures to know because of lack, impairment, or misuse of recognitional abilities, and failures to know arising from other sources. I have not shown how to draw this distinction in a principled manner, and some may doubt that it is possible to do so. The only way to quiet such qualms is to draw the distinction in a principled manner.

The term of art, 'counter-possibility', will prove convenient: a *counter-possibility* is a possibility which a claimant to knowledge must be able to rule out to qualify as a knower. Here 'rule out' is a convenient shorthand for "know that the possibility does not obtain." Thus, in the fox-hologram example, the possibility that the apparent fox might be a hologram is a counter-possibility; you have to be able to rule out that possibility to count as knowing. To draw the desired distinction in a principled way, we need to distinguish between two kinds of counter-possibilities: if one cannot rule out the first sort, one fails to know because of "other sources"; if one cannot rule out the second sort, one fails to know because of lack, impairment, or improper use of the relevant ability.

The fox-hologram example illustrates the first sort of counter-possibility. Suppose I have the ability to recognize foxes by sight; the ability is unimpaired and properly employed. I may still fail to know because I am unable to rule out a counter-possibility. Suppose that, after I raise the hologram possibility in the fox case, you want to rule out the counter-possibility that what you see is a hologram. You might rule out the counter-possibility by looking at the apparent fox from another perspective; if it is a hologram, it may not seem as foxlike from some perspectives. Or, you could try to touch the apparent fox; if your hand will not go through it, it is not a hologram. But suppose you are unable to change your perspective; you cannot move, and the 'fox' does not move either. All you can do is look at the apparent fox. In this situation, you will never know whether you are looking at a real fox. Or that is almost right. You might, after an hour, infer that the apparent fox is not real on the ground that real foxes do not stand still for so long; or, if it suddenly vanished into thin air, you might, on the ground that real foxes do not simply vanish, reasonably infer that someone turned off the machinery generating the hologram.

However, even where you can know by appeal to such empirical regularities, change of perspective or change of sense modality would still be *relevant* to ruling out the hologram counter-possibility. It would be relevant in this way: the evidence would consist in the fact that change of perspective or sense modality would lead to a certain result. Thus, suppose you try to pass your hand through the apparent fox and encounter impenetrable resistance; your encountering this resistance is evidence that the apparent fox is not a hologram. Note that the change in perspective is a change in perspective *on the object (or apparent object) about which one claims to have knowledge;* similarly, the change in sense modality leads to a new perception *of that same object (or apparent object).* [15] The reason for this is that the hologram counter-possibility is a claim that a mind-independent portion of the world is a certain way. In such a case, change of perspective or sense modality with respect to just this portion can in principle provide evidence as to whether the claim is true. This turns out to be essential — for reasons that will be clear later.

The hologram counter-possibility illustrates a general type of counter-possibility. I will call them *object-oriented.* A counter-possibility is object-oriented if and only if change of perspective or sense modality is relevant to ruling out the counter-possibility, where: the change in perspective is a change in perspective on the object (or apparent object) about which one claims to have knowledge, and the change in sense modality leads to a new perception of that same object (or apparent object). [16]

Lack, impairment, and improper employment of the relevant recognitional ability are not object-oriented counter-possibilities. They are counter-possibilities of a quite different type, which I will call *subject-oriented.* A counter-possibility is subject-oriented if and only if change of perspective or sense modality is *not* relevant to ruling out the counter-possibility. As before, the relevant change in perspective is a change in perspective on the object (or apparent object) about which one claims to have knowledge, and the relevant change in sense modality leads to a new perception of that same object (or apparent object). I will focus initially on the lack of the recognitional ability, arguing that it is a subject-oriented counter-possibility.

I begin with an example. Suppose you are studying a guidebook to the identification of wild life, but your mastery is incomplete. Last week, on several occasions, you misidentified dogs as foxes, so, when you claim to know by sight that the animal is a fox, I challenge your claim by raising the counter-possibility that, despite further study of the guidebook, you may still lack the ability to recognize foxes by sight. You point out that you remember making several identifications yesterday verified as correct by competent third parties. This shows that you have the ability, given I have no reason to doubt your memory. But note that the appeal to memory rules out the counter-possibility with*out* change of perspective or sense modality. The question is: could change of perspective or sense modality be relevant to ruling out the counter-possibility?

It is difficult to see how. Change of perspective or sense modality with respect to a particular object may reveal something about the features of that particular object, but why should they reveal something about *your mind,* about your ability to recognize a kind of object? Examples confirm that they cannot. Thus: looking at the fox from the side instead of the front will not show you have, through study of the guide book, acquired the ability to recognize foxes by sight. Nor will touching the fox; you would learn how the animal felt but not whether you could recognize it by sight.

Here it is essential that the relevant change in perspective is a change in perspective on the object (or apparent object) about which one claims to have knowledge, and that the relevant change in sense modality is one that leads to a new perception of that same object (or apparent object). To see why, suppose you can recognize a fox by the feel of its coat; we line up a hundred randomly arranged dogs and foxes. You walk down the line twice; the first time you visually identify the foxes; the second time you feel each animal thereby corroborating your visual identifications. These correlations between sight and touch are evidence that you have the ability to recognize a fox by sight. But this does not show that lack of a recognitional ability is really an object-oriented counter-possibility, for this example involves investigating a *series* of objects, not just the object perceived. The evidence consists in the result of the *series*. This is just one of many examples that show the need to restrict the change of perspective or sense modality to a single object. Here is another: A blood test would reveal whether you have the ability; you simply need to see if a piece of test paper turns pink or blue. Performing the test yields the desired evidence via changes in perspective and sense modality. So this is a case in which changes in perspective and sense modality provide relevant evidence. But, again, the change in perspective is *not* a change in perspective on the apparent fox, and the change in sense modality does not lead to a new perception of the apparent fox.

But, even where we restrict the change of perspective or sense modality to a single object, can't we come up with examples in which the change produces relevant evidence? Consider this fanciful example: Suppose that, if you have the ability to recognize foxes by sight, then, whenever you walk around a fox twice clockwise, it glows a strange, eerie green. The change of perspective thus produces relevant evidence. But it is no accident that this example is fanciful. In the real world, no such magical correlations exist between objects and recognitional abilities. Objects do not change to signal the possession or lack of a recognitional ability. If they did, our conception of the relation between mind and world would be profoundly different. Our conception — the one I am explicating — is premised on the non-existence of such correlations.

I conclude that lack of a recognitional ability is a subject-oriented, not an object-oriented, counter-possibility. Similar remarks hold for impairment and improper employment. I will be extremely brief.

Impairment: Suppose you are a subject in a double blind experiment;

some subjects are given a drug that greatly blurs their vision; others are given a placebo. I have reason to think you were given the vision-blurring drug, so, when you claim that you know by sight that a certain animal is a fox, I challenge your claim on the ground that your vision is too blurred to make the identification. Change of perspective or change of sense modality will not help rule out this challenge: touching the fox or looking at it from a different angle will not show that your vision is not blurred.

Another example: Suppose that you may have taken the drug that makes dogs look just like foxes to you. However, you have the ability to recognize foxes by feel. So, when the animal in front of you looks like a fox, you feel it and find that it feels like a fox. So you know it is a fox. Isn't this a case in which change in sense modality rules out the possibility that you took the drug? No, the fact that the animal both looks and feels like a fox does not show that you have not taken a drug that makes dogs look like foxes to you. All it shows is that the animal in front of you is a fox. But, to change the example, what if the animal looks like a *fox* but feels like a *dog?* Wouldn't this show that you took the drug? Yes, but this does not *rule out* the counter-possibility. It does not show that your ability is unimpaired – quite the opposite. So this example does not show that you can rule out impairment counter-possibilities by a change in perspective or sense modality.

Improper employment: You merely glance for a second at the animal and announce that it is a fox. I think you did not look long enough to tell if the animal is a fox, and I raise this possibility. Again, change of perspective or change of sense modality is simply irrelevant to ruling out this possibility. Touching the fox, for example, will not show that you paid sufficient attention to the item in your visual field.

I suggest that lack, impairment, and improper use of a recognitional ability are the only subject-oriented counter-possibilities. I will not argue for this claim as it is sufficient that these counter-possibilities be included in the class of subject-oriented counter-possibilities; there is no need to claim that they exhaust it. But assuming they do makes it easy to state in a principled way the distinction between failures to know because of lack, impairment, or misuse of recognitional abilities and failures to know arising from other sources. Thus: One fails to know because of lack, impairment, or improper employment if and only if one fails to know because one cannot rule out a subject-oriented counter-possibility.[17] One fails to know because of "other sources" if and only if one fails to know because one cannot rule out an object-oriented counter-possibility. These definitions are not arbitrary; they reflect a fundamental difference in the kinds of challenges we make to knowledge claims. So the fact that (*) rests on these definitions is not a reason for skepticism.

I contend then that (*) is true and that it follows that the body is not fully mind-independent. In a way, this result should not be surprising. It is through the body that the mind affects the mind-independent world, ·so perhaps it should not be surprising that the medium that joins mind and world is not itself fully mind-independent. The dualist flavor of this observation may not, of course, be to everyone's taste.[18]

There is a last objection to consider. Some will think that I have completely failed to make my case. They will grant that — in a sense — (*) expresses a necessary truth; the objection is that no anti-physicalist conclusions follow. To see the idea consider that we act and think within a conceptual scheme — our network of commonsense psychological concepts and explanations; (*) is a part of this conceptual scheme, and to accept the conceptual scheme is in part to recognize (*) as a necessary truth. The objection grants this much. The crucial claim is that we do not have to commit ourselves to the *truth* of the conceptual scheme. We can regard our use of it as a kind of *façon de parler*. We just, so to speak, pretend that (*) expresses a necessary truth — just as we sometimes pretend that Newtonian mechanics is true when we use it to predict the motions of bodies at speeds significantly below the speed of light. The true theories, according to this objection, are the physical sciences; at least, these are the only theories to be taken seriously as attempts to delineate reality. On this view, commonsense psychology is only a very crude approximation to some future neurophysiological and/or psychophysiological theory of human beings. These are, by the way, sciences of the *very distant* future; neurophysiology and psychophysiology are in their infancy. But be that as it may, the usual reason given for this view is the success of physics over the last three centuries; physics has explained an increasingly broad range of phenomena, and this is offered as a reason to think it will explain all phenomena.

It is a comment on the hold that naturalism has on contemporary philosophy that this is a position to be taken seriously. Consider what you are saying if you hold this position: "I think and act in terms of commonsense psychology; however, I do not think that theory is true; I think that there is some other theory — to be formulated in the distant future — that is true and to which commonsense psychology is a crude approximation (in somewhat the way phlogiston theory was a crude approximation to thermodynamics)." How can this make sense? Consider the assertion, "I do not think that commonsense psychology is true." How can it make sense to assert, from within the theory that gives the concept of thinking its sense, that one *thinks* the theory is false? What are we to make of a person who thinks and acts within — i.e., believes — and who nonetheless espouses the *belief* he does not believe the theory? This sounds more like self-deception than anything else. We must forever resist the devil of scientism, who would have us think that we do not think.

Notes

1. There are alternative terms: 'kinesthetic sense', 'proprioception', and 'inner sense', for example. The advantage of 'inner feeling' is that it lacks the theoretical associations the alternatives may carry.

2. See, e.g., Israel Scheffler, *Science and Subjectivity* (Indianapolis: Bobbs-Merrill, 1967).

3. I take this to be the prevailing conception, not the universal one. Some, for example, will define the physical as that which exists in space. The difficulty here is to see why spatial existence makes a thing physical. That would seem to depend on what one's views about the nature of space were.

4. Scheffler, *Science and Subjectivity,* 1.

5. Thomas Nagel, "Subjective and Objective," in Thomas Nagel, *Mortal Questions* (Cambridge: Cambridge University Press, 1979), 118.

6. Austin draws a similar, if not entirely explicit, distinction in "Other Minds," in J. L. Austin, *Philosophical Papers,* ed. J. O. Urmson and G. J. Warnock (Oxford: Oxford University Press, 1979), 79–80.

7. Strictly speaking, where one fails to know because one *lacks* the relevant recognitional ability, the belief cannot result from the exercise of that ability. In such cases, one mistakenly thinks one has the ability.

8. Richard Warner, "Incorrigibility," in *Objections to Physicalism,* ed. Howard Robinson (Oxford: Oxford University Press, forthcoming).

9. An example involving a distortion as opposed to an illusion: Suppose you decide — mistakenly — after careful attention that the blurred item in your visual field is a fox. The problem is not lack of attention, it is distortion.

10. You fail to know because I have given you good reason to think that what you see might be a hologram; having been given such a reason, to know that what you see is a fox, you have to know that it is not a hologram. The reason you fail to know is not that to know that *p* (that the animal is a fox) one must know whatever is entailed by *p* (that it is not a hologram). Indeed, it is probably not true that to know that *p* one must know everything entailed by *p;* see, e.g., Robert Nozick, *Philosophical Explanations* (Cambridge, Mass.: Harvard University Press, 1981), chap. 3. However, to know that *p* one must know that not-*q,* in those cases in which *q* and *p* cannot both be true, and one has (at least in light of certain considerations) good reason to think *q* might be true. See Austin, "Other Minds."

11. In "Incorrigibility" I require that the recognitional ability be the ability *non-inferentially* to recognize pain. I would now rephrase this requirement in favor of talk of the ability to recognize pain by inner feeling — pointing out that this ability is non-inferential.

12. Oliver Sacks, *The Man Who Mistook his Wife for a Hat* (New York: Harper & Row, 1970), 68.

13. Public speaking is a fertile source of examples — e.g., you think you are not drumming on the side of the podium with your fingers, but as the video tape will show, you are. Anxiety impairing your recognitional ability explains the false belief.

14. A good source of examples here is learning dances or sports. In the learning process, you have to pay attention to so many positions and changes of position that, invariably, through inattention, you form false beliefs. You think you have it right, but the mirror or the video will reveal that you are wrong.

15. This talk of a new perception of an apparent object is not literally coherent, but of course it is obvious what I mean: a new perception of that part of the external world where the object appears to be. *Mutatis mutandis,* the same point holds for changes of perspective on apparent objects.

16. One may wonder about theoretical entities. Suppose I claim that some theoretical entity has a certain property. You point out that my instruments do not allow me to distinguish between that property and another quite similar one. I rule out this counter-possibility by "observing" the entity with additional instruments. This additional observation involves a change of perspective, but isn't it a change of perspective with respect to the *instruments,* not the entity? If so, the counter-possibility is not object-oriented. And this would be wrong, for it is exactly analogous to the fox-hologram counter-possibility. However, there is really not a problem here, for, while the later observation does involve a change of perspective on the instruments, it *also* involves a change of perspective on the theoretical entity.

17. What about false logical and mathematical beliefs? Do they not all come out false because of lack, impairment, or misuse of an ability? Change of perspective or type of sense experience is irrelevant to forming true logical and mathematical beliefs. I have argued that the result is correct for first-order logic in "Why Is Logic A Priori?" *Monist* 72, no. 1 (January 1989): 40–50. Restricting the definition to beliefs about contingent matters will avoid the result.

18. Janet Levin read and discussed early versions of the essay, and I am indebted to her for suggestions and encouragement — despite her skepticism.

Analysis and the Attitudes

Ian Pratt

If I believe, as I do, that the Loch Ness monster does not exist, then my having that belief is one thing; the nonexistence of the monster (or otherwise) is, of course, another. If I fear, as I do, that war will break out in Europe during the next decade, then my having that fear is one thing; the occurrence of such a cataclysm (or otherwise) is another. So it is with all of the so-called *propositional attitudes.* Whenever I *believe* or *doubt* or *fear* or *desire,* we have two things: on the one hand, my believing or doubting or fearing or desiring; on the other, that state of affairs which, in having these thoughts, I thereby represent to myself. Question: what, in general, can we say about the relationship between the two?

The problem, known to contemporary philosophy as the problem of intentionality, is to provide an account of the relationship which holds between a state of affairs *P,* and the state of affairs in which a person entertains a given attitude (typically, belief) towards *P.* It is widely accepted, among naturalistically minded philosophers, that a solution can be given which is at once general, succinct, and non-trivial. By *general,* I mean an account that works for all possible states of affairs that one may believe: what we seek is a schema that will produce, for any given state of affairs *P,* a specification of what it means to believe *P.* By *succinct,* I mean an account which generates these specifications in a principled way: it would hardly constitute an explanation of the propositional attitudes to compile a titanic, perhaps infinite, listing containing a separate entry for each possible content *P.* By *non-trivial,* I mean an account couched in terms devoid of intentional (or semantic) idiom: if there are any facts about representation, those facts must surely be identifiable within a physicalistic scheme which does not number irreducible psychological (or linguistic) properties among its basic categories. For ease of reference, I shall speak of an account satisfying these criteria — *generality, succinctness* and *non-triviality* — as an *analysis* of the attitudes. Thus, received wisdom among naturalistically minded philosophers is that an analysis of the attitudes can in principle be given. The aim of this essay is to unearth the reasons underlying this received wisdom and to show that these reasons are bad ones. The conclusion I then draw is that, since there is no reason to believe the propositional attitudes to be analyzable, it would be a miracle if they were. Therefore they are not.

1. Analyzing the Attitudes

It is an oft-made point that a normal English speaker's command of the attitude-verbs is thoroughgoingly systematic, in that each of the galaxy of English sentences he can understand can properly form the complement of an attitude-report. Consider the attitude-verb "believes." For just about any declarative sentence P you care to mention, anyone who understands P also understands [S believes that P].[1] Moreover, this command of the attitude-verbs survives the learning of new vocabulary. If someone coins the term "bandersnatch" to denote a newly discovered animal species, then no sooner do we understand the sentence "Bandersnatches are highly intelligent," than we also understand "Karl believes that bandersnatches are highly intelligent." Knowledge of which state of affairs is described by the former brings with it knowledge of which state of affairs is described by the latter. And as for "believes," so for the other attitude-verbs: "doubts," "fears," "desires," etc.

I speak thus of our systematic command of attitude-*verbs* in English (and possible extensions thereof); but this phenomenon is really just the linguistic façade of an underlying conceptual systematicity. For the fact is that anyone who can *think* that P can also think that S believes P, that S doubts P, that S fears P, and so on, for just about any proposition P.[2] And, just as our command of attitude-verbs survives the learning of new vocabulary, so our grasp of the attitude-concepts survives the enlargement of our conceptual repertoire. In coming to know what bandersnatches are (whether or not we know the English word for them), no sooner can we entertain the thought that bandersnatches are highly intelligent than we can also entertain the thought that Karl believes that bandersnatches are highly intelligent. That is, there are no gaps in our ability to think about the attitudes of people (either ourselves or others) concerning any of the indefinitely many states of affairs which we can think about ourselves. It is these systematic linguistic and conceptual abilities, I shall claim, that lie at the root of the belief in the analyzability of the attitudes.

So much, then, for our systematic grasp of the attitudes. But what sort of thing is a belief or desire? What, in general, does philosophy have to say about the nature of these psychological states? Currently, the most widely accepted answer to this question is *functionalism,* the thesis that psychological states are defined by their functional roles. Take, for example, the state of *believing that it is raining.* According to functionalism, to believe that it is raining is to be in a state which is endowed with a certain ensemble of causal powers: it must tend to be produced by rain in good perceptual conditions, it must tend to interact with the desire not to be wet and with knowledge about umbrellas and hats so as to produce appropriate behavior, and much else besides. Notice that a functionalist definition of *believing that it is raining*—if one were ever completed—would make reference not only to environmental causes such as the presence of rain, and to behavioral effects such as the donning of a hat, but also to other psychological states—sundry beliefs, desires, and intentions—states which themselves have functionalist definitions in terms of other psychological states, including, perhaps, the state of believing that it is raining. But such circularity is not vicious; it merely requires that psychological states be defined in whole battalions rather than as single spies. As Lewis puts it:

> Think of common-sense psychology as a term-introducing scientific theory, though one invented long before there was any such institution as professional science. Collect all the platitudes you can think of regarding the causal relations of mental states, sensory stimuli, and motor responses. Perhaps we can think of them as having the form:
>
> > When someone is in so-and-so combination of mental states and receives sensory stimuli of so-and-so kind, he tends with so-and-so probability to be caused thereby to go into so-and-so mental states and to produce so-and-so motor responses.
>
> Add also all the platitudes to the effect that one mental state falls under another—'toothache is a kind of pain', and the like. Perhaps there are platitudes of other forms as well. Include only platitudes which are common knowledge among us—everyone knows them, everyone knows that everyone else knows them, and so on. For the meanings of our words are common knowledge, and I am going to claim that the names of mental states derive their meaning from these platitudes.[3]

Commonsense psychological knowledge—*folk psychology,* Lewis elsewhere calls it—can thus be seen as a theory which specifies the functional role of every belief, desire, intention, etc., it is possible to have. Lewis's suggestion is then that, since it is the platitudes of folk psychology that govern the use of psychological idiom, we should think of phrases such as "belief that it is raining," "desire to stay dry," "puzzlement as to where one's umbrella is," as theoretical terms—terms, that is, whose referents are defined to be the occupants of the functional roles assigned to them by folk psychology.

It is important to see how functionalism, as characterized above, meshes with the above observations on our systematic grasp of the attitudes. If, as functionalism holds, the defining characteristic of any psychological state is its causal signature, then our ability to grasp what it is for an agent to have any of an indefinite number of beliefs — an ability which, remember, survives the enlargement of our conceptual repertoire — amounts to implicit knowledge of a function mapping any state of affairs P onto the causal signature definitive of the belief that P. Such knowledge cannot, bearing in mind the computational limitations of our brains, be encoded as a separate set of clauses for each possible content P; there are just too many, perhaps infinitely many, possible contents. So there must, it would appear, exist some relatively succinct theory able to generate these mappings, for then our systematic grasp of the attitudes could be explained as knowledge of such a theory. That is, our systematic grasp of the attitudes, together with the limited computational resources of our brains, imposes an upper bound on the complexity of the most succinct specification of the relationship between a state of affairs and the functional role definitive of some attitude towards that state of affairs.

The natural — and quite reasonable — response of the functionalist to this observation is to go schematic. Rather than have one set of platitudes concerning the belief that it is raining, another set concerning the belief that Caesar crossed the Rubicon, yet another concerning the desire to be rich and famous and so forth, the platitudes of folk psychology are assumed to *quantify* over belief-contents. Indeed, these platitudes might be highly general affairs such as: "People tend, by and large, not to be massively mistaken in their beliefs"[4] or "People tend, by and large, to act in ways which would secure their desires if the world were such that their beliefs were true."[5] As before, ascriptions of psychological states are supposed to be constrained to conform to — or to conform as nearly as possible to — a collection of folk-psychological platitudes, and this collection of platitudes is then taken as giving meaning to such ascriptions. But quantifying over attitude-contents as suggested holds out the prospect of a relatively succinct set of such defining platitudes. Here, the theoretical terms defined by folk psychology are the small band of attitude-verbs themselves — "believes," "desires," etc. — rather than the numberless hordes of complete psychological states — "believes that it is raining," "desires to stay dry," etc. Such a relatively succinct theory would have the desirable property of rendering our systematic grasp of the attitudes explicable: understanding the attitudes is simply a matter of knowing the quantified platitudes that define them. No problems about the effectively infinite supply of content sentences or about our ability to combine psychological notions with newly acquired concepts.[6] And, of course, to say that such a theory exists just *is* to say that the attitudes are analyzable.

The quest for a general, succinct, and non-trivial account of the attitudes is by no means confined to functionalist analyses in the style of Lewis. Consider, for example, the approach of Hartry Field. Field proposes to factor the relation of believing — whereby a person is related to a proposition — into two relations: first, a relation called *believing**, which relates a person to sentences in that person's language of thought; and second, a relation of *meaning,* which relates sentences in that language to propositions. Thus, according to Field, for S to believe that P is for S to believe* some sentence σ such that σ means that P. In factoring the notion of *believing* into the notions of *believing** and *meaning,* Field trades the problem of how a person can entertain a thought with proposition P *as content* for the (he thinks) easier problem of how a sentence can *mean* that P. The latter problem is easier because, according to Field, to say what proposition a sentence means is simply to say in what possible worlds that sentence is true.[7] And an account of whether a given sentence is true in a given possible world can be provided by a compositional truth-theory in the style of Tarski. For simple languages, such as those based on first-order predicate logic, such a truth theory would have axioms falling into three classes. First, a large set of axioms specifying the referents of all the proper names in the language: "'Hesperus' denotes Hesperus," "'Bismarck' denotes Bismarck," and so on. Second, a large set of axioms specifying the intentions of all the predicates in the language: "'is a planet' denotes the property of being a planet," "'is a politician' denotes the property of being a politician," etc.[8] Third, a handful of axioms specifying the meaning of the combinator functions and syntax: "[Fa] is true at world w if a denotes an individual ξ and F denotes an intension Ψ such that ξ is in the extension of Ψ at w," "[$P\&Q$] is true at w if P is true at w and Q is true at w," etc. Of course, languages capable of expressing the full range of human thought might have truth theories considerably more complicated than that just sketched; however, Field believes this fact poses no difficulties in principle for his strategy.

But Field is adamant that to leave matters here would not constitute a satisfactory analysis of the attitudes. For the above account helps itself to the semantic notion of *denotation;* and the litany of axioms specifying the denotation of each of the names and predicates in the language in question ("'Bismarck' denotes Bismarck," "'is a planet' denotes the property of being a planet," etc.) hardly constitutes an analysis of that notion. What is needed, Field urges, is a general, succinct, and non-trivial account of what denotation *is,* of *why* a symbol having such-and-such physical characteristics, embedded in such-and-such a physical environment has this or that individual as its referent, or this or that property as its intension.

The kind of account Field has in mind is a causal theory of denotation:

> the fact that 'Cicero' denotes Cicero and that 'muon' denotes muon are to be explained in terms of certain kinds of causal networks between Cicero (muons) and our uses of 'Cicero' ('muon'): causal connections both of a social sort (the passing of the original word 'Cicero' down to us from original users of the name, or the passing of the word 'muon' to laymen from physicists) and of other sorts (the evidential and causal connections that gave the original users of the name "access" to 'Cicero' and gave physicists "access" to muons).[9]

There must be something, Field would maintain — and something like a network of causal connections to boot — which unifies the notion of denotation, which binds together the infinitely many pairings of mental symbol with what that symbol is about. And unless we provide an account, however sketchy it may be, of that general causal nexus between symbols and their denotations, unless we can do better than a mere enumeration, we have not given a satisfactory explanation of the phenomenon of intentionality.[10]

The underlying idea is a familiar one which has appeared in various incarnations in the recent philosophy of mind. In its simplest form, the idea is that what makes a type of data-structure in my head the concept of — say — a *horse* is, to a zeroth approximation, the fact that tokens of that type tend to be caused, in good perceptual conditions, by horses, by all horses, and only by horses.[11] Of course, matters must be more complicated than that. For one thing, fake horses can cause beliefs about horses, and camouflaged or concealed horses can fail to do so. For another, while the concept of *horse* is at least often activated by real horses (rather than by books or newspapers), the corresponding connection between concept and object is standardly less direct in cases like *muon* or *Cicero* — hence Field's deliberately vague talk of *causal networks*. Nevertheless, defenders of causal theories all take as axiomatic the conviction that it constitutes no sort of explanation of intentionality to give an account of the causal relations holding between "horse" and horses, "muon" and muons, etc., one by one, for all the various concepts we can have. There must be something, the causal theorists maintain, that is common to the cases of all these symbol-denotation pairs. To solve the problem of intentionality is to say something about what this common factor is.

What I have labored most to draw attention to in this section is the pervasive demand for an analysis of the attitudes — an account, that is, of what it means to adopt an attitude towards a given state of affairs *P,* which is *general* in that it will work for all possible contents *P, succinct* in that it at least avoids degenerating into an analysis-by-enumeration, and *non-trivial* in that it does not appeal to psychological or semantic notions. I have tried to elicit the natural feeling that only such an account would be intellectually satisfying, and — harder to shrug one's shoulders at — the conviction that only on the supposition that such an account exists would our systematic command of the attitudes be explicable. If these ideas seem too obvious to bear mention, all well and good: I intend to spend the remainder of this essay arguing against them. If, on the other hand, they seem shaky and ill-justified, then I hope at least to have provided evidence of their widespread acceptance.[12]

2. A Theory of Psychological Inference

In this section, I sketch a theory of psychological inference. By "psychological inference," I understand inference essentially to involve descriptions of persons as doubting, perceiving, affirming, willing, not willing various things — to involve, that is, the attitude-concepts. The object of the exercise is to sketch a possible explanation of our systematic grasp of the attitude-concepts without implying or presupposing their analyzability. In so doing, I am not particularly concerned with the plausibility of my 'theory' as a piece of human psychology; for present purposes, I am merely interested in the logical possibilities it opens up. These possibilities will be explored in the next section.

The theory I shall put forward takes as its point of departure an observation made by Hobbes.

> But there is another saying not of late understood, by which they might learn truly to read one another, if they would take the pains; and that is, *Nosce teipsum, Read thy self* . . . [which is meant] to teach us, that for the similitude of the thoughts, and Passions of one man, to the thoughts, and Passions of another, whosoever looketh into himself, and considereth what he doth, when he does *think, opine, reason, hope, feare &c,* and upon what grounds; he shall thereby read and know, what are the thoughts, and Passions of all other men, upon the like occasions.[13]

Recommending one's own psychological states as an important source of information about the psychological states of others only makes sense on the assumption that knowledge of the former is less problematical than knowledge of the latter. So Hobbes was taking for granted a faculty — call it *introspection* — whereby we can monitor and know our own psychological states. Though we be not always aware of what we think, though we sometimes deceive ourselves, though our lives obey subliminal urges of which we have not an inkling, we nevertheless enjoy fairly extensive awareness of much of what goes on within our minds. Thus, we frequently know whether we believe something, and we frequently remember what we used at one time to believe, even if we have since changed our minds. And as for beliefs, so for other psychological states as well. But I do not propose to catalog our introspective abilities and proclivities here. I merely point out that, often at least, if it is possible for us to believe that P, it is also possible for us to be in another psychological state — the belief that we believe P — which can arise through the operation of our faculty of introspection upon the former. Similarly with beliefs about our types of psychological states. The introspectibility of psychological states has tended to be downplayed in the modern philosophy of mind, being portrayed as a contingent fact insofar as it is a fact at all. I propose, by contrast, to promote it to a key role.

Introspecting one's attitudes can yield information about their causes. If I can monitor when I came to the belief that there was a cat sitting on the mat in front of me, and if I can thereby observe that I have in the past come to that belief when positioned in conditions of good visibility in front of an unoccluded cat, then I can judge, from this observation and from other of my beliefs, that the latter tends to bring about the former. (Objection: mere observation of conjunctions does not establish causality! Reply: knowledge of the causation of beliefs is, in this regard, no different from our knowledge of the causation of anything else.) Notice that, by remembering what I believed at an earlier time, I can with hindsight come to know under what conditions I falsely believed the cat was on the mat, or under what conditions I failed to believe the cat was on the mat even though it was. Notice also that I may draw conclusions not only about the many possible environmental causes of my beliefs (and other attitudes), but about their psychological causes. I might, for example, observe the patterns of inference that I often follow in reasoning.

There seems to be no limit, in principle, to the sophistication and detail of the knowledge concerning the aetiology of my attitudes that I can garner in this way. And, of course, as Hobbes recommends, these observations of my own psychological states can be generalized to the case of other persons. I can trade on the presumed similarity of other persons' minds to my own by assuming that what caused the belief in me that there is a cat on the mat will cause the same belief in them. So if I know of some person that he is staring at a cat, and I know that that is the sort of thing that causes me to think there is a cat before my eyes, it is a good bet that person is thinking the same thing.

Similar remarks apply to the *effects* of psychological states. I observe that an unqualified intention to move a part of my body in a normal way, to pick up small, liftable objects, to cross the street, to utter sentences of my mother tongue, and so on, will standardly be followed by my doing those things. I observe that clashes of desires often precede hesitation. I observe that desires for immediate gratification can often win out over more considered and rational plans to secure my long-term flourishing, and so on. Insofar as I can observe these constant conjunctions, I can form conclusions about the causal powers of my various attitudes, conclusions which can again be generalized from my own case to that of other persons.

The foregoing account — according to which one can reason about the psychological states of others by introspecting one's own psychological states — may, however, be thought implausible. After all, effective reasoning about other people's psychological states would require a large number of these introspective generalizations. And it is arguably unlikely that we make such assiduous use of our introspective faculties that we could form all the requisite generalizations, to say nothing of the problems of storing and accessing the resulting mountain of data. Absent any more detailed proposals as to how such introspectionist methods would actually work, this objection is hard to evaluate. Fortunately, however, there is a far more plausible suggestion as to how we reason about the many and complex interactions between psychological states. And it is to this suggestion that I now turn. [14]

In 1943, Kenneth Craik published a small but influential volume, *The Nature of Explanation,* in which he argued that thought should sometimes be understood as a kind of *simulation*. In order to predict the behavior of physical systems, Craik conjectured, people construct inside their heads mental models of those systems — representations which are, in the relevant ways, functionally isomorphic to the things they represent. [15] Now, as various authors have noted, one obvious domain for reasoning by simulation is that of psychological inference. We have, in the shape of our own brains, ready-made analogues of the brains of others. If only we could take another person and somehow temporarily set ourselves up as believing what he believes, as desiring what he desires and so on, and if only we could observe the progress of these thoughts as they develop in our own minds, we would have a good idea as to how that person's thought is likely to develop. [16]

How might such psychological simulation work? Let us introduce two characters, *Basil* and *Florence*. Basil is trying to reason about what Florence is thinking and is using psychological simulation to do this. And let us indulge in a little fictional physiology for the purpose of definiteness: we shall imagine that psychological simulations of Florence occur in one part of Basil's brain—call it the "Florence-simulacrum"—and ordinary, non-psychological thought in another. Suppose, then, Basil thinks Florence believes $P, Q, R, \ldots$, and desires $X, Y, Z, \ldots$. In simulating Florence's mind, Basil builds, in his Florence-simulacrum, copies of brain-states which, if they occurred in the part of his brain given over to normal thought, would count as his own beliefs $P, Q, R, \ldots$ and as his own desires $X, Y, Z, \ldots$. Basil also copies into the Florence-simulacrum certain background beliefs and desires that he takes everyone to share. We might call the ersatz beliefs and desires in Basil's Florence-simulacrum *virtual* beliefs and desires. There may be a certain amount of consistency-checking and maintenance required in order to square Basil's explicit beliefs about Florence's psychological states with his presumption of background knowledge and abilities, but we need not concern ourselves with the details of how this might be achieved. Having cloned a suitable collection of virtual beliefs and desires in the Florence-simulacrum, Basil can just let matters take their course. Being *copies* of the sorts of psychological states that Basil might be in, they interact exactly as those psychological states would interact in normal thought, producing further psychological states—perhaps the (virtual) decision to perform some action—which Basil, viewing the progress of the psychological simulation, can observe by introspection.

We can assemble the foregoing ideas into a story about how it is that one such as Basil (or such as we) uses his faculty of introspection to determine what it is that another person—Florence, for example—is thinking. Basil's first source of knowledge concerns the *causes* of Florence's psychological states; those conditions—including environmental conditions—which he has found by introspection to cause in him a collection of psychological states ψ, he may likewise suppose to cause ψ in Florence. Basil's second source of knowledge concerns the effects of Florence's psychological states; those effects—including behavioral effects—which Basil knows to be caused by a collection of psychological states ψ in himself, he may likewise suppose are so caused in Florence. Basil's third source of knowledge concerns causal interactions *between* psychological states; when imagining himself in what he takes to be Florence's cognitive predicament, Basil can, in observing the evolution of that imagined state of mind, suppose Florence's real thoughts to evolve along similar lines.

Of course, the supposition that psychological simulation proceeds by producing literal *copies* of the simulator's psychological states in a specially designated part of the brain is only by way of an implementation story. The point I wish to draw attention to here is not the *physical* relationship between, for example, the belief that P and the virtual belief that P, or between the desire that X and the virtual desire that X, but their *functional* relationship. What makes Basil's simulation of Florence a simulation in which Florence is represented as believing $P, Q, R \ldots$, and desiring $X, Y, Z, \ldots$ is that, in that simulation, there are states which interact in just the way Basil's *own* beliefs $P, Q, R, \ldots$ and desires $X, Y, Z, \ldots$ would interact if they occurred in normal thought. Now literal copying is one way, but not the only way and doubtless not the most efficient way, to achieve the requisite identity of function between virtual psychological states and their real counterparts. But it is the identity of function that is important here, not the means by which it is achieved. To reason about Florence's belief P, Basil must employ a brain state which functions in his simulation of Florence just as Basil's own belief P would function in ordinary thought. To reason about Florence's desire X, Basil must employ a brain state which functions in his simulation of Florence just as Basil's own desire X would function in ordinary thought. As for beliefs and desires, so for other psychological states: hopes and fears, moods and passions and feelings, and so on: the important thing about simulating them in order to reason about others is similarity of function to their originals in the mind of the simulator.

Now we are in position to describe the characteristic functional relationship between a belief of the form: "S believes P" and the corresponding belief P. Let the functional role of the belief P be given; then, as a first approximation, the belief that S believes P functions so as to dispose one to include, in any simulation of the mind of S, a state which, in that simulation, has the functional role that the belief P has in ordinary thought. Similarly with desires: let the functional role of the desire X be given; then, as a first approximation, the belief that S desires X functions so as to dispose one to include, in any simulation of the mind of S, a state which, in that simulation, has the functional role that the desire X has in ordinary thought. And so on, *mutatis mutandis* for other attitudes.

This formulation is nearly correct, but not quite, because the functional similarity between Basil's real belief P and his ersatz belief P used in simulating Florence does not extend to their environmental causes and behavioral effects. Let P be the belief "There is a cat sitting in front of me." For a brain-state of Basil's to qualify as a belief with this content, that brain-state must tend to be caused, under suitable conditions, by the proximity of a suitably positioned cat. That is as important an aspect of the functional role of that belief as are the interactions with other of Basil's psychological states into which it may enter. By contrast however, Basil's representation of Florence as believing that there is a cat on the mat should not be caused by the appearance of a cat to Basil. Rather, Basil's disposition to include the ersatz belief P in the simulation of Florence should be prompted by (among other things) knowledge of *Florence's* proximity to cats in conditions of good visibility. So we have a difference between the functional role of the real belief P and the ersatz belief P used in the simulation of Florence: where the former is caused by perception, the latter is caused by knowledge of Florence's situation.

Corresponding remarks apply to the causation of behavior by means of psychological states. Suppose Basil believes that the cat is on the mat, and desires to punish the cat for some violation of domestic hygiene; such attitudes might cause Basil's foot to swing aggressively catward. Again, this kind of effect constitutes an important aspect of the functional role of the psychological states involved. By contrast, Basil's representation of Florence as believing or desiring these things should not make Basil swing his foot. Psychological simulation of others does not have the immediate and direct effects of ordinary thought. Conclusion: we must amend the above view, according to which the belief that S believes P disposes one to include in any simulation of S a state whose functional role within that simulation is identical to the functional role of one's belief P in ordinary thought. The identity of function in question must be restricted to internal interactions between psychological states; those aspects of function concerning perceptual causation and behavioral effects are exempt.

We are now in a position to assemble the foregoing observations into an outline of the functional roles which characterize some simple beliefs involving the attitude-concepts. The belief that S believes P has the following characteristic function: it functions so as to induce one to include, in any mental simulation of S, a psychological state which, input-output conditions excepted, functions within that simulation is just the way that the belief P would function in ordinary thought. Similarly for the other attitudes: the belief that S desires P has the following characteristic function: it functions so as to induce one to include, in any mental simulation of S, a psychological state which, input-output conditions excepted, functions within that simulation is just the way that the desire P would function in ordinary thought. In regard to input-output conditions, where a collection of attitudes is caused by a certain environmental condition, the belief that S has those attitudes should be caused by the belief that S is in a corresponding condition; likewise, that where a collection of attitudes causes certain behavior, the belief that S has those attitudes should cause the belief that S will exhibit that behavior. Of course, the above is very much by way of a thumbnail sketch. In addition, it depends upon a simulation-based model of psychological inference whose psychological reality, if true, is surely contingent. However, I hope it illustrates *the kind of* story that could be told about the systematic functional relationship between any belief P and the corresponding belief that S believes P, between any desire P and the corresponding belief that S desires P, and so on through the gamut of the attitudes. And that is all I need for the present.[17]

3. The Problem of Intentionality

Let us take stock. I began by trying to motivate the demand for an analysis of the attitudes, the demand, that is, for a succinct, general, and non-trivial solution to the problem of intentionality. Such a demand arises, I said, from the need to explain our systematic grasp of the attitudes. If the defining characteristic of any psychological state is its causal signature, then the ability to understand what it is for an agent to have any of an effectively unlimited number of beliefs amounts to implicit knowledge of a function mapping any state of affairs P to the causal signature definitive of the belief that P. But our having this implicit knowledge seems to imply the existence of some relatively succinct theory which generates the required mappings, in which case, analyzing the attitudes can then be seen as articulating that knowledge. In the previous section, I sketched my own account of psychological inference and used that account to draw out the systematic functional relationships which hold between any belief P and the belief that S *believes* P, between any desire P and the belief that S *desires* P, and so on. In brief: the belief that S believes P has the following characteristic function: it functions so as to induce one to include, in any mental simulation of S, a psychological state which, input-output conditions excepted, functions within that simulation in just the way that the belief P would function in ordinary thought. Similarly, *mutatis mutandis,* for the other attitudes. I wish in the present section to consider how the account of psychological inference offered in the previous section might be implemented: what sorts of data-structures might be useful for representing beliefs about people's beliefs, desires, intentions, and so forth, and what cognitive mechanisms might be required to process those data-structures in the proper way. In answering these questions, I hope to show how our systematic command of the attitude-concepts can be explained without implying or presupposing their analyzability.

I begin with a suggestion made in the previous section: that Basil's belief that Florence believes P might be implemented by giving Basil a disposition to include in a special part of his brain devoted to simulations of Florence (the Florence-simulacrum), a data structure Δ_P which, if it occurred in the part of Basil's brain devoted to normal thought, would encode the belief P.[18] Now, one way for Basil to have such a disposition would be for him to encode the belief that Florence believes P using a data-structure Δ_P^{Flo} which contains Δ_P as a proper part. We should think of tokens of Δ_P^{Flo} as being "wrapped" versions of Δ_P, where the wrapping-paper indexes the data-structure as suitable for simulations of Florence. Setting up a simulation of Florence would then involve copying the kernels of all similarly wrapped data-structures into the Florence-simulacrum (together, perhaps, with certain background beliefs and desires). By "copying," I mean just that: making physical copies of the kernels of all the data-structures which Basil uses to encode beliefs about Florence's state of mind. This copying having been accomplished, the simulation of Florence will take its course, with the ersatz beliefs and desires within the simulation interacting just as if they were Basil's own beliefs and desires. Small wonder that the ersatz attitudes should have this property: if the relevant data-structure were in another part of Basil's brain, they would be Basil's own beliefs and desires!

To repeat, this is all by way of a fanciful implementation story: something to illustrate how some of Basil's data-structures might have the functional roles definitive of beliefs about the attitudes of one such as Florence. But — and here is the crux of the matter — on this story, *the systematicity of Basil's grasp of the attitudes is entirely unproblematic*. It is unproblematic, if a belief "S believes that P" is a wrapped version of the corresponding belief P, how the former can be formed whenever the latter can and can be formed, moreover, in such a way that, input-output conditions excepted (I will come to these presently), it functions in Basil's simulations of Florence in just the way that Basil's belief P would function in normal thought. Moreover, if implemented thus, Basil's ability to engage in psychological inference will survive the enlargement of his conceptual repertoire. When Basil acquires the ability to think about bandersnatches, then the copying and wrapping mechanisms alluded to above can be expected to work on whatever novel data-structures Basil used to encode his concept of bandersnatch. The situation can be illustrated by considering a computer program whose job is to copy various types of computer files. There are many types of computer file — text, executable, bitmap, raster — and more types yet to be invented. But there is usually no difficulty in writing a program capable of shunting just about any type of file from one location in memory to another: the copying program need have no idea of what the files it operates on are about, or what their functions within the computer system are. So may it be also with the labeling and copying mechanisms that underpin Basil's ability to engage in psychological inference.

We must augment this implementation story to accommodate the differences in functional role between the belief that S believes P and the belief P, in respect of their perceptual causes and behavioral effects. Recall that, according to our rough approximation, where a collection of attitudes is caused by a certain environmental condition, the belief that Florence has those attitudes should be caused by the belief that Florence is in a corresponding condition. Likewise, where a collection of attitudes causes certain behavior, the belief that Florence has those attitudes should cause the belief that Florence will exhibit that behavior. Let us see whether, on the above implementation story, there is any problem about Basil's systematic command of the attitudes in regard to these aspects of their functional roles.

I argued in the previous section that knowledge of the environmental causes and behavioral effects of psychological states could be gleaned by introspection, and that these introspective observations on one's own psychological states could then be simply assumed to apply to other people. How might this process be implemented in Basil conformably with the implementation details that we have fixed so far? Quite simply, as it turns out. What I propose is that Basil, in judging, introspectively, that he believes P, takes the data-structure Δ_P which encodes the belief P, and wraps it in some appropriate packaging, resulting in a data-structure Δ_P^I which contains Δ_P as a proper part. Similarly for Basil's other attitudes: in observing in himself the desire X, Basil takes the data structure, Γ_X which encodes the desire X, and wraps it in some appropriate packaging, resulting in a data-structure Γ_X^I which contains Γ_X as a proper part. We can also suppose Basil time-stamps these wrapped data-structures so he later remembers when he had the attitudes in question. These wrappings then protect the data structures against future deliberations that may affect the original attitudes. Thus, should Basil later come to doubt P, he will retain the belief that he once believed P; should he later come to loathe and detest X, he will retain the belief that he once desired X. The important point about this proposal for encoding beliefs about one's own earlier attitudes is that it allows generalizations about the environmental causes and behavioral effects of attitudes to be encoded in a form which makes them suitable for interfacing to psychological simulations. Let me explain.

Let P be the proposition that Basil's cat is sitting on the mat. The previous section offered the following account of how one such as Basil might obtain information about the environmental causes of the belief that P. After a certain amount of experience, Basil may be in a position to judge that, in various situations in the past—e.g., when he stood in front of the cat sitting on the mat in broad daylight—he came to believe P. Hence or otherwise, he may draw various conclusions about the typical aetiology of this belief—for instance, that whenever he stands in front of his cat sitting on the mat in broad daylight, that tends to cause him to believe P. Proceeding in accordance with Hobbes's dictum, Basil may then make judgments about the causes of the belief P in other people — for instance, that if *they* stood in front of the cat sitting on the mat in broad daylight, that would tend to cause *them* to believe P.[19] Following the implementation story sketched in the last paragraph, we might suppose that Basil encodes the generalizations about the causes of *his* belief P using data-structures of the form: $C \Rightarrow \Delta_P^I$, where C is a data-structure representing conditions which may cause the belief, and Δ_P^I, as before, a wrapped copy of Δ_P. We might further suppose that Basil encodes the corresponding generalizations about the causes of *Florence's* belief P using corresponding data-structures of the form: $C \Rightarrow \Delta_P^{Flo}$, where Δ_P^{Flo} is a differently wrapped copy of Δ_P. That would be sensible, since then the process of turning the former into the latter could be effected by systematically exchanging one kind of wrapping for another. Thus, the resulting generalizations about the conditions under which Florence will believe P will be encoded, in Basil's head, using data-structures which contain Δ_P^{Flo}, and hence Δ_P, as proper parts. This means that, should Basil use one of these generalizations to judge that Florence is indeed in such circumstances as are likely to cause her to believe P, he will have a copy of the data-structure Δ_P ready to transfer into his simulation of Florence. That is what I mean when I say that, on the proposed implementation, Basil's beliefs about the environmental causes of Florence's beliefs will be encoded in a form suitable to interface directly to Basil's simulations of Florence. Similarly for Basil's beliefs about the causes of Florence's other attitudes. Similarly also for Basil's beliefs about the behavioral effects of Florence's attitudes: these beliefs will be encoded in a form which allows them to be activated by the occurrence of the relevant data-structure in a mental simulation.

Again, the crux of the matter is that, on this implementation, there is no problem about the systematicity of Basil's grasp of the attitudes. The monitoring and copying mechanisms alluded to in the previous paragraphs will work whatever the functional roles of the data-structures Δ_P on which they operate. Moreover, such mechanisms will respond effortlessly to any enlargement of Basil's conceptual repertoire: new types of thoughts, connected no-matter-how with the outside world and with other of Basil's existing thoughts, will just be treated like any other data-structure, to be wrapped-up, made the subject of causal generalizations, copied, and run in simulations. Whatever the external aspects of the functional role of the new thought are, Basil's introspective mechanisms can in principle recover arbitrarily detailed information about them in a form which can be usefully interfaced to mental simulations of persons whom Basil may later take to have that thought.

Thus, the account of psychological inference set forth in the last section takes our systematic mastery of the concept of belief, indeed, of all our attitude-concepts, in its stride. But nowhere does that account allude to any succinctly specifiable mapping between the state of affairs in which S believes P and the corresponding state of affairs P. Rather, the account is given at the psychological level — in terms of the characteristic functional relationships between the *belief P* and the *belief* that S believes P. I therefore claim that our account of psychological inference bodes ill for the project of analyzing the attitudes. For it explains away what I claimed was the only reason for supposing that the attitudes should be analyzable at all: our systematic grasp of them. And, I contend, since there is no other reason to believe in a general, succinct, and non-trivial mapping between the state of affairs in which S believes P and the corresponding state of affairs P, we should suppose that there is not one.

The implementation story sketched above makes it clear how Basil can form data structures having the functional roles definitive of the beliefs that S believes P, that S desires P, etc., assuming only that he can form data structures having the functional roles definitive of the belief P, the desire P, etc., respectively. Moreover, this is so no matter what — within limits — those latter functional roles may be. Thus, if Basil acquires the capacity to think about bandersnatches, then no matter how, exactly, beliefs about bandersnatches are caused by the external world, Basil's introspective mechanisms could, in principle, record arbitrarily detailed information concerning the relevant patterns of causation. Basil might, for instance, notice that, upon being confronted with a bandersnatch in broad daylight, then he has the belief "There's a bandersnatch," but that he also has that belief when, as he later discovers, a trickster was projecting realistic holograms of certain sorts in his vicinity, and so on. Certainly, among Basil's beliefs about the typical aetiology of his beliefs about bandersnatches, bandersnatches themselves will, no doubt, loom large: beliefs about bandersnatches (let us pretend) get caused by bandersnatches in certain regular ways. But, on the present view, this fact is quite incidental. If beliefs about bandersnatches were typically caused by quite different things than bandersnatches, Basil could discover that, too. Indeed, Basil will make observations concerning the typical aetiology of his beliefs about, for example, *muons* or *Cicero* which do not relate either of these concepts so directly to their originals, to say nothing of his beliefs about prime numbers, hermeneutics, or God.

This is where we see the present account of intentionality clashing most sharply with the intuition underlying the traditional view which I tried to elicit in the first section, the view that has it that there must be some succinct and general connection between a representation and what it represents. There must, according to the traditional view, be some core relation which beliefs about muons bear to muons, which beliefs about horses bear to horses, and, if there were such things, beliefs about bandersnatches would bear to bandersnatches. Or, to whistle the same tune in a more propositional key: there must be some core relation which any state of affairs in which S believes P bears to the corresponding state of affairs P. Not so, according to the view developed here. The possible relationships between these two states of affairs can be open-ended; what determines that relationship in the case of a new belief will be the functional role of that new belief; and there is no reason, as far as one's abilities to engage in psychological inference are concerned, why that new functional role cannot be more or less anything.[20]

The present account, it should be stressed, is compatible with—nay, presupposes—functionalism, considered merely as the thesis that psychological states are defined by their functional roles. That is, the present account accepts that to believe that it is raining is to be in a brain state which functions thus-and-so, that to believe that the cat is on the mat is to be in a brain state which functions thus-and-so, and so on, for any psychological state one could possibly be in. The thrust of my argument concerns the lack of any need for a common thread running through this list. For there is, I ween, no general, succinct, non-trivial account of the relation between the state of affairs of S's believing that P and the corresponding state of affairs P.

Our conclusion has an idealistic flavor: the primary—and, so far as we know, the only—way to identify the relation between a state of affairs P and the corresponding state of affairs in which S believes P, or desires P, etc., is to describe the way our *thoughts* about believing and desiring, etc., function, rather than to reduce believing and desiring to terms and constructs taken from whatever metaphysical catalog is currently in vogue. If you ask me what it is, in general, for someone to *believe* something, then all I can tell you is what sort of brain-state you will need in order to have the concept of belief; for there is nothing that believing is, other than that which is thought therewith. Needless to say, this is no idealism which rejects the material world as an illusion, or which denies the objectivity of our judgments about it. No: I really believe there to be no Loch Ness monster; and, as it happens, there really is not one. Our conclusion is idealistic in this sense: it says that the only general, succinct, and non-trivial account of belief takes the form of a specification, at the psychological level, of how the concept of belief functions in thought and adds thereto that there is no reason to suppose that this specification can be mapped down to the objective level. All that is rejected is the wild goose chase of trying to provide an analysis of the attitudes. There is nothing for philosophy to say about the attitude concepts, about their unity and their utility, that is not best said at the psychological level.[21]

4. Summary

In this essay, I have addressed the problem of intentionality. I characterized that problem as the task of giving an account of the relationship between a state of affairs P, and the state of affairs in which a person entertains a given attitude (typically, belief) towards P. I claimed that the widespread belief in the existence of a general, succinct, and non-trivial solution of this problem arises from the fact that our systematic grasp of the attitudes, together with the limited computational resources of our brains, seems to impose an upper bound on the complexity of the best specification of this relationship. I then went on to sketch a theory of psychological inference, and, in doing so, specified the characteristic functional roles of beliefs of the form "S believes that P," "S desires that X," etc., in terms of the functional roles of the corresponding belief P, desire X, etc. I showed that these characteristic functional roles could be implemented without supposing the existence of a general, succinct, and non-trivial relationship between a state of affairs P, and the state of affairs in which a person entertains a given attitude towards P. I inferred that we have no reason to believe such a relationship exists.

Notes

1. For brevity's sake, I shall ignore the obviously false implication that normal English speakers can understand sentences with arbitrarily iterated attitude-verbs. I also ignore the grammatical changes, such as those of tense and mood, which English attitude-verbs frequently demand. In addition, throughout this essay, I allow myself some imprecision when it comes to quantifying over the contents of beliefs (e.g., in alternating between "S believes P" and "S believes that P").

2. Provisos corresponding to those of the previous footnote also supply here.

3. David Lewis: "Psychophysical and Theoretical Identifications," *Australasian Journal of Philosophy* 50 (1972): 256.

4. Davidson: "Radical Interpretation," in *Essays on Actions and Events* (New York: Oxford University Press), 152–153; David Lewis, "Radical Interpretation" in *Philosophical Papers,* vol. 1, p. 112.

5. Lewis, "Radical Interpretation," 113; Robert Stalnaker, *Inquiry* (Cambridge, Mass.: MIT Press, 1984), 82.

6. Lewis himself suggests that folk-psychological platitudes might quantify over attitude-contents in "Psychophysical and Theoretical Identifications," note 13. For a more up-to-date account, see, for example, David Lewis, *On the Plurality of Worlds* (New York: Oxford University Press, 1986), 36 ff. There is one important respect in which I have deliberately misrepresented the views of some of the radical interpretation theorists, including Stalnaker and Lewis. I have represented folk psychology as taking beliefs, desires, intentions, etc., to be identifiable, count-

able internal states or events which stand in certain causal relations to each other. Lewis (at least in his later papers) and Stalnaker urge that the attitudes not be thought of in this way. It does not make sense, they say, to talk of individual beliefs and desires as if they were identifiable states or events: in particular, it would not make sense to *count* the number of beliefs and desires a person has. However, I propose to ignore this feature of their views here, since it does not impinge upon the observations to follow.

7. Actually, Field rejects the possible-worlds construal of propositions, adopting it only for expository purposes. I likewise.

8. By "intension" of a predicate I mean something which determines the extension of that predicate (i.e., the set of things to which that predicate applies) for every possible world. I do not wish to become embroiled in the questions of what such intensions are, or how they 'determine' intensions.

9. Hartry Field, "Tarski's Theory of Truth," *Journal of Philosophy* 69 (1972): 369. See also his "Mental Representation," *Erkenntnis* 13, no. 1 (1978), for some discussion of the relation of denotation holding between a predicate and its intension.

10. Interestingly, Stalnaker (*Inquiry,* 30–32) criticizes Field's envisaged analysis for, among other things, not being succinct (in our sense) enough. Field proposes only that the plethora of axioms specifying the denotations of names and predicates be generated by some succinct causal theory; Stalnaker points out that to do so leaves the axioms specifying the meaning of the combinators (such as &, ¬, etc.) unexplained. A naturalistically plausible theory of truth, Stalnaker urges, ought to explain *why* the symbol & denotes logical conjunction as much as it explains why the name "Cicero" denotes Cicero, a suggestion he bolsters by pointing out that the number of possible combinators is limitless. But Stalnaker's criticism is all grist to my mill: he, too, is moved by the desire to achieve generality with succinctness.

11. For developments of this idea, see also David Armstrong, *Belief, Truth and Knowledge* (Cambridge: Cambridge University Press, 1973); F. I. Dretske, *Knowledge and the Flow of Information* (Cambridge, Mass.: MIT Press, 1981); Jerry Fodor, *Psychosemantics* (Cambridge, Mass.: MIT Press, 1987), chap. 4.

12. For a notable voice of dissent, see S. Schiffer, *Remnants of Meaning* (Cambridge, Mass.: MIT Press, 1987).

13. Thomas Hobbes, *Leviathan,* ed. C. B. Macpherson (Harmondsworth, Middlesex: Penguin Books, 1968), 82.

14. Notice that we cannot necessarily tell, by introspection, when we are using our introspective faculties. Introspection, as I understand the term here, is merely a *monitoring* process: as such, it need not be conscious (whatever that means); indeed, it need not even be monitored.

15. K. J. W. Craik, *The Nature of Explanation* (Cambridge: Cambridge University Press, 1943), chap. 5.

16. For other writers who have either developed or touched on this idea see: Daniel Kahneman and Amos Tversky, "The Simulation Heuristic," in Daniel Kahneman, Paul Slovic, and Amos Tversky, *Judgment Under Uncertainty: Heuristics and Biases* (Cambridge: Cambridge University Press, 1982); W. V. O. Quine, *Word and*

Object (Cambridge, Mass.: MIT Press, 1960), 219; Stephen Stich in "Dennett on Intentional Systems," *Philosophical Topics* 12, no. 1 (1981), and in *From Folk Psychology to Cognitive Science* (Cambridge, Mass.: MIT Press, 1983), chap. 5; D. K. Lewis, "Prisoners' Dilemma is a Newcomb Problem," in his *Philosophical Papers,* vol. 2 (New York: Oxford University Press, 1986), 299–304; Daniel C. Dennett, "Making Sense of Ourselves," in his *The Intentional Stance* (Cambridge, Mass.: MIT Press, 1987), 100; Lewis G. Creary, "Propositional Attitudes: Fregean Representation and Simulative Reasoning," *Proceedings, Sixth International Joint Conference on Artificial Intelligence,* Tokyo (1979); and Andrew R. Haas, "A Syntactic Theory of Belief and Action," *Artificial Intelligence* 28, 3 (1986).

17. In speaking, in the same breath, of the *belief P,* and the *desire P,* I have, in the foregoing explanation, helped myself to the notion of a belief's and a desire's *having the same content;* I need, therefore, to say how I intend this notion to be cashed out. Briefly, what I envisage is a story about the systematic psychological relations holding between a belief P and the corresponding desire P. Such a story would tell, for example, of how the belief P functions so as to terminate planning activity initiated by the desire that P, while tending not to affect (or not to affect so directly) the planning activity initiated by desires with content other than P. No doubt such a story would tell much else besides; but I will not attempt to go into the details here. What I do wish to claim is that such a story about the systematic psychological relationships between a belief P and a desire P could then be taken as *constitutive* of what it is for a belief and desire to have the same content. Similarly, with the other attitudes: intending P, doubting P, entertaining the thought P, etc. We can give a general account of what it is for two thoughts to have the same state of affairs as content, even though these thoughts are instances of different attitudes. Needless to say, a general account of what it is to have two thoughts with the same content is far from being a general account of what it is to have a thought with a *given* content.

18. I say that a data-structure Δ *encodes* the belief P for an agent if that agent is so constituted that a tokening of Δ in his brain constitutes his having the belief P.

19. I ignore, for simplicity, variations in the descriptions under which different people are likely to think of Basil's cat, and of the mat on which it is sitting.

20. Might there not be *some* constraints on the new kinds of functional roles that we are prepared to countenance as definitive of beliefs or other attitudes? Perhaps so. Admissible functional roles might, for example, be required to secure a suitably rich interaction with existing attitudes, and might perhaps be required to respect certain constraints imposed by the framework of beliefs, desires, intentions, etc. Thus, if the belief P is a new belief, then we might require that it be possible to believe conjunctions of the form $P\&Q$ for all existing beliefs Q, that it be possible to form the corresponding *desire P* and *intention P,* and so on. Or again, we might impose a ban on concepts — call them *viral* concepts — whose functional role is to gobble up and destroy all one's existing attitudes. To get an idea of what we would be legislating against here, let us consider a concept *tonk* which combines beliefs in the following way: from A, one may infer A *tonk* B; from A *tonk B* one may infer B. The adoption of such inferential policies would soon lead

me to infer anything that came into my head, so obliterating all my existing beliefs. Thus, *tonk* has a functional role which our minds could not endure; so maybe we should say that it does not count as a proper concept. And of course, it would not be difficult to think up other sensible constraints. But whatever exactly these constraints turn out to be, they may yet leave a great latitude for beliefs and concepts having all sorts of novel functional roles—in particular, having all sorts of novel causal relationships with various aspects of the world.

21. There is a connection between the conclusion reached here and the debate over 'procedural' versus 'truth-theoretic' semantics. See, e.g., J. Fodor, "Tom Swift and his Procedural Grandmother," *Cognition* 6 (1978): 229–247. See also P. N. Johnson-Laird's "What's wrong with Grandma's Guide to Procedural Semantics: A Reply to Jerry Fodor," in the same volume, and, for a more recent discussion, R. F. Hadley, "A Default-Oriented Theory of Procedural Semantics," *Cognitive Science* 13 (1989): 107–137. The account of the attitude concepts given here might be regarded as a procedural semantics for the attitude verbs. What is interesting about these procedural semantics (if I am right) is their lack of any general succinct, non-trivial, truth-theoretic counterparts.

Nonreductive Materialism and the Explanatory Autonomy of Psychology

TERENCE HORGAN

In this essay I will address some philosophical issues concerning the relationship between neurobiology and mentalistic psychology. For present purposes I will largely take for granted a realist view of the mental antecedents of behavior—as opposed to eliminativism, instrumentalism, or any other anti-realist position. I will argue for the following claims. First, the mental and the neurobiological explanatory frameworks are compatible, rather than excluding each other. Second, their compatibility does not require that mentalistic psychology be reducible to neurobiology; indeed, psychology probably is not so reducible. Third, mentalistic causal explanations have an important kind of autonomy vis-à-vis neurobiological causal explanations.

As a metaphysical naturalist, I believe that all human behavior is susceptible in principle to neurobiological explanation. But because of the three claims just mentioned, I deny that this materialist premise forces us to choose between reductionism on the one hand, or unpalatable views like eliminativism or ephenomenalism on the other hand. I advocate instead a non-reductive form of naturalism or materialism—a form that is robustly realist about mentality itself, about mental causation, and about mentalistic causal explanation.[1]

Although I eschew reductionism while embracing realism about the mental, I do not take a casual live-and-let-live, have-your-cake-and-eat-it-too, attitude toward metaphysical questions about inter-level connections generally, or about the connection between neurobiology and psychology. On the contrary, I view these questions as profoundly difficult, all the more so once reductionism is repudiated. And I consider the concept of supervenience considerably less helpful in this regard than it is often thought to be. The problem of explaining psychophysical supervenience relations has now emerged, I think, as a new and puzzling incarnation of the perennial mind-body problem.

1. Causal Explanation and Multiple Theoretical Levels[2]

In causal explanation the effect phenomenon e, described as instantiating a phenomenon type E, is shown to depend in a certain way upon the cause phenomenon c, described as instantiating a type C. Often the dependence involves the fact that c and e are subsumable under a counterfactual-supporting generalization — either a generalization that directly links C to E, or else a more complicated generalization whose antecedent cites a combination of properties that includes C. But in order for the cited properties C and E to be genuinely explanatorily relevant to the causal transaction between c and e, it is not enough that c caused e and that c and e are subsumable under such a generalization. Rather, C and E must fit into a suitably rich pattern of counterfactual relations among properties. The following passage from James Woodward gives a sense for how such patterns figure in explanation:

> A scientific explanation not only shows that the explanandum phenomenon was to be expected, but also enables us to answer questions of the form 'What would have happened if. . . .' A successful explanation accomplishes this by exhibiting the explanandum phenomenon as one of a range of states, any one of which might have occurred had initial conditions, boundary conditions, and so forth been different in various ways from what they actually were. We are shown why, conditions being what they were, the explanandum phenomenon rather than one of these alternative outcomes occurred. In effect we are not just shown why the explanandum phenomenon had to occur, but are given some sense of the range of conditions under which it would have occurred. . . . But why should this additional information have any explanatory significance? One way to appreciate the significance . . . is to note that if we simply require that an explanans provide a nomically sufficient condition for the explanandum we do not insure that the explanans is relevant to the explanandum. When we require, in addition, that the laws answer a set of what-if-things-had-been-different questions, we help to insure that the explanans will perspicuously identify those conditions which are relevant to the explanandum being what it is.[3]

To illustrate these remarks, Woodward cites an example from Wesley Salmon. Suppose that Mr. Jones, a man who has been taking birth control pills regularly, fails to get pregnant. Even though the generalization 'All men who take birth control pills regularly fail to get pregnant' satisfies certain standard criteria for being lawlike, this generalization will not sustain a genuine explanation of why Mr. Jones failed to get pregnant. In his case the property *taking birth control pills regularly* is explanatorily irrelevant. For, the pertinent what-if-things-had-been-different question — viz., 'What

would have happened had he not taken birth control pills regularly?' —
receives the wrong answer.

On the other hand, suppose that Mrs. Jones, a female who has been
taking birth control pills regularly, fails to get pregnant. Now the very
same property becomes explanatorily relevant: and a very similar lawlike
generalization (pertaining to women) undergirds a genuine explanation
(albeit a crude one, too crude to count as scientific) for now we have a
pattern of counterfactual relations that makes for genuine explanatory
relevance. Thus Woodward:

> In an explanation involving [the lawlike generalization about pregnancy] there
> are in effect two possible initial conditions which may obtain — Mrs. Jones
> either may or may not take birth control pills — and two possible explananda
> — Mrs. Jones either may or may not get pregnant. In a successful scientific
> explanation we have a kind of generalized analog of this feature — the ex-
> planation identifies not two but a great range of possible explananda, and
> a range of possible initial conditions under which these different explananda
> will be realized. The explanation explains in part in virtue of showing us
> how it is that it was the explanandum rather than one of these many alter-
> nate possibilities that was realized and in doing so, perspicuously identifies
> those conditions which are relevant to the obtaining of these various ex-
> plananda.[4]

As Woodward stresses in this passage, a successful scientific explanation identifies an extensive pattern of counterfactual dependencies of
possible explananda upon possible initial conditions. It is important to
understand how this feature is related to the structure of scientific laws.
The generality of the fundamental laws of the natural sciences does not
consist merely in their having the logical form, All A's are B's. It consists,
rather, in the fact that they are systematic in scope and structure, so that
a wide range of phenomena are subsumable under relatively few laws. One
major source of their systematicity is that (i) the laws cite *parameterized*
properties — viz., quantitative magnitudes, where the parameters are numerical values that these magnitudes can take on when instantiated; and
that (ii) the laws contain universal quantifiers ranging over the values of
these parameters (in addition to the universal quantifiers ranging over the
non-numerical entities in a law's domain). Newtonian velocity, for example, is not a single property but an infinite array of determinate properties,
one for each real value of V. The resultant generality of a physical law
consists largely in the existence of a whole (typically infinite) set of specific
nomically true principles, each of which is a specific instantiation of the
law with specific numeric values "plugged in" for the quantitative parameters.[5] Rich patterns of counterfactual dependence, of the sort that are a

crucial feature of successful scientific explanation (as Woodward stresses), are reflected by the truth of such sets of specific law-instantiations.

I will refer to this generic approach to explanatory relevance as the *counterfactual pattern* conception (for short, the CP conception). On this general view, the explanatory relevance of a pair of properties *C* and *E*, instantiated respectively by a pair of causally related events or states *c* and *e*, consists largely in the fact that *C* and *E* fit into a pattern of counterfactual relations of the kind Woodward describes.[6] (I will refer to such patterns as *CR patterns*.)

Under the CP conception, a single phenomenon can perfectly well be subject to a variety of different explanations, involving properties from a variety of different CR patterns. Often several distinct patterns, all explanatorily relevant to a single phenomenon, will involve different levels in the hierarchy of the sciences — e.g., microphysical, neurobiological, macrobiological, and psychological. Typically, certain context-relative features of discourse will determine, in a given situation of inquiry, which sort of explanation is most appropriate for the purposes at hand. (These features operate in much the way that context-relative features typically determine, in a given discourse situation, what counts as the proper referent of a given definite description that is satisfied by several distinct objects in the contextually pertinent universe of discourse.)[7]

Explanations at the level of intentional psychology evidently fare quite well, under the CP conception of explanatory relevance. Consider first commonsense intentional psychology, so-called folk psychology. There are robust patterns of counterfactual dependence among the state types (including act types) posited by folk psychology — patterns systematizable via generalizations containing universal quantifiers ranging over suitable parameters. These parameters are not quantitative, but instead are *propositional* (or *intentional*); i.e., they are the kinds typically specified by 'that'-clauses. Take, for instance, explanations of actions on the basis of reasons. The intentional mental properties that constitute reasons (viz., belief types, desire types, and other attitude types), in combination with act types, clearly figure in a rich and robust pattern of counterfactual dependence of actions upon reasons that rationalize them, a pattern undergirded by the following generalization:

(G) (*S*) (*D*) (*A*) (If *S* wants *D* and *S* believes that doing *A* will bring about *D*, then *ceteris paribus, S* will do *A*).

There also are rich patterns of counterfactual dependence among folk psychological mental states themselves, undergirded by generalizations like the following:

    (x) (p) [If Wants(p)x & Discovers(p)x, then *ceteris paribus,*
       Pleased(p)x]

    (x) (p) [If Fears(p)x then *ceteris paribus,* Wants(−p)x]

    (x) (p) (q) [If Believes(p)x & Believes(if p then q)x, then *ceteris*
       paribus, either Believes(q)x or Reconsiders(p) x or Reconsiders(if
       then q)x]

    (x) (p) (q) [If Wants(p)x & Believes(if q then p)x, then *ceteris paribus,*
       either Wants(q)x or (∃s) (Wants(s)x & Believes(if q then −s) x)][8]

Wanting, believing, etc., figure in these generalizations as vast (possibly infinite), highly structured, arrays of properties, a different specific property for each specific value of each propositional variable.

Theoretical intentional psychology, in order to be a viable scientific discipline, also will need to advert to rich patterns of counterfactual dependence over the state types it posits. So its laws, too, if they are to have the kind of generality that is essential to science, will contain universal quantifiers ranging over its parameters. (A mature theoretical psychology might or might not turn out to employ *quantitative* parameters, but its concepts will certainly have *propositional* parameters. It will contain either the intentional concepts of folk psychology, or some refinement or replacement of them; it may also contain additional intentional concepts, too, which themselves have propositional/intentional parameters.)

It should be stressed at this point that the *'ceteris paribus'* clauses in the above sample generalizations from folk psychology do not undermine the claim that these generalizations reflect rich patterns of counterfactual dependence among psychological state types. Nor do these clauses undermine the use of such generalizations in causal explanation; for, normally a folk psychological causal explanation implicitly assumes that *ceteris* was *paribus* in the given situation, with respect to the applicable folk psychological generalization. (Jane went to the refrigerator because she wanted a beer and she believed there was beer in the refrigerator. The explanation of Jane's behavior, when reconstructed in fully explicit form adverting to the above generalization (G), is this: (G), Jane wanted a beer and believed she could get one from the refrigerator, and *ceteris* was *paribus;* so she went to the refrigerator for a beer.)

Furthermore, one should expect the laws of the special sciences generally, and those of theoretical intentional psychology in particular, to be *ceteris paribus* laws—a point emphasized by Jerry Fodor. "I assume," says Fodor, "that the laws of the basic sciences are strictly exceptionless, and I assume that it is common knowledge that the laws of the special sciences are not."[9] He elaborates the point this way:

> [I]t simply isn't true that we can, even in principle, specify the conditions under which — say — geological generalizations hold *so long as we stick to the vocabulary of geology*. Or, to put it less in the formal mode, the causes of exceptions to geological generalizations are, quite typically, not themselves *geological* events. . . . Exceptions to the generalizations of a special science are typically *inexplicable* from the point of view of (that is, in the vocabulary of) that science. . . . But of course, it may nevertheless be perfectly possible to explain the exceptions *in the vocabulary of some other science*. In the most familiar case, you go 'down' one or more levels and use the vocabulary of a more 'basic' science. . . . [T]he same pattern that holds for the special sciences seems to hold for common-sense psychology as well.[10]

As applied to intentional psychology, these remarks point to the ubiquitous presence of potential exceptions that fall outside the domain of psychology itself, and hence are stateable only in some other vocabulary: had-a-stroke or hit-by-a-bus exceptions, i.e., equipment failure or external catastrophe. But in addition, John Tienson and I have argued elsewhere (i) that there are very good reasons to expect the laws of intentional psychology to have essentially limitless *same-level* exceptions, i.e., exceptions describable in the language of psychology itself; and (ii) that this feature does not undermine their theoretical legitimacy or their role in causal explanation.[11]

The upshot so far is this. Under the CP conception of explanatory relevance, there can perfectly well be multiple levels of causal explanation for a single phenomenon. The phenomenon and its cause can respectively instantiate multiple pairs of properties; and several instantiated pairs, at different theoretical levels, can perfectly well each belong to some pattern of counterfactual relations among properties that makes for explanatory relevance. Furthermore, *prima facie* there are strong grounds for thinking that intentional mental properties figure in CR patterns of the requisite kind, and thus that explanations at the level of intentional psychology are compatible with explanations at other more fundamental theoretical levels such as neurobiology. When a given phenomenon is multiply explainable, factors specific to the situation, including the conceptual vocabulary of the 'why'-question being asked and the purpose(s) that motivated asking it, normally will determine which level of explanation is the contextually appropriate one.

This kind of context/purpose relativity is entirely compatible, as far as I can see, with the contention that facts about explanatory relations are objective and mind-independent. Hence the CP conception does not embody any commitment to what Jaegwon Kim calls *explanatory irrealism*. This he describes as "the view that the relation of being an explanans for, as it relates C and E within our epistemic corpus, is not, and need not be, 'grounded' in any objective relation between events c and e"[12] — where C and E are statements or propositions that respectively constitute the (putative) explanans and explanandum of a single causal explanation, and c and e are the causally related events respectively characterized by C and E. An advocate of the CP conception can plausibly maintain that the explanans/explanandum relation does indeed have an objective grounding, even in cases where the phenomenon e is causally explainable at other theoretical levels in addition to the level of C and E. The grounding consists of the fact that C and E respectively cite properties, instantiated in c and e respectively, which figure in the kind of rich, robust pattern of counterfactual dependence that constitutes causal/explanatory relevance.

2. Inter-Level Constraints

What are the appropriate constraints on inter-level connections among distinct theories or explanatory frameworks, given the compatibilist conception of explanation just sketched, and given a broadly naturalist (or materialist, or physicalist) metaphysical orientation?

In addressing this question one cannot simply proceed by first laying out the key theses of a naturalist/materialist metaphysics, and then reading off from these the appropriate inter-level constraints, for our notion of what constitutes naturalism or materialism is somewhat vague and inchoate. Articulating plausible inter-level constraints goes hand-in-hand with articulating a physicalistic metaphysical *Weltanschauung*.

Each constraint I shall propose will be characterized here in somewhat generic terms; thus each will be susceptible to further articulation or explication. But for present purposes I think these generic characterizations are appropriate, since the general position I am sketching in this essay is potentially refinable in a variety of different ways.

2.1. The Causal/Explanatory Completeness of Physics

Metaphysical naturalism includes the view that physics is causally and explanatorily complete, within its own domain: i.e., every fact or phenomenon describable in the language of physics is fully explainable (to the extent that it is explainable at all) entirely on the basis of facts and laws of physics itself. There are no causal "gaps," in the nexus of physically describable events and processes, that get "filled in" by causes that are not themselves physically describable; and there are no explanatory gaps, vis-à-vis physical phenomena as physically described, that get filled in by higher level non-physical explanations. Accordingly, inter-level connections among distinct theories or distinct explanatory frameworks must be consistent with the internal causal/explanatory completeness of physics.

2.2. Physical Supervenience

Metaphysical naturalism also includes the view that in our world, and in any other physically possible world, the facts of physics synchronically fix, or determine, all the facts. One dimension of this supervenience idea is purely global, pertaining to physically possible worlds considered in their entirety:

> Any two physically possible worlds which are exactly alike physically are also exactly alike in all other respects.

A second, non-global, dimension pertains to individuals and their intrinsic properties:

> For any two individuals i and j, either in two distinct physically possible worlds or in a single such world, if i and j are exactly alike in all intrinsic physical respects then they are exactly alike in all other intrinsic respects.

And yet a third dimension pertains to individuals and their non-intrinsic properties — properties like propositional attitude state-types with wide content. It can be roughly characterized this way:

> For any two individuals i and j, either in distinct physically possible worlds or a single such world, if (i) i and j are exactly alike in all intrinsic physical respects, (ii) i has a non-intrinsic property F, and (iii) i and j are exactly alike with respect to all non-intrinsic physical features that are pertinent to i's possession of F, then j also possesses F.

Inter-level connections among distinct theories or distinct explanatory frameworks must be consistent with all three dimensions of physical supervenience. [13]

2.3. Physical Causal Mechanisms

A third inter-level constraint concerns causal explanations that cite properties from higher-level theories or explanatory frameworks. For any causal transaction where some higher-level property F is cited as causally explaining the effect, there must be an *underlying mechanism* in virtue of which the transaction occurs — a mechanism involving a physical property (or a complex of physical properties) which, on the given occasion, *physi-*

cally realizes the property *F*. That is to say, causal transactions involving higher-order properties must be grounded in causal mechanisms involving the nexus of physical causes and effects, mechanisms describable and explainable at the level of physics.[14]

When a single phenomenon is causally explainable at a variety of different levels, typically there will be a hierarchy of causal mechanisms involved, some more fundamental and more complete than others. Take, for instance, a case where a person's behavior is caused by a certain combination of desires and beliefs. These state types will be *neurobiologically* realized in a certain way (on this occasion), and there will be an underlying neurobiological story about how those realizing properties causally generated the bodily motion that constituted (on this occasion) an instance of the relevant action-type. But the relevant neurobiological properties, in turn, will be *physically* realized in a certain way (on this occasion), and there will be an even deeper underlying physical story about how these *physical* realizing properties causally generated (on this occasion) the bodily motion in question.[15]

2.4. Non-Coincidentality of Higher-Level Generalizations[16]

In order for higher-level CR patterns to have genuine causal/explanatory relevance to phenomena that exhibit higher-level properties, the higher-level generalizations that systematize those CR patterns must themselves satisfy a certain constraint vis-à-vis lower-level theory. These generalizations must be *non-coincidental*, when viewed from a lower-level perspective.

Suppose, for instance, that a certain fatal disease always causes certain symptoms (say, a distinctive kind of skin rash) shortly before it causes death, and that these symptoms are never caused in any other way. Then there will be higher-level CR pattern involving presence or absence of skin rash, and presence or absence of subsequent death. But this pattern will be explanatorily spurious: having the skin rash does not causally explain a person's subsequent death; rather, the rash and the death are both the effects of a single common cause. Thus, from a lower-level perspective, the generalization linking the skin rash to subsequent death is merely coincidental.

In this example there is also a violation of the causal mechanism constraint, set forth above; there is no underlying physical causal mechanism linking the presence of the skin rash to subsequent death. But cases can be imagined where there does exist an appropriate causal mechanism underlying the higher-lever CR pattern, and yet this pattern is merely coincidental anyway. Suppose, for instance, there is an all-female society of Amazons, each of whom can produce, and can perceptually distinguish, sounds with the properties that shatter glass. Suppose, also, that sounds instantiating these properties — regardless of any other acoustic properties they do or do not possess — mean 'shatter' in the Amazon language. When Amora, queen of the Amazons, first encounters something made of glass, she reacts by saying 'shatter' (in Amazon), and it promptly shatters.

In this case there is indeed an underlying physical causal mechanism linking Amora's utterance to the glass's shattering. Moreover, there is also a certain CR pattern of the kind that sometimes undergirds explanatory relevance: glass's shattering or not shattering depends counterfactually upon uttering or not uttering a sound that means 'shatter'. The pattern is systematizable by a generalization something like:

> If an Amazon utters 'shatter' in the presence of an object composed of glass, then *ceteris paribus,* that object will shatter.

(This generalization is quite crude and limited, but it does seem comparable, for instance, to the operative generalization in Woodward's example of Mrs. Jones and the birth control pill.) But the sound's meaning is explanatorily irrelevant anyway. The generalization in question is merely coincidental; it is not linked in an appropriate way to other, lower-level, CR patterns that do sustain genuine explanatory relevance.

Needless to say, there is much to be done philosophically in getting a conceptual handle on what does, and does not, count as a generalization that is "merely coincidental." I will not attempt to address this issue at any great length here. But let me mention one general line of thought, currently much in the air in philosophy of mind, which I find highly suggestive — especially in connection with laws and CR patterns involving intentional mental states. The leading idea is that the tendency of a given kind of creature both (i) to instantiate certain higher-level properties when it does, and (ii) to satisfy the relevant higher-level laws, is plausibly viewed as the product of nature's "design," through evolutionary natural selection. Colin McGinn puts crisply the theme I want to stress:

> Let us start with the idea of *relational proper function.* The proper function of some organ or trait or process is what it is designed to do, what it is supposed to do, what it ought to do. Proper functions can come about either through the intentions of a designer or through a mindless process like natural selection. . . . An organism must be designed (by natural selection) according to the environmental constraints; indeed the given environment is the chief *architect* in constructing a species of organism, since it does the selecting of characteristics. And here is where relational proper function comes in: proper functions are generally defined *relatively* to some environmental object or feature. Thus the function of the chameleon's pigmentation mecha-

nism is to make it the same colour as its immediate environment. . . . In each case we specify the function of the characteristic in terms of a relation to some environmental item. . . . What natural selection must do is to install a causal mechanism of some kind which carries out the function selected for in a specific environment. . . . It is not difficult to see how this idea might be applied to traits of mind as well as to traits of body. The mind and its characteristic powers and properties are evolutionary products too, and as such may be expected to exhibit functional features: mental states will have their own distinctive relational proper functions. On general grounds, then, we may anticipate environment-directed functions on the part of such states as desire, belief, and perception; they too will play their part in helping the organism adapt itself to the environmental contingencies.[17]

Representational content and relational proper function are so intimately connected, in the case of propositional attitudes, that it is clearly no mere coincidence that attitude types and act types figure as they do in robust CR patterns. On the contrary, the requirement that propositional attitudes should figure in such patterns is crucial to their relational proper function; it is their *raison d'etre,* from the point of view of Nature-as-Designer.

3. Reduction and Multiple Realizability

Notably absent from my list of proposed inter-level constraints is the requirement that higher-level laws, theories, or properties be reducible to lower-level ones. As I said at the outset, I deny that a naturalist/material-ist position in metaphysics must embrace any such constraint. In particu-lar, I deny that mentalistic psychology must be reducible to neurobiology; and in fact I very much doubt whether the former is *in fact* reducible to the latter. My reasons for holding these views will seem fairly familiar. But the issue deserves reopening, especially in light of recent arguments[18] that nonreductive materialism is a conceptually unstable position and that one must therefore choose between reductionism or some anti-realist posi-tion like eliminativism.

3.1. Fodor's Multiple Realization Argument Against Reductionism

Reduction, as standardly conceived, involves (universally quantified) biconditional bridge laws linking the predicates and properties of a higher-level theory with predicates and properties of the lower-level reducing the-ory. The higher-level theory, or perhaps a modestly corrected version of it, is logically entailed by the conjunction of the lower-level theory and the bridge laws. The bridge laws express either *identities* between entities and properties posited by the two theories, or at least nomic coextensiveness between higher-level and lower-level properties and thing-kinds.[19]

The classical conception of reduction also requires that the properties posited by the higher-level theory be *uniquely realizable* under the bridge laws, rather than multiply realizable. This requirement can be cashed roughly as follows: even though a bridge law might correlate a given higher-level property with a lower-level property whose characterization in lower-level terms is fairly complex (rather than, say, correlating the higher-level property with a property expressed by a single lower-level theoretical term), nevertheless the lower-level property must not be *disjunctive*. To be correlated with a disjunctive lower-level property is to be multiply realizable, with each disjunct expressing a distinct mode of realization.

During the past two decades, skepticism about reductionism has largely focused on this requirement of unique realizability. In an important and influential essay, Jerry Fodor argued that this demand is excessively stringent, and that it is very likely violated all the time. He wrote:

> The reason it is unlikely that every kind corresponds to a physical kind is just that (a) interesting generalizations (e.g., counterfactual supporting generalizations) can often be made about events whose physical descriptions have nothing in common; (b) it is often the case that *whether* the physical descriptions of the events have anything in common is, in an obvious sense, entirely irrelevant to the truth of the generalizations, or to their interestingness, or to their degree of confirmation, or indeed, to any of their epistemologically important properties; and (c) the special sciences are very much in the business of formulating generalizations of this kind.[20]

To illustrate these claims he offered the example of Gresham's 'law' in economics:

> Suppose, for example, that Gresham's 'law' really is true. (If one doesn't like Gresham's law, then any true and counterfactual supporting generalization in any conceivable future economics will probably do as well.) Gresham's law says something about what will happen in monetary exchanges under certain conditions. . . . [B]anal considerations suggest that a physical description which covers all such events must be wildly disjunctive. Some monetary exchanges involve strings of wampum. Some involve dollar bills. And some involve signing one's name to a check. . . . What is interesting about monetary exchanges is surely not their commonalities under *physical* description.[21]

In my view, the line of argument in these passages constitutes a very convincing case against the appropriateness of imposing classical reducibility as a constraint on inter-level fit among theories or explanatory frameworks. Fodor's argument also constitutes quite a plausible case against the view that the special sciences all will turn out *in fact* to be reducible to lower-level sciences (and thus ultimately to physics). What I have to say in the remainder of this section will largely be commentary on the passages just quoted.

3.2. The Strong Realization-Neutrality of Special Science Concepts

The example of the concept *monetary exchange* reveals an important, and quite general, point about the theoretical concepts of the special sciences. Higher-level theoretical concepts typically are, as I shall put it, *strongly realization-neutral.* By this I mean that they are neutral both (i) about *how* they are realized at lower theoretical levels (and ultimately at the level of physics), and (ii) about whether or not they are *uniquely* realized at lower levels (and ultimately at the physics level). Because of this feature, the integrity and applicability of special science concepts is not undermined if they turn out to be multiply realizable at lower theoretical levels of description (and ultimately at the level of physics). Accordingly, multiple realizability also would not undermine the truth, or the explanatory potential, of higher-level theoretical generalizations either.

Examples abound. In biology, for instance, consider the concept of *cell.* Cells are entities that have certain biologically characterizable distinctive features, and that constitute functional "building blocks" of complex organisms of all sorts. They come in a huge variety of shapes and sizes, and different kinds of cells perform a huge variety of different functions within living organisms. *Maybe* there is some interesting, non-disjunctive, physics-level property that is possessed by all and only cells; or maybe there is not. (I myself have no idea.) If not, this would not impugn the existence of cells, or the scientific legitimacy of the concept of cell, or the truth of biological generalizations about cells. Should it turn out that the entities playing the cell-role within living organisms do not constitute a single kind under any physics-level description, this would mean not that cells do not exist after all, nor that cells do not constitute a biological natural kind, but rather that the sortal property *being a cell* turns out to be multiply realizable at the level of physics.[22]

The concepts of intentional psychology are even more abstract than those of biology. They are strongly realization-neutral vis-à-vis not only the physico-chemical level of description, but also vis-à-vis the neurobiological level. Often in philosophy of mind this point is made vivid by pointing out the possibility that there are intelligent Martians who are composed out of a very different kind of stuff than humans (e.g., silicon rather than organic molecules); who have beliefs, desires, and other intentional states, just as humans do; and in whom these intentional states are realized very differently than in humans — so differently that Martian realizations and human realizations have no interesting, non-disjunctive, physical characteristics in common.

But the Martian example tends to obscure the full extent to which intentional mental concepts are strongly realization-neutral. Multiple realizability might well begin at home. For all we now know (and I emphasize that we really do *not* now know), the intentional mental states we attribute to one another might turn out to be radically multiply realizable at the neurobiological level of description, *even in humans;* indeed, even in *individual* humans; indeed, even in an individual human *given the structure of his central nervous system at a single moment of his life.* A single person S at a single moment t might be capable of undergoing (at t) any of a variety of different physico-chemical states which are quite disparate from one another at the physico-chemical level of description (and perhaps even involve different parts of the brain), each of which would realize (in S) the same intentional mental property — e.g., the property *believing that the Chicago Cubs will win a World Series before the year 2000.* (Henceforth I shall refer to this possibility as *fully* multiple realizability.) Even if intentional mental states turn out to be fully multiply realizable in humans, this outcome would not impugn the integrity of our intentional mental notions, or show that humans do not really have beliefs and desires.[23]

3.3. The Epistemic Autonomy of the Special Sciences

The two above-quoted passages from Fodor also bring into a focus the following important epistemic fact: Generalizations in the special sciences, and statements attributing to individuals the properties that figure in these generalizations, can possess — and often do possess — a high degree of epistemic warrant, quite *independently* of whether or not those higher-level properties are multiply realizable. (The same goes for folk psychology.)

Given that the concepts of the special sciences typically are strongly realization-neutral, and given that the special sciences (and also folk psychology) are very much a going enterprise, this epistemic autonomy should not seem terribly surprising. Since the concepts themselves do not carry any built-in demand for unique realizability, why should the evidential warrant for the generalizations of the special sciences, or for statements attributing higher-level properties to individuals, depend upon whether or not there is evidence of unique realizability? To insist on such evidence would be to shackle the special sciences (and folk psychology) with an epistemic demand that is incommensurate with the strong realization-neutrality of their concepts, a demand that also contravenes established scientific practice. Thus Fodor:

> Reductionism . . . flies in the face of the facts about the scientific institu-
> tion: the existence of a vast and interleaved conglomerate of special scien-
> tific disciplines which often appear to proceed with only the most casual
> acknowledgment of the constraint that their theories must turn out to be
> physics 'in the long run'. Why is this so?[24]

It is so because the integrity of the special sciences just does not require their ultimate reducibility to physics. Metaphysical materialism is consistent with the existence of multiply realizable higher-level natural kinds, and with counterfactual-supporting generalizations over these kinds. It is overwhelmingly likely that there are such kinds — and that intentional mental state types are among them. Once again, Fodor:

> [T]here are special sciences . . . because of the way the world is put together:
> not all kinds (not all the classes of things and events about which there are
> important, counterfactual supporting generalizations to make) are, or corre-
> spond to, physical kinds.[25]

3.4. Local Reduction

It is sometimes suggested that even if the classical conception of reduction is too strong to be a plausible constraint on inter-level fit, nevertheless any naturalistically acceptable higher-level theory or explanatory framework still must be reducible in some *weaker* sense to lower-level theories, and ultimately to physics. In particular, intentional psychology allegedly must be so reducible to neurobiology.

Jaegwon Kim holds such a view.[25] The weakened kind of reduction he demands, which he dubs *local* reduction, involves biconditional bridge laws that are restricted to a class of systems with a specific physical or biological structure. In the case of psychology, the canonical form of such laws would be

$$S \rightarrow [M_i \leftrightarrow P_i],$$

to be read this way: for any physical system with structure S, it is in psychological state M_i at a time just in case it is in physical state P_i at that time.

But even local reduction is too strong a constraint to impose upon inter-level relations, and upon the relation between neurobiology and psychology. For, the considerations of the preceding three subsections are still applicable, *mutatis mutandis*. Take folk psychology, for example. Human beings, as the result of nature's "engineering" activities in the course of evolution and natural selection,' have a physico-biological architecture that implements the design requirements for being a full fledged "true believer" — a (largely) rational agent with beliefs, desires, intentions, and other propositional attitudes. Because of the abstractness of mental concepts, nature might very well have implemented these design requirements in a way that employs *fully* multiple realizations of mental states, in the sense of section 3.2 above. For all we now know (and again I emphasize that we really do *not* know), mentality is implemented in humans in just this way. And, however the story might go for humans, surely the design requirements for being a true believer could be thus implemented in certain *physically possible* kinds of true believers. Accordingly, it is a mistake to insist upon local reducibility as a constraint on inter-level fit between psychology and the physical or biological sciences.[27]

It will be instructive at this point to consider an argument Kim employs in defense of his proposed local reducibility constraint. He writes:

> Consider *jade:* we are told that jade, as it turns out, is not a mineral kind, contrary to what was once believed; rather, jade is comprised of two distinct minerals with dissimilar molecular structures, *jadeite* and *nephrite*. Consider the following generalization:
>
> (L) Jade is green
>
> We may have thought, before the discovery of the dual nature of jade, that (L) was a law, a law about about jade; and we may have thought, with reason, that (L) has been strongly confirmed by all the millions of jade samples that had been observed to be green (and none that had been observed not to be green). We now know better: (L) is really a conjunction of these two laws:
>
> (L₁) Jadeite is green
> (L₂) Nephrite is green
>
> . . . Does (L), "Jade is green," pass the projectibility test? Here we seem to have a problem. For we can imagine this: on re-examining the records of past observations, we find . . . that all positive instances of (L) . . . turn out to have been samples of jadeite, and none of nephrite! If this should happen, we clearly would not, and should not, continue to think of (L) as well confirmed. . . . Let us now . . . [turn] to pain. . . . If pain is nomically equivalent to . . . [a] property claimed to be wildly disjunctive, *then why isn't pain itself equally heterogeneous and nonnomic as a kind?*[28]

The trouble with this argument is that 'jade', insofar as it is employed as a natural-kind term, purports to pick out a *physico-chemical* natural kind. There is simply no distinction to be drawn between a determinate physico-chemical natural kind on the one hand, and its "physico-chemical realization" on the other. Hence, if the purported natural kind exists at all, it cannot be "multiply realizable" physico-chemically. Thus 'jade', *qua* natural-kind term, lacks a crucial feature possessed by intentional mental terms: strong realization-neutrality. So although 'jade' is arguably non-projectible by virtue of applying to two distinct physical natural kinds, this does not sanction the conclusion that intentional mental terms are non-projectible over a domain of creatures for which these terms are — or might be, for all we know — multiply realizable. Kim's argument from analogy is therefore unpersuasive.

The argument does, however, raise an important philosophical question: How, if at all, does the abstractness of intentional mental terms affect their projectibility? This is an intriguing and complex issue, which I cannot discuss here. But this much seems hard to deny: in ordinary life, and also in the special sciences, we routinely project abstract terms without having any idea whether or not they are multiply realized within the domain of individuals over which the projection ranges. In particular, we routinely project *intentional mental* terms, even though (as I stress yet again) we have *no* idea whether or not these terms are fully multiply realized in humans. So although there are interesting epistemological questions about when such projections are epistemically warranted and when they are not, the claim that they are *never* warranted runs violently contrary to actual epistemic practice. Thus the contention that terms are projectible only if we have evidence that they are physically reducible just is not credible. Again I quote Fodor:

> A way of stating the classical reductionist view is that things which belong to different physical kinds ipso facto can have none of their projectible descriptions in common: that if x and y differ in those descriptions by virtue of which they fall under the proper laws of physics, they must differ in those descriptions by virtue of which they fall under any laws at all. But why should we believe that this is so? Any pair of entities, however different their physical structure, must nevertheless converge in indefinitely many of their properties. Why should there not be, among those convergent properties, some whose lawful interrelations support the generalizations of the special sciences? Why, in short, should not the kind predicates of the special sciences *cross-classify* the physical natural kinds?[29]

4. Explanatory Autonomy

Intuitively and pre-theoretically, one thinks of psychological explanation as possessing a certain autonomy or independence, vis-à-vis neurobiological explanation—notwithstanding the fact that psychological states undoubtedly must be realized neurobiologically. One also thinks of higher-level special sciences in general as having this sort of independence, vis-à-vis lower-level ones. In this section I shall propose a way of cashing this intuitive notion of autonomy. If the explication is adequate, and if my discussion in preceding sections is correct, then psychological explanation does indeed possess the autonomy we pre-theoretically think it has. (I will confine the discussion to psychology and neurobiology; but what I say will be generalizable, *mutatis mutandis,* to other special sciences vis-à-vis lower-level ones.)

Terms like 'autonomy' and 'independence' are rather vague. Although this vagueness is actually quite useful, it means that one must proceed with caution in attempting to capture or explicate certain inchoate intuitive beliefs that we are inclined to express using these terms. This is especially true when the very same terms can also be used, in a seemingly contradictory way, to express certain other inchoate intuitive beliefs concerning the same subject matter.

Such is the case with respect to the relation between psychological and neurobiological explanation—especially for someone who espouses a naturalist/materialist metaphysical orientation. On the one hand, there clearly is a sense of 'autonomy' (better: a resolution of its vagueness) under which psychological explanation is *not* autonomous: psychological properties supervene upon non-psychological ones, and psychological causal transactions require underlying neurobiological causal mechanisms.[30] On the other hand, there still seems to be another sense (another vagueness resolution) under which psychological explanation is autonomous anyway. This latter is what I now seek to capture.

As I emphasized in section 3, intentional psychological properties are *abstract* properties, in a certain sense: they are strongly realization-neutral. And according to the CP conception of explanatory relevance I described in section 1, to explain a phenomenon psychologically is to fit it into a CR pattern involving psychological properties and related properties (e.g., act types). Thus, when we explain a phenomenon by fitting into it such a CR pattern, it makes no difference *how* the abstract properties involved in this pattern are neurobiologically realized in humans, as long as they are realized somehow or other. Moreover, it makes no difference whether or not these properties are *uniquely* realizable in humans—as opposed to being either multiply realizable from one human to another, or even fully multiply realizable in each particular human.

Precisely because these things do not matter, psychological explanation has a degree of independence from neurobiological explanation. Thus the strong realization-neutrality of the properties figuring in psychological explanations is, I suggest, a feature that answers directly to our pre-theoretic belief in the explanatory autonomy of psychology. It answers well to that belief, while also accommodating the inter-level constraints described in section 2.

Not surprisingly, this explanatory autonomy goes hand-in-hand with the epistemic autonomy of psychology described in section 3.3. We can, and surely do, possess excellent empirical warrant both for many of our specific attributions of intentional mental states to people, and also for counterfactual-supporting generalizations involving such mental states. This is the case despite the fact that there is currently very little evidence one way or the other concerning unique vs. multiple realizability of these states in humans.

There is another, related, kind of explanatory autonomy for psychology. This kind comes in degrees, and it is an open empirical question how extensive it is. It involves the extent to which mental properties and the neurobiological properties which realize them diverge in their extensions, both in the actual world and in other physically possible worlds—i.e., the extent to which psychological kinds "cross-classify" neurobiological kinds (as Fodor puts it).

That there is *some* cross-classification seems virtually guaranteed by the fact that psychological properties are strongly realization-neutral. Surely there are physically possible creatures in which psychological properties are realized quite differently than in humans; and surely there are also physically possible creatures in which psychological properties are fully multiply realizable. But psychology might or might not turn out to cross-classify neurobiology *locally*, i.e., among humankind.

The more local cross-classification there is, the greater is the extent to which psychology is autonomous from neurobiology in this second way. But of course nonreductive materialism cannot insist upon local cross-classificatory autonomy, since it is entirely an *empirical* question whether, and to what extent, psychology locally cross-classifies neurobiology. What nonreductive materialism does insist upon, rather, is the first kind of autonomy: the strong realization-neutrality of the properties that figure in psychological explanation.

5. Explaining Supervenience Relations

To what extent does the idea of supervenience help deal with the interrelations between mental and neurobiological causal explanation? In my view, the concept of supervenience actually raises more questions than it answers. For, in any metaphysical framework that deserves labels like 'materialism', 'naturalism', or 'physicalism', supervenience facts must be explainable rather than being *sui generis.*

This is a large topic, but I do want to address it very briefly. So I will conclude this essay in sharply staccato fashion, by making a series of rapid-fire remarks without pausing for qualification, elaboration, or argument.[31]

First, any form of materialism/naturalism should assert that if there are any unexplainable facts about world, they are certain explanatorily fundamental physical facts. (Fundamental *physical regularities,* as opposed to certain *particular* physical facts, are perhaps the most plausible candidates for this status.)

Second, metaphysical materialism/naturalism should therefore include the requirement that inter-level supervenience facts be explainable, rather than being themselves included among the fundamental, unexplainable facts about the world. (From a materialist/naturalist perspective, one important reason to reject G. E. Moore's meta-ethical position is his claim that certain synthetic necessary truths of the form 'Anything with natural property N is intrinsically valuable' are utterly *sui generis* and unexplainable.)

Third, even if a higher-level theory or explanatory framework happens to be classically or locally reducible to physics, inter-level supervenience facts need to be explained anyway. Biconditional bridge laws are not part of physics either, and hence should not themselves be *sui generis* and unexplainable.

Fourth, the requirement that supervenience relations be explainable is inherently problematic, however, because of what I call the *standpoint problem:* the problem of finding allowable explanatory resources. On the one hand, it would seem that the only kosher resources are the fundamental facts of physics, the ultimate unexplained explainers. On the other hand, it is hard to see how one could possibly explain inter-level supervenience facts without allowing oneself *some* sort of information about higher-level properties, concepts, or terminology.

Fifth, one potential strategy for meeting the explanation requirement is to allow oneself, as a supplemental explanatory resource, *semantic* facts about higher-level terms and concepts. Perhaps semantic facts plus physical facts can, in principle, explain all supervenience facts.

Sixth, perhaps the supervenience of semantic facts can itself be explained without vicious circularity, even though semantic facts also are employed as an explanatory resource. (This would finesse the standpoint problem.) Imagine, for instance, the hermeneutic perspective of an English-speaking LaPlacean Demon who is given a complete physics-level description of the world and must deduce from this, plus his knowledge of English, a complete description (in English) of all higher-level facts about the world. The Demon would have to deduce, "from the ground up," the semantic facts about the various languages spoken by Earthlings. His knowledge of English would not necessarily help him deduce the semantic facts about the Earthling sentences that happen to be in English, since he would have to work from raw *physics-level* descriptions of Earthlings and their verbal/symbolic output.

Seventh, there is reason to suspect, however, that semantic facts themselves are dependent upon certain facts about the intentional mental states of language users — for instance, communicative intentions, intentions to refer, and the like. If so, then psychological facts too would perhaps have to figure among the resources required to explain physical/nonphysical supervenience relations. And this, in turn, would seriously exacerbate the standpoint problem, threatening vicious circularity in the explanatory project.

Eighth, certain important supervenience relations, over and above those that figure in ethics, involve normativity — and thus an is-ought gap. In particular, there is a normative element involved in *intentional content* — both the content of public-language expressions, and the content of intentional mental states. The "Kripkenstein problem,"[32] for instance, can be seen as a skeptical challenge about whether there are any objective facts or properties, there in the world, that could ground semantic *correctness* (like the putative correctness of answering '125' to the query '68 + 57'). And a parallel problem can be raised about the objective groundability of a putative correct/incorrect distinction for the putative semantic content of people's mental states.

Ninth, the task of explaining supervenience facts, including psychophysical supervenience facts, therefore apparently includes the task of explaining how certain objective, in-the-world, is-ought gaps get bridged. No small task!

Tenth, metaphysical skepticism about in-the-world normative facts — a kind of skepticism which after all has been very prominent in metaethics — now threatens to spill over into philosophy of mind and philosophy of language (not to mention epistemology, since *epistemic warrant* is a normative concept, too). This threat, plus the standpoint problem, constitute potential motives for going eliminativist about mentality (and/or intentionality in language, and/or epistemic warrant). Just when one thought one had the eliminativists on the defensive, the world as we know it threatens to disappear!

To summarize this section: In my view, the concept of supervenience is considerably less helpful in dealing with quandaries about psychophysical relations than it is often thought to be. Supervenience facts should be naturalistically explainable, rather than being metaphysically *sui generis,* but it is far from clear how this constraint could be met satisfactorily, and the difficulties largely center upon the intentionality of mentality. So supervenience does not solve the mind/body problem, but only points us toward yet another version of it.[32]

Notes

1. My view is "robustly realist" insofar as it treats these as no less real, and/or no less legitimate, than (say) tables, persons, molecules, physical causation, or physicalistic causal explanation. But I am not a so-called "metaphysical realist" about any of these things. In my "Metaphysical Realism and Psychologistic Semantics," *Erkenntnis* 34 (1991): 297–322, I espouse a general ontological position that countenances only one entity (the entire physical universe) within its ontology and denies that the cosmos literally contains any proper components. This view, which I call "Parmenidean materialism," has affinities with Kantian transcendental idealism.

2. My discussion on this section draws largely on section 5.i of my "Actions, Reasons, and the Explanatory Role of Content," in B. McLaughlin, ed., *Dretske and His Critics* (Oxford: Basil Blackwell, 1991); and section 2 of Terence Horgan and John Tienson, "Soft Laws," *Midwest Studies in Philosophy* 15 (1990): 256–279.

3. James Woodward, "Scientific Explanation," *British Journal for the Philosophy of Science* 30 (1979): 41–67, pp. 54–55.

4. Ibid., 57.

5. This point has been widely under-appreciated in philosophy of science.

6. For one proposed way of further elaborating the generic CP conception of explanatory relevance, with specific attention to the explanatory role of intentional mental properties, see my "Mental Quausation," *Philosophical Perspectives* 3 (1989): 49–76.

7. I elaborate this point in "Actions, Reasons, and the Explanatory Role of Content," section 5.iii. There I also address the currently widespread belief that intentional mental properties with so-called "wide content" cannot be explanatorily relevant to human behavior. I hypothesize that this belief — which under the CP account of explanatory relevance is just mistaken — arises largely through failure to notice subtle shifts in the context-relative parameters that govern explanation. (Under the parameters that normally govern the neurobiological explanation of behavior, explanatorily relevant properties must supervene upon what is in the head. Not so under the parameters that normally govern psychological explanation.) A similar account can be harnessed, I believe, to explain away a related, but broader, intuition that sometimes takes hold when one reflects on psycho-physical relations: viz., that if human bodily motions are fully explainable neurobiologically, then human behavior cannot also be explainable psychologically.

8. These examples are taken from Paul Churchland, *Scientific Realism and*

the Plasticity of Mind (Cambridge: Cambridge University Press, 1979), 184. The *'ceteris paribus'* clauses are my own addition.

9. Jerry Fodor, *Representations* (Cambridge, Mass.: Bradford-MIT, 1981), 141.

10. Jerry Fodor, *Psychosemantics* (Cambridge, Mass.: Bradford-MIT, 1987), 5-6.

11. Terence Horgan and John Tienson, "Representations without Rules," *Philosophical Topics* 17 (1989): 147-174; and "Soft Laws."

12. Jaegwon Kim, "Explanatory Realism, Causal Realism, and Explanatory Exclusion," *Midwest Studies in Philosophy* 12 (1988): 225-240, pp. 226-227.

13. In my "Supervenience and Microphysics," *Pacific Philosophical Quarterly* 63 (1982): 29-43, I proposed a single supervenience thesis that sought to capture all three dimensions and also sharpen the third one. I introduced the notion of a *P-region:* roughly, a spatio-temporal region of a physically possible world. I also introduced the notion of a *qualitative* intrinsic feature of a P-region: roughly, an intrinsic feature whose instantiation does not depend logically upon the existence of a specific individual (e.g., Oscar Peterson), over against a distinct molecule-for-molecule replica (e.g., an Oscar Peterson *doppelganger*), within the region. And I employed the term 'microphysics' to refer to the most fundamental aspects of (ideal) physics. Using these notions, I formulated the proposed supervenience thesis this way:

> There do not exist any two P-regions that are exactly alike in all qualitative intrinsic microphysical respects but different in some other qualitative intrinsic microphysical respect.

For further relevant discussion see Jaegwon Kim, "'Strong' and 'Global' Supervenience Revisited," *Philosophy and Phenomenological Research* 48 (1987): 315-326; and "The Myth of Nonreductive Materialism," *Proceedings of the American Philosophical Association* 63 (1989): 31-47.

14. Jerry Fodor is describing essentially the same constraint, I take it, in the following passage in his "Making Mind Matter More," *Philosophical Topics* 17 (1989): 59-79:

> [A] metaphysically interesting difference between basic and nonbasic laws is that, in the case of the latter but not the former, there always has to be a *mechanism in virtue of which* the satisfaction of its antecedent brings about the satisfaction of its consequent. If 'Fs cause Gs' is basic, then there is no answer to the question *how* do Fs cause Gs; they just do, and that they do is among the not-to-be-further-explained facts about how the world is put together. Whereas, if 'Fs cause Gs' is *nonbasic,* then there is always a story about what goes on when—and in virtue of which—Fs cause Gs (p. 66).

I agree with the substance of these remarks, *provided* they are interpreted as leaving open the possibility that the story about the underlying causal mechanism can differ from one *F*-causing-*G* transaction to another. Although the quoted passage is ambiguous about this point, I think Fodor himself should prefer my recommended reading because of other views of his that will figure prominently in section 3 below.

15. Sometimes when a single phenomenon is causally explainable at a variety of different levels, there also will be a hierarchy of supervenience relations among properties at the different levels. However, one cannot assume that the properties figuring in a higher-level explanation of the phenomenon are directly supervenient upon the lower-level properties that realize them (on the given occasion). For example, when a person instantiates a propositional attitude state-type with wide content, this property is realized by some neurobiological state-type intrinsic to what is going on neurally in the person's head at the time; yet a lower-level supervenience base for the wide-content intentional state must include, in addition the instantiation of this intrinsic neurobiological property, lower-level facts that are extrinsic to what is in the head.

16. This subsection draws largely upon section 5.ii of my "Actions, Reasons, and the Explanatory Role of Content."

17. Colin McGinn, *Mental Content* (Oxford: Basil Blackwell, 1989), 145–147. McGinn acknowledges his strong indebtedness to Ruth Millikan, *Language, Thought, and Other Biological Categories* (Cambridge, Mass.: Bradford-MIT, 1984). It should be noted that the notion of relational proper function can be invoked in at least three ways in philosophy of mind: (i) for an account of mental content itself; (ii) for an account of the explanatory relevance of content; or (iii) for an account of the non-accidentality of generalizations and CR patterns involving intentional mental states. Millikan, as I understand her, explicitly envisions employing the notion for purpose (i). McGinn evidently envisions using it for both (i) and (ii); and the same goes for Fred Dretske, *Explaining Behavior* (Cambridge, Mass.: Bradford-MIT, 1988). I myself, however, am only suggesting invoking relational proper function for purpose (iii). I am officially neutral—and unofficially rather skeptical—about its usability for purpose (i). And although I think it has *some* import for the explanatory relevance of intentional mental properties—viz., its connection to non-accidentality—I would deny that an adequate account of explanatory relevance can be framed directly in terms of relational proper function. For elaboration of this last point, see my "Actions, Reasons, and the Explanatory Role of Content."

18. Kim, "The Myth of Nonreductive Materialism"; and "Multiple Realization and the Metaphysics of Reduction," *Philosophy and Phenomenological Research* 52 (1992): 1–26.

19. See, for instance, Ernest Nagel, *The Structure of Science* (New York: Harcourt, Brace, and World, 1961); Kenneth Schaffner, "Approaches to Reduction," *Philosophy of Science* 34 (1967): 137–147; Lawrence Sklar, "Types of Inter-Theoretic Reduction," *British Journal for the Philosophy of Science* 18 (1967): 109–124; and Hilary Putnam, "On Properties," in N. Rescher, ed., *Essays in Honor of Carl G. Hempel* (Dordrecht: Reidel, 1969). In light of the fact that scientific generalizations usually involve parameterized magnitudes (as stressed in section 1), it is worth noting that a biconditional bridge law really identifies, or nomically correlates, not just a *single* higher-level property with a single lower-level property, but rather a whole array (typically an infinite array) of property pairs. (There are infinitely many

determinate temperature properties, for instance, one for each value of the numerical variable in a predicate like 'has temperature r in degrees centigrade'. Likewise, there are infinitely many mean-molecular-kinetic-energy properties.) But for convenience of exposition, in the text I will defer to the common philosophical practice of talking about bridge laws as though they each involve just a single higher-level and lower-level property.

20. Jerry Fodor, "Special Sciences," *Synthese* 28 (1974): 77–115, reprinted in his *Representations*. Quoted from p. 133 of the reprinted version.

21. Ibid., 133–134.

22. For a detailed defense of the multiple realizability of certain key theoretical properties in biology, see Harold Kincaid, "Molecular Biology and the Unity of Science," *Philosophy of Science* 57 (1990): 575–593.

23. For further defense of this claim, see Terence Horgan and George Graham, "In Defense of Southern Fundamentalism," *Philosophical Studies* 62 (1991): 107–134.

24. Fodor, *Representations*, 144.

25. Ibid.

26. Kim, "The Myth of Nonreductive Materialism"; and "Multiple Realization and the Metaphysics of Reduction."

27. Thus it is also a mistake to construe mental terms as (functionally definable) non-rigid designators of physico-chemical state-types, as does David Lewis, "An Argument for the Identity Theory," *Journal of Philosophy* 63 (1966): 17–25; and "Psychophysical and Theoretical Identifications," *Australasian Journal of Philosophy* 50 (1972): 249–258. Allowing such terms to designate in a population-relative way (as does Lewis in "Mad Pain and Martian Pain," in N. Block, ed., *Readings in the Philosophy of Psychology, Volume One* [Cambridge, Mass.: Harvard University Press 1980], 216–222) does not overcome the problem, because this refined construal still is committed to local type-type psychophysical identities, and thus to local reducibility. For further related discussion, including an account of how Lewis's general format for functionally defining mental terms can be adapted to suit a position that eschews type-type psychophysical identities or correlation laws, see my "Functionalism and Token Physicalism," *Synthese* 59 (1984): 321–338.

28. Kim, "Multiple Realization and the Metaphysics of Reduction," 11–15.

29. Fodor, *Representations*, 144–145.

30. Jaegwon Kim, in "Explanatory Realism, Causal Realism, and Explanatory Exclusion" and "Mechanism, Purpose, and Explanatory Exclusion," *Philosophical Perspectives* 3 (1989): 77–108, defends a principle he calls *explanatory exclusion*, which states that "two or more complete and independent explanations of the same event or phenomenon cannot coexist" ("Mechanism, Purpose, and Explanatory Exclusion," 89). Although he does not attempt to characterize in general terms what he means by completeness and independence, it seems clear in context that he is using these notions in such a way that the inter-level constraints I described in section 2 prevent all psychological causal explanations from being either "complete" or "independent" explanations. So as far as I can tell, my discussion in this essay is fully compatible with Kim's thesis. I do think, however, that the phrase 'explanatory exclusion principle' is a somewhat misleading name for the thesis,

since this label suggests that explanations which are not "complete" and "independent" in Kim's sense cannot be autonomous in *any* interesting or important sense — or anyway, not in any interesting or important sense involving metaphysical aspects of explanation (over and above mere epistemological ones). This suggestion I would deny.

31. Some of the themes I shall mention are pursued at greater length in my "Supervenient Bridge Laws," *Philosophy of Science* 45 (1978): 227–249; "Token Physicalism, Supervenience, and the Generality of Physics," *Synthese* 49 (1981): 395–413; and "Supervenience and Cosmic Hermeneutics," *Southern Journal of Philosophy* 22 (1984), Spindel Conference Supplement, 19–38; and in Terence Horgan and Mark Timmons, "Troubles on Moral Twin Earth: Moral Queerness Revived," *Synthese,* in press.

32. Saul Kripke, *Wittgenstein on Rules and Private Language* (Cambridge, Mass.: Harvard University Press, 1982).

33. This essay was presented at a conference on Mental Causation at the Center for Interdisciplinary Research of the University of Bielefeld, in April 1990. I thank David Henderson, Jay Rosenberg (my commentator at the conference), and John Tienson for helpful discussion and comments.

What Beliefs Are Not

LYNNE RUDDER BAKER

In recent years, philosophers have come to take it for granted that beliefs are inner states of individuals that cause behavior. Since it is assumed to be the business of science to discover causes, the view that beliefs are internal causes of behavior leads to an obvious research question: Are beliefs (and other attitudes) understandable as scientifically respectable entities, or should we deny their existence altogether? I want to consider a presupposition about the nature of belief that lies behind this research question. The presupposition is that beliefs have tokens that are identical with, or supervene upon, instances of brain states. Although I take Cartesian dualism to be dead, I am also skeptical that beliefs are internal states in the sense that contemporary philosophers assume,[1] all the more so since the attempts to spell out such a view, I believe, have been unsuccessful.[2]

My aim here is further to undermine conceptions of beliefs as physically realized inner causes by presenting two arguments — one against views that combine the notion of belief as physically realized inner cause with a language-of-thought hypothesis, the other against a leading view that combines the notion of belief as physically realized inner cause with an account of belief-as-indication. The first argument questions the physical reality of syntactic properties; the second questions the causal efficacy of semantic properties. Then, I shall suggest a way to understand belief other than as an internal state without courting Cartesian dualism.

According to the view that I want to consider, to believe that p is to have an internal state that means that p or has the content that p. On this view, being a belief that p is (or purports to be) a property of particular internal states, and a belief that p is an internal state that has that property; a person, then, *has* a belief that p in virtue of having an internal state that *is* a belief that p. What makes a particular internal state a belief that p may be determined in part by its relations to the environment; but even if the property of being a belief that p is a relational property, on the view under consideration, the bearer of the property of being a belief that *p* is an internal state. So, the notion that belief is an internal state does not require that beliefs be construed individualistically or narrowly.

Such a view of belief is, I think, almost universally accepted today both by philosophers who think that there are beliefs and by philosophers (eliminative materialists) who think that there are not any beliefs. The eliminative materialists, of course, deny that there are any beliefs, but, they think, if there were any, they would be internal states. Indeed, the eliminative materialists' arguments *require* that beliefs, if there were any, be internal states for their arguments infer from the (alleged) fact that the sciences that study internal states have no use for beliefs (or anything like them) that there are no beliefs. Such an argument obviously rests on the tacit premise that if there are beliefs, then they are internal states. So, to discredit the conception of beliefs as internal states would be to discredit eliminative materialism along with what Fodor calls Intentional Realism.

Let us turn to two attempts by friends of belief to fill out a picture of beliefs as internal states.

Syntax and the Problem of the Parameter

To account for the compositionality and generativity of beliefs, many philosophers have argued that beliefs must be syntactically structured internal states. To hold that internal states have syntactic structure is to embrace a minimal hypothesis of a language of thought.[3] The idea is that syntax is, as William G. Lycan says, "psychologically real," that is, syntax is physically realized by structures in the brain. Since syntax is assumed to be fully determined by, or to supervene on, brain structure, syntactic properties are thought to cause behavior.

Since the language-of-thought hypothesis seems made to order to explain linguistic behavior, I shall focus on utterances as caused by internal states with syntactic structure. Let me make a simplifying assumption: Suppose that we can identify certain utterances as "standard" in the following way: They are sincere, assertive utterances that *p* that are directly produced by a belief that *p* and a desire to assert that *p*. (Call the belief that *p* that produces a standard utterance that *p* the 'associated belief.') This assumption may be grossly implausible, but, as we shall see, even sticking with standard utterances, matters are not simple.

How is the syntactic structure of a belief to be determined? One prominent suggestion that is reasonably well worked out is Lycan's: Associated with every sentence is a "semantic representation," which displays the logical form of the sentence and which can serve as input for syntactic transformations. For each belief that one tokens, say, that snow is white, there is an internal sentence that gives the logical form of the sentence 'snow is white'. Now suppose that someone issues a standard utterance of 'I am tired now'. What is the appropriate syntax to attribute to the associated belief? One obvious suggestion is that the syntax has parameters for the indexical elements. So, we must allow for indexical and other contextual elements to be provided for in the syntax of beliefs.

Call features of context that affect the truth conditions of a sentence or belief 'semantically relevant features'. In public language, a hearer's appreciation of context may contribute to the causal relevance of an utterance. For example, suppose that Jill's shouting to Jack, "There's a charging bull," causes Jack to jump a fence. The utterance has its effect in part in virtue of its meaning: Jack understands it; as an English speaker, he knows what it means. With the language of thought, however, the situation is different. If Jack's jumping the fence is caused by his belief that there is a charging bull—a belief that he may have acquired by understanding Jill's warning—the belief has its effect (of propelling Jack's body over the fence) solely in virtue of the syntax of the internal sentence. (As Lycan says, concurring with Harman, "I do not 'understand' my own language of thought in the same sense in which I understand a natural language."[4]) In the language of thought, those features of context that can make a difference in behavior must be explicitly represented in the brain. There is not a similar constraint on the representation of the logical forms of sentences in public languages, where salient features of context may be taken for granted.[5]

Since the causal efficacy of sentences in the language of thought is wholly determined by internal states of the agent, every element whose presence or absence can affect behavior must be represented in the brain. So, whether or not public language requires that every semantically relevant feature be represented in logical form, the function of the syntax of the language of thought in causing behavior requires that every semantically relevant feature be explicitly represented in logical form and physically encoded in the brain.

So, the syntactic structure of any belief must have a "slot" (a parameter or a variable) for each semantically relevant feature. For example, in the case of "I am tired now," the syntactic structure of the belief must have parameters for speaker and for time. Obviously, there are many other contextual elements that must be syntactically represented in the internal state. For example, there are all sorts of hidden parameters in ordinary discourse ("I gave it to the woman on the left"—on the left of what?). The belief that standardly would cause assertion of "I gave it to the woman on the left" must have a "slot" for the hidden parameter to be filled in by whatever the woman was to the left of.[6]

For this picture to serve its purpose of showing how syntactically structured internal belief states cause behavior, it must impose two constraints on the syntactic structure of beliefs:

(A) Syntactically distinct beliefs have physically distinct realizations in the brain.

(B) A belief with n parameters is syntactically distinct from a belief with $n + 1$ parameters.

(A) is simply the requirement that syntax is to be physically represented in the brain. (B) may seem more controversial: after all, semantical indices are not always marked in surface sentences; so why must they be marked in neural entities? Regardless of how we think of the semantics of public language, semantical indices would still have to be marked in the language of thought if the language of thought is to play its causal role in producing behavior. The neural entity is supposed to be a syntactically structured inner cause: it must be able to cause behavior in virtue of its syntactic properties. Anything that can make a difference in behavior must be represented syntactically in the brain. Differences in number of parameters are differences in number of semantically relevant features; this kind of difference in truth condition (as opposed to twin-earth differences) can make a difference in behavior, and hence must be reflected in different physical realizations in the brain.

Unfortunately, (A) and (B) lead straight to trouble. The problem arises for any term that some people take to be relational, and others take to be nonrelational; terms of morals and manners come readily to mind. It also arises for terms, like 'tall,' which apply to objects only relative to some implicit reference class; again, semantically relevant features that may remain implicit in a public language must be made explicit in the language of thought. I shall illustrate the general difficulty by an example from science since we agree on its correct truth conditions, but I emphasize that the problem is not confined to theoretical contexts. Consider various standard utterances of the following English sentence:[7]

(s) An event on the sun is not simultaneous with anyone's seeing it.

The first utterance is by a nineteenth-century Newtonian physicist; the second utterance is by a twentieth-century Einsteinian physicist. Do the associated beliefs, realized in the brains of the speakers, have the same syntactic structure or not?

Suppose this is the case. Assuming that Einstein's theory, with a frame-of-reference parameter for simultaneity, gives the actual truth conditions of (s), then the Einsteinian's associated belief must represent all the semantically relevant features of (s) and the internal sentence must have a frame-of-reference parameter. On the current alternative, the Newtonian's associated belief must also have a frame-of-reference parameter. Question: How did a frame-of-reference parameter get into the Newtonian's head?

In the unlikely event that we could answer that question, more are waiting in the wings. Since the Newtonian would deny that simultaneity was relative to inertial frame, must we conclude that the Newtonian did not understand Newtonian physics? What about Newton himself? Must we say that in maintaining absolute simultaneity, he did not know what he was talking about? What are *we* saying when we say, "Newton believed that simultaneity was absolute"? And when Aristotle said: "Those things are called *simultaneous* without qualification and most strictly which come into being at the same time" (Categories 14b25), did he have a frame of reference parameter in his head?

On the current alternative of saying that all the standard utterances of (s) have the same truth conditions, which are given by relativity theory, there is no way even to entertain the possibility of absolute simultaneity. For if all standard utterances of (s) have a frame-of-reference parameter, then it is difficult to see how even to formulate truth conditions for an assertion of absolute simultaneity. Assuming that there is no difference in meaning between two tokens of an expression, one in a standard utterance, and the other in a counterfactual, the following becomes unintelligible (on the current alternative): "If Newton had been right, then simultaneity would have been absolute" (= 'it would have been the case that: simultaneity is absolute').

Moreover, if the correct truth conditions for (s) are already encoded in Newton's brain, then the correct theories are already represented in our brains before they are 'discovered.' In that case, to find out about the physical world, we should not do physics, but psychology and linguistics. Thus, it seems hopeless to suppose that the beliefs associated with standard utterances of (s) of the Newtonian and Einsteinian physicists are internal states with the same syntactic structure. So, turn to the other alternative.

Suppose that the physically realized beliefs associated with the Newtonian's and Einsteinian's standard utterances of (s) have different syntactic structures. Then, presumably, the Einsteinian's internal state has a frame-of-reference parameter that the Newtonian's lacks. In that case, 'simultaneous' would be ambiguous. Of course, on some radical conceptions of theory-change, it is ambiguous. Let us investigate the implications of ambiguity for the language-of-thought hypothesis.

To bring out the difficulty, I shall set up an example in a way that highlights exactly the relevant points. In order to avoid extraneous issues,

I am making the example empirically improbable; but the empirical improbability is a feature of the example, not of the phenomena being illustrated. Suppose that the Newtonian and Einsteinian each has a daughter and a son; it happens that the daughters, who have been brought up in restricted environments, have been subjected to exactly the same sensory stimulation over their lifetimes, and that at the time we encounter them, their brains are in the same state. Suppose that both parents, emitting exactly the same noises, tell their respective daughters that it takes time for light to get to Earth from the sun, and hence that (s). Now, suppose that, in each scene, the brother arrives, and each daughter (flushed with new knowledge) issues a standard utterance of (s).

On the current alternative, internal states that are the beliefs associated with Newtonian and Einsteinian physicists' respective standard utterances of (s) differ in truth condition: the Einsteinian's, but not the Newtonian's, internal state has a frame-of-reference parameter. If we also assume that their daughters' similar beliefs inherit their parents' truth conditions (otherwise, it would be miraculous that anyone ever learned a language), then at least one of the constraints, (A) or (B), is violated. Since up until their parents informed them about simultaneity, the daughters' brains were in the same state, and the information about simultaneity was transmitted by means of physically identical sounds, they do not now have different physical realizations in their brains; so by (A), their internal states are syntactically the same. But since, by assumption, one internal state has a frame-of-reference parameter but the other does not, their beliefs have syntactic structures with different numbers of parameters; hence, by (B) their internal states are syntactically distinct. Hence, (A) and (B) lead to contradiction.

Lycan has replied to this by holding, at least tentatively, that "'simultaneous' remains a two-place predicate for ordinary people but has become a three-place predicate for the *cognoscenti*."[8] Then, since neither daughter knows physics, "presumably neither has the three-place predicate on board." First, note that this implicitly denies that language-learners inherit the truth conditions of their teachers; as I said parenthetically, this consequence would seem to make language-learning generally a mystery. Perhaps one could say that usually learners inherit truth conditions from their teachers, but in this case they do not. However, such a move sounds ad hoc to me. What reason, other than a need to solve the problem, is there to think that this case of language-learning differs from standard cases in which learners do inherit truth conditions from their teachers? In any case, the reply seems empty in the absence of some account of how learning a theory affects the syntax of an internal sentence.

Moreover, the current alternative adds to the difficulties of the incommensurability thesis of the relation between theories, by supposing the incommensurable relations between theories to be reflected in the physical structures of the brain. On the current alternative, the Newtonian says nothing false when she says, "Simultaneity is not relative to a frame of reference." For the Newtonian's utterance has different truth conditions from the Einsteinian's; on the current alternative, the Newtonian's utterance is true if and only if simultaneity construed as a two-place relation is not relative to frame, and it obviously is. Moreover, the Einsteinian and the Newtonian do not disagree when one says, "Simultaneity is absolute," and the other says, "Simultaneity is relative." Lycan's reply seems to subject his view to all the counterintuitive consequences of the "incommensurability" view of theory change.

Therefore, it seems that either answer to the question — Do standard utterances of (s) by both Newtonians and Einsteinians have the same truth conditions? — comes to grief when we assume that syntax is "psychologically real." So, I think that the language-of-thought hypothesis is afflicted with what we might call 'the problem of the parameter'.[9]

Actually, to use an example like 'simultaneity' underestimates the problem of the parameter for the language-of-thought hypothesis. For, as already suggested, the problem of the parameter may be generated by any hidden parameter: Consider representations of 'slurping soup is impolite' in the heads of an absolutist and a relativist. In the scientific case, theories provide accounts of which features are the semantically relevant ones. But in most ordinary contexts, things are not so tidy. We have no general theory of semantically relevant features, nor will we until we solve the frame problem.

And until we do solve the frame problem, it seems to me that we have no theory whatsoever, only a relabeling of the problem. To say, as Lycan does, that all contextual elements are handled via an all-purpose assignment function is not to say anything informative, in the absence of some account of what features are semantically relevant in general. Otherwise, the only available specification of the assignment function is that it takes as arguments all the different parameters realized in the brain and returns as values all and only semantically relevant features of the context, whatever they may be.

Note that I am not talking here about empirical work on how the brain functions to encode the requisite parameters, nor am I asking for mechanisms that show how the brain computes the values for the assignment function. I am asking the prior question of what parameters need to be encoded (by whatever mechanisms). For the language-of-thought proposal to work, we need a context-free theory of context. However, I see no such theory in the offing. Lycan remains unmoved: "our present or even future inability to specify a context does not matter to the thesis that a determinate assignment function exists."[10] Inability to specify a context may not count against whether or not a determinate assignment function exists, but it does count against the usefulness of such a postulated function for the theoretical purposes to which it is put.

In any case, the problem of the parameter would seem to afflict any account of beliefs as syntactically structured internal states. Since any language-of-thought hypothesis assumes that syntax is physically realized in brains and any such hypothesis must accommodate semantically relevant features of context in some way, the problem of the parameter is not peculiar to Lycan's view. Rather, any view that takes the syntax of internal sentences to cause behavior must have some way to specify the syntactical features of the language of thought that avoids these difficulties. These examples show that we can not simply assume that it makes sense to think of the brain as organized in terms of states that generally realize syntactic properties.

Semantics and the Problem of the Circle

The second kind of problem with the idea that beliefs are internal causes concerns the meanings of intentional states. While the possibility of internal states with syntactic properties has largely gone unquestioned, the possibility of internal states with semantic properties has been fiercely debated. It is now generally agreed that semantic properties like meaning or content — properties in virtue of which states have truth conditions — are relational properties. The truth conditions of a person's beliefs depend in part on the character of the person's environment. Assuming again that beliefs are internal states, this recognition leads to the task of showing how relational semantic properties of an internal state can be causally relevant to behavior.[11] Meaning, or a state's having meaning, must help explain the behavior produced. Otherwise, meaning is simply epiphenomenal.

The *prima facie* problem is this: Meaning or content is a relational property of internal states, but the properties that actually cause bodily movements are nonrelational. If this is right, how can relational properties have any kind of causal or explanatory role in behavior? Fred Dretske tries to meet this challenge by showing how meaning, though a relational property of internal states, can have a causal role in behavior. Dretske's account, like other naturalistic accounts of meaning for internal states, is two-tiered. At the ground level, meaning is linked directly to the (nonintentional, nonsemantic) physical world; then, with those naturalistic credentials in hand, other kinds of meaning may have social, linguistic, and intentional components. I shall focus solely on the ground-level account.

On Dretske's view, the idea of cause as a nonrelational property of an agent that produces a particular bodily movement is too narrow. Suppose that an internal token of type C causes a token of bodily-motion type M on a certain occasion. Then the token of C is a triggering cause: given the background conditions in which a $C \rightarrow M$ process is (in some sense) realized in the brain, the token of C brought about the token of M. However, Dretske says, the behavior also has another kind of cause: the fact that the $C \rightarrow M$ process is structured the way that it is. What brought it about that the $C \rightarrow M$ process is structured the way that it is Dretske calls the 'structuring cause' of the behavior.[12] The causal role for meaning, on Dretske's view, is to be found in structuring causes, not triggering causes.[13]

Dretske builds up his account from the basic relation of indication. Since beliefs are identified by their meanings, the idea is to give an account of what an internal state means or represents in terms of what it indicates. Indication is a relation between token events: token event b of type B indicates a token event a of type A iff (i) a caused b and (ii) there is a reliable covariation between type-B-events and type-A-events. If a B-token indicates an A, then we may say that 'A' is the natural meaning of the B-token. Obviously, indication or natural meaning is insufficient for representation. For there is no representation without the possibility of misrepresentation, and there is no possibility of "misindication." So, an indication theorist must move from indication (or natural meaning) to something that allows for error. One way to do this is to define a new relation: having the function of indicating something. C may have the function of indicating F even if, on occasion, a token of C fails to indicate F (e.g., the token of C is caused by something that is not F).

What is needed, and what Dretske supplies, is a naturalistic, ground-level account of how a natural indicator of F acquires the function of indicating F. Let C be a natural indicator of F. Then C acquires the function of indicating F if C is "recruited" (by a learning process) as a cause of M, where M is a bodily movement, and C is so recruited because C indicates F. The recruitment structures a $C \rightarrow M$ process, so that, after the learning period, tokens of C cause tokens of M. Since it is because C indicates F that C is recruited as a cause of M, C's indicating F is (in Dretske's terms) a structuring cause of the behavior M. C then has the function of indicating F when the fact that C indicates F becomes a structuring cause of some behavior. Finally, C's meaning or representing F is understood in terms of C's having the function to indicate F, where C acquired that function via a naturalistic learning process. ('F' becomes the non-natural meaning of C.)

Now suppose that, after a $C \rightarrow M$ process is established in this naturalistic way, a token of C occurs and produces the bodily motion M. Then, on Dretske's view, meaning has a causal (and hence explanatory) role in the production of M, in virtue of the fact that C's indicating F is a structuring cause of the $C \rightarrow M$ process. I believe that my remarks, though compact, accurately represent the structure of Dretske's view. What I wish to show now is that it is thoroughly circular.

On the account just given, a state has meaning in the first place in virtue of its causal role in behavior. We begin with the notion of a (structuring) causal role, and derive the meaning of a state. That is, Dretske's naturalistic account of meaning entails:

(a) A state C has meaning in virtue of its causal role in behavior.[14]

However, Dretske's goal is to show "how ordinary explanations, explanations couched in terms of an agent's *reasons,* explain" (*EB* 52). The assumption is that reasons are attitudes like beliefs, desires, and intentions construed as internal state types and individuated by what they mean. So the goal is to show how an internal state's having meaning has an explanatory role in behavior. Like other physicalists, Dretske equates explanatory role and causal role. If this is the goal, then Dretske is committed to the following:

(b) A state C has a causal role in behavior in virtue of having meaning.

(a) and (b) form a tight circle.[15] The circle is apparent in Dretske's characterization of beliefs as "those representations whose causal role in the production of output is determined by their meaning or content — by the way they represent what they represent" (*EB* 52). If, as the account has it, meaning is itself determined by (structuring) causal role, then that same (structuring) causal role cannot in turn be determined by meaning.

Let me anticipate two objections: (i) Perhaps 'causal role' is used equivocally. (a) and (b) do not really form a circle if 'causal role in behavior' does not refer to the same thing in both theses. The reply is that 'causal role' does refer to the same in both: the causal role in structuring the $C \rightarrow M$ process. The only causal role for meaning, on Dretske's view, is as a structuring cause of behavior. By contrast, the triggering cause "causes the process to occur *now*" (EB 42); and Dretske explicitly eschews a triggering causal role for meaning (see, e.g., *EB* 80).[16]

(ii) Perhaps 'behavior' is used equivocally. (a) and (b) do not really form a circle if a state C has meaning in virtue of its causal role in one kind of behavior, but it has a causal role in some other kind of behavior in virtue of having meaning. The reply is this: if we can not assume that the same behavior is at issue in both (a) and (b), then C's meaning is not a candidate for explaining the behavior M for which C's indicating F is a structuring cause. In that case, the theory crumbles for it would break the explanatory link between C's meaning and any occurrence of M.

Thus, I see no way to maintain both (a) and (b) without circularity. What Dretske is trying to show is that C's meaning something can give C a causal role. If meaning something were solely a matter of indicating something, there would be no problem: C would mean 'F' in virtue of the fact that C indicates F, and meaning 'F' would have a (structuring) causal role if C were recruited to cause M. But meaning is not indicating. Meaning is having the function of indicating: C means 'F' in virtue of having the function of indicating F. But by definition 'having the function of indicating F' already includes 'being a structuring cause of M' for some behavior. So, what Dretske is saying is that C means 'F' in virtue of the fact that C's indicating F is a structuring cause of M, and that C's indicating F is a structuring cause of M in virtue of C's meaning 'F.' The former conjunct follows directly from Dretske's definitions, and the latter conjunct is what Dretske is arguing for — namely, a place for reasons in a world of causes.

Let me put it another way: Dretske takes meaning to be a structuring cause of behavior — whence the causal role of belief. C's meaning 'F' (at the ground level) is identified with C's having the function of indicating F. C's having the function of indicating F depends on the fact that C's indicating F is a structuring cause of the $C \rightarrow M$ process. Therefore, Dretske cannot — without circularity — take meaning, or the fact that a state has meaning, to be the structuring cause of behavior M. For the structuring of the $C \rightarrow M$ process is a precondition of C's having meaning. The circularity slips in because meaning is implicitly identified both with C's indicating F (meaning as structuring cause) and with C's having the function of indicating F (meaning as representing F).

There is a way out of the circle that maintains the materialism, but only at the cost of giving up the explanatory or causal role of belief. The circle is generated, as we have seen, by a slide from the notion of C's indicating F to the notion of C's having the function of indicating F. It is only the former that is (noncircularly) a structuring cause of behavior; but it is only the latter that gives C a meaning. So, the circle may be broken by consistently taking C's indicating F (not C's having the function of indicating F) both to be a structuring cause of behavior and to be a relation that *underlies* meaning or representation. But to say that a single relation both is a structuring cause and underlies meaning gives no causal role whatever to meaning. Meaning, on this noncircular rendition, remains wholly epiphenomenal.

Therefore, I believe that the most detailed attempt to provide an explanatory role for belief, construed as an internal state, does not succeed. For either it is circular or it accords the meaning of internal states no causal role at all. Although I cannot be sure, I believe that other naturalistic accounts of meaning, if developed in the detail of Dretske's, would fall to similar arguments.

What Are Beliefs?

As I see it, contemporary philosophy of mind has misconceived belief. Beliefs are not entities — material or immaterial — at all. 'Belief' is a nominalization, a mere grammatical device derived from 'believes that . . . ,' where 'believes that . . . .' points to complex patterns of thought and behavior. But when someone believes that p, there is no other fact — in particular, no nonintentional and nonsemantic fact — in virtue of which she has that belief.

The language of belief is irreducible, as Quine argued so forcefully. Of course, Quine took irreducibility to reveal "the baselessness of intentional concepts," since they are infected with the indeterminacy of translation and hence promise "little gain in scientific insight."[17] However, as I have argued at length elsewhere, pursuit of scientific insight is not the only good reason to employ a cognitive framework.[18] To limit our cognitive interests to science would be to impoverish our cognitive lives considerably.

The original Cartesian bifurcation, honed down to materialistic proportions, has misled us about the nature of belief (and other so-called mental states). Cartesian materialism takes belief on the analogy of water. To find the nature of water, identify the matter that constitutes it: H_2O. But the analogy with belief does not hold: it does not follow that to find the nature of belief, identify the matter that constitutes it.

Indeed, there is a problem of location with respect to belief as an internal state that the unproblematic cases like water lack. In the water/H_2O case, one can determine the spatiotemporal location of a sample of water, and thereby determine the location of its molecular constituents, without knowing what those constituents are. But the only means of identifying the spatiotemporal location of a belief construed as an internal state is already to have identified the spatiotemporal location of the constituents.

To put this last point another way: If you ask what makes these particular molecules constituents of this sample of water, the answer may be that they are at the same spatiotemporal location, and the location of the water sample is discoverable without knowing anything about its constituents. But if you ask what makes this neuronal configuration a physical realization of that belief token, you cannot have a parallel answer. There is no independent way (short of "brainwriting") to locate the belief in the brain, and then to discover its constituents.

If I am right about the difficulties of construing beliefs as physically realized internal states, does it follow that neurophysiology is irrelevant to beliefs (and other commonsensical mental states)? Absolutely not. But the relations between a belief that p and brain states cannot be simple. There is no reason to think that there is a single relation between brain states and beliefs, even within an individual — much less that there is a single relation between brain states and intentional states generally. There may well be ascertainable physically necessary conditions for having a belief that p, but it would be unwarranted to suppose that neurophysiology will reveal a neurophysiological difference between a belief that p and a belief that q, where p and q are similar in some respect. (We could end up with reliable predictions that taking a certain drug will make a person paranoid, without the more fine-grained prediction that the person will believe that there are rats rather than pink elephants before her.)

So my worries about beliefs as internal states do not suggest that beliefs are beyond illumination by neurophysiology. Even before the rise of neurophysiology, it was obvious that being kicked in the head by a mule, or having a high fever, or drinking a lot affected beliefs and other states in many ways. If I am right, however, the "nature" of belief, or what beliefs really are, is not revealed by neurophysiology or any other physical science. No physical science will reveal what beliefs really are, because there is no one way (such as realization in the brain) that beliefs are related to the nonintentional world.

In the first instance, beliefs pertain, not to internal states, but to persons — whole persons.[19] We use beliefs to predict, to explain, and to hold people responsible for what they do. Our concern with behavior is primarily with intentional action, not with bodily motion. A physical explanation of a bodily motion — in terms of a brain state, say — is no explanation of an intentional action, even if the action consisted in moving one's finger.

Let me anticipate an objection: "If beliefs are to be genuinely explanatory, they must cause behavior. Behavior, even intentional behavior, typically consists in bodily motion, and the causes of bodily motion must be wholly in the brain: The intrinsic properties of the brain must suffice for all its causal powers. So, if beliefs are to explain behavior causally, they must be understood as internal states." My reply is that the idea of causality implicit in the objection is too narrow to be useful, not just for belief/desire explanation, but for explanation generally.[20]

The idea of causality in the objection is that "causal powers" must supervene on internal physical states.[21] If 'causal powers' is a technical term, according to which causal powers are defined as supervening on intrinsic physical states, then we can simply reject the notion that causal explanations require recourse to causal powers. Causal explanations generally do not cite intrinsic physical states: for example, we causally explain the devastation of a certain area in terms of an airstrike, not in terms of any intrinsic properties of the rubble; we causally explain someone's enormous wealth in terms of what she inherited, not in terms of her internal states.

In the causal explanations that are actually produced and accepted, we commonly attribute causal powers to individuals that do not supervene on the individuals' intrinsic states. For example, the U.S. president has the power to nominate members to the Supreme Court; or the policeman has the power to put the mayor in jail. These are real powers, and they are explanatory. The fact that these are cases of causal powers as authority to effect certain changes leaves the explanatoriness of these powers undiminished: We explain why a particular person is appearing before the Judiciary Committee by the fact that the president has nominated her to the Supreme Court. We explain why the mayor did not come home to dinner by the fact that the policeman had her jailed.

Yet, neither of these powers supervenes on internal physical states of the president or the policeman. A molecular duplicate of George Bush, in a world in which he lost the election, would lack the power to nominate members to the Supreme Court; a molecular duplicate of the policeman who, unbeknownst to himself, has just been fired, would not have the power to put the mayor in jail. Such causal powers, although they do not fit the narrow conception of causal powers required by the objection, are commonly explanatory.

My proposal is to focus on explanation. If we do so, we can see the enormous explanatory power of ascriptions of beliefs and other intentional states. If we must reify, we can think of beliefs as explanatory states. We often explain phenomena in terms of states whose instances have no interesting connection to instances of fundamental physical properties: Think of explanations that cite states of war, states of emergency, states of bankruptcy, states of disgrace, states of intoxication, states of being in violation of parade ordinances. Why should a state of belief be any more suspect than, say, a state of matrimony? Both have explanatory potential, and neither is connected in any interesting way to physical realizations.

I believe that the conception of beliefs as internal states of the brain has led to a philosophical dead-end, which we best avoid by trying to get beyond our Cartesian (albeit materialistic) habits. A belief may explain behavior, but not because it is an internal state — just as the state of being counterfeit explains why the dollar bill lookalikes were exhibited by the prosecutor, even though the state of being counterfeit is not an internal state. The presence or absence of an internal distinguishing feature of counterfeit dollars is simply irrelevant to their being counterfeit. Similarly, I want to suggest, the presence or absence of an internal distinguishing feature of a belief that p is irrelevant to someone's having a belief that p.

Conclusion

I have tried to do two things. First, I have presented two major arguments against taking beliefs to be internal states realized in the brain: One concerns syntax and the problem of the parameter; the other concerns semantics and the problem of the circle. Although for the sake of definiteness, these arguments have been directed against specific proposals in the literature, I believe that they cut deeply against the general conception of beliefs as physically realized internal states. Second, I have suggested an alternative general conception of belief, one that puts belief on a par with other states used in commonsense causal explanations. Belief/desire explanations are part of the commonsense apparatus that we use in everyday life. They allow us to make sense of our own and others' behavior in the ways that matter to us. The metaphysical fear — that unless we find a physical basis for beliefs, we are stuck with Cartesian dualism — is unfounded.

In sum: The explanatory connection between what we believe and what we do no more requires belief to be an internal state than does the explanatory connection between arson and the smoldering rubble require arson to be an intrinsic property of the fire. But if belief is not an internal state, then we need not be lured into thinking that belief states must either be detected by scientists, or failing detection, cast off as "mythical posits of a bad theory."[22] This false dichotomy is the excess baggage of our metaphysical heritage.[23]

Notes

1. See, for example, *Psychosemantics: The Problem of Meaning in the Philosophy of Mind* (Cambridge, Mass.: MIT-Bradford, 1987); *Explaining Behavior: Reasons in a World of Causes* (Cambridge, Mass.: MIT-Bradford, 1988); Stephen P. Stich, *From Folk Psychology to Cognitive Science: The Case Against Belief* (Cambridge, Mass.: MIT-Bradford, 1983); William G. Lycan, *Logical Form in Natural Language* (Cambridge, Mass.: MIT-Bradford, 1984); Patricia Smith Churchland, *Neurophilosophy: Toward a Unified Science of the Mind/Brain* (Cambridge, Mass.: MIT-Bradford, 1986); Paul M. Churchland, *A Neurocomputational Perspective: The Nature of Mind and the Structure of Science* (Cambridge, Mass.: MIT-Bradford, 1989).

2. See my *Saving Belief: A Critique of Physicalism* (Princeton, N.J.: Princeton University Press, 1988), chaps. 1–5; "On a Causal Theory of Content" in *Philosophy of Mind and Action Theory, 1989,* vol. 3 of *Philosophical Perspectives,* ed. James E. Tomberlin (Altascadero, Calif.: Ridgeview, 1989), 165–186.

3. This view has been promoted by Fodor (see the Appendix of *Psychosemantics*) and by Lycan, *Logical Form in Natural Language.* Even eliminative materialists tend to see the brain as a "syntactic engine." (They deny, of course, that it is a semantic engine.)

4. *Logical Form in Natural Language,* 237.

5. This was pointed out to me by Max Cresswell.

6. These ideas are taken from *Logical Form in Natural Language.*

7. This and other criticisms of Lycan's version of the language of thought hypothesis may be found in greater detail in my "Truth in Context," *Philosophical Perspectives* 2 (1989): 85–94.

8. William G. Lycan, "Reply to Baker," *Philosophical Psychology* 2 (1989): 97.

9. The example has implications beyond the language-of-thought hypothesis. First, it suggests that there are syntactic as well as semantic issues of theory-change; second, it suggests that any theory of meaning based on syntactic primitives is at least liable to the problem of the parameter. I hope to explore these matters elsewhere.

10. Lycan, "Reply to Baker," 99.

11. In "Anomalous Monism and the Problem of Explanatory Force," *Philosophical Review* 98 (1989): 153–188, Louise Antony has shown, conclusively, I think, that Davidson's view of reasons as causes fails to account for the explanatory power of reasons.

12. Fred Dretske, *Explaining Behavior: Reasons in a World of Causes* (Cambridge, Mass.: MIT-Bradford, 1988), 42. (Hereafter, references to this work will appear in the text as *EB* followed by a page number.) In *EB,* Dretske identifies behavior with the causal process $C \rightarrow M$; however, in "Mental Events as Structuring Causes," a paper presented at a Conference on Mental Causation at the University of Bielefeld (March 1989), Dretske applies his view to the more standard conception of behavior as the resulting $M.$

13. Even if Dretske's account is successful in showing how meaning can have a structuring role in behavior, it still cannot explain any actual tokening of a $C \rightarrow M$ process. Particular actions (such as Booth's assassinating Lincoln) would not be explained by showing how beliefs had a role in Booth's being "structured" in such a way that when a certain internal event occurred, it caused a shooting.

14. In "Dretske on the Explanatory Role of Behavior," I show in elaborate detail that Dretske's theory commits him to (a). 'In virtue of' is to express an (asymmetric) explanatory relation.

15. It may be thought that Dretske is giving a logical analysis of 'having meaning,' in which case, (a) and (b) may be tautologous rather than circular. However, I believe that Dretske aims to give an informative account of "the place of reasons in a world of causes."

16. Indeed, if a token of C *triggered* a token of M in virtue of its meaning

(as opposed to its intrinsic physical properties), then Dretske's position would be an overt mind/body dualism inasmuch as it would countenance nonphysical causation. But I take Dretske at his word: he is no dualist. So, the circle is genuine.

17. W. V. O. Quine, *Word and Object* (Cambridge, Mass.: MIT, 1960), 221.

18. In *Saving Belief,* chaps. 6–7, and in "The Cognitive Status of Common Sense" (in preparation).

19. Dennett recognized this early on, but his recent insistence on an analogy between intentional states and centers of gravity suggests that he has now bought into the idea of beliefs as internal states. He now seems to differ from the mainstream only by taking beliefs to be "abstracta" rather than theoretical entities. See Daniel C. Dennett, "Real Patterns," *Journal of Philosophy* 88 (1991): 27–51.

20. See my "Metaphysics and Mental Causation" in *Mental Causation,* ed. John Heil and Albert Mele (Oxford: Oxford University Press, forthcoming).

21. For a defense of narrow causal powers, see Fodor's *Psychosemantics,* chap. 2.

22. Stitch, *From Folk Psychology to Cognitive Science,* 9–10.

23. I want to thank Derk Pereboom, Hilary Kornblith, Steven Wagner, Max Cresswell, and the Five-College Propositional Attitudes Task Force (especially John Connolly) for illuminating critical comments on earlier drafts.

Index